# Disability Research and Policy

*Current Perspectives*

# Disability Research and Policy

## Current Perspectives

*Edited by*

**Richard J. Morris**
*University of Arizona*

LONDON AND NEW YORK

First published 2006 by Lawrence Erlbaum Associates, Inc.

2 Park Square, Milton Park, Abingdon, Oxfordshire OX14 4RN
52 Vanderbilt Avenue, New York, NY 10017

*Routledge is an imprint of the Taylor & Francis Group, an informa business*

First issued in paperback 2019

Copyright © 2006 Taylor & Francis

All rights reserved. No part of this book may be reprinted or reproduced or utilised in any form or by any electronic, mechanical, or other means, now known or hereafter invented, including photocopying and recording, or in any information storage or retrieval system, without permission in writing from the publishers.

Notice:
Product or corporate names may be trademarks or registered trademarks, and are used only for identification and explanation without intent to infringe.

Cover design by Kathryn Houghtaling Lacey

**Library of Congress Cataloging-in-Publication Data**

Disability research and policy : current perspectives / edited by Richard J. Morris.
      p. cm.
Includes bibliographical references and index.
ISBN 0-8058-5337-5 (cloth : alk. paper)
1. People with disabilities—United States. 2. People with disabilities—Research. 3. Sociology of disability—Research. 4. People with disabilities—government policy—United States. I. Morris, Richard J.
HV1553.D5486 2005
362.4'0973—dc22

                                                  2005042043
                                                         CIP

ISBN 13: 978-0-8058-5337-7 (hbk)
ISBN 13: 978-1-138-00414-6 (pbk)

*In Memory of Lee Meyerson (1920–2002),
Nancy Kerr Meyerson (1933–2001),
and Jacqueline Anne Morris (1978–2000)
—three people who taught me about compassion,
commitment, advocacy, honesty,
and the value of friendship*

# Contents

Preface ix

List of Contributors xi

## I. INTRODUCTION

1 Introduction and Overview 3
   *Richard J. Morris and Gretchen Schoenfield*

## II. DISABILITY RESEARCH AREAS

2 Physically Disabled Offenders in Prison 17
   *Nicole S. Kitei and Bruce D. Sales*

3 The Use of Existing Videoconferencing Technology to Deliver Video Remote Interpreting Services for Deaf Vocational Rehabilitation Clients 39
   *Joyce S. Steinberg*

4 The Use of Computer Technology for People Having a Disability 69
   *Deepti Joshi and Richard J. Morris*

5 Philosophical Congruence in Health Care 85
   *Tina Buck, Amos Sales, Charlene Kampfe, Leslie McAllan, and Cela Archembault*

6 Pictorial Illustrations, Visual Imagery, and Motor Activity: Their Instructional Implications for Native American Children With Learning Disabilities 103
   *Scott C. Marley and Joel R. Levin*

| | | |
|---|---|---|
| 7 | Cognitive and Behavioral Effects of Children's Exposure to Pesticides: Critical Issues and Research Trends<br>*Patricia Sánchez Lizardi, Richard J. Morris, and Mary Kay O'Rourke* | 125 |
| 8 | Disability and Juvenile Delinquency<br>*Kimberly A. Morris, Gretchen Schoenfield, Priscilla Bade-White, Deepti Joshi, and Richard J. Morris* | 141 |
| 9 | Fears and Related Anxieties in Children Having a Disability: A Synthesis of Research Findings From 1937 to 2004<br>*Huijun Li and Richard J. Morris* | 163 |
| 10 | School Bullying and Victimization of Children With Disabilities<br>*Árni Víkingur Sveinsson and Richard J. Morris* | 187 |

## III. DISABILITY POLICY AREAS

| | | |
|---|---|---|
| 11 | Mental Retardation and the Death Penalty: Current Issues for Attorneys and Psychologists<br>*Julie C. Duvall and Richard J. Morris* | 205 |
| 12 | ADHD and the Law: Students' Rights, Schools' Responsibilities, and Educational Issues<br>*Susan Ampriester and Richard J. Morris* | 221 |
| 13 | Access to E-Texts for Disabled Students: A Practical Reality or Just a Myth?<br>*Michael S. Somsan* | 237 |
| 14 | Making the Case for Meaningful Reasonable Accommodations for Employees With Physical Disabilities: A Legal Analysis of Part-Time and Flexible Work Schedules Under the Americans With Disabilities Act (ADA)<br>*Nonnie L. Shivers* | 265 |
| 15 | The Adequacy and Enforcement of Emergency Evacuation Laws in the Workplace for People With Disabilities<br>*Marina Hadjioannou* | 301 |
| | Author Index | 323 |
| | Subject Index | 335 |

# Preface

This book is based on the research and scholarship produced by the Meyerson Disability Research Project (MDRP) at the University of Arizona. The MDRP was conceived by Dr. Lee Meyerson, Regents Professor and professor of psychology at Arizona State University, and Dr. Nancy Kerr Meyerson, professor of educational psychology at Arizona State University. The funding for the MDRP came from the David and Minnie Meyerson Foundation, a private foundation created by Dr. Lee Meyerson. The purpose of the MDRP was to support student–faculty mentor research, advocacy, and/or policy studies projects that focused on the amelioration of personal and social issues associated with having a disability. The overarching goal of the foundation was to contribute to the advancement of knowledge and policy matters that enhance the lives of people with disabilities—especially people with physical disabilities.

The MDRP began in July 2000 and was continuously funded through July 2004 by the Meyerson Foundation. During this time period, a total of 36 student–faculty mentor research, public policy, or scholarly projects were funded, with each student receiving a research assistantship with the MDRP or research funding plus financial support to present her or his research or policy studies project at a professional association meeting and/or to publish his or her findings in a professional journal. The chapters included in this book were each prepared under the mentorship of a faculty member at the University of Arizona.

Many people have worked for or been associated with the MDRP over the years to ensure its smooth operation. These people include Mary Lucker, Brenda Ann Gatterer, Pamela de Steiguer, Ann Ferarro, and Mary Ann Bescript. Each of these persons has been invaluable in the day-to-day operations of the MDRP, and I thank them for their advice and professionalism. I also want to thank Jackie Collins and Gretchen Schoenfield for their assistance in preparing this book for publication. I also wish to acknowledge the following students whose various projects were funded by the MDRP: Susan L. Arnpriester, Priscilla Bade-White, Ernistina Buck, Kathryn E. Cherbini, Sarah Collier, Julie C. Duval, Peter English, Alberto Gamarra, Jennifer Guerrero, Marina Hadjioannou, Scotia Hicks, Sunggye Hong, Deepti Joshi, Jason Laker, Huijun Li, Scott Marley, Amy Morefield, Kimberly A. Morris, Modurki Ramkishore, Melanie V. Romo, Patricia Sanchez Lizardi, Nicole R. Schneider, Nonnie Shivers, Staci Skall, Michael Somsan, Gretchen Schoenfield, Scott Stein, Joyce Steinberg, Arni Vikingur Sveinsson, and Judson Ward. The faculty mentors who worked with these students include Jane Erin, PhD, Salim A. Hariri, PhD, Elaine G. Jones, RN, PhD, Charlene Kampfe, PhD, Jane B. Korn, JD, Joel R. Levin, PhD, Leslie C. McAllan, PhD, Richard J. Morris, PhD, Mary Kay O'Rourke, PhD, Rachel Pfister, PhD, Amos Sales, EdD, and Bruce D. Sales, JD, PhD. It was their cooperative scholarly endeavors with their respective graduate students that made the MDRP a success and demonstrated beyond a doubt how Lee Meyerson's and Nancy Kerr Meyerson's model for graduate student–faculty mentor scholarship could be turned into a reality.

Lastly, I want to thank my wife, Yvonne P. Morris, for her support and love over more than 37 years of marriage. She was with me when I first enrolled in graduate courses with Drs. Meyerson and Kerr Meyerson, and she spent many, many long hours listening to the mentoring discussions that I had with the Meyersons about the field of psychology and, specifically, psychological aspects of disability in children and adults. Ultimately, she became as close a friend as I was of Lee Meyerson and Nancy Kerr Meyerson. She loved them as I did, and we were both forever touched by their caring, respect, and regard for people, as well as by their strong opposition to discrimination of any kind. This book is a tribute to the devotion and commitment of Lee Meyerson and Nancy Kerr Meyerson to the mentoring of graduate students in research and scholarship in the area of disability.

—*Richard J. Morris*
*November 2004*

# List of Contributors

Cela Archambault
*Integrative Pain Center of Arizona*

Susan Arnpriester
*University of Arizona*

Priscilla Bade-White
*University of Arizona*

Tina Buck
*University of Arizona*

Julie C. Duvall
*University of Arizona*

Marina Hadjioannou
*University of Arizona*

Deepti Joshi
*Intel Corporation, Portland, Oregon*

Charlene Kampfe
*University of Arizona*

Nicole S. Kitei
*University of Arizona*

Joel R. Levin
*University of Arizona*

Huijun Li
*Florida State University*

Patricia Sánchez Lizardi
*Chula Vista Elementary School District, Chula Vista, California*

Scott C. Marley
*University of New Mexico*

Leslie C. McAllan
*University of Arizona*

Kimberly A. Morris
*University of Arizona*

Richard J. Morris
*University of Arizona*

Mary Kay O'Rourke
*University of Arizona*

Amos Sales
*University of Arizona*

Bruce D. Sales
*University of Arizona*

Gretchen Schoenfield
*University of Arizona*

Nonnie L. Shivers
*Arizona Court of Appeals Division One*

Michael Somsan
*Department of Justice, United States Attorney's Office, District of Arizona*

Joyce S. Steinberg
*The State of Arizona Rehabilitation Services Administration*

Árni Víkingur Sveinsson
*University of Arizona*

# I

# Introduction

# 1

# Introduction and Overview

Richard J. Morris and Gretchen Schoenfield

There have been many changes over the past 50 years in the study of disability. For example, research in the areas of assessment, rehabilitation planning, and service delivery has expanded from studying primarily the psychological, sociological, and medical aspects of physical disabilities in adults and children (e.g., orthopedic impairments, hearing and visual impairments, and acute and chronic physical illnesses) to studying also specific learning disabilities, emotional disabilities and mental illnesses, developmental disabilities and pervasive developmental disorders, substance abuse disorders, traumatic brain disorders, burn injuries, and several additional chronic and disabling physical illnesses (e.g., acquired immune deficiency syndrome and human immunodeficiency virus, Alzheimer's disease, blood disorders, cancers, cardiovascular disorders, diabetes, neuromuscular disorders, and rheumatoid diseases).

In addition, with the advent of the *Civil Rights Act* passed by the U.S. Congress in 1964, the *Voting Rights Act* passed in 1965, the *Rehabilitation Act* of 1973, the *Education for All Handicapped Children Act* of 1974 (renamed in 1990, *Individuals With Disabilities Education Act*), the *Americans With Disabilities Act* of 1990, and the *Family Medical Leave Act* of 1993 (see, e.g., Bruyere & DeMarinis, 1999; Sales, Powell, & Van Duizend, 1982), advocacy movements and public policy programs emerged across the United States which focused on protecting the rights of people with disabilities in virtually every facet of their lives (e.g., employment settings, school settings, independent living and housing settings, public buildings and spaces, public transportation, web-site access, etc.). These laws also contributed to establishing legal mandates at state government levels regarding protecting the rights of people with disabilities, and ensuring them equal access to the same opportunities, services, and settings as their peers who did not have a disability (Sales et al., 1982).

As these changes were occurring, there were also major advancements taking place in the area of computer sciences and information technology. Specifically, the large main-frame computers that were being used by researchers in the 1960s and early 1970s were being set aside in favor of the smaller, less expensive, and more commercially available personal computer (PC). The PC proved to be quite versatile and capable of being programmed to assist people with disabilities in such areas as rehabilitation and education, as well as advance the area of disability research (see, e.g., Floyd, McKinley, Reed, Sitter, & Tewksbury, 2004; Holmes, 1999; Klaus, Miesenberger, & Zagler, 2002; Patterson, 2000). These PCs and their peripherals, including the keyboard and monitor, were also found to be modifiable in order to be accessible to people with a disability (e.g., Amaya et al., 2000). With increased accessibility, advocacy and public policy groups also campaigned for equal access to web sites for people with disabilities. There has been increased interest over the past 15 years in using computers for videoconferencing and to provide various telehealth services to people having a disability (e.g., Glueckauf et al., 1999). Each of these changes, as well as progress in the area of disability law and the necessary accommodations needed for people having a disability, has also contributed to an increased public awareness of people who have a disability, and an increased opportunity for individuals who have a disability to lead independent and productive lives.

The chapters in this book are divided into two major sections: Disability Research Areas and Disability Policy Areas. The first section addresses some relatively new areas of research and scholarship with adults and children within the area of disability, whereas the second section critically examines various public policy and legal areas that impact the daily lives of many persons having a disability.

The first section begins with chapter 2 by Nicole S. Kitei and Bruce D. Sales. These authors present an overview of the literature regarding inmates with physical disabilities and discuss the problems these individuals encounter despite the existing laws that serve to protect them. Kitei and Sales first discuss the epidemiology of physically disabled (PD) offenders in prison and present data regarding prevalence and the difficulties associated with obtaining epidemiological information within the prison system. The authors describe the unique problems prison inmates with physical disabilities may encounter, addressing the two issues they deem most important: the inaccessibility of prison programs and the resulting lack of vocational and educational opportunities, and the potential for emotional and physical abuse. In addition, they discuss the lack of mental health services available to PD offenders, as well as the boredom and loneliness that these individuals may experience because of the lack of work and other opportunities. Moreover, the authors describe some of the barriers to social relationships that these inmates face. With respect to the issue of potential for emotional and physical abuse, the authors cite several cases in which inmates filed suit against prison systems and/or prison personnel for instances of physical, emotional, and sexual abuse, as well as physical neglect. Kitei and Sales draw comparisons between PD offenders' experiences and those of individuals outside of the prison system with physical abilities versus non-physically disabled individuals within the prison system. Kitei and Sales argue that PD inmates face greater difficulties than these comparator groups and address the implications of this disparity. The authors provide recommendations regarding future directions for research addressing the unique needs of PD offenders, which include developing new tools for collecting epidemiological information and more comprehensive evaluation of services and accommodations appropriate for these individuals. In addition, the authors address the need for research examining the nature, frequency, and magnitude of abuse, resulting mental health issues, and the availability and efficacy of intervention programs, services, and other accommodations. The authors conclude by addressing the divide between the laws regarding protection and accommodations for PD offenders and actual implementation of these laws.

In chapter 3, Joyce Steinberg presents a study intended to evaluate the effectiveness of a real-time videoconferencing initiative completed by the Arizona Rehabilitation Services Administration (ARSA) in supporting video remote interpreting (VRI) for individuals with hearing impairment. Steinberg notes the lack of data evaluating whether the ARSA videoconferencing network, originally designed to facilitate distance learning activities, can effectively support VRI. She provides a rationale for the study by citing research reporting that approximately 8.6% of the total Arizona population has a hearing impairment, and by addressing the fact that many Arizona counties are rural communities with limited or no access to rehabilitation counselors for the deaf and therefore have limited access to appropriate services. Steinberg provides an overview of the literature regarding vocational rehabilitation services and rehabilitation counselors for the deaf and the roles, issues, and laws regarding interpreters. Emerging technologies for individuals with hearing impairments, such as telemedicine and various videoconferencing projects, are also explored. Steinberg describes the technical and practical issues associated with this technology, and presents research addressing consumer satisfaction. Steinberg's study addressed two research questions: whether there was a significant difference in clients' comprehension of VRI compared to local interpreting, and whether there were significant differences in levels of satisfaction reported in local versus remote interpretation settings. The study also evaluated the quality of the video transfer rate and whether fingerspelling and signs could be understood. The author concludes by reporting that there were no significant differences in comprehension of VR programmatic information and no significant differences in consumer satisfaction in local versus remote interpretation delivery. Steinberg acknowledges that VRI will not likely replace traditional interpreting, yet it provides a compelling option that may yield tremendous benefits to deaf and hard of hearing populations in rural and/or underserved communities.

In chapter 4, Deepti Joshi and Richard J. Morris discuss recent advancements in assistive technology for individuals with various types of disabilities, as well as computer and information technology that has the potential to improve the quality of life for these individuals. Joshi and Morris begin by providing a brief overview of the history of technology, citing several advances that have proven useful in a variety of domains. The authors present specific software and hardware technology and advancements that address the needs of individuals with visual impairment and blindness; hearing impairment and deafness; physical disability, mobility impairment, and chronic medical conditions; learning disabilities; and developmental disabilities. Joshi and Morris intersperse their descriptions of these technologies with research literature that supports the utility and benefits to individuals with disabilities. The authors conclude by addressing the barriers to the commercial availability of some of these technologies, and recommend further efforts for collaboration to directly address the technological needs of individuals with disabilities.

In chapter 5, Tina Buck, Amos Sales, Charlene Kampfe, Leslie McAllan, and Cela Archembault discuss the use of complementary and alternative medicine (CAM) practices among individuals with disabilities. The authors provide an overview of the literature of Pepperian worldviews (as defined by how an individual perceives the world and processes the instrumentality between events) as they apply to health care and examine the relationship between this approach and the benefits of evaluating philosophical congruence for the delivery of health care services. Buck et al. begin by exploring the literature regarding increasing consumer demand for CAM practices, particularly among individuals with disabilities. The authors present Pepperian worldviews that include the following: formism, mechanism, contextualism, and organicism. The authors present two scales that measure Pepperian worldview preferences and review the literature regarding the use of these scales. The authors then discuss philosophical congruence between worldview and the perceived benefits of a variety of health care services, claiming that preference for health care service correlates with preference for worldview. The authors present research literature that addresses personality traits, counseling preferences, physician compatibility and patient satisfaction, health promoting behavior, and conventional and alternative medicine. Buck et al. argue for a connection between philosophical congruence and health care, stating that the perceived benefit of certain matched health care choices may maximize the placebo effect. The authors discuss the placebo effect extensively as it applies to Pepperian worldviews and psychophysiological responses to various health care treatment modalities. The authors posit that health care providers have an ethical responsibility to assist clients in drawing on their individual worldviews to experience health benefits. Therefore, matching of client and practitioner based on shared worldview is encouraged. The authors conclude by recommending that rehabilitation professionals become further educated in integrative health care practices, such that they can assist clients with disabilities in making appropriate and efficacious choices.

In chapter 6, Scott C. Marley and Joel R. Levin discuss the instructional implications of three types of activities for Native American children with learning disabilities: pictorial illustrations, visual imagery, and motor activity. The authors begin by providing an overview of the characteristics of Native American children with learning disabilities. Marley and Levin specifically address the overrepresentation of Native American children in the population of children diagnosed with learning disabilities, issues related to second-language learning, and risks for academic failure. The authors present research literature regarding indications that Native Americans may learn differently. As an example, some studies suggest that Native Americans may have particular strengths in the area of visual/performance orientation, which conflicts with typical public school instruction, which traditionally has emphasized written and verbal learning approaches. As a result, the authors believe that instructional interventions with Native American youth should emphasize visual and motor modalities. However, Marley and Levin caution educators against making generalizations regarding the efficacy of emerging instructional strategies in Native American populations, emphasizing that empirical research must be first performed across multiple Native American communities. The authors follow this discussion by presenting research findings that highlight the impacts of the following instructional strategies on Native American children: activity- and imagery-based learning strategies; pictures, activity, and students' learning from text; and Glenberg's activity-based model of comprehension, learning, and memory. The authors conclude by suggesting that Native American students may benefit from learning strategies that utilize multiple representations—specifically, enactive and iconic modalities. Given the paucity of research regarding Native American children with learning disabilities, future endeavors may serve to address the needs of this population and seek to determine the efficacy of the various theoretical frameworks the authors discuss.

In chapter 7, Patricia Sánchez Lizardi, Richard J. Morris, and Mary Kay O'Rourke provide an overview of the research literature regarding the cognitive and behavioral effects of children's exposure to pesticides, specifically addressing the critical issues and research trends therein. The authors also discuss research and methodological issues that have limited study in this area. Sánchez Lizardi et al. begin by discussing one of the most commonly used pesticides, organophosphate (OP), for agricultural and common household purposes, and describe its characteristics and misuse. The authors note the existence of only one study to date that evaluates the effects of OP pesticide on children's growth and development. The findings of this study suggest that OP pesticides have adverse effects on children's development. The authors review the literature regarding the effects of OP pesticides and discuss research findings regarding the impact of OP pesticides on cognitive and behavioral functioning. Sánchez Lizardi et al. indicate that the majority of the research in this area has been with adults. They also cite the few studies that have evaluated the effects of these pesticides on children's neurodevelopment and growth and address the implications of exposure to OP pesticides on children's classroom functioning. The authors conclude that further research efforts must be initiated to generalize findings to children.

Chapter 8, by Kimberly A. Morris, Priscilla Bade-White, Deepti Joshi, Gretchen Schoenfield, and Richard J. Morris, focuses on youths with disabilities in the juvenile justice system. Morris et al. address definitional issues, prevalence and incidence data, and the types of educational and mental health services provided to incarcerated and non-incarcerated youths. The authors also present preliminary findings from a large-scale research project examining disability and juvenile delinquency. Morris et al. begin by providing an overview of the evolution of the juvenile justice system, describing the shifts in approaches since inception. Although prevalence and incidence of disability among juvenile offenders is discussed in the literature, there is considerable variability in reported frequency. In addition, there are few studies that address the contribution of a youth's disability to sentencing decisions, recidivism, and best practices regarding educational and mental health services. Morris et al. discuss definitional issues regarding disability diagnoses under federal and state laws, in addition to clinical guidelines set forth by the *DSM-IV*. The authors present prevalence and incidence data regarding youths with disabilities in the juvenile justice system, drawing attention to the most commonly diagnosed disabilities found in this population—learning disability, emotional disorder, and mental retardation—and to the services provided these youths. The unique issues of females within the juvenile justice system are also addressed. The preliminary findings from the research study suggest that there is an overrepresentation of youths with disabilities in the juvenile justice system. The authors conclude that future research endeavors should include examining whether there are significant relationships between gender, ethnicity, offense, type of sentence, and disability, in addition to evaluating the efficacy of treatment within the juvenile justice system.

In chapter 9, Huijun Li and Richard J. Morris discuss fears and related anxieties in children and adolescents having a disability, providing a synthesis of the literature published between 1937 and 2004. The authors draw on 27 studies that examine fears and related anxieties in children with hearing impairment, health impairment, autism, visual impairment, mental retardation, and learning disabilities. Additionally, the authors review studies that draw comparisons across disability groups. Based on this extensive review, Li and Morris indicate that children with disabilities experience more specific fears and higher anxiety levels than their non-disabled peers. Research also suggests that young children report more fears and higher levels of anxiety than older children, which is consistent with normative data. Other research findings have revealed gender differences in the frequency and intensity of fears and anxiety. Li and Morris also discuss findings that address methodological issues in the research on fears and anxieties in children. The authors conclude that few studies actually have examined treatment of fears and anxieties in children with disabilities and in children at the preschool age. They suggest that further study should be conducted in these areas to determine successful intervention and prevention.

Until recently, less obvious forms of aggression in the school system have rarely been addressed in the literature; the attention primarily has focused on observable acts such as assault, theft, and vandalism. In chapter 10, Árni Víkingur Sveinsson and Richard J. Morris discuss bullying and victimization of children with disabilities in the school system. The authors provide a brief overview of the research on school bullying, discuss current models that serve to explain bullying behavior, and explore theories regarding bullying in children with disabilities. Sveinsson and Morris note that the majority of the research regarding school bullying has originated in Sweden and Norway. International studies documenting school bullyism have reported variable prevalence rates, with some reports estimating rates between 15% to 30% and others ranging from 8% to 78%. Sveinsson and Morris indicate that this variability may be due, in part, to incongruity in definitions and methods of assessment employed in research on bullying. The most commonly used assessment instrument to date is an adapted version of a self-report questionnaire that originated in Norway and Sweden. The authors remark that the paucity of research regarding the validity of this instrument yields problems when generalizing to a population on which it was not normed. Sveinsson and Morris present literature regarding theoretical frameworks regarding bullyism that address the characteristics of individuals who become bullies or victims, situational factors, ecological models, and social learning perspectives. The authors explore research that emphasizes characteristics of victims of school bullyism, which has received less attention in the literature than characteristics of aggressors. In this section, the authors highlight potential risk factors such as physical attributes, social skill deficits, and the presence of a disability. Sveinsson and Morris indicate that the research on bullyism in disabled populations suggests that these youths face a greater risk of victimization than their non-disabled peers. Sveinsson and Morris conclude with recommendations for further research to address whether the presence of a disability is an actual risk factor for victimization, and the need to study methodological and psychometric issues regarding the use of assessment instruments, as well as to compare rates of bullying across different disability categories.

The section on Disability Policy Areas begins with chapter 11 by Julie C. Duvall and Richard J. Morris. These authors examine the controversial topic of mental retardation (MR) and the death penalty, and the ensuing issues that attorneys and defendants face. Duvall and Morris first provide an overview of the legal history of MR defendants and the death penalty leading to the landmark 2002 *Atkins v. Virginia* decision, which held that individuals with mental retardation could not be executed for capital crimes. The authors note that the *Atkins* decision neither specified criteria for diagnosing mental retardation nor established a judicial procedure for determining whether an individual meets the diagnostic criteria. The result of this lack of criteria and procedures has placed the onus of MR determination on the individual states. Duvall and Morris extensively discuss definitional issues with regard to mental retardation, addressing the differences between clinical diagnostic criteria set forth by the American Association on Mental Retardation (AAMR) and the *Diagnostic and Statistical Manual of Mental Disorders*, 4th ed. (DSM–IV; American Psychiatric Association [APA], 2000) and statutory definitions, which have largely been determined by legal precedent. Duvall and Morris review the statutory definitions of MR in the 38 states that permit execution for certain crimes, classifying those states into one of the following requirements for MR determination: (a) adherence to the standard clinical definition; (b) adherence to a "cutoff" score on qualifying IQ tests; (c) adaptive behavior limitation requirements; (d) extension of age of onset; and (e) no adherence to standard clinical definitions. The authors then describe how the states have been permitted to create their own definitions of mental retardation as well as mandate the procedures through which an MR determination is made and the legal problems that have ensued. The authors conclude by arguing that the lack of adherence to clinical definitions of mental retardation and the inconsistent determination procedures have yielded a cumbersome process for all individuals involved, as well as the potential for unconstitutional executions of MR defendants having committed certain crimes.

Attention deficit hyperactivity disorder (ADHD) and the law is the subject of chapter 12 by Sue Arnpriester and Richard J. Morris. Arnpriester and Morris provide an overview of the history of ADHD, addressing the varying definitions and symptomatology. The authors describe the diagnostic criteria using the DSM–IV (APA, 2000) guidelines and discuss the chasm between clinical diagnostic procedures and federal special education criteria for special education services. The authors note that the presence of a psychiatric diagnosis does not guarantee the provision of special education services, which has led school personnel to rely on state and federal disability definitions for identification and placement decisions. Arnpriester and Morris review the laws that address disability in the school system—namely, the *Individuals With Disabilities Education Act* (IDEA, 1997) and Section 504 of the *Rehabilitation Act* (1973)—and review the research literature regarding the identification and services provided to children with ADHD. The authors specifically focus on the following issues: (a) problems associated with the assessment of ADHD in the school system, and the reliability and validity of assessment instruments; (b) developmental issues and the associated changing educational needs of children with ADHD in the classroom; (c) the overrepresentation of ADHD in children from diverse cultural and linguistic backgrounds; (d) the difficulties associated with differentiating between those behaviors specifically linked to ADHD and other inappropriate behaviors; and (e) the potential danger involved when an extremely disruptive student is classified as disabled and is therefore exempt from the disciplinary measures of the non-disabled peers. Arnpriester and Morris conclude by offering recommendations for the development of procedures to monitor the need for accommodations for those children diagnosed as having ADHD, to impart knowledge of the guidelines outlined in IDEA and Section 504, and to offer training for personnel on classroom and behavior management with children having an ADHD diagnosis. In addition, the authors recommend that school personnel inform parents of the rights regarding children with an ADHD diagnosis, as well as provide information regarding community resource and advocacy centers.

In chapter 13, Michael Somsan asserts that the increasing creation and cataloguing of textbooks into electronic formats and the emerging speech software applications substantiate the need for improved access and availability to blind college students. Somsan emphasizes that publishers and universities have not embraced the full potential of such technologies, arguing that publishers and universities may not realize the necessity to provide blind students with the accommodations to achieve success at the higher education level. Somsan posits that the lack of emphasis that universities and publishers place on reasonable access to electronic textbooks may reflect the absence of federal and/or state laws addressing this issue. Federal laws that address reasonable accommodations for individuals with disabilities, such as the ADA or the Rehabilitation Act of 1973, do not specifically set forth specific guidelines. Somsan provides a legal analysis of Titles I, II, and II of the ADA, as well as state laws that address the issue of accessibility to electronic textbooks. Somsan explores policy objectives and seeks to provide a practical approach for educators, rehabilitation counselors, and blind college students with regard to problems of access to reasonable accommodations. The status of electronic textbook availability is inconsistent, according to Somsan. Individuals who may benefit from this technology generally receive little guidance regarding how they may pursue these options effectively. Somsan concludes by emphasizing that change in the accessibility of electronic textbooks and other forms of adaptive technology must arise from the recognition that full and meaningful participation by individuals with disabilities is required.

Chapter 14, by Nonnie L. Shivers, offers a legal analysis of the reasonable accommodations for employees with physical disabilities mandated by the Americans With Disabilities Act (ADA). Shivers examines the extent to which legal decisions have interpreted the measures ADA has defined to protect employees with disabilities in the workplace, specifically addressing how courts have interpreted ADA's stated "reasonable accommodations" to include or exclude part-time or flexible work schedules. In the second part of the chapter, Shivers argues that an ongoing employment crisis exists for individuals with disabilities, largely due to legal interpretations of ADA's reasonable accommodations, the inability of individuals with disability to secure employment, and the alleged discrimination that has yielded a disproportionately high number of unemployed individuals with disabilities. Shivers details the relevant provisions of Title I of the ADA (1990), describing the terms and processes of reasonable accommodations. She also indicates that full-time work schedules are often considered an essential function, but that this requirement may yield an undue hardship for individuals with disabilities in the workplace. Shivers then provides analysis of how part-time, flexible, and sporadic work schedules are in accordance with ADA's reasonable accommodations requirements. In the final section of the chapter, Shivers recommends legislative action to conduct further study regarding interpretation and implementation of ADA's definitions, and to amend these definitions such that the ADA could more effectively meet the needs of individuals with disabilities in the workplace. Shivers also offers a critical interpretation of ADA for employers and provides recommendations for effective accommodation practices, as well as recommendations for assisting individuals with disabilities seeking part-time and flexible work schedules.

Chapter 15, by Marina Hadjioannou, addresses the issue of the adequacy and enforcement of emergency evacuation procedures in the workplace for individuals with disabilities. Hadjioannou begins by recalling the terrorist attack on the World Trade Center on September 11, 2001, stating that New York Port Authority's revised evacuation plan (motivated by the 1993 terrorist attack on the World Trade Center) proved successful for some individuals with disabilities, yet unsuccessful for others. Hadjioannou explains that as a response to recent events, government initiatives and funding have been set aside to reevaluate and create disaster response plans. Hadjioannou deems this post-9/11 era a crucial time to evaluate whether individuals with disabilities are adequately protected by evacuation plans in the event of a situation like a terrorist attack or other type of emergency. Hadjioannou explains that there is an employers' obligation to protect individuals with disabilities by providing accessible emergency evacuation plans as described under the ADA, the Federal Emergency Management System (FEMA), U.S. Fire Administration (USFA), and the Equal Employment Opportunity Commission (EEOC). She argues that the obligation to provide accommodations when evacuating individuals with disabilities is not consistently practiced, supporting her claim by citing several legal decisions stating that various public facilities were in violation of the ADA. Specifically, building guidelines and fire codes often do not provide accessible evacuation accommodations for individuals with disabilities, despite the requirements of the antidiscrimination statutes. Hadjioannou advocates that states should take proactive measures to legislate specific provisions that require protection for individuals with disabilities. Hadjioannou concludes by offering recommendations that include consulting experts in the field of disability accommodation and disaster planning and educating the public about current inadequacies of the system.

## REFERENCES

Amaya, C., Civit, A., Jimenez, G., Rio, F. D., Rodriguez, M. A., & Sevillano, J. L. (2000). Analysis of tremor in handicapped people for design of computer interfaces. *Technology and Disability, 13,* 117–131.

American Psychiatric Association. (2000). *Diagnostic and statistical manual of mental disorders* (4th ed.). Washington, DC: Author.

Bruyere, S. M., & DeMarinis, R. K. (1999). Legislation and rehabilitation service delivery. In M. G. Eisenberg, R. L. Glueckauf, & H. H. Zaretsky (Eds.), *Medical aspects of disability* (2nd ed., pp. 679–695). New York, NY: Springer.

Floyd, S., McKinley, W., Reed, J., Sitter, P., & Tewksbury, M. A. (2004). Assistive technology and computer adaptations for individuals with spinal cord injury. *Technology and Disability, 19*, 141–146.

Glueckauf, R. L., Hufford, B., Whitton, J., Baxter, J., Schnieder, P., Kain, J., & Vogelgesang, S. (1999). Telehealth: Emerging technology in rehabilitation and health care. In M. G. Eisenberg, R. L. Gluecckauf, & H. H. Zaretsky (Eds.), *Medical aspects of disability* (2nd ed., pp. 625–639). New York, NY: Springer.

Holmes, L. (1999). The computer revolution and assistive technology. In M. G. Eisenberg, R. L. Glueckauf, & H. H. Zaretsky (Eds.), *Medical aspects of disability* (2nd ed., pp. 640–650). New York: Springer.

Klaus, J., Miesenberger, K., & W. Zagler, W. (Eds.). (2002). *Computers helping people with special needs*. 8th International Conference, ICCHP 2002. New York, NY: Springer.

Patterson, J. B. (2000). Using the internet to facilitate the rehabilitation process. *Journal of Rehabilitation, 66*, 4–11.

Sales, B. D., Powell, D. M, & Van Duizend, R. (1982). *Disabled persons and the law*. New York, NY: Plenum Press.

# II

# Disability Research Areas

# 2

# Physically Disabled Offenders in Prison

Nicole S. Kitei and Bruce D. Sales

There are laws in effect to protect prisoners with disabilities. Title II of the Americans With Disabilities Act (ADA, 1990), The Architectural and Transportation Barriers Compliance Board (ADAAG, 1994), the Rehabilitation Act (1973), Civil Rights of Institutionalized Persons Act (1980), and the Eighth Amendment to the U.S. Constitution are the most common laws referred to by physically disabled inmates bringing lawsuits. Although it may appear that physically disabled (PD) inmates have sufficient legal protection, numerous lawsuits brought by these individuals suggest otherwise (discussed later).

Why might this be the case? Perhaps these laws are not being applied to inmates with disabilities or not being implemented appropriately. Perhaps they are not having their intended effects, or are having unintended negative consequences. Unfortunately, there is no empirical literature examining these possibilities, the specific and unique problems PD inmates encounter in prison, the psychological sequelae of these problems, and the types and quality of service programs and other interventions offered to this population. To partially address this void in the scholarly literature, this chapter considers the epidemiology of PD inmates; the problems these people experience in prison that non-PD inmates do not encounter; the services and accommodations prisons provide for PD inmates so that they can operate as well as non-PD inmates; and what scientific research must do to understand the PD inmate experience in prisons.

## EPIDEMIOLOGY OF PD OFFENDERS

For the purposes of understanding PD offenders in prison, the following distributional issues must be considered: the definition of physical disability for purposes of epidemiological classification, the prevalence or proportion of the prison population that is physically disabled, the characteristics of these PD offenders (e.g., age, sex, race), the number of these individuals in need of special services, and the correctional environments in which they are placed. For example, as the number of persons in need increases, budget planning, treatment planning, and the pressure for special services will increase, creating new administrative complexities. Identifying the location of these inmates becomes critical for developing a sound financial plan. Age information is required to understand the changing needs of the individual across the life span, whereas socioeconomic factors may be relevant to treatment strategies (Schneider & Sales, 2004). Finally, epidemiological information can be instrumental in prevention. If almost all PD inmates incur their specific disorder prior to incarceration, it becomes important to ask questions about whether their disorder contributed to their antisocial behavior, and, if so, what prevention strategies reduce the likelihood of criminality. If almost all PD inmates become disabled following incarceration, other questions arise.

An individual with a disability is defined by the ADA as a person who has a physical or mental impairment that substantially limits one or more major life activities, a person who has a history or record of such an impairment, or a person who is perceived by others as having such an impairment. Unfortunately, epidemiological research has not adopted this definition nor adhered to any other specific one. The result is that the research does not accurately tell us the exact number of PD offenders in prison. Additionally, many correctional institutions have extremely poor reporting and record-keeping procedures, and overlook the special needs of PD inmates during intake and subsequently. Although data do exist on PD prisoners, they are often inaccurate and must be interpreted cautiously.

Keeping in mind these limitations, let us take a look at what the extant literature suggests. Inmates with physical disabilities make up 29.6% of the total number of state inmates and 26.5% of federal inmates (Maruschak & Beck, 2001). In raw numbers, this constitutes 371,773 state inmates and 28,325 federal inmates with either a hearing, speech, visual, or other physical disability. Broken down by disability, this includes: 60,054 (5.7%) state inmates and 4,921 (5.6%) federal inmates with a hearing disability; 39,166 (3.7%) state and 1,956 (2.2%) federal inmates who reported having a speech disability; 87,242 (8.3%) state and 6,688 (7.6%) federal inmates who reported having a visual disability; and 125,257 (11.9%) state and 9,839 (11.1%) federal inmates who reported having another type of physical disability (Maruschak & Beck, 2001). If learning disabilities were included among the statistical inventory of physical disabilities in prison, this population would constitute 103,789 or 9.9% of state inmates and 4,477 or 5.1% of federal inmates within the United States prison system. Learning disabilities are not considered further in this chapter because the category is arguably not a physical disability.

How do these numbers compare to the prevalence of physical disability in the general population? Standardizing the general population to simulate the age and gender distribution of state inmates, Maruschak and Beck (2001) found the following. The prevalence of speech impairment among state inmates (3.7% or 39,166) is more than three times higher than in the U.S. general population (1.3% or 3,802,427). If we compare the rates of hearing impairment in the prison population (5.7% or 64,975) to the general population (6.6% or 19,304,633), however, we find that the rate of impairment is higher in the general population. The prevalence of visual impairment in prison (8.3% or 93,930) is more than twice as high as in the U.S. general population (3.5% or 10,237,305) (U.S. Department of Health and Human Services, National Health Interview Survey, 1996). In summary, the rates of speech and vision impairment are higher among inmates than in the U.S.general population.

Excluding reports of a cold, virus, or the flu, the most commonly reported medical problems fell into nine categories: HIV/AIDS, heart problems (e.g., heart attack, angina), circulatory problems other than heart (e.g., anemia, aneurysm, vascular, blood clots/transfusions), cancer, kidney/liver problems (e.g., hepatitis), respiratory disorders (e.g., emphysema, asthma), neurological disorders (e.g., seizures, epilepsy), skeletal problems (e.g., back/spine, muscle/tendon, joint, fracture), and diabetes. In 1998, there were 1,299,096 state and federal prisoners in the United States (U.S. Department of Justice, 2002). Since the time of their admission, 2.2% (28,580) of inmates reported having HIV/AIDS, 2.4% (31,178) reported a heart condition, 4.8% (62,356) reported a circulatory impairment, 5% (6,495) reported cancer, 2.3% (29,879) reported kidney or liver problems, 2.6% (33,776) reported a respiratory problems, 1.1% (14,290) reported a neurological impairment, 5.7% (74,048) reported a skeletal disability, and 2.4% (31,178) reported having diabetes.

In regard to the prevalence of physical injury occurring in prison, whether accidental or due to a fight, 318,000 state and federal inmates reported being injured since admission to the facility. This is constituted by 28% (294,683) of state and 26% (23,038) of federal inmates reporting being injured in an accident since admission, versus 10% (105,244) of state and 3% (2,658) of federal inmates who reported that they had been injured in a fight. Inmates who had reported having a physical disability were more likely to report an injury than were other non-physically disabled inmates. More specifically, among those who reported having a physical disability, 22% (231,537) of state and 25% (22,151) of federal inmates reported being injured in an accident, compared to 19% (199,963) of state and 22% (19,463) of federal inmates without such a disability.

Finally, what level of medical treatment do inmates receive in the correctional facility at the time of admission and subsequently? The only reported data cover state inmates. Approximately 60% of them reported that they had been checked by staff to see if they were sick, injured, or intoxicated at the time of admission, while 80% of them reported having a medical exam since their admission. The problem with these data is that because no criteria were provided to guide respondents, it is not clear what constitutes a medical exam and whether PD inmates received one whenever it was needed.

Moreover, all of the data are suspect because they fail to address a number of relevant characteristics. For example, the data was derived from one to two questions at most per disability on a self-report survey that was given to inmates regarding their physical and mental well-being. To assess the presence of a speech disability, inmates were asked, "Do you have a speech disability, such as a lisp or stutter?" (Maruschak & Beck, 2001, p. 2). One potential problem with the use of such a question is that there are myriad variations in the presenting pathology of speech, and to ask only one question that exemplifies only two types of speech disability is by no means comprehensive. To assess the presence of a visual impairment, inmates were asked, "Do you have difficulty seeing ordinary newsprint even when wearing glasses?" (Maruschak & Beck, 2001, p. 2). In this case, not only are the researchers assuming that the condition of the inmate's eyewear is up to medical standards, they are neglecting the various degrees of visual impairment that may not be detected by such a question (e.g., disorders affecting peripheral vision).

Additionally of concern is the fact that because the survey was given in paper and pencil format, those answering the question must have been able to read the print. Six words are used to assess physical disability in the sample that they used to generalize to the entire prison population, namely, "Do you have a physical disability?" (Maruschak & Beck, 2001, p. 2). Not only are most inmates unaware of what constitutes a disability, but the researchers themselves provided no means of standardizing or of operationalizing their own definition of what it means to have a physical disability. The only other question employed to assess physical disability reads, "Do you have a physical, mental, or other health condition which limits the kind or amount of work you can do?" (Maruschak & Beck, 2001, p. 2). Obviously there may be ulterior motivation in such a population to answer this question affirmatively (e.g., expectation that prison officials would remove them from a work assignment). Further epidemiological research is therefore crucial to understand the true state of affairs for members of this population whose numbers appear substantial.

## UNIQUE PROBLEMS PD INMATES FACE IN PRISON[1]

Even for the physically healthy offender, prison life is often an intimidating, violent, and grueling experience. Boredom, anger, abuse, domination, and fear permeate the lives of all prisoners (*Ruiz v. Estelle*, 1980). The negatives of prison life are often exacerbated for the PD inmate. Not only do these offenders need to become accustomed to the brutalities encountered in prison, but they also must learn how to be at a greater physical disadvantage in a hierarchical and dangerous environment. For example, an inmate with a disabled leg can fall in the shower area because of the slippery floors and lack of hand rails, fall while trying to carry his food tray and operate his crutches at the same time, or injure himself trying to navigate a large number of stairs if no special assistance is provided (*Frost v. Agnos*, 1998). This section addresses the two most important problem areas affecting PD prisoners and their consequences: the inaccessibility of prison programs and opportunities, and the potential for being emotionally and/or physically abused.

### Inaccessibility of Prison Programs and Opportunities

In some prisons, various programs and services are available to inmates with special needs. For example, drug and alcohol treatment programs are available for inmates seeking treatment for substance abuse problems (Mumola, 1999); psychotropic medications are available to inmates meeting criteria for a mental disorder; individual therapy is available for inmates who prefer one-on-one counseling (Beck & Maruschak, 2001); sex offender therapy is often mandatory for inmates convicted of sexual offenses (e.g., *Key v. Grayson et al.*, 2001); and educational opportunities and skills training workshops are available to help the offender obtain a job upon release (see Harlow, 2003). Often these same programs and services are inaccessible to PD offenders. For example, in some prisons, the meeting rooms for group therapy sessions may be on the third or fourth floors of the facility. A wheelchair-bound inmate may be unable to participate in the session due to accessibility limitations (*Evans v. Dugger*, 1990).

Prison work programs present an opportunity for offenders to reduce boredom and loneliness. Although participation is contingent on good behavior and the willingness of prisoners to follow rules, PD prisoners may be excluded for several reasons. They may feel incapable of performing the work because of their impaired skills. For example, an offender with a speech disability may be

---

[1]Because Schneider and Sales (2004) reviewed the plight of deaf and hearing-impaired persons in prison, the rest of this chapter focuses on the other categories of PD offenders.

offered a job serving food in the prison cafeteria, but may decline the offer because of the potential humiliation and ridicule that may ensue when attempting to communicate. The offender also may be afraid to be in an open area where he or she could be easily confronted or attacked. An inmate with a visual impairment, for example, may feel vulnerable working in the library out of fear of not being able to do the job efficiently, or of being unprotected and potentially more exposed to attack.

Decreased ability to work can exacerbate the problems of boredom and loneliness that exist in prison. To address these latter concerns, inmates are often permitted (depending on the level of security in the facility) time to exercise, play sports, watch TV, listen to the radio, use the library, day rooms, and chapel, and visit with friends and relatives. Inmates also often make friends during group activities, to provide relief from what can be overwhelming solitude. Many of these avenues of potential boredom alleviation fail the PD offender. For example, in some facilities, the visiting rooms are in another part of the prison and inmates must be transported back and forth in a van. For wheelchair-bound inmates in some institutions, accommodations cannot be made because the vans are not wheelchair accessible (*Candelaria v. Greifinger*, 1998). In other cases, PD offenders have a difficult time making social contacts as the stigma of befriending a PD inmate can dissuade another offender from becoming close. Inmates with ambulatory disabilities are unable to take advantage of the exercise or sport activities, and if an institution's day rooms, libraries, or chapels are inaccessible, the boredom alleviation tactics employed by non-PD offenders fail the PD offender.

Reading material, for example, is of no or limited use to a blind or visually impaired offender, leaving radio or other auditory material as the only distraction. Even if Braille is available in some texts, not all blind or visually impaired inmates may feel comfortable or competent with this system. Additionally, not all inmates, including visually impaired inmates, may be satisfied with a radio as their only source of information or stimulation. In addition, a blind or visually impaired inmate may worry that listening to an auditory device will result in missing an important auditory cue (e.g., via a loudspeaker) that is crucial for participating in other activities (e.g., mealtime or recreation time) (*Brown v. King County Department of Adult Corrections*, 1998).

Social contacts inside the prison are also made difficult because other offenders often do not trust PD offenders because they frequently need to communicate with correctional staff. PD offenders require additional consideration from staff in order to meet daily prison requirements and engage in daily prison activities. This makes other inmates skeptical, as anyone who befriends the "opposing side" is viewed with suspicion. An inmate who converses with a correctional officer can be labeled "a rat" and treated as a traitor. A rat is an inmate who befriends guards in exchange for privileges. Given their added reliance on prison staff, PD inmates can be unfairly labeled a rat and suspected of ill intentions (Schneider & Sales, 2004).

Non-PD prisoners also might stay away from PD offenders because they are viewed as holding up or delaying prison procedures. For example, most correctional facilities operate by mandating frequent line-ups for cell counts and entry onto the yard for recreation time, and activities may be delayed while special attempts are made to accommodate PD inmates. PD inmates are blamed for holding up lines and cutting into very desirable outdoor time. In some facilities, in order to enter the yard for recreation time, inmates must pass through a turnstile. If a wheelchair-bound or visually impaired inmate wants to participate in recreation time, the other inmates often must wait for these offenders. When finally in the yard, these inmates may become the targets of abuse and pent-up aggression. Similar situations occur in the cafeteria, where PD inmates hold up lines while trying to convey their meal preferences to the servers or make their way through the line. These factors can and often do ostracize the PD inmate from engaging in and building positive social contacts within the prison.

Contacts with those outside the prison are equally thwarted for PD inmates. For example, if visitation areas are not accessible to wheelchair-bound inmates, it becomes an undue burden to take part in this activity to which they are entitled and that provides the offender something to look forward to and, in many cases, keep him or her going. If a separate visiting area is not made available for inmates with HIV/AIDS, not only is a health issue raised, but many inmates suffering this disease may not be able to have contact with their loved ones.

## Potential for Abuse

The already noted problems of inaccessibility increase the potential for PD inmates to experience abuse (*Ruiz v. Estelle*, 1980). In this type of environment, PD inmates are often left to protect themselves and are at increased risk for encountering emotional and/or physical harm. For example, almost all activities in prison pose a potential threat. PD inmates on the yard during recreation time are easy targets for physical attacks. If a PD inmate is in line to use equipment, other inmates can and do take advantage of the individual. If the PD offender has an item of value that another, stronger inmate wants (e.g., cigarettes), the item is often confiscated forcefully or without permission. This often results in an emotional, and sometimes physical, insult.

Simply going to prison places blind or visually impaired offenders at high risk for psychological harm because they are no longer a part of what may have been a protective and supportive feeling of community. In the community outside of prison, there are social, educational, advocacy, and work groups that serve only blind or visually impaired individuals. These groups help to foster a sense of support and camaraderie, but when a blind or visually impaired inmate enters prison, the community to which they may have belonged, as well as its support and tolerance, is no longer available.

The potential for the abuse of visually impaired offenders is quite significant. In *Bellamy v. Bradley* (1984), for example, a blind inmate, with the approval of prison authorities, was allowed "runners" to help him with tasks such as retrieving meals and escorting him to the yard, cafeteria, and restrooms. Yet correctional officers denied the runners permission to retrieve meals and other necessities and did not allow them access to the inmate in need. As a result, the complainant in this case went without meals on some days. Other known instances of abuse include housing a blind inmate with other inmates who end up physically, emotionally, and sexually abusing the visually impaired offender (*Stanciel v. Gramley*, 2001), beatings of PD offenders by staff and fellow inmates for what is thought to be the intentional violation of prison rules but is in actuality the inability to conform to prison procedure due to a physical limitation (*Harris v. O'Grady*, 1992), and inadequate instructional materials necessary for PD offenders and the staff responsible for their maintenance to learn and comply with important security and/or educational protocols (e.g., *Durham v. Roberts*, 1996).

The potential for the abuse of inmates with HIV/AIDS also runs high. In 1999, Lydia Kay Onishea, representing a class of HIV/AIDS offenders in Alabama's prison system, sued the warden and commissioner of the Alabama Department of Corrections (*Onishea v. Hopper*, 1999). Onishea claimed that she and others in her class were not allowed to participate in most of the programs and activities available at the prison. For example, they claimed they were unable to participate in prison jobs (e.g., maintaining the grounds, working on the prison farm, trash detail jobs, laundry jobs), classes (e.g., upholstery classes, electrical classes, welding classes, mechanics classes), or sporting events (e.g., basketball and baseball tournaments), and that all of these activities are available to HIV-negative offenders (see also *Bowman v. Beasley*, 2002). Other instances of potential abuse include inadequate medical attention (*McNally v. Prison Health Services*, 1999), teasing (*Bennett v. Maier*, 1998), and inaccessibility of family overnight visitations for HIV/AIDS offenders (*Bullock v. Gomez*, 1996).

Another category of physically disabled offenders at risk for abuse are those individuals with ambulatory disabilities (e.g., paraplegia, quadriplegia, tetraplegia, amputations, skeletal or spinal problems). The majority of cases brought by these offenders fall into three subcategories. First, the inadequacies of prison medical care are of paramount concern to inmates with ambulatory disabilities. Many cases have cited problems with wheelchair fit (*Hallett v. New York State Department of Correctional Services*, 2000), denial of pain and other medications (*Johnson v. Bendheim*, 2001), and neglect of and indifference to medical need (*Beckford v. Portuondo*, 2001; *Daniel v. Fields*, 1995; *Hucks v. Artuz*, 2003; *Wetzel v. Sheahan*, 2000). Second, inmates with ambulatory disabilities often cite inaccessibility of prison institutions as a pervasive problem. Numerous cases have been brought alleging that appliances and amenities are not accessible to them (e.g., microwave or refrigerator) (*Shariff v. Artuz*, 2000); shower chairs and hand rails, bed rails, and toilet hand rails are not provided, causing injury (*Beckford v. Irvin*, 1999; *Bryant v. Madigan*, 1996; *Evans v. Dugger*, 1990; *Frost v. Agnos*, 1998; *Herndon v. Johnson*, 1996; *Navedo v. Maloney*, 2001); and simply moving about the facility, including entering and exiting their cells, often required abandoning their wheelchairs and pulling themselves along the floor, resulting in further physical injury (*Hallett v. New York State Department of Correctional Services*, 2000; *Love v. Westville Correctional Center*, 1996; *Navedo v. Maloney*, 2001; *Schmidt v. Odell*, 1999).

Offenders with ambulatory disabilities claim that they have been the targets of emotional abuse (*Beckford v. Portuondo*, 2001; *Hucks v. Artuz*, 2003). For example, in *Hucks v. Artuz* (2003), a paraplegic inmate alleged that he was harassed and threatened by correctional officers and that on one occasion one of the officers "dumped him out of his wheelchair and onto the floor while other officers stood by." In another case, an inmate was not allowed his one hour per day of recreation time because the wheelchair access ramp to the outdoor facility was broken (*Beckford v. Portuondo*, 2001). In yet another instance (*Stanciel v. Gramley*, 2001), a visually impaired inmate alleged that correctional officers intentionally led him into objects such as gates, doors, and rails because they were angry at him for filing a grievance against the Department of Corrections.

For inmates with diabetes, who comprise a significant proportion of the state and federal prison population (*Green v. Corrections Corporation of America*, 1999; *Parker v. Michigan Department of Corrections*, 2001; *Rouse v. Plantier*, 1997), the majority of legal complaints seem to center around the inadequacy of medical and nutritional care (*Rouse v. Plantier*, 1997). For example, plaintiffs in the *Rouse v. Plantier* (1997) case named blood sugar control, nutrition and diet, patient education, prevention and management of acute and long-term complications of diabetes, and diabetic-specific primary care needs as missing components of a much needed program of diabetic care in prison. Other grievances included the inaccessibility of prison programs and services, including the correctional staff's failure to administer insulin injections at the most appropriate times (*Green v. Corrections Corporation of America*, 1999).

A common complaint of many physically disabled offenders from all mentioned populations is their inability to receive honors points or rewards that are established to promote good behavior in prisons (*Amos v. Maryland Department of Public Safety and Correctional Services*, 1997; *Daniel v. Fields*, 1995). Acquisition of good behavior points translates into increments of time to be taken off of the sentence the inmate has been ordered to serve. There is an issue of potential discrimination if the difference between one inmate earning these good time points and another inmate being unable to is caused by physical disability. For example, if an offender ambulates in a wheelchair and the prison cell he lives in does not adequately accommodate the device, the inmate may be late for cell count line-ups, meal time, recreation time, or other regimented activities that allow for the acquisition of good behavior points. Another problem arises for inmates who, despite their physical disability, manage to acquire enough of these honors points or rewards. In *Shariff v. Artuz* (2000), the prison facility in which the inmates were housed maintained a separate housing unit called the "Honor Block" for inmates who kept up high standards of behavior. Residence in the Honor Block was "noted in an inmate's record" and increased the inmate's chances of parole or clemency. Honor Block inmates also were awarded privileges not available to inmates in the general population. For example, Honor Block inmates were allowed extra time for recreation, increased mailing privileges, access to appliances (including refrigerators, microwave ovens, pots, irons, and ironing boards), and the opportunity to live among other "well-behaved" inmates. To qualify for the Honor Block, an inmate must have: (1) resided at the facility for 2 years; (2) successfully completed unspecified "programs"; and (3) maintained a record free of disciplinary convictions for a 1-year period prior to application for, or placement in, the Honor Block. The plaintiffs in this case contended that the prison facility in question did not permit disabled inmates to live on the Honor Block. The Honor Block facility lacked widened cell doors, hand rails, and shower chairs required by inmates in wheelchairs. If prisons reward good behavior with admission to a less secure part of the facility and with added privileges, all inmates should have the same opportunity to gain points, to access the special part of the facility, and otherwise benefit from the reward system.

It is clear that PD offenders are often subject to a significantly more adverse experience in prison compared to non-PD offenders. In order to fully appreciate the scope of this abuse experience, we next compare the effects of having a physical disability in prison to two other relevant groups: individuals in the general population, and non-PD offenders in prison.

## COMPARATOR POPULATIONS

### Physically Disabled Individuals Outside of Prison

The social psychological processes affecting people with disabilities, those receiving rehabilitative services, and non-disabled observers are undeniable (Dunn, 2000). Coping with a physical disability often requires the support of family, friends, and the community, as less satisfaction with social contacts is closely related to more symptoms of depression (Williamson, Shulz, Bridges, & Behan, 1994). In this section, we describe some of the challenges facing individuals with spinal-cord injuries, amputations, visual impairments, speech impairments, and HIV outside of the prison environment.

Spinal-cord injuries (SCIs) can be devastating injuries to both the physical and psychological integrity of individuals (Donelson, 1998). Mental health problems encountered in the general population, such as depression, anxiety, suicide, and substance abuse, are encountered in the SCI population, but depression is also associated with the initial impact of recognizing that a physical limitation exists. The level of physical disability is predictive of scores on measures of overall sexual self-concept, sexual esteem, sexual depression, prevalence of depression, and positive outlook (Donelson, 1998). Psychosexual maladjustment due to SCI, for example, contributes to the development of indecisiveness and ambivalence in many life activities, while sexual dysfunction frequently results in a sense of inadequacy (Berger & Garrett, 1952). In addition, adjustment problems following SCI, cognitive deficits, chronic pain, and secondary conditions are also often present (Richards, Kewman, & Pierce, 2000). Not surprisingly, then, the personality characteristics and attitudes revealed most frequently in connection with SCIs are situational depression, immature emotional expression, ambivalence and indecision, and unrealistic thinking (Mueller, 1950).

In addition to being physically demanding, undergoing an amputation and the training required to acquaint oneself with a prosthesis can be a psychologically distressing experience. All people with amputations must come to terms with the loss of their limb(s) and the associated functional setbacks (Rybarczyk, Szymanski, & Nicholas, 2000). Persons with amputations express significantly more neuroticism, less extraversion, more body distortion, and more alienation compared to their normal counterparts. In addition, they are more dissatisfied with their present life and expected more dissatisfaction in the future as compared to controls (Bhojak, Nathawat, & Swami, 1989).

People with poor vision are more likely to manifest indicators of psychological distress (e.g., depressive feelings, anxiety, worry, intrusive thoughts, isolation, and loneliness) (Karlsson, 1998). Sudden blindness, in particular, may result in a psychological process marked by psychic numbness, denial, mistrust, obsessional thoughts of blame, and posttraumatic stress disorder (Dale, 1992). In Hudson's (1994) review of 27 works explaining reactions to blindness, 15 of the works considered social factors to be the primary influence on reactions to blindness, 4 considered personal factors to be the primary influence, and 8 considered the combination of the two the primary influence in determining reactions to blindness. Based on these results, Hudson argued that rehabilitation agencies should place greater emphasis on the social aspects of blindness. Additionally, research indicates that adolescents with visual impairment had fewer friends and dates with other young people than those without visual impairment, and reported feelings of loneliness and difficulties in making friends more often than controls. Female adolescents had lowered self-esteem, school achievement, and social skills compared with the control girls (Huurre & Aro, 1998).

Excessive anxiety, musculoskeletal tension, and difficulties in expressing feelings or being assertive have been commonly reported among individuals with speech disorders, and are usually associated with unsatisfactory interpersonal relationships, especially with members of their family (Butcher, Elias, Raven, Yeatman, & Littlejohns, 1987). Non-speech-disordered persons even perceive those who have lost their voice as having a mental disability (Weitzel, 2000). There also is an increasing amount of evidence linking emotional and behavioral problems with communication difficulties (Cross, 1998). For example, there are significant differences in the degree of internalizing, social, and attentional problems between children with language impairments and those without them, with teachers rating children with language impairment as having more social and internalizing behavioral problems than their peers (Redmond & Rice, 1998). In addition, children with pervasive speech/language problems at age 5 demonstrate greater behavioral disturbance than children without such impairment (Beitchman et al., 1996).

Finally, individuals infected with the human immunodeficiency virus (HIV) often experience significant levels of psychological distress, particularly depression and anxiety (Watts, 2001). These psychological and emotional difficulties may occur as a result of associated medical conditions, including secondary opportunistic conditions, central nervous system HIV infection and medication side effects, primary psychiatric disorders (Balderson, Halman, & Jones, 2000), and stigmatization of HIV persons and needed changes in lifestyle (Campbell, 1997; Davies, 1997). Psychological consequences almost always result, not only for the HIV patient but also for his or her friends and family, and it is argued that, irrespective of the route of transmission of HIV infection, the burden of care usually falls on the family (Bor & du Plessis, 1997).

## Non-Physically Disabled Individuals in Prison

Research indicates that prison can be psychologically and emotionally traumatic even to the most physically and psychologically well-adjusted inmate for several reasons (Morris & Rothman, 1995; Toch, 1992). First, inmates attempt to portray the image of the "manly man," an individual who does not experience depression, anger, despair, or self-doubt. (Goffman, 1961; Toch, 1992). It is often tough for inmates to successfully portray this image. Those who fail are sometimes the subjects of ridicule, sexual dominance, and physical violence (*Ruiz v. Estelle*, 1980).

Second, many prisoners experience loneliness and boredom. In the outside world, a solution would be to create significant interpersonal contacts. When an inmate makes a friend, life behind in prison can be bearable. In truth, many inmates isolate themselves in an attempt to gain protection, as a result of depression, or due to difficulties securing a compatible friend. Solitude, boredom, sadness, and fear can and often do perpetuate a cycle that leads to physical and psychological breakdown (Goffman, 1961; Toch, 1992).

Third, boredom is accompanied by intense understimulation. Life in prison is routine, with little to look forward to on a day-to-day basis. Meal time, recreation time, visitations, phone calls, television, and reading are about the extent of the extracurricular activities inmates rely on for stimulation (*Ruiz v. Estelle*, 1980). An inmate who experiences understimulation often cannot concentrate, function appropriately, or make sense of his or her environment, and anxiety, paranoia, depression, and a host of other schizophrenic-like responses may result (Morris & Rothman, 1998; Toch, 1992).

Fourth is the problem of segregation in prison. Inmates often want to socialize with those who are similar to themselves which can and does lead to segregation in prison. The sense of belonging that is often stripped away in the prison environment can be gained by associating with similar others. Social groups are formed according to racial identification, gang identification, or assigned prison family identification (Morris & Rothman, 1998).

It can be difficult for an inmate who identifies with more than one racial group to be accepted into a social circle that defines itself by a single race. For example, a Mexican American inmate who equally identifies with his or her Mexican and American backgrounds may not be considered "Mexican enough" or "American enough" to meet criteria for in-group status in either group.

Problems also arise for those inmates who do identify with a particular group when their group is not adequately represented in prison or there is no group with which to identify. It is difficult enough to cope with the mundane, isolating aspects of prison, but segregation and separatist attitudes increase the likelihood that those without their own group suffer even more.

Finally, qualified mental health staff in prison are lacking (*Ruiz v. Estelle*, 1980), whereas the number of inmates in need of their services is increasing. Inmates who feel their psychological needs are too overwhelming or are not being attended to often attempt suicide or self-mutilation, hoping to be transferred to a mental health unit (Ashford, Sales, & Reid, 2001a; Ivanoff & Hayes, 2001; Toch, 1992).

## Implications of Comparator Groups for Physically Disabled Offenders

All of these difficulties will arguably affect the physically disabled more deleteriously than the non-physically disabled inmate. For example, it is often much more difficult for an inmate who uses a wheelchair or crutches to successfully manifest the "manly man" image. PD offenders are often seen as weak, vulnerable, and of little or no threat. Making social contacts is often more difficult for the PD offender. The physical impairment itself is a deterrent to other inmates because befriending a stigmatized person often has a social price for the non-PD offender. In addition, boredom alleviation tactics are less often available for PD inmates. Recreation activities may be limited for the offender using a wheelchair to ambulate, library materials may be inaccessible to offenders with visual impairments, television or radio may be inaccessible to deaf or hard-of-hearing offenders, and socializing opportunities may be thwarted for inmates with HIV or AIDS.

In addition, given that individuals with physical disabilities in the general population often require mental health services, PD offenders may feel the effects of the prison system's inadequacy in this arena more than other inmates. Just as the non-PD offender in prison suffers anxiety, paranoia, depression, and a host of other schizophrenic-like responses (Morris & Rothman, 1998; Toch, 1992), the PD offender may also be at increased risk for psychological breakdown. The combination of confinement, little access to stimulation including social contact, and an environment that is riddled with hostility and provides no assurance of safety places PD offenders in an especially precarious emotional situation.

Finally, the problem of segregation in prison may place the PD offender in an especially disadvantageous situation. Although an offender may be Caucasian, for example, the identity most salient to other inmates as far as inclusion in a particular group may be his or her disability. So it may be that rather than being included in a racial or ethnic group, PD offenders may have to form their own group. The number of members and hence chance of the successful creation of a group becomes small if, for example, category membership is solely contingent on having a visual impairment.

## ACCOMMODATIONS AND SERVICES FOR PD INMATES

Given the risks facing, and the problems encountered by, PD inmates, it is important to identify potential accommodations and services that should be implemented to address their needs. First, PD inmates need to have auxiliary aids provided to them. Auxiliary aids are any assistive service or device a person with a sensory disability could utilize. Examples of auxiliary aids for visually impaired offenders include books on audiotape, in-cell radios, auditory options for written rules or other text present in prison facilities, and navigational devices such as walking canes or facilitators. For deaf or hard-of-hearing inmates, examples of auxiliary aids include assistive listening devices, notetakers, interpreters, and closed captioning. For wheelchair users, auxiliary aids include shower chairs, hand rails, wider doors and ramps for accessibility, and lowered shelves and appliances. The U.S. Department of Justice has stated that "in determining what type of auxiliary aid and service is necessary, a public entity shall give primary consideration to the requests of the individual with disabilities" (28 C.F.R. 35.160 (b)(2)). This means that prisons should defer to the ability of the PD inmate to assess for him- or herself which of the auxiliary aids will be most effective (*Chisolm v. Mcmanimon*, 2001).

Second, given the added level of vulnerability of these inmates, their safety becomes a central issue. A special device could be attached to their person that, when pushed, alerts guards that they are in danger. Inmates who abuse the use of such a device could be penalized for their misconduct. Supervision should be mandatory for the visually impaired while recreating, showering, and navigating. If a PD offender is to have a cellmate (*Walker v. Snyder*, 2000), this inmate must be screened for previous violent conduct to assure the safety of the disabled offender.

Third, PD offenders need to be able to access and gain potential benefit from prison benefits and programs (*Cassidy v. Indiana DOC*, 1999; *Crawford v. Indiana DOC*, 1997; *Daniel v. Fields*, 1995; *Love v. Westville Correctional Center*, 1996; *Nelson v. Norris*, 2001; *Stanciel v. Gramley*, 2001). If an inmate merits inclusion into an educational program, he or she should not be denied access to it solely because of a physical disability. For example, offenders who use a wheelchair should not be prohibited from participating in programs or services such as an Alcoholics Anonymous meeting or a group therapy session because of architectural barriers. Meeting places for programs and activities should be accessible to all who otherwise qualify for inclusion in them. Similarly, educational materials available to sighted offenders must be made accessible to nonsighted offenders.

## RESEARCH NEEDS

Although the preceding discussion represents the most accurate picture of the potential problems facing PD inmates in prison today, it is a portrait largely based on case reports because of the lack of empirical research. Addressing PD inmate problems and needs in the absence of such research is a problem given that it is impossible to know with any certainty PD inmates': (a) specific problems and needs, (b) magnitude of problems and needs, (c) the mediating and moderating variables affecting them, (d) the causal pathways that lead to them, and (e) the interventions and services most appropriate for responding to them.

### Epidemiological Research on Physical Disability

As already noted, most of the epidemiological data are derived from a few poorly formulated and grossly deficient questions in written form. Questions like "Do you have difficulty seeing ordinary newsprint even when wearing glasses?" or "Do you have a physical disability?" (Maruschak & Beck, 2001, p. 2) must be treated as suspect due to the myriad ulterior motives possible in the responses to them. For example, an offender who thinks he or she may receive benefits such as a private cell or immunity from physical labor might answer affirmatively to these questions. A new tool for measuring the occurrence of physical disability must be created.

Furthermore, epidemiological research cannot study those with a physical disability as a homogeneous group. A new tool for more accurately measuring the epidemiology of PD offenders should take into account the multiple types and levels of impairment, coping styles, and psychological ramifications employed by this diverse population. For example, an inmate with partial paraplegia will have a different set of needs and hence necessary accommodations than an inmate with complete paraplegia or quadriplegia. An inmate with partial vision will have a different set of needs and necessary accommodations than an inmate who is completely without sight.

## Physical and Emotional Abuse in Prison

In prison, all offenders are at risk for abuse. The PD offender, however, is at a substantially greater risk due to his or her impaired ability to see, hear, ambulate, communicate, or use full body capacity for protection. It is important to know the frequency and magnitude of the abuse that is occurring, the environmental and social conditions that may incite or facilitate it, and any differences between the types, frequency and magnitude of abuse experienced by PD and non-PD inmates. Existing and necessary types of prison monitoring for abuse, reporting and record-keeping of it, and interventions to prevent it also need to be carefully considered. It is not acceptable to rely on anecdotal evidence about abuse because this type of information does not support the construction of causal models to explain and predict when and how abuse is likely to occur. A multitrait, multimethod approach may be necessary for gathering reliable and valid information (see Campbell & Fiske, 1959). Self reports, interviews with inmates, family, and/or friends, skilled observation, and archival research should all be considered in collecting relevant data.

## Psychological Breakdown of PD Inmates in Prison

If offenders in the general prison population are at risk for psychological breakdown induced by the pervasive threat of violence, the incessant boredom, and the often cruel and callous treatment of inmates by one another as well as by correctional officers and other prison staff (*Evans v. Dugger*, 1990; *Frost v. Agnos*, 1998; *Stanciel v. Gramley*, 2001), then offenders who encounter the same environment but who also have physical disability should be at an even greater risk. Thus, future research must consider techniques to screen and assess for psychological disorder prior to entering prison, at numerous points throughout incarceration, and after release if the person is on parole. The administration of a periodic inventory of offender adjustment is necessary to understand, predict, and control the threat of psychological breakdown among both PD and non-PD offenders.

An assessment of psychological well-being prior to entry into the facility provides a baseline measure of psychological functioning, and would allow us to know if inmates with physical disabilities come to prison with adjustment problems or if these are the result of life behind bars. If it appears that inmates with physical disabilities are differentially deleteriously affected by prison life, to which inmates does the concern apply most? Are visually impaired inmates fairing better than inmates with ambulatory disabilities, and if so, why? Are certain moderating and mediating variables better able explain adverse outcomes? It is important for researchers to start identifying what causal pathways might be leading to breakdowns in prison over time and for what disability types in particular.

## Availability and Quality of Prison Services

Once the epidemiological, mental health, abuse, and adjustment concerns are addressed, the availability and efficacy of intervention programs, work opportunities, and other services (e.g., problem-solving skills workshops) and accommodations for the PD offenders must be empirically considered. Research must address not only the accessibility of these programs and services, but also their respective levels of effectiveness. Given the variable nature of individual differences in response to treatment, inclusion in such programs is not enough. Questions of response to inclusion in specific programs must be assessed for inmates with varying disabilities. It may be that certain programs and services prove beneficial to inmates with visual but not speech disabilities. The type of treatment research detailed earlier can lead to a new generation of interventions, which are empirically validated for and normed on specific subpopulations and presenting problems (e.g., Ashford, Sales, & Reid, 2001b).

## Implementation of Existing Law

Finally, research must examine the difference between law on the books versus law in action. The way law is implemented depends on the exercise of discretion by legal actors (e.g., correctional administrators) and and lay citizens (e.g., other inmates and/or their families). The result is that law as it is applied in action often differs significantly from the law on the books. This point is particularly applicable to ADA's mandated accommodations for PD inmates. Rules need to be implemented and employed appropriately. Unless future research monitors the law in action, and examines how and why the intent of the law is being thwarted, an atmosphere in which PD offenders are neglected and even abused will likely occur.

## REFERENCES

Americans With Disabilities Act 42 U.S.C. § 12101 (1990).
Americans With Disabilities Act Accessibility Guidelines, 36 C.F.R. § 1191(1994).
*Amos v. Maryland Department of Public Safety and Correctional Services*, 126 F. 3d 589 (D.Md. 1997).

Ashford, J. B., Sales, B. D., & Reid, W. (2001a). Introduction to treating offenders with special needs. In J. B. Ashford, B. D. Sales, & W. H. Reid. (Eds.), *Treating adult and juvenile offenders with special needs* (pp. 3–27). Washington, DC: American Psychological Association.

Ashford, J. B., Sales, B. D., & Reid, W. (Eds.). (2001b). *Treating adult and juvenile offenders with special needs*. Washington, DC: American Psychological Association.

Balderson, K., Halman, M., & Jones, K. (2000). Psychiatric aspects of HIV disease. *Primary Care Psychiatry, 6*(3), 83–92.

Beck, A. J., & Maruschak, L. M. (2001). *Mental health treatment in state prisons, 2000*. U.S. Department of Justice, Office of Justice Programs, NCJ 188215.

*Beckford v. Irvin*, 60 F. Supp. 2d 85 (W.D.N.Y. 1999).

*Beckford v. Portuondo*, 151 F. Supp. 2d. 204 (N.D.N.Y. 2001).

Beitchman, J. H., Wilson, B., Brownlie, E. B., Walters, H., Inglis, A., & Lancee, W. (1996). Long-term consistency in speech/language profiles II. Behavioral, emotional, and social outcomes. *Journal of the American Academy of Child and Adolescent Psychiatry, 35*(6), 815–825.

*Bellamy v. Bradley*, 729 F.2d 416 (6th Cir. 1984).

*Bennett v. Maier*, U.S. Dist. LEXIS 10191. (E.D.Pa. 1998).

Berger, S., & Garrett, J. F. (1952). Psychological problems of the paraplegic patient. *Journal of Rehabilitation, 18*(5), 15–17.

Bhojak, M. M., Nathawat, S. S., & Swami, D. R. (1989). Psychological consequences following lower limb amputation. *Indian Journal of Clinical Psychology, 16*(2), 102–104.

Bor, R., & du Plessis, P. (1997). The impact of HIV/AIDS on families: An overview of recent research. *Families, Systems & Health, 15*(4), 413–427.

*Bowman v. Beasley*, 535 U.S. 1121 (2002).

*Brown v. King County Department of Adult Corrections*, 1998 U.S. Dist. LEXIS 20152 (W.D.Wash. 1998).

*Bryant v. Madigan*, 84 F.3d 246 (7th Cir. 1996).

*Bullock v. Gomez*, 929 F. Supp. 1299 (C.D.Cal. 1996).

Butcher, P., Elias, A., Raven, R., Yeatman, J., & Littlejohns, D. (1987). Psychogenic voice disorder unresponsive to speech therapy: Psychological characteristics and cognitive-behavioral therapy. *British Journal of Disorders of Communication, 22*(1), 81–92.

Campbell, D. T., & Fiske, D. W. (1959). Convergent and discriminant validation by the multitrait-multimethod matrix. *Psychological Bulletin, 56*, 81–105.

Campbell, T. (1997). A review of the effects of vertically acquired HIV infection in infants and children. *British Journal of Health Psychology, 2*(1), 1–13.

*Candelaria v. Greifinger*, 1998 WL 312375 (N.D.N.Y 1998).

*Cassidy v. Indiana Dep't of Corrections*, 59 F. Supp. 2d 787 (S.D. IN 1999).

*Chisolm v. Mcmanimon*, 97 F. Supp. 2d 615 (D.N.J. 2000), *aff'd*, 275 F. 3d 315 (3rd Cir. 2001).

Civil Rights of Institutionalized Persons Act of 1980, 42 U.S.C. §1381 (1997).

*Crawford v. Indiana Dep't of Corrections*, 115 F. 3d. 481 (7th Cir. 1997).

Cross, M. (1998). Undetected communication problems in children with behavioural problems. *International Journal of Language & Communication Disorders, 33*, 509–514.

Dale, B. (1992). Issues in traumatic blindness. *Journal of Visual Impairment & Blindness, 86*(3), 140–143.

*Daniel v. Fields*, 66 F. 3d 338 (10th Cir. 1995).

Davies, M. L. (1997). Shattered assumptions: Time and the experience of long-term HIV positivity. *Social Science & Medicine, 44*(5), 561–571.

Donelson, E. G. (1998). The relationship of sexual self-concept to the level of spinal cord injury and other factors. *Dissertation Abstracts International: Section B: The Sciences & Engineering, 58*, 12-B (6805).

Dunn, D. S. (2000). Social psychological issues in disability. In R. G. Frank & T. R. Elliott (Eds.), *Handbook of rehabilitation psychology* (pp. 565–584). Washington, DC: American Psychological Association.

*Durham v. Roberts*, 103 F.3d 138 (9th Cir. 1996).

*Evans v. Dugger*, 908 F. 2d 801 (11th Cir. 1990).

*Frost v. Agnos*, 152 F.3d. 1124 (9th Cir. 1998).

Goffman, E. (1961). *Asylums: Essays on the social situation of mental patients and other inmates.* New York: Doubleday.

*Green v. Corrections Corporation of America*, 198 F.3d 245 (6th Cir.1999).

*Hallett v. New York State Department of Correctional Services*, 109 F. Supp. 2d 190 (S.D.N.Y 2000).

Harlow, C. W. (2003). Education and correctional populations. U.S. Department of Justice, Office of Justice Programs, NCJ 195670.

*Harris v. O'Grady*, 803 F. Supp. 1361 (N.D.Ill. 1992).

*Herndon v. Johnson*, 970 F. Supp. 703 (S.D.Ala.1996).

*Hucks v. Artuz*, 2003 WL 22853047 (S.D.N.Y. 2003).

Hudson, D. (1994). Causes of emotional and psychological reactions to adventitious blindness. *Journal of Visual Impairment & Blindness, 88*(6), 498–503.

Huurre, T. M., & Aro, H. M. (1998). Psychosocial development among adolescents with visual impairment. *European Child & Adolescent Psychiatry, 7*(2), 73–78.

Ivanoff, A., & Hayes, L. M. (2001). Preventing, managing, and treating suicidal actions in high risk offenders. In J. B. Ashford, B. D. Sales, & W. H. Reid (Eds.), *Treating adult and juvenile offenders with special needs* (pp. 313–331). Washington, DC: American Psychological Association.

*Johnson v. Bendheim*, 2001 LEXIS 3636 (S.D.N.Y 2001).

Karlsson, J. S. (1998). Self-reports of psychological distress in connection with various degrees of visual impairment. *Journal of Visual Impairment & Blindness, 92*(7), 483–490.

*Key v. Grayson et al.*, 163 F. Supp 2d 697 (E.D.Mich. 2001).

*Love v. Westville Correctional Center*, 103 F. 3d 558 (7th Cir. 1996).

Maruschack, L. M., & Beck, A. J. (2001). Medical problems of inmates, 1997. *Bureau of Justice Statistics*, 1–11.

*McNally v. Prison Health Services*, 52 F. Supp. 2d 147 (D.Me. 1999).

Morris, N., & Rothman, D. J. (1998). *The Oxford history of the prison: The practice of punishment in Western society.* New York: Oxford University Press.

Mueller, A. D. (1950). Personality problems of the spinal cord injured. *Journal of Consulting Psychology, 14*, 189–192.

Mumola, C. J. (1999). *Substance abuse and treatment, state and federal prisoners, 1997.* U.S. Department of Justice, Office of Justice Programs, NCJ 172871.

*Navedo v. Maloney*, 172 F. Supp. 2d 276 (D.Mass. 2001).

*Nelson v. Norris*, 242 F.3d 376 (8th Cir. 2001).

*Onishea v. Hopper*, 171 F. 3d. 1289 (11th Cir. 1999).

*Parker v. Michigan Department of Corrections*, 2001 LEXIS 18931 (W.D.Mich. 2001).

Redmond, S. M., & Rice, M. L. (1998). The socioemotional behaviors of children with SLI: Social adaptation or social deviance? *Journal of Speech, Language, & Hearing Research, 41*(3), 688–700.

Rehabilitation Act, 29 U.S.C. § 504 (1973).

Richards, J. S., Kewman, D. G., & Pierce, C. A. (2000). Spinal cord injury. In R. G. Frank & T. R. Elliott (Eds.), *Handbook of rehabilitation psychology* (p. 11–27). Washington, DC: American Psychological Association.

*Rouse v. Plantier*, 987 F. Supp. 302 (D.N.J. 1997).

*Ruiz v. Estelle*, 503 F. Supp. 1265 (S.D.Tex. 1980).

Rybarczyk, B., Szymanski, L., & Nicholas, J. J. (2000). Limb amputation. In R. G. Frank & T. R. Elliott (Eds.), *Handbook of rehabilitation psychology* (pp. 29–47). Washington, DC: American Psychological Association.

*Schmidt v. Odell*, 64 F. Supp. 2d 1014 (D.Kan. 1999).

Schneider, N. R., & Sales, B. D. (2004). Deaf and hard of hearing inmates in prison. *Disability and Society, 19*, 77–89.

*Shariff v. Artuz*, 2000 LEXIS 15523 (S.D.N.Y. 2000).

*Stanciel v. Gramley*, 267 F. 3d. 575 (7th Cir. 2001).

Toch, H. (1992). *Mosaic of despair: Human breakdowns in prison*. Washington, DC: American Psychological Association.

U.S. Department of Health and Human Services, National Center for Health Statistics. (1996). *National Health Interview Survey, 1996* [Computer file]. ICPSR version. Hyattsville, MD: U.S. Department of Health and Human Services.

U.S. Department of Justice, Office of Justice Programs, Bureau of Justice Statistics. (2002). *Correctional populations in the United States, 1998*. A BJS Internet Report. NCJ 192929.

*Walker v. Snyder*, 213 F. 3d 344 (7th Cir. 2000).

Watts, M. S. (2001). Hope, coping, and psychological adjustment in HIV-infected gay men (immune deficiency). *Dissertation Abstracts International: Section B: The Sciences & Engineering, 62*, 3-B (1605).

Weitzel, A. (2000). Overcoming loss of voice. In D. O. Braithwaite & T. L. Thompson (Eds.), *Handbook of communication and people with disabilities: Research and application* (pp. 451–466). Mahwah, NJ: Lawrence Erlbaum Associates.

*Wetzel v. Sheahan*, 210 F.3d 377 (7th Cir. 2000).

Williamson, G. M., Shulz, R., Bridges, M. W., & Behan, A. M. (1994). Social and psychological factors in adjustment to limb amputation. Psychosocial perspectives on disability [Special Issue] *Journal of Social Behavior & Personality, 9*(5), 249–268.

# 3

# The Use of Existing Videoconferencing Technology to Deliver Video Remote Interpreting Services for Deaf Vocational Rehabilitation Clients

Joyce S. Steinberg

In 2002, the Arizona Rehabilitation Services Administration (ARSA) completed a technology infrastructure project that included a separate network dedicated to real-time videoconferencing. As part of this initiative, video training sites in Phoenix, Tucson, Flagstaff, and Yuma were designed and equipped to facilitate distance learning activities, including in-service training and academic coursework.

This study was designed to evaluate the effectiveness of using the ARSA videoconferencing system, originally intended for distance learning activities, to support video remote interpreting (VRI) for the deaf. VRI is defined as a situation in which the vocational rehabilitation (VR) counselor and the client are located together at one video site and the sign-language interpreter is viewed on video from a remote video site. This is in contrast to what would be considered a "traditional" VR interview, where the counselor, the client, and the interpreter comprise a triad, in a local office setting.

## STATEMENT OF THE PROBLEM

There were no data to evaluate whether it would be an appropriate use of ARSA resources to expand the original scope of the videoconferencing network to support video remote interpreting, within the context of the VR process. Informal video interpreting had been attempted on a few occasions when a deaf staff person showed up for an in-service training without previously requesting an interpreter. The accommodation in these situations was to adjust the camera at the remote site so that the interpreter, who was hired to interpret for a different deaf individual at that remote location, was seen on the monitor at the local site. Feedback from staff involved in these "impromptu" VRI sessions was that it was "acceptable" (personal communications, 2000). However, these situations were not evaluated and there was no way to know if the individual was able to understand everything that was discussed or any specifics related to satisfaction with the services.

## Rationale for the Study

Arizona is principally a rural state spread out over 113,909 square miles. Based on population estimates from the *2000 Census of Population and Housing*, there are only 45.2 persons per square mile in Arizona, as compared to the national population density of 79.6 (2002). More than half of the state's population (2,784,075) resides in Maricopa County, where Phoenix, the capital and largest city is located. Most of the remaining counties, with the exception of parts of Pima County, where the second largest city of Tucson is located, are considered rural counties.

Because the U.S. Bureau of Census has not included a question related to hearing loss since 1930, and only recently changed the sampling strategy to include state and regional estimates for the deaf and hard of hearing population, it is difficult to get definitive numbers (Holt, Hotto, & Cole, 1994). The most recent *National Center for Health Statistics* data published by Adams, Hendershot, and Marano (1999) reported 8.3% of the United States population has a hearing loss. However, the numbers of deaf persons varies depending on the terms used to describe them. For the purpose of this study, the following operational definitions for coding sensory impairments taken from the *ARSA Policy Handbook* (Article 2, Section 11, H), effective July 1997, were used:

> Deafness—A hearing impairment; of such severity that the individual must depend primarily upon visual communication such as writing, lip-reading, manual communication, and gestures.
>
> Hard of Hearing (HoH)—A hearing impairment, resulting in a functional loss, but not to the extent that the individual must depend primarily on visual communication.

According to self-reported data from the *1999–2000 Annual Survey of Deaf and Hearing Children and Youth* conducted by Gallaudet Research Institute (2001), approximately 398,422 or 8.6% of the total Arizona population of 4.6 million were estimated to be deaf/hard of hearing. *The National Health Interview Survey (NHIS)*, conducted by the Center for Assessment and Demographic Studies at Gallaudet University (1994), estimated that 123,460 or 31% of the total population of hard-of-hearing/deaf individuals reside in the two urban centers of Phoenix and Tucson. This means that the remaining 69% are dispersed throughout the remaining rural cities and counties (Blackwell, Collins & Coles, 2002).

Part of the problem in delivering VR services equitably to deaf persons, wherever they may reside, is that out of 290 rehabilitation counselors in Arizona, there are only 7 rehabilitation counselors for the deaf (RCDs), with the training and experience to work with deaf and hard of hearing consumers. All of these counselors are located in offices in either Phoenix or Tucson (ARSA, 2003). This means that 100% of the staff resources for the deaf and hard of hearing are allocated to the two urban cities, where only 31% of the individuals are estimated to reside.

## REVIEW OF THE LITERATURE

### Vocational Rehabilitation Services for the Deaf

The public rehabilitation program has been in existence for over 75 years. "The plight of individuals who are deaf and have failed to reach their optimum levels of functioning has been of concern to rehabilitation professionals for more than 30 years" (Long & Ouellette, 1994, p.1). In spite of the increase in the incidence of hearing loss (Ries, 1994), the federal Rehabilitation Services Administration (RSA) reported a 10-year decline, between 1989 and 1999, in the total number of consumers with hearing loss, closed as "successfully rehabilitated" (RSA, 2000). The definition for successfully rehabilitated, according to the federal RSA, is a client who has been suitably employed for a minimum of 90 days. This case is coded a "Status 26" closure in the Federal 9-11 Report.

Although the number of deaf/HoH clients served from 1997 through 1999 increased in the Arizona VR program, only 1,327 VR clients with either a primary disability coding of deafness or hard of hearing were closed as rehabilitated in 1999 (ARSA, 2000). This represented less than 5% of all VR clients closed as Status 26 in 1999, which was below the 7.3% national average (RSA, 2000) for the same period.

In a recent report from the University of Arkansas Rehabilitation Research and Training Center for Persons Who Are Deaf or Hard of Hearing, Capella (2003) compared differences in outcomes for 23,992 VR consumers with hearing loss with a random sample of the same size comprised of VR consumers from other disability groups. For those consumers who were unemployed at time of application, 77% of the hearing loss group was successfully closed in competitive employment, versus 86% for those from the other disability groups.

The federal RSA has called for states to reexamine their policies for providing VR services to consumers with hearing loss (Capella, 2003) and on improving access for individuals who had previously been underserved or underrepresented, including those who are deaf and hard of hearing (Kosovich, 1994). In order to be more responsive to these mandates, state agencies have begun to place greater emphasis on outreach activities and on encouraging consumer involvement in the VR process.

## Rehabilitation Counselors for the Deaf

In order to accommodate deaf consumers, the *ARSA Handbook*, effective April 2000, states, "Clients who are deaf require specialized services from counselors knowledgeable in the rehabilitation of deaf persons and skilled in manual communication. Individuals who are deaf will be referred to such a specialist if one is available within the geographical area" (Article 2, Section 4, iv, p. 6).

The deaf specialist originally was created through cooperative agreements between state rehabilitation agencies and state residential schools for deaf students (Danek, 1992). The RCDs' value to a deaf or hard of hearing VR client lies in the fact they have a clearer understanding of the impact of hearing loss on the person's daily life. Although both the Rehabilitation Act Amendments and the Individuals With Disabilities Education Act (IDEA) reference "qualified" staff, other than the Commission on Rehabilitation Counseling certification, a generic discipline certification, there exists no certification or licensure standard for counselors who work specifically with deaf or hard of hearing consumers (Danek, 1994). There are few rehabilitation counselor education programs nationwide that train rehabilitation counselors for the deaf (RCDs). The limited educational opportunities in the area of deafness have resulted in fewer personnel to fill positions within state VR agencies. Anderson, Boone, and Watson (2002) surveyed state VR agency administrators and program specialists from 43 state agencies and reported that one-third experienced significant shortages of rehabilitation counselors for the deaf to work with consumers with hearing loss.

In rural areas, population density may not support the justification for a specialist to work only with persons with hearing loss. Because all the ARSA deaf specialists are located in either Phoenix or Tucson (ARSA, 2003), generalist counselors most often are the counselors who provide services for deaf consumers seeking VR services in rural counties. Few, if any, generalist counselors can communicate in American Sign Language (ASL), which is the visual language used by 1.5 million deaf individuals in the United States and English-speaking parts of Canada (Nakamura, 2003).

## Interpreters

Communication is a difficult task when people are speaking different languages. The role of an interpreter is to receive the message in one language and transmit the meaning into a second language (Bourquin, 1996). When there is a need for accurate communication between a deaf consumer who uses ASL and a hearing nonsigning person, a sign-language interpreter is an integral part of the process (Kampfe, 1990). According to the Registry of Interpreters for the Deaf (RID), the official certifying body for interpreters, "Interpreting is a complex process that requires a high degree of linguistic, cognitive and technical skills" (RID, 1997). In sign-language interpreting, the interpreter is also dealing with two different modes, one visual and the other audiological (Bourquin, 1996).

Contrary to what many believe, the interpreter is not present only for the deaf person. The interpreter acts as a communication link between the hearing person and the deaf individual, and each party is a consumer of the interpreter's services (Bourquin, 1996). The outcome and the success of a VR plan developed between the deaf client and a VR counselor are often dependent on the skills of the interpreter. Within the context of the interview, the counselor must rely on the interpreter's ability to grasp the meaning of the questions asked and convey them in such a way that the consumer can understand and respond to them (Prosser, 1993).

In Arizona, as in many other states, there is a great demand for qualified interpreters, due in part to disabilities rights legislations enacted in the last decades (Bahan, Hoffmesiter, & Lane, 1996; Danek, 1994; Gammlin, 2000). Interpreter services were considered a "reasonable accommodation" under Section 504 of the Rehabilitation Act of 1973. The Rehabilitation Act Amendments of 1978 required the hiring of personnel, either interpreters or counselors, who could use the client's preferred mode of communication (Danek, 1992). This was further strengthened with the Rehabilitation Act Amendments of 1992, where states were mandated to provide the necessary information in the mode of communication most appropriate for the client [RSA,

Sec 101 (a)(7)(c)(2)]. Title I of the Americans with Disabilities Act (ADA) of 1990 required that employers and other covered entities to make reasonable accommodations to the work environment to provide equal opportunity for a qualified employee with a disability. For deaf employees, interpreters are a reasonable accommodation (National Association of the Deaf [NAD] Information Center; 2002).

According to Danek (1994), the provision of interpreters, unlike other accommodations under the ADA, is a need that must be continuously met. Although there are more than 60 interpreter training programs (ITP) across the nation (Stauffer & Brandwin, cited in Siple, 1993), the number of qualified interpreters has not kept pace with the demand (Siple, 1993). In Arizona, interpreters are hired under the Arizona State Procurement Office (SPO) Sign Language Interpreter contract (AD020140). The current contract lists 12 vendors who are either sole proprietors or have one or more interpreters working under their contract number (SPO, 2000).

For deaf consumers in rural parts of the state, the shortage of interpreters translates into longer times between appointments or delays in the provision of services. According to ARSA (2001), during 1999–2000, the average time between referral and application for deaf individuals was almost 2 weeks longer than for nondeaf clients. The average time between eligibility determination and movement into an individualized plan for employment (IPE) was twice the number of days.

When an interpreting assignment is over 2 hours in length, the counselor must contract for a team of two interpreters (ARSA Sign Language Interpreter Fee Schedule, 2001). Hourly rates for interpreting range from $42 to $60 per hour. In addition, the SPO contract permits travel and per diem expenses for interpreters who provide services more than 50 miles from the contractor's location or last work site. This results in higher cost cases for deaf VR clients when compared with other disability groups. An analysis of case costs per service for the SFY 1999 reveals that for the 1,696 deaf and hard-of-hearing clients who received VR services, 1,149 received services that involved expenditures of federal/state monies, totaling $3,350,884.21. Of this amount, interpreter services accounted for more than 56% of all case costs, or approximately $1.9 million (ARSA, 2000).

## Telemedicine: A Model for Video Remote Interpreting

In rural communities, telemedicine has been used for over 50 years to overcome the problems of distance when access to health care and some social services is limited. It generally involves using telecommunications technology to bring together a team to transfer medical information for diagnosis, therapy, and education (Harper, 2001). The information shared may include medical images, live two-way audio and video, output data from medical devices, and patient records (*Telemedicine*, 1999).

Wittson and colleagues are credited in the literature as the first to employ telehealth services, connecting the Nebraska Psychiatric Institute in Omaha and the state mental hospital 112 miles away (Whitten, Kingsley, Cook, Swirczynski, & Doolittle, 2001). Telemedicine projects now are global in scope. Many federal agencies have been involved in telemedicine projects, among them the U.S. Department of Defense (DOD) and the U.S. Department of Veterans Affairs (VA). The VA has invested heavily in telemedicine with a network of hospitals and health facilities. The DOD projects have been directed toward bringing medical care to soldiers on the front lines of battle (ATA). According to Harper (2001), through the medium of telemedicine, health care can be delivered in a more cost-effective, holistic, patient-centered manner.

Typically, patient satisfaction with telemedicine has been measured by several factors, including improved access to care, satisfaction with the technology, satisfaction with the communication during a consultation, and satisfaction with the consultation, overall (Whitten et al., 2001). Patients surveyed in small-scale studies revealed generally positive responses to telemedicine. There was agreement among patients that telemedicine reduced waiting times and costs and increased the thoroughness of the examination. Disadvantages included nervousness about the use of the technology, difficulty talking candidly with doctors over video, and a sense of emotional detachment (Whitten et al., 2001).

## Videoconferencing Technology and Deafness

Because video telecommunications technology is relatively new and continually improving, there are limited studies of its effectiveness in the area of deafness. Previous research conducted with the deaf primarily involved one-way communication, with the deaf person viewing a signed video (Barnicle et al., 2000; Blades & Collins, 1998a). The SignWorks project, funded by the British Centre for the Deaf, used real-life situations such as scheduling a doctor's appointment, making travel reservations or handling a banking transaction to develop role play scenarios (Blades & Collins, 1998b).

In the SignWorks Project (Blades & Collins, 1998b), the effectiveness of a Motion Media Technology videophone with a 4-inch screen for the transmission and reception of sign language was tested. Transmission was over high speed ISDN. Participants had varying signing skills ranging from fluent British

Sign Language (BSL) to competent BSL. One of the trials examined the comparison of participant comprehension between finger-spelled words, single signed words, and signed narration. This research replicated the FORUM project trials (1997), reported in Blades and Collins (1986), which used a Picture Tel 100 videoconferencing system with a 17-inch screen. Researchers concluded that signing appeared natural and, based on participative responses, participants were "happy" to use the system. However, finger spelling was harder for the participants to comprehend than signing, and the researchers reported that finger spelling should be undertaken with more care and attention than in face-to-face conversations (Blades & Collins, 1998b).

One problem with desktop systems is that for sign-language interpreting, signers need to sit far enough away from the camera so that they can sign in their normal signing space, from waist level to above the head, and about a foot on either side of the body. Because the user will probably sit a couple of feet back from the screen, size of image is important. If the image is very small the signer may have difficulty seeing the other person's signs from a distance (*Video Telecommunications Fact Sheet*, 1998).

Although digitized video has been in place for several years, there are two technical issues that may affect the quality of the video. One is delay, sometimes referred to as "jitter." This refers to the variation in the delay from one frame to the next. The reason this is critical is that video requires a constant stream of data bits in order to maintain the image (Young, 1998). The second problem is dropped frames. A lost frame may cause a click or pop in the audio and some *pixilization* of the video. Pixilization refers to situations when the thousands of pixels or digital blocks that make up the video image break up, creating obvious squares of wrong colors on the screen (Young). The only way to avoid these problems is to maintain constant transmission of packets and constant transmission speed. Even companies with high-speed Internet connections cannot guarantee the required bandwidth will be continuously available when needed throughout the entire videoconference call (Barnicle et al., 2000).

According to the Gallaudet University Technology Access Program (TAP) *Video Telecommunications Fact Sheet* (1998), products that operate over POTS (plain old telephone service) analog phone lines or basic rate ISDN (integrated service delivery networks) cannot adequately handle "full-motion video," which requires 30 still pictures or frames per second (fps). This is generally the accepted rate for sign language and lip movements to look natural. At lower frame rates, especially below 15 frames per second (fps), the video appears jerky. Below 15 fps, finger spelling becomes distorted, especially if done at the normal rate for ASL of 6–7 letters per second (Blades & Collins, 1998a, 1998b; Hazelwood, 1999). Most researchers and professionals in the field of telecommunications agree that although 384 kbps will support full-motion video, larger bandwidth is required to achieve full motion with high-quality, large-screen pictures suitable for interactive signing (Barnicle et al., 2000; Blades & Collins, 1998a; Williams, 1998).

## Satisfaction

Because the intent of this research was to determine how effective the existing ARSA videoconference system was for delivering VRI, the researcher was concerned not only with the technology, but also with the consumers' satisfaction with video interpreting services. This required some understanding of what comprised quality services and customer satisfaction.

Early researchers in the area of quality and customer service used psychological theories to explain the internal processes involved in customer satisfaction. They demonstrated that there was more to customer service than just the product or service and introduced the link with customer expectations (Forsyth, 2002). Garvin (1984) recognized that quality is a subjective multidimensional concept and identified six performance features: reliability, conformance, durability, serviceability, aesthetics, and perception (cited in Seawright & Young, 1996). This multifaceted approach was expanded to the service delivery sector by Parasuraman, Zeithaml, and Berry (1985, 1991). Their SERVQUAL instrument utilized a questionnaire to measure the gap between customer expectations and customer perceptions of the services received, on five dimensions: (a) tangibles, which includes physical facilities or equipment used to provide service; (b) reliability; (c) responsiveness, which includes timeliness of service; (d) assurance, which includes four sub-dimensions dealing with communication, credibility, security, and competence of the service providers; and (e) empathy (Richard, 2000). Empathy is the caring, individualized attention the organization provides its customers. It includes knowing the customer's specific requirements and providing individualized attention. Empathy also includes access, meaning that telephones (TTYs) are accessible and that locations and hours of operations are convenient (Richard, 2000).

Zeithaml, Parasuraman, and Berry (1985) found that service attributes cannot easily be evaluated, because they are tied to experience. In this study the researcher needed to take into account not only the dynamics between the client and the counselor and how they were affected by the interaction with the interpreter, but in the case of the VRI scenario, the technology. Therefore, the use of a multidimensional model of customer satisfaction, which considered various attributes of the experience, was chosen in developing the methodology.

## RECRUITMENT STRATEGY

Because the purpose of this project was to evaluate the use of remote video interpreting within the vocational rehabilitation (VR) program, the participant pool for recruitment was limited to those VR clients of the Arizona Rehabilitation Services Administration (ARSA) with a primary disability code of deafness who indicated American Sign Language (ASL) was their language preference when they applied for services. This participant pool was further limited to those clients residing in Maricopa County. The total number of individuals with open VR cases who met these criteria was 298 (ARSA, 2003).

Rehabilitation counselors for the deaf (RCDs), VR counselors who specialize in the provision of services for the deaf, were asked to present information about the research study to their current clients residing in Maricopa County. The counselors were instructed not to discuss the specifics of the study, nor the technology to be used. However, potential participants were told that the outcome of the study could possibly improve services for the Deaf. Clients who expressed an interest were asked to sign a release form so that information could be shared with the researcher. In the case of minors, parents and/or guardians were asked to sign the releases as well. After these forms were signed, the RCDs referred the clients' information to the researcher with an ARSA confidentiality cover sheet.

Forty-five referrals were received, representing 15% of the potential participant pool. The researcher contacted these individuals by e-mail, or by phone using the relay service or a TTY, to discuss their participation in the study. These contacts followed a prescribed script. Clients were assured that their choice to participate or not to participate would in no way affect their VR program. Clients who agreed to participate were randomly assigned to one of two groups. The participants in the local [control] group consisted of those consumers who participated in a traditional meeting, where the interpreter was physically in the same location as the counselor and the consumer. The VRI [experimental] group utilized remote video interpreting services, with the client and counselor in the same location and the interpreter in a remote location and viewed on a video monitor.

Once interviews were scheduled, a request for a certified ASL interpreter was completed and sent to the Community Outreach Program for the Deaf (COPD) interpreter coordinator. This vendor is one of several agencies with contracts to provide sign-language interpreter services for the ARSA (Arizona State Procurement Office [SPO] Sign Language Interpreter contract AD020140, 2000). As a condition of that contract, all interpreters must be nationally certified. To ensure consistency, all interpreters requested for this study were Registry of Interpreters for the Deaf (RID), Certificate of Interpretation (CI) certified. Interpreting assignments were made by the provider without identification of the study participants.

## Interview Protocol

All interviews were conducted by a certified rehabilitation counselor (CRC) with a master's degree in Rehabilitation Counseling and more than 8 years of experience with ARSA vocational rehabilitation. This counselor, who had no signing skills, conducted all interviews using a prescribed interview script that was interpreted into ASL. During the entire interview meeting, the interpreter was either at the local site with the counselor [control group], or at the remote site and viewed on video [experimental group]. When several interviews were scheduled in a row, two interpreters at the site were scheduled to allow for breaks.

Before the counselor/client interview began, the study participant and the interpreter were given time to converse. This provided an opportunity for the interpreter to gain some understanding about the participant's ASL skills and body language and for the participant to become accustomed to the interpreter's style of signing. This was done for both the local and video remote interpreting group participants.

Prior to beginning the interview, participants were asked to sign an informed consent statement, provided in written form and also interpreted into ASL by the interpreter. All participants were asked for permission to videotape the sessions, and those who agreed were asked to check a separate box on the consent form.

Because all interviews were completed at one meeting, neither history nor maturation was a threat to validity. There was no pretest to sensitize the participant to the instrument or the technology. Although all questions and answer choices were interpreted into ASL, participants had their own copy of the answer sheet and were asked to check the answer boxes themselves. These written responses were kept from the view of the counselor and the interpreter. An assigned ID number was used to identify all participants. No names, VR case ID numbers, or other personal information appeared on the answer sheets. Only the researcher had access to the data. No information was shared with the referring VR counselor.

## Instrumentation

The interview script, which included the questionnaire items, was developed by the researcher. To ensure content validity, a panel of experts comprised of rehabilitation counselors for the deaf (RCDs), both Deaf and hearing, and two certified interpreters, one of whom was a child of deaf adults (CODA), participated in the development and pretest of the instrument. This panel of experts discussed the intended meaning of each item with the researcher and translated the questions into ASL several times to gain consensus. The total number of items in the questionnaire was kept to a minimum to ensure that the interview did not become too lengthy when interpreted in American Sign Language. The group was also asked to comment on the clarity of the instructions. Based on input from the group of experts, anything in the script or questionnaire that was not straightforward and concrete was revised.

Part I of the questionnaire was designed to collect standard demographic information about the individuals participating in the study. Part II consisted of five true/false questions to assess comprehension of VR programmatic information. The material discussed during the interview was taken from the introductory chapter of the ARSA "Owner's Guide to Work." This workbook was implemented for use with VR clients in 2002, to encourage more active client participation in the VR planning process. Each question had only one correct answer, and each correct response had a value equal to 1. A maximum comprehension score for each participant equaled a score of 5. The participant comprehension scores were used to compute the mean scores for the two groups (local and VRI).

Part III of the questionnaire was developed to measure consumer satisfaction with the total interview experience. A Likert scale ranging from a 5 (*strongly disagree*) to 1 (*strongly agree*) was used to capture the participant responses to the statements in Part III. The numerical responses to each item were added together and divided by the number of participants who responded to each statement. A mean score for each of the five statements, ranging from 1 to 5, was used to compute a mean satisfaction score for each group (VRI and local) for each statement.

Because some VR programmatic terms do not have ASL signs, finger spelling of words is a critical component in providing the client with accurate information. Based on the previous SignWorks trials by Blades and Collins (1998b), one statement was included in Part III to capture data about the participants' abilities to read finger-spelled words at the transmission speed of the video network.

## Logistical Considerations

To minimize threats to reliability, all participants were interviewed by the same counselor at the ARSA Phoenix videoconferencing site, regardless of whether the interpreter was local or on video from the remote site. For the video interpreting, the ARSA Tucson videoconference site was used as the remote site. This ensured consistency of the physical facilities and standardized the conditions under which the study was conducted.

Prior to beginning interviews, several trials were done to evaluate camera angles, lighting, sound quality, and placement of the furniture. These were videotaped for later review by the researcher and panel of experts. After reviewing the tapes it was determined that a solid background was needed, both behind the interpreter at the remote site and behind the participant in the local site, to minimize visual distractions. A fabric-covered blue/gray partition was constructed that could be moved out of the way when the video room was used for trainings or meetings. Solid black was tried first, but it created too much of a contrast, making people appear flat or two-dimensional on video. The blue/gray color was chosen because most skin tones looked more natural against this neutral background. The background also provided additional sound absorption to reduce echoing.

Because the rooms were originally designed for videoconferencing, lighting was not a concern. The rooms were designed with uniform overhead lighting, at a minimum of 70 candlepower, throughout the room. This eliminated harsh shadows that might have obscured the participants' faces. There were also two soft spotlights in the front of the room that could be turned on to ensure the interpreter's face and lips could be seen clearly. Finally, the camera had an adjustable iris to capture more light, if needed.

The ARSA video cameras were fully adjustable, with pan-tilt and zoom capability, permitting the interpreter to sign in a normal signing space without concerns about portions of the signs being cropped when viewed on the screen. The 36-inch monitors, larger than desk-top monitors used in trials described in the literature, permitted the participants to sit comfortably in the room during the interview, without having to lean forward or crowd close to the monitors.

## RESULTS

This study was designed to evaluate the effectiveness of video remote interpreting (VRI) in a two-way communication exchange between a hearing VR counselor and a deaf VR client. The study was designed to test the following alternative hypotheses:

1. VR clients in the local interpreting group will score higher in comprehension than clients in the VRI group.
2. Clients in the VRI group will be less satisfied with the VR interview experience than those in the traditional local interpreting group.

3. Clients in the VRI group will have more difficulty in understanding the interpreter's finger spelling than those in the local group.

The statistical analysis strategy for all three hypotheses involved computing the mean and standard deviation from data collected for the VRI and the local group. A statistical pretest (Levene's equality of variance) was done to satisfy the assumption that the variances of the two groups were equal and the data were normally distributed. Finally, data were analyzed using $t$-tests of independent means, to determine if statistically significant differences existed between the means of the two groups. The level established as the criterion for significance for this study was .05. Statistical analysis was computed using SPSS11.5 for Windows.

## Part I—Participant Demographics

Of the 45 participants originally referred to the researcher by the vocational rehabilitation counselors for the deaf (RCDs) in Maricopa County, 5 were never interviewed. One participant asked to withdraw due to a family medical emergency, one moved out of state suddenly, and a third asked that her VR case be voluntarily closed, thereby no longer meeting one of the prescribed selection criteria. Two individuals did not show up for their interviews and did not respond to repeated attempts to reschedule the appointments. In total, 37 participants (54% female and 46% male) completed the study. This represented 82% of the total number of subjects who were referred to the researcher and 12% of the total number of active VR clients who met the study criteria.

The sample population ranged in age from 16 to 57 years old, with 27% between the ages of 15 and 24; 57% between the ages of 25 and 39; 13% between the ages of 40 and 54; and 3% 55 years old and older. More than half (59%) of the study participants self-identified as congenitally deaf, and 19% reported age of onset of deafness at less than 1 year old. The remaining 22% of the participants had no knowledge of when they became deaf. The participants self-reported race/ethnicity, with 46% identifying themselves as Caucasian, 16% identifying themselves as African American, 30% classifying themselves as being of Hispanic descent, 5% identifying as Asian/Pacific Islander, and 3% reporting American Indian heritage.

In response to the Part I demographic question about education, 84% of the VRI group and 83% of the local group participants reported attending a special class or school for the deaf. For those individuals who responded in the affirmative, 53% of the VRI group and 44% of the local group were schooled in residential schools. One individual did not respond to this question. Among those individuals who did not attend residential programs, 42% of the VRI participants and 56% of those in the local group attended deaf programs in day schools. Training in lip (speech) reading was reported by 62% of participants (32% VRI and 30% local).

Although all participants self-identified themselves at time of referral as ASL users, they were asked in Part I to identify *all* the different ways they communicated at home, work, or school. Expressive communication modes are represented in Table 3.1. Participants were also asked about their receptive communication styles. Responses to the question "*What are the ways other people tell you what they want?*" are represented in Table 3.2.

## Part II—Comprehension

In Part II, a total comprehension score was computed for each participant based on the total number of correct answers to the five true/false questions. Each

**TABLE 3.1**

Expressive Communication Modes

| Setting | I voice n | % | I write notes n | % | I fingerspell n | % | I sign n | % | I use gestures (mime) n | % |
|---|---|---|---|---|---|---|---|---|---|---|
| VRI n = 19 | 11 | 58% | 6 | 32% | 2 | 11% | 15 | 79% | 2 | 11% |
| Local n = 18 | 6 | 33% | 9 | 50% | 8 | 44% | 17 | 94% | 6 | 33% |
| Total n = 37 | 17 | 46% | 15 | 41% | 10 | 27% | 32 | 87% | 8 | 22% |

**TABLE 3.2**

Receptive Communication Modes

| Setting | They voice n | % | They write notes n | % | They fingerspell n | % | They sign n | % | They use gestures (mime) n | % |
|---|---|---|---|---|---|---|---|---|---|---|
| VRI n = 19 | 10 | 53% | 9 | 47% | 3 | 16% | 11 | 58% | 2 | 11% |
| Local n = 18 | 8 | 44% | 14 | 78% | 5 | 28% | 9 | 50% | 5 | 28% |
| Total n = 37 | 18 | 49% | 23 | 62% | 8 | 22% | 20 | 54% | 7 | 19% |

correct response was scored as 1; each incorrect response was scored as 0. A perfect individual comprehension score was a total of 5.0. Participant scores in each group were added and a mean and standard deviation were computed. For the VRI subject group the mean score was 4.42 (SD = 0.84). The mean score for the local group was 4.78 (SD = 0.55).

Because the groups were normally distributed, with equal variance ($F = 8.24, p = .007$), an independent groups $t$-test was used to compare the mean scores for comprehension between the VRI and local groups. The data analysis (two sided $t$-test, $t(35) = -1.52, p = .137$) did not support the alternative research Hypothesis 1. Therefore the null hypothesis, that there were no significant differences in comprehension scores between the video remote interpreting and local interpreting groups, was not rejected.

## Part III—Satisfaction

Part III of the questionnaire was used to collect data to measure consumer satisfaction with the total interview experience. Subjects were asked to rate their level of agreement with five statements. The responses constituted a 5-point Likert scale with the following values assigned: *strongly disagree* = 1; *disagree* = 2; *no opinion* = 3; *agree* = 4; and *strongly agree* = 5. All statements were stated in the positive, with the exception of statement number 2. Response values for each item were summed and divided by the number of responses, to obtain the average score for each item, for both the groups. Raw scores were converted to percents. Response data for statements numbered 1 through 5 are presented in the Tables 3.3 through 3.6.

A statistical pretest, Levene's test of equality of variance, was performed to verify the assumption that the data were normally distributed and the variances were equal. For statement 1 ($F = .149; p = .702$), statement 3 ($F = 2.407; p = .130$), and statement 4 ($F = .485; p = .491$), the variances were equal. The $p$ value for statement 5 ($F = 11.51; p = .002$) was less than .05, demonstrating unequal distribution of scores. For this item only, a modified $t$-test for unequal variances (Welch's $t$-test) was performed and the $p$ value was adjusted accordingly.

The results of all four $t$-tests, presented in Table 3.7 and Table 3.8, indicate there were no significant differences in mean scores for participant satisfaction, whether interpreting was delivered by means of VRI or locally, for any of the four statements. Thus the alternative research Hypothesis 2, that participants in the local group would be more satisfied with their interview experience, was not supported. Therefore the null hypothesis assuming no significant differences in satisfaction with the interview process was not rejected.

**TABLE 3.3**

Client Responses to Statement 1—"time between questions"

| Setting | Strongly disagree n | % | Disagree n | % | No opinion n | % | Agree n | % | Strongly agree n | % |
|---|---|---|---|---|---|---|---|---|---|---|
| VRI n = 19 | 1 | 5% | 1 | 5% | 2 | 11% | 10 | 53% | 5 | 26% |
| Local n = 18 | 0 | 0% | 0 | 0% | 2 | 11% | 6 | 33% | 10 | 56% |
| Total n = 37 | 1 | 3% | 1 | 3% | 4 | 11% | 16 | 43% | 15 | 40% |

**TABLE 3.4**

Client Responses to Statement 3—"ability to ask the counselor questions"

| Setting | Strongly disagree n | % | Disagree n | % | No opinion n | % | Agree n | % | Strongly agree n | % |
|---|---|---|---|---|---|---|---|---|---|---|
| VRI n = 19 | 1 | 5% | 0 | 0% | 2 | 11% | 8 | 42% | 8 | 42% |
| Local n = 18 | 0 | 0% | 0 | 0% | 0 | 0% | 6 | 33% | 12 | 67% |
| Total n = 37 | 1 | 3% | 0 | 0% | 2 | 5% | 14 | 38% | 20 | 54% |

**TABLE 3.5**

Client Responses to Statement 4—"counselor seemed to understand"

| Setting | Strongly disagree n | % | Disagree n | % | No opinion n | % | Agree n | % | Strongly agree n | % |
|---|---|---|---|---|---|---|---|---|---|---|
| VRI n = 19 | 2 | 10% | 3 | 16% | 3 | 16% | 8 | 42% | 3 | 16% |
| Local n = 18 | 3 | 17% | 1 | 6% | 3 | 17% | 5 | 27% | 6 | 33% |
| Total n = 37 | 5 | 14% | 4 | 11% | 6 | 16% | 13 | 35% | 9 | 24% |

## TABLE 3.6

Client Responses to Statement 5—"comfortable talking with the counselor today"

| Setting | Strongly disagree n | % | Disagree n | % | No opinion n | % | Agree n | % | Strongly agree n | % |
|---|---|---|---|---|---|---|---|---|---|---|
| VRI n = 19 | 0 | 0% | 0 | 0% | 1 | 5% | 15 | 79% | 3 | 16% |
| Local n = 18 | 0 | 0% | 0 | 0% | 3 | 17% | 4 | 22% | 11 | 61% |
| Total n = 37 | 0 | 0% | 0 | 0% | 4 | 11% | 19 | 51% | 14 | 38% |

## TABLE 3.7

Group Means and Standard Deviation for Satisfaction—Statements 1, 3, 4, and 5

| | | Setting | n | M | SD |
|---|---|---|---|---|---|
| #1 | I had enough time between questions to watch the interpreter. | VRI | 19 | 3.89 | 10.6 |
| | | Local | 18 | 4.44 | .71 |
| #3 | I was able to ask the counselor questions when I didn't understand. | VRI | 19 | 4.16 | 1.02 |
| | | Local | 18 | 4.67 | .49 |
| #4 | The counselor understood me even though she did not sign. | VRI | 19 | 3.37 | 1.26 |
| | | Local | 18 | 3.56 | 1.46 |

## TABLE 3.8

$t$-Tests for Group Satisfaction Scores—Statements 1, 3, 4, and 5

| | t | df | P |
|---|---|---|---|
| #1 I had enough time between questions to watch the interpreter. | –1.86 | 35 | .071 |
| #3 I was able to ask the counselor questions when I didn't understand. | –1.93 | 35 | .062 |
| #4 The counselor understood me even though she did not sign. | –.42 | 35 | .679 |
| #5 I felt comfortable talking with the counselor today. | –1.60 | 27.13[a] | .122 |

[a] $df$ Calculated on the sample size and the SD.

**TABLE 3.9**

Client Responses to Statement 2—"difficulty reading the fingerspelling"

| Setting | Strongly disagree n | % | Disagree n | % | No opinion n | % | Agree n | % | Strongly agree n | % |
|---|---|---|---|---|---|---|---|---|---|---|
| VRI n = 19 | 8 | 42% | 3 | 16% | 4 | 21% | 3 | 16% | 1 | 5% |
| VRI n = 18 | 10 | 55% | 1 | 6% | 4 | 22% | 1 | 6% | 2 | 11% |
| VRI n = 37 | 18 | 49% | 4 | 11% | 8 | 22% | 4 | 11% | 3 | 8% |

Table 3.9 displays data for statement 2 in Part III of the questionnaire, "*I had difficulty reading the interpreter's fingerspelling.*" It is important to note that this statement was the only one of the five items in Part III stated in the negative.

The mean score for the VRI group for this statement related to ability to read the interpreter's fingerspelling was 2.26 (SD = 1.327) and the mean score for the local subjects was 2.11 (SD = 1.451). Equality of variance ($F = .224$; $p = .639$) and normal distribution of the data were assumed. The data analysis (two sided t-test, $t(35) = .333$, $p = 0.741$) demonstrated that there was no significant difference in means scores for clients in either group, regardless of whether the interpreter was local or viewed on video from a remote site (null hypothesis). Therefore the alternative research Hypothesis 3 was not accepted.

## DISCUSSION

In Arizona, out of 290 VR counselors statewide, there are only 7 RCDs (ARSA, 2000). These counselors who specialize in serving deaf and hard of hearing clients are located in the two urban cities of Phoenix and Tucson, where only 31% of the deaf and hard of hearing population resides (Gallaudet Research Institute, 2001). As a result of this unequal distribution, generalist counselors must provide rehabilitation services for deaf clients in rural parts of Arizona. Unfortunately, few can communicate with a deaf client in American Sign Language, the first language for many deaf and hard-of-hearing consumers. Therefore, general counselors must contract for ASL interpreters, who are limited in number, to assist in the communication process.

This research project was designed to evaluate whether the ARSA videoconferencing network, originally implemented to support distance learning activities, would support video remote interpreting (VRI). VRI would enable a hearing counselor and a deaf client located in one location to communicate using the services of an interpreter located in another remote site, through video. This situation is in contrast to what would be considered a "traditional" VR interview, where the nonsigning counselor, the deaf client, and the interpreter comprise a triad in a local setting.

The first research question this study was designed to answer was whether there was any difference in clients' comprehension of VR programmatic information, when sign language interpreting was delivered through VRI, as compared to local interpreting. The second question of interest was whether the interpreting setting, whether local or VRI, had any impact on the clients' satisfaction with the VR interview process. Finally the research examined the quality of the video transfer rate and whether fingerspelling and signs could be read and understood.

## Research Findings and Future Directions

Participant demographics reveal a higher percentage of females (54%) than males (46%) in the study population. This is in contrast to the U.S. population data reported in the 1999–2000 Regional and National Summary Data, from the *Annual Survey of Deaf and Hard of Hearing Children and Youth* (2000) (Gallaudet Research Institute [GRI], 2001), which reported higher percentages of males (54%) with some form of hearing loss, than females (46%). In this study population, there was a smaller percentage of American Indian participants (3%), compared to the 6% of Arizonans who reported American Indian ethnicity in the 2000 Census. This discrepancy can be explained by the subject pool being restricted to Maricopa County (*Arizona Quick Facts*, 2000).

Fluency in ASL may depend on many things, including age of onset of deafness, parental hearing status, and school environment (Allen, 1994). Although participants all self-identified themselves as ASL users at time of referral, two questions were included in the demographic section of the questionnaire to assess the "communication environment" of the study participants (i.e., what modes of expressive and receptive communication were used by the participants to communicate with friends and family members).

Because all participants self-identified ASL as their preferred mode of communication, it was consistent that "*I sign*" was the most frequently selected response (87%) to the question of how "*I communicate with others.*" However, within the local group, 94% identified this method of communication, compared to 79% for participants in the VRI group. Also, although 57% of the combined study participants reported sign was used most frequently by family and friends to communicate with them, more than twice the rate reported in the

GRI *Annual Survey* (2001) for deaf/HoH, there were differences in the rankings between the groups. After sign (58%), VRI participants responded that friends and family members most often voiced (53%) when communicating with them, followed by writing notes (47%). For the local participants, the most frequently used receptive communication mode was writing notes (78%), followed by sign (50%), and then voice (44%).

Analysis of these data at the alpha level of .05 established no statistically significant differences between the two group means for comprehension of material discussed during the VR interview. Therefore, the researcher was 95% confident that any chance differences between the participants' comprehension scores were attributed to natural variation within the measurements, and not to whether interpreting was delivered remotely on video or face-to-face in a local setting. Also because the mean comprehension scores for each of the participant groups exceeded 4.4, out of a possible 5.0, the researcher did not have sufficient evidence to reject the null hypothesis of equality. Therefore, the assumption that both methods of interpreting were equally effective, and both facilitated the clients' understanding of the material, was accepted.

The second research question explored whether traditional or VRI had any impact on the clients' satisfaction with the VR interview process. The ability to ask questions (statement 1) and have questions answered (statement 3) related to the SERVQUAL satisfaction dimensions of assurance, including the subdimension factors of communication, creditability, and competence. Statement 5, which asked about comfort level during the interview, related to the dimensions of empathy, and the assurance subdimension of security.

The Cronbach alpha correlation coefficient $a = .8017$ for Statements 1, 3, and 5 indicated a strong internal consistency for these three questionnaire items. Therefore, the results were considered together as reliably representing consumer satisfaction with the interview experience. Although there were no significant differences, the mean scores for satisfaction for the local group were slightly higher on all three statements. This could be the result of VRI participants not being able to establish the same rapport with the counselor as the local group participants, or possibly be due to some distractions associated with the technology.

Statement 4, "*The counselor understood me even though she did not sign,*" was intended to assess from the client's perspective whether or not the counselor understood the client, even though the counselor was not proficient in sign. This statement may not have been clear to the participants, because responses had more variability than for any other item on the questionnaire. Although in both groups more than half the respondents either *agreed* or *strongly agreed* (58% VRI and 61% local) with the statement, there were more *no opinion* responses

(16% VRI and 17% local), and higher percentages for *disagree* and *strongly disagree* (26% VRI and 23% local).

Because all interpreters hired for the study were CI/CT certified, the researcher assumed that client dissatisfaction with the communication exchange was not a function of interpreter skill. Further examination of the communication variables for the nine participants who responded that they either *disagreed* or *strongly disagreed* with the statement "*The counselor understood me even though she did not sign*" was completed. All of the nine (five VRI and four local), in responding to communication questions in Part I, stated they used sign to communicate with others, but two-thirds reported that others did not use sign when communicating with them. The researcher contends that the perception that the hearing counselor did not understand may have been the result of the individual's own difficulty in comprehending the ASL signs. This may be an outcome of having limited opportunities for signing in day-to-day activities.

In a study by Maher and Walters (1984), interpreters identified advantages to utilizing their services, including guarding against miscommunication, putting clients at ease in unfamiliar situations, and providing the counselor with some insight into deafness. Because the questionnaire used in this study was intended to gather client data only, the counselor was not interviewed. The researcher suggests any future research on VRI should include a follow-up survey with the counselor to assess satisfaction with video remote interpreting.

Although there were no significant differences between the two groups in terms of comfort level with the interview experience, it was noteworthy that more participants in the remote group either agreed or strongly agreed (95%) with statement 5, "*I was comfortable talking with the counselor today*," than those in the local group (83%).

Based on reviews of the taped sessions, it appeared that younger participants seemed more at ease being on camera. They tended to focus less on their own images and were less self-conscious (i.e., smoothing their hair or adjusting their clothing). However, because only 79% of the remote group participants were between the ages of 15 and 24, as compared to 83% of the local group, age does not appear to be a factor in the higher satisfaction scores for the VRI group on statement 5. These results may therefore reflect the Hawthorne effect. The experience of being selected to participate in a research study with some new technology, or perhaps seeing oneself on camera, may have contributed to the high agreement scores on this statement.

Because there were insufficient data to accept an alternative hypothesis, the researcher contends that the method of delivering interpreting, whether VRI or traditional, was not a consideration in client satisfaction. Therefore for this study, the null hypothesis stating equal satisfaction between VRI and face-to-face interpreting was not rejected.

The results of the analysis for statement 2, "*I had difficulty reading the interpreter's fingerspelling,*" confirmed that at this point in time, video telecommunication technology has evolved to the point where communication can take place across distances in real time. The concern that because finger spelling exists in three dimensions (Porter, 1999) participants might have difficulty comprehending finger-spelled words when viewed on video in two dimensions (Hazelwood, 1999) was apparently not an issue. In addition, because the ARSA system had dual monitors, it was possible for both the interpreter at the remote site and the client at the local site to see him- or herself at all times. This allowed the signers to stay within the natural signing space, without any of the signs being lost on-screen (Hazelwood, 1999).

In contrast to earlier trials (Barnicle et al., 2000; Blades & Collins, 1998a), the current study demonstrated that the ARSA network was more than adequate for VRI services. The ARSA videoconferencing system is a "closed" or private network, running over T-1 land lines. The T-1 transmits 1.54 mbps, the equivalent of 24 POTS channels (64 kbps), or 3 high-speed (384 kbps) ISDN lines. This means faster connectivity and extremely fast data transfer rates, resulting in improved quality for audio and video transmission (*Videoconferencing Cookbook*, 2002; Williams, 1998). In addition, the RSA videoconference network does not suffer from bandwidth loss due to other data packet transmissions across the network. Review of the taped sessions confirmed there was no blurring or pixilization, even when signing or finger spelling was quite fast.

This video remote interpreting project, if expanded, will utilize the existing videoconferencing infrastructure at no additional costs, and with no modifications to the network. Because the T-1 lines are within the private network, there are no long-distance phone charges beyond the monthly charge to maintain the lines. In addition, because the technology is not proprietary (i.e., limited to products from one manufacturer), the system can be expanded to include non-ARSA sites, as long as the video telecommunications equipment in use is compatible with the International Telecommunications Union (ITU-T) standards. This would further expand the geographic limits of the ARSA VRI network to include community colleges, universities, local governments, and human service providers with videoconferencing networks.

## Limitations of the Study

*Population validity* is the term used by Borg and Gall (1983) to describe the degree to which the sample of individuals in a study are representative of the population from which it was selected (p. 99). The primary problem with volunteer samples, according to Bellini and Rumrill (1999), is that systematic sampling error can be introduced.

Although all deaf VR clients had an opportunity to participate in this study, only those with current open VR cases who were either contacted by their counselor or had an appointment with the counselor during the recruitment period were provided with information about the study. Others may have learned about the research through friends, or colleagues at work or school. However, the sampling response rate of 82%, representing the ratio of those who agreed to participate (37) compared to those who indicated an interest in participating (45), argues for less likelihood that systematic sampling error was introduced into the process (Bellini & Rumrill, 1999).

A larger sample would certainly have increased the population validity. However, confidentiality of VR client information was a concern of the agency. Thus, the researcher was only permitted to contact those clients who signed a release form, expressing an interest in the study, and giving permission for the RCD to provide their contact information to the researcher. Because it was not possible to increase the sample size in this study, additional care was taken to ensure that sample characteristics (i.e., deaf VR clients; residing in a single county in Arizona; whose language preference was ASL) closely matched the characteristics of the larger population (Salkind, 2000). Because these characteristics were very relevant to the variables studied, a small $n$ was sufficient to test the hypotheses.

The researcher recognizes that with a small sample there is always a possibility of a Type II error; accepting the null hypothesis when it is false. A single study on VRI may not be sufficient to demonstrate significant differences in comprehension or satisfaction between the two modes of interpreting, even if these differences exist. Therefore, demographic variables, particularly those related to age of onset of deafness, self-reported communication preferences, and education, should be closely examined by future researchers who plan to replicate this study.

Furthermore, it is the opinion of this researcher that self-reported communication preferences cannot be easily translated into predictions about ASL competency. National data suggest that approximately 10% of deaf students attend school in integrated settings, where oral education is stressed (Allen, 1994). In interpreting the study results, there was no way to know whether the 16% of participants who reported they attended integrated schools were oral in school but ASL users at home. There was also no way to determine whether, at some later point in life, they abandoned oralism in favor of ASL. Therefore it is recommended that an assessment of ASL competency be considered for those planning future studies of video remote interpreting.

## Best Practices

To insure the most effective use of the medium, the following recommendations for VRI should be considered as best practices (Covell, 1996; Hazelwood, 1999; see also *Videotelecommunications Fact Sheet*, 1998; VTEL, 2001):

Before the videoconference:

• A warmup time should be factored into the appointment scheduling to give the client and interpreter time to get accustomed to each other's style of signing.

• The best seating arrangement, which permits optimal visual contact between the client and the interpreter, should be determined in advance for each individual site.

• Standards should be developed for the physical environment, including wall or background colors. Minimal lighting requirements should be set based on the room size and shape.

• If appointments are scheduled in advance, both interpreters and clients should be prepped about what to wear. They should be made aware that patterns, horizontal stripes, and glittery jewelry create distracting visual effects onscreen. They should also avoid all-light or all-dark clothes, because they trick the camera's automatic brightness control.

• Fax machines and computers should be available at all remote locations to ensure that interpreters have copies of all materials to be covered during the interview. This will assist in interpreting rehabilitation and medical terms.

During the videoconference:

• Participants should be encouraged to avoid excess movements, such as rustling papers or tapping pencils. These can produce sounds that may be magnified by the microphones.

• For those individuals who are not as proficient in manual communication, the interpreter should be advised to sign and fingerspell more slowly.

• As there is sometimes a very slight time lag time between audio transmission and reception, speakers should pause to allow the other person to respond before speaking.

## CONCLUSION

In discussing technology, during his keynote speech at the 2002 ALDA Conference in Orlando, I. King Jordan, the first deaf president of Gallaudet University, said, "I sat down recently and tried to make a list of what I think are the most important advances technologically, which impact directly on deaf people .... One is communication—and telecommunications, especially" (Jordan, 2003). This research study demonstrated first hand the impact of this technology. Deaf VR clients and nonsigning hearing counselors successfully communicated using video remote interpreting, delivered over a telecommunications network.

When sign-language interpreting, by certified interpreters, was delivered remotely on video, as compared to locally, there were (a) no significant differences in comprehension of VR programmatic information, and (b) no significant differences in consumer satisfaction with the interview experience. VR clients involved in this study were representative of the larger population of deaf VR clients in the state. Therefore, it is hoped that the results of this study will encourage expansion of the existing ARSA videoconference network to support VRI.

Although it is unlikely that video remote interpreting will replace traditional interpreting altogether, there is definitely a place for VRI within the array of vocational rehabilitation services in Arizona. In situations where a deaf consumer lives in a rural community, when interpreters and rehabilitation counselors for the deaf may not be available, VRI satisfies the desire to communicate in ASL, the deaf person's preferred language. Video remote interpreting may be one answer to improving outreach to an underserved group within the deaf and hard-of-hearing population. VRI can contribute to more individuals with hearing loss participating in the VR program, leading to increased representation in the workforce.

## REFERENCES

Adams, P. F., Hendershot, G. E., & Marano, M. A. (1999). Current estimates from the National Interview Survey, 1996. *Vital and Health statistics, 10*(200). Hyattsville, MD: National Center for Health Statistics.

Allen, T. E. (1994). *Question: How many people in the USA and Canada use ASL as a primary language and how many use it as their second or other language?* Retrieved July 24, 2000, from the Gallaudet Research Institute web site, http://www.gri.gallaudet.edu/Demographics.html

American Society for Quality. (2002). *Quality basics.* Retrieved September 12, 2003, from http://asq.org/portal

Anderson, G. B., Boone, S. E., & Watson, D. (2002). *Impact of legislation and policy on provision of VR services to consumers who are deaf or hard of hearing: Perspectives of agency administrators and program specialists.* Little Rock: University of Arkansas, Rehabilitation Research and Training Center for Persons Who Are Deaf and Hard of Hearing.

*Arizona QuickFacts from the U.S. Census Bureau.* (2000). Retrieved November 2, 2002, from http://quickfacts.census.gov/qfd/states/04000.html

Arizona Rehabilitation Services Administration. (2001). *Deaf/hoh expenditures by county-FFY/1999* (Ad Hoc VWQISJ36). Phoenix, AZ.

Arizona Rehabilitation Services Administration. (2001). *Sign language interpreter fee schedule.* Phoenix, AZ.

Arizona Rehabilitation Services Administration. (2000). *Expenditure report SFY1997–1999* (Ad Hoc Report QCM-340). Phoenix, AZ.

Arizona Rehabilitation Services Administration. (2000). *Intake, application, eligibility. ARSA Policy Handbook: Article 2-Vocational rehabilitation program* (Section 4; iv). Phoenix, AZ.

Arizona Rehabilitation Services Administration. (2000). *Personnel database.* Phoenix, AZ.

Arizona State Procurement Office (SPO). (2000). Retrieved March 6, 2002 from the State Procurement web site http://www.purchasing.state.az.us

Bahan, B., Hoffmeister, R., & Lane, H. (1996). *A journey into the Deaf-world.* San Diego: DawnSign Press.

Barnicle, K., Vandenheiden, G., Gilman, A., Reinberg, J., Schauer, J., Kelso, D., et al. (2000). Sign language interpretation over an Internet 2 network. *Proceedings of the RESNA 2000 Annual Conference: Technology for the New Millennium,* Orlando, FL.

Bellini, J. L., & Rumrill, P., Jr. (1999). *Research in rehabilitation counseling.* Springfield, IL: Charles C. Thomas.

Blackwell, D. L., Collins, J. G., & Coles, R. (2002). Summary health statistics for U.S. adults: National Health Interview Survey, 1997. *Vital Health Statistics, 10*(2005). Hyattsville, MD: National Center for Health Statistics.

Blades, F., & Collins, J. (1998a). *Remote sign language interpreting.* Retrieved August 28, 2003, from http://www.sign-works.org.uk/D223.htm

Blades, F., & Collins, J. (1998b). *Sign recognition from a fixed remote source: BSL videophone use.* Retrieved January 31, 2001, from http://www.sign-works.org.uk/D221.httm

Borg, W. R., & Gall, M. D. (1983). *Educational research.* New York: Longman.

Bourquin, E. A. (1996). Using interpreters with deaf–blind clients: What professional service providers should know. *Re: View, 27,*(4), 149–154.

Capella, M. E. (2003). Evaluating differences in demographics, services, and outcomes for vocational rehabilitation consumers with hearing loss versus consumers with other disabilities. *Journal of Rehabilitation, 69*(3), 39–46.

Covell, A. B. (1996, March 15). *Network Design Manual: Designing a videoconference solution.* Network Computing. Retrieved October, 9, 2003, from http://www.networkcomputing.com/netdesign/video1.html

Danek, M. (1992). Working with people who are deaf or hard of hearing. *American Rehabilitation, 18*(2), 12–17.

Danek, M. (1994). Rehabilitation Act Amendments and the Helen Keller National Center Act of 1992: Implications for consumers with hearing loss. *American Rehabilitation, 19*(4), 8–16.

Forsyth, E. M. (2002). *Measuring and delivering quality in open employment services for people with disability: Is a system of compliance to performance standards in conflict with furthering quality in service delivery for customers?* Unpublished master's thesis, Adelaide University, Graduate School of Management, South Australia. Retrieved on July, 5, 2002, from http://www.workable.org

Gallaudet Research Institute. (2001, January). *Regional and national summary report of data from the 1999–2000 annual survey of deaf and hard of hearing children & youth.* Washington, DC: Gallaudet University.

Gammlin, B. (2000, April 24). *Attracting qualified interpreters to Maine. American Sign Language Interpreting Resources.* Retrieved September, 19, 2003, from http://asl_interpreting.tripod.com/misc/index.htm

Harper, P. (2001). Distance no object. *HD: Hospital Development, 32*(4), 33–35.

Hazelwood, D. (1999). *TSD presents: Videoconferencing systems for the Deaf.* Retrieved April, 14, 2001, from the Texas School for the Deaf web site, http://www.tsd.state.tx.us/videoconferencing/index.htm http

Holt, J., Hotto, S., & Cole, K. (1994). *Demographic aspects of hearing impairment: Questions and answers* (3rd ed.). Center for Assessment and Demographic Studies, Gallaudet University. Based mostly on the Health Interview Study 1994. Washington, DC: Gallaudet Research Institute.

Jordan, I. K. (2003). Special guest speaker I. King Jordan. In L. Piper & D. Watson (Eds.), *Selected proceedings of the 2002 conference of the Association of Late-Deafened Adults.* Retrieved September 23, 2003, from http://www.alda.org/aldapubs.htm

Kampfe, C. M. (1990). Communicating with persons who are deaf: Some practical suggestions for rehabilitation specialists. *Journal of Rehabilitation, 56*(4), 41–45.

Kosovich, G. N. (1994). VR and people who are hard of hearing: Where do we go from here? *American Rehabilitation, 19*(4), 16–19.

Long, N., & Ouellette, S. (1994). Historical overview of services to traditionally underserved persons who are deaf. *American Rehabilitation, 19*(4), 2–7.

Maher, P., & Walters, J. E. (1984). The use of interpreters with deaf clients in therapy. *Journal of Rehabilitation of the Deaf, 17,* 11–15.

Nakamura, K. (2002). *About American Sign Language: Sign language linguistics.* Retrieved August 28, 2003, from http://www.deaflibrary.org/asl.html

National Association for the Deaf (NAD) Information Center. (2000). *I have heard that Deaf people are against technology. Is that true?* Retrieved August 28, 2003, from http://www.nad.org/infocenter/infotogo/tech/against.html

National Association for the Deaf [NAD] Information Center. (2002). *Reasonable accommodations for deaf employees under the Americans with Disabilities Act.* Retrieved October 19, 2002, from http://www.nad.org/infocenter/infotogo/legal/accom.html

National Technical Institute for the Deaf. (1992). *Tips you can use when communicating with Deaf people.* Rochester, NY: Rochester Institute of Technology.

Parasuraman, A., Zeithaml, V. A., & Berry, L. L. (1985, Fall). A conceptual model of service quality and implications for future research. *Journal of Marketing, 49,* 41–50.

Parasuraman, A., Zeithaml, V. A., & Berry, L. L. (1991). Understanding customer expectations of service. *Sloan Management Review, 32,* 39–48.

Porter, A., (1999, Spring). Sign-language interpretation in psychotherapy with deaf patients. *American Journal of Psychotherapy, 53*(2), 164–177.

Prosser, F. (1993). Finding a way in. *Youth Studies, 12*(1), 21–28.

Rehabilitation Services Administration. (2000). *Information on the provision of vocational rehabilitation services to individuals with hearing loss (deaf and hard of hearing).* [Information Memorandum RSA-IM-00-21, March 21]. Washington, DC: Department of Education, Office of Special Education and Rehabilitative Services.

Registry of Interpreters for the Deaf. (1997). *Professional sign language interpreting.* Retrieved on January 5, 2001, from http://www.rid.org/prof.html

Richard, M. A. (2000). A discrepancy model for measuring consumer satisfaction with rehabilitation services. *Journal of Rehabilitation, 66*(4), 37–43.

Ries, P. W. (1994). Prevalence and characteristics of persons with hearing trouble: United States, 1990–1991. *Vital and Health Statistics, 10*(188). Hyattsville, MD: National Center for Health Statistics.

Salkind, N. J. (2000). *Exploring research.* Englewood Cliffs, NJ: Prentice Hall.

Seawright, K. W., & Young, S. T. (1996). A quality definition continuum. *Interfaces, 2*(3), 207–213.

Siple, L. A., (1993). Working with the sign language interpreter in your classroom. *College Teaching, 41*(4), 139–142.

Telemedicine, A brief overview. (1999). Developed for the Congressional Telehealth Briefing, June 23, 1999. Retrieved March 10, 2002, from the American Telemedicine Association (ATA) web site, http://www.atmeda.org/news/overview.htm

U.S. Bureau of the Census. (2000). *2000 Census of population and housing.* Retrieved November 2, 2002, from the U.S. Census Bureau web site, http://www.census.gov/prod/cen2000

U.S. Bureau of the Census. (2000). *Arizona QuickFacts from the U.S. Census Bureau.* Retrieved on November 2, 2002, from the U.S. Census Bureau Quick Facts web site, http://quickfacts.census.gov/qfd/states/04000.html

*Videoconferencing cookbook.* (2002). Retrieved June, 17, 2003, from the Video Development Initiative web site, http://www.videnet.gatech.edu/cookbook.html

*Video telecommunications fact sheet.* (1998). Retrieved January 1, 2001, from Gallaudet University, Technology Assessment Program (TAP) web site, http://tap.gallaudet.edu/video.htm

VTEL. (2001). *Digital visual communication—Tutorials: Learn about videoconferencing.* Retrieved January 18, 2001, from http://www.vtel.com/newsinfo/tutorial/Default.htm

Whitten, P., Kingsley, C., Cook, D., Swirczynski, D., & Doolittle, G. (2001). School-based telehealth: An empirical analysis of teacher, nurse, and administrator perceptions. *Journal of School Health, 71*(5), 173–181.

Williams, N. (1998). *ISDN video tutorial.* Retrieved October 19, 2002, from Gallaudet University, Technology Access Program (TAP) web site, http://tap.gallaudet.edu/ISDNTutorial.htm

Young, D. J. (1998). *Video over frame relay: White paper.* Retrieved September 24, 2003, from http://www.memotec.com/technology/vofrwp.htm

Zeithaml, V. A., Parasuraman, A., & Berry, L. L. (1985). Problems and strategies in services marketing. *Journal of Marketing, 49,* 33–46.

# 4

# The Use of Computer Technology for People Having a Disability

Deepti Joshi and Richard J. Morris

Computer technology has increased exponentially over the past 50 years. From the bulky vacuum tubes used in the early 1950s to the use of transistors in the late 1950s and 1960s, and personal computers (PC) beginning in the mid-1970s, scientists and engineers have been constantly working to improve computer technology in order to make it more accessible and useful to the general public. In addition, the Internet has opened a whole new chapter in global communications. People can now connect to anyone across the globe and access information about almost any topic at a click of the mouse. Not only can one access web sites that contain a plethora of knowledge, but people can communicate with experts about a wide range of topics, obtain feedback on specific questions through web postings and online bulletin boards, and engage in online activities for the sole purpose of entertainment.

This evolution in technology is not limited to computers alone. Mobile phones have made it possible to stay connected to people who are on the go. Automatic teller machines (ATMs) ensure that people do not need to go to a bank or currency exchange each time cash is needed or a check needs to be deposited in a bank account. There is also ongoing research and development in the field of robotics, and it may not be too far in the future when robots will become a part of everyday living. For example, robots have now been developed to perform highly specialized tasks, work in environments that are hazardous for humans, and/or do mundane tasks such as vacuuming the house or washing floors.

Recent advancements in the field of signal and image processing have also been impressive. For example, speech synthesis using digital signal processing is one of the most popular research areas, finding use in numerous applications (Lazarro, 1993). Speaker/speech recognition as well as face recognition techniques are already being used as forms of identification in the public domain (Cheok, Kaynak, Ko, & Sengupta, 2001). Artificial intelligence and neural networks are also yielding "smarter" computers, thereby making them more useful in a diverse range of applications (Bassano, Braunwarth, & Mekaouche, 1994).

Given these various technological advancements for the general population, such advances can be easily modified and/or expanded to accommodate the needs of people who have a disability. Such accommodations, in turn, have the potential not only to improve the quality of life for people having a disability, but to appreciably contribute to their feelings of self-sufficiency and autonomy. Moreover, through the use of the Internet, chat rooms, and e-mail, people can develop ongoing communications and camaraderie with others (Bradley & Poppen, 2003).

The present chapter reviews the recent advancements in assistive technology for people having various types of disabilities, including those having visual impairment or blindness, hearing impairment or deafness, physical disability and related mobility difficulties, chronic medical conditions, and/or learning disability. A discussion is also presented on how computers and information technology can be used to improve the daily living of people, as well as a discussion of future directions for research.

## VISUAL IMPAIRMENT AND BLINDNESS

Use of computers by people having visual impairment or blindness was initially a major challenge. However, it was soon discovered that the MS Office Suite provided features that could alter the text size in an MS Word document via font size (in 1-point increments), zoom (in 1% increments), and/or bold. These features, in turn, made text on computer screens readily accessible to people having low vision. Graphs in MS Excel were also found to be more visible by making high-contrast backgrounds, widening the curves, and enlarging and highlighting the axis labels. In addition, researchers discovered that MS PowerPoint could be a good tool for visually impaired persons because it was easy to create, edit, and see graphics on the screen (Gilden, 2002). Moreover, to make MS PowerPoint more useful to people having a visual impairment, a screen reader program could be employed that obtains the information displayed on the screen and processes it into a controlled speech output or Braille display (Bexten & Jung, 2002).

Work has also been conducted to assist blind students in learning mathematics. Although Braille is good for regular text, it is difficult for Braille to represent mathematical expressions because they are not linear. A better tactile method for representing mathematical expressions is an 8-dot Braille representation, which increases the character set from 64 to 256 characters and also provides some ability to display graphics. Furthermore, standard markup languages like Standard Generalized Markup Language (SGML) or Extended Markup Language (XML) are used to offer teachers tools to prepare instructional materials in electronic format and have it translated into Braille (Bledsoe & Karshmer, 2002).

The Windows graphic user interface (GUI) has eliminated the need for users to remember and type long text commands, but it has made it more difficult for people who are blind or visually impaired to use the computer. Haptic technology (i.e., controlling the movements and obtaining feedback via the sense of touch) can be used to assist these individuals (Rassmus-Gröhn & Sjöström, 1999). For example, the PHANTOM (developed by Sensible Technologies, Inc.), as shown in Fig. 4.1, is one such haptic interface device that can add a three-dimensional (3-D) touch to 3-D graphic programs. The user puts one finger in a thimble connected to a metal arm, and by moving the finger, the user can feel virtual three-dimensional objects that are programmed in the computer. As a result, a Windows interface that has frames, icons, buttons, and menus touchable via a haptic interface can aid users having visual impairment or blindness to navigate and access various programs on the computer.

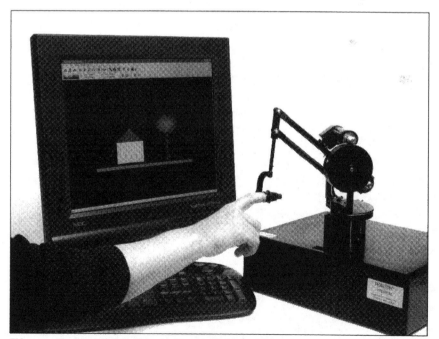

FIG. 4.1. The PHANTOM. Photo by Sensable Technologies, Inc.

Image processing is also being used to obtain useful information from technical drawings such as circuit diagrams, unified modeling language (UML) diagrams, and architectural plans. The TeDUB System classifies the type of diagram to be analyzed and then extracts the relevant diagram content (Alafaci et al., 2002). The output can be synthetic speech, nonspeech sounds, three-dimensional presentation of speech and sound, commercial force feedback devices, and the use of a touch tablet with graphic overlays. This technique can be further extended to be used with other kinds of graphics as well.

In addition to image processing, several Braille printing systems have been developed that cater to the specific needs of individuals who are blind. For example, a Braille printing system developed by Fujiyoshi, Hara, Kawamitsu, Kusunoki, and Sato (2002) can print Braille text in various sizes. A further improvement is the 3-D laser printer, constructed with inexpensive linear motors and a semiconductor laser, producing less noise compared to the mechanical Braille printers (Itoh, Oda, Osada, & Sudoh, 1999). This printer can print tangible letters for persons who are blind, as well as those for whom Braille is too difficult to learn, and it can print Braille letters of optimal size for people. In addition, it can print tactual maps with multilayered thicknesses.

The use of assistive technology for persons with visual impairment or blindness is not limited to computer usage alone. For example, a global positioning system (GPS) and electronic maps can be used to develop a navigational assistance system in an urban environment (Guillet, Pinon, & Rumpler, 2002). In addition, several methods are being tested to assist these individuals in the use of ATMs. One technique is to use ATMs with raised buttons that have Braille symbols. Another possibility is to employ raised pictorial symbols (Wake, 1999). A third technique is "talking ATMs," where telephone receivers are attached to the ATM and the user obtains auditory instructions through the telephone.

In addition to the adaptations just described, software developers have been modifying multimedia games for visually impaired or blind persons. For example, the TiM project (Archambault, Buaud, Burger, & Svensson, 2002) developed a tactile and sound interface system for multimedia games that can be used to design multimedia-based games. Moreover, a new programming language named Tim Language (TL) has been developed to create games for visually impaired and blind children and adolescents (Archambault, Dutot, & Olivier, 2002). Blind and visually impaired individuals also have difficulty often in accessing print news on demand unless they have direct and immediate access to a computer that also has Internet accessibility. Modukuri and Morris (in press) addressed this issue using Voice XML. This system requires no additional hardware other than a regular everyday touch-tone telephone or cellular phone and indirect access to a centralized computer with a functional voice browser, which interfaces with a newspaper's daily news web site. The news articles printed on a newspaper web site are synthesized by the centralized computer into speech, and the user navigates the web site's news sections and/or specific news articles via the use of the standard telephone or cell phone and by speaking commands such as "Back," "Forward," and "Skip" or by pressing keys on the touch-tone pad of the phone. News articles are then read directly to the user into the telephone or cell phone. The only requirement for the use of this device is that the centralized computer (which can be housed in a social services office) has to be turned on.

## HEARING IMPAIRMENT AND DEAFNESS

Many people having a hearing impairment or deafness often lip-read in addition to using a hearing aid(s) in order to comprehend what another individual is saying. Though effective at close range, lip-reading becomes more difficult in large auditoriums or lecture halls where the speaker is at a considerable distance from the audience or even when the speaker is more than 15 to 20 feet away from the person reading lips. In such cases, a technique called "augmented reality," which is an extension of virtual reality, can be used to assist these persons. This technology displays information that is obtained by overlapping data from external sensors and the physical world. An optical see-through head mount display (ST-HMD) equipped with a holographic optical element (Nishioka, 2002) is used to implement the augmented reality. The device is similar in appearance to a pair of eyeglasses and contains a 320 × 240 Quarter Video Graphics Array (QVGA) display on which the combined images of the physical world and computer-generated graphics are displayed. This method has been found useful in places such as classrooms and auditoriums because the device's user is granted the ability to see a magnified image of the speaker and therefore to analyze lip movements and gestures.

Furthermore, digital speech signal processing is being used to develop aids that would compensate for severe auditory loss. For example, people who are unable to gain full benefit from conventional hearing aids, and are not good candidates for cochlear implants, could find such aids very helpful (Bauer, Finke, & Plinge, 2002). In addition to compensating for losses in the spectral sensitivity and spectral dynamic ranges, these aids would also compensate for the loss of selectivity in phonetic cortical pattern recognition, thereby improving speech reception.

Advances in technology have also taken place for those individuals who prefer to communicate with others and receive information via sign language. For example, broadband networks provide high bandwidth and data transfer capacity for video communications, and this advancement in Internet technology can be successfully used to create a virtual remote sign-language interpretation system (Ishihara, Kato, Minagawa, Murakami, & Naito, 2002). This could be especially beneficial for online counseling and/or lectures, where people who have deafness or a hearing impairment would not be required to be accompanied by an interpreter. It has also been observed that these individuals do not have the same experiences or reactions when viewing various television shows. The primary reason for this is that the current closed captioning system for television provides only limited bandwidth for verbatim text and sparse background and contextual information to reach the viewer. To overcome this problem, a graphics and haptics caption editor is being developed that would result in emotive captioning (Fels & Silverman, 2002).

## PHYSICAL DISABILITY, MOBILITY IMPAIRMENT, AND CHRONIC MEDICAL CONDITIONS

To determine proper assistive technology devices for persons with physical disability, a computer access assessment (CAA) procedure has been developed (Li, Meng, Wang, Wu, & Wu, 2002). The following four components are analyzed and special equipment needs are provided at the end of the evaluation: (a) seating and positioning needs, (b) keyboard adaptation needs, (c) potential anatomical control site allocations, and (d) mouse adaptation needs. CAA has been successfully used in cases involving cerebral palsy, muscular dystrophy, spinal-cord injury, and other physical disabilities. Another useful software is *Habitat Mobile pour Personnes Handicapées* (HMPH), which can be used to design a home that provides greater autonomy to the person who is disabled (Gaucher & Leloup, 2002). Some areas that can be adapted to the specific needs of the disabled person are home automation, architecture, and furniture. Computer-aided design (CAD) is used to generate the layouts for each area, and the user can select the ones that are best suited to his or her needs and/or modify them automatically or manually.

A technical assistance (TA) system developed at the Vienna University of Technology is aimed at providing motor-disabled and multiply disabled children means to be more independent while exploring their material and social environment. The interface uses a PC with MS Windows operating system. The input/output hardware can be chosen from a range of standard and special devices to meet the specific needs of the user (Beck, Mina, Panek, Seisenbacher, & Zagler, 2002). The system can be installed to control all appliances in the room and the remote is placed on a trolley. The user needs only to face the trolley in the direction of the targeted object and, in turn, be in a position to control the operation of the TV, CD, VCR, computer, multimedia games, electric toy trains, and so on.

Specialized computer interfaces have also been developed for those users who exhibit tremors in their upper limbs (Amaya et al., 2000). These interfaces reduce tremor effects on the user's activities and thus increase the level of independence of these users. Specifically, a digitizer sketch board is used as the input device and a dedicated background process receives and stores samples from the sketch board. These samples are then used for tuning the filter that is contained in the strategy routine, which separates the problem of the user's tremor from the software developer writing an application code. In this way, a valid coordinate zone on the sketch board is detected and the desired task is performed. An automatic gesture recognition system has also been developed for people having a motor impairment (McKenna & Morrison, 2002). This system uses hidden Markov models (HMM) and is a real-time computer vision system for recognition of one- and two-handed gestures, providing a more autonomous and unobtrusive alternative to physically attaching sensors to the user. Digital image analysis is used to detect skin regions from the image obtained from a camera that is installed on the desktop or the wheelchair, and HMM are trained using hundreds of examples of each gesture. Thus, gestures can be used by such people to access computers even though they lack fine motor skills to control the keyboard or mouse.

Another system that has been developed involves a unique gait training system for computer-aided rehabilitation (Arakane et al., 2002). This system provides the user with a feeling of self-directed walking through the relaxing and tensing of the muscles in the legs. The hybrid assistive leg (HAL) has also been developed to control walking speed and step length in people during their rehabilitation process (Nozawa & Sankai, 2002). The HAL system is designed to generate stable walking motions and thus prevent people from falling down. The HAL-3 is an extension of the HAL and is used with those persons who locomote with a wheeled walker or wheelchair. This device has three parts: skeleton and actuator, controller, and sensor. Electromyogram (EMG) signals are used as estimators of joint torques for knee and hip joints, and the power assist is realized according to the operator's intention of walking and standing up, thus improving the mobility of gait disorder persons.

Another assistive technology innovation has been developed for those people who have limited or no functional use of their arms or legs. For example, Curran, DiMatta, Gates, Gips, and Lees (2002) used measures of electro-oculographic potential (EOG) from electrodes placed around a person's eyes. These measures, in turn, are used to control a mouse pointer via the movement of the person's eyes or head. An alternative method involves the use of a "camera mouse," where the type of camera commonly associated with videoconferencing is focused on the person's head. Slight movements of the head are then connected through the camera system to the movement of the mouse pointer, resulting in the person selecting particular icons on the computer or, in the case of the word processor, selecting certain letters to compose text.

Children with cerebral palsy who have limited or no upper limb movements can benefit from assistive drawing devices to communicate and express themselves. One such device has been developed using the USERfit framework for user-centered design (Chang, Chen, Chen, & Wu, 2003). The user's hand grip, arm movements, and body posture are considered when designing the assistive drawing device. It consists of a hand-grip assistive device, which is used to stabilize the pen and helps in grip tightness, an arm support assistive device, which can be adjusted to match the table height and user's arm weakness and disability, and a moving drawing board that can be easily positioned as desired.

It has been found that children with severe motor disabilities often develop "learned helplessness" as they are unable to explore and control their environment (Hay, Howell, & Rakocy, 1989, cited in Brooks & Rose, 2003). To assist such children, a robotic arm has been developed that can be used to engage in play activities (Cook, Gu, Howery, & Meng, 2000), contributing to these children being more independent and socially active. A further adaptation to the robotic arm is the use of single-switch scanning for children with very severe motor disabilities. The robotic arm used is the CRS A465 that can rotate about its base, flex and extend at the elbow and shoulder, flex, extend, supinate, and pronate at the wrist, and open and close the gripper.

Assistive technology can also be useful to individuals with spinal-cord injury. For example, Table 4.1 lists various assistive technology options for job-site accommodation and the cost of such technology (Floyd, McKinley, Reed, Sitter, & Tewksbury, 2004). Because nearly 60% of the people with spinal-cord injuries are between 16 and 30 years of age, these adaptations can be particularly beneficial in assisting these individuals in continuing their education and/or employment.

In addition, telecommuting can be used as an employment alternative for people with disabilities (Anderson, Bricout, & West, 2001). Telecommuting implies performing work at a distance using information and communication technology (ICT), such as computers, telephones, faxes, and videophones. For example, people having multiple sclerosis, spinal-cord injuries, respiratory or heart conditions, asthma, allergies, agoraphobia, and other conditions that limit mobility can therefore work and earn a living without having to actually travel to their place of work. The kind of jobs that can effectively use telecommuting are word processing, customer service, programming, account-

TABLE 4.1

Technology Options for People With Spinal-Cord Injury

| Type of technology | Approximate cost of technology |
|---|---|
| Low-tech options | |
| Mouthstick | $33–60 |
| Dorsal wrist splints, long Wanchik splints, ratchet splints, typing stick, right angle pocket Wanchik typer, universal cuffs, slip-on typing/keyboard aid, ClearView typing aid, weaving typing stick between fingers | $6–43 $1–30 |
| Ergorest forearm supports—provide support to the shoulder musculature; allows the individual to move easily in a horizontal plane; can be attached to the armrest of the wheelchair | $140 |
| Overhead slings—provides shoulder support; primarily used as a strengthening tool with a new injury | $100–205 |
| Accessibility options (standard feature of windows) | |
| Sticky keys—allow the user to depress more than one key simultaneously; this feature is very helpful to any individual who is using a mouth stick, typing stick, or one finger to type | $0 |
| Filter keys—allows the user to adjust the time a key is held down before it will repeat; the keys on some keyboards are more sensitive than other keyboards | $0 |
| Mouse keys—allows the user to use the numeric keypad to control the mouse | $0 |
| Computer workstation needs | |
| Height-adjustable workstation (Deskalators [low-tech], modular furniture, manually adjustable, power height adjustable tables) | $50–2,000 |
| Adjustable keyboard trays | $40–500 |
| Adjustable monitor arms or monitor stands | $15–200 |
| Alternative keyboard devices | |
| Small modules (Space Saver—curved and flat versions available, Mini-Thin, Wireless, Little Fingers, USB Mini) | $30–100 |
| Small membrane or stylus (EKEG Mini, Magic Wand) | $475–2,000 |
| Keyboards with built-in trackballs | $50–105 |
| Notetakers (AlphaSmart 3000, DreamWriter, Link) | $200–300 |

(continued)

## TABLE 4.1 (continued)

| Type of technology | Appropriate cost of technology |
| --- | --- |
| Mouse alternatives | |
| Trackballs (Kensington, Ergo-Trackball, Evolution Mouse Trak, Roller Plus, Roller II) | $50–400 |
| Mouth-controlled joystick (QuadJoy) | $600 |
| Head-controlled joystick (JOUSE—no longer available) | $1095 |
| Touchpads (Easy Cat, Smart Cat, Cruise Cat) | $50–80 |
| Head-pointing mice (Tracer, HeadMouse, Tracker, Smart NAV, Headmaster) | $300–2,840 |
| Software applications | |
| On-screen keyboards (ScreenDoors, Keystrokes, REACH Interface Author, IMG's OnScreen, SofType, Wivik); on-screen keyboards are used in conjunction with head-pointing mice and head-controlled joysticks | $95–495 |
| Mouse emulators (Dragger, Gus! Dwell cursor, MagicCursor, Qpointer keyboard, Joystick to Mouse, Click It); a mouse emulator imitates and takes the place of a mouse, and can be switch operated or used with one of the head-pointing mice | $50–195 |
| Speech recognition software (Dragon Naturally Speaking, Dragon Dictate, Qpointer Voice) | $200–700 |

Note. From Floyd, McKinley, Reed, Sitter, and Tewksbury (2004), with permission.

ing, billing, claims processing, data entry, dispatching, editing, filling orders, researching, report writing, and scheduling.

Moreover, videophones can make it possible for people with mobility disabilities to interact and talk to their friends and family without having to actually visit their homes—a technology called *televisits*. Similarly, such videophones could be set up in the home of a particular individual who has a disability and then family members and friends could "televisit" him or her everyday without traveling to the person's house.

Virtual reality is also being used to assist people with disabilities. For example, it has been used to help assess the driving ability of persons with cognitive disabilities (Al-Shihabi, DeLuca, Lengenfelder, Mourant, & Schultheis, 2002) and train patients with neurological impairments to operate powered wheelchairs (Attree, Derwent, Enticknap, Harrison, & Rose, 2002). Virtual reality has also been successfully used to achieve near normal walking patterns among patients with Parkinson's disease (Dutton, 1994).

## LEARNING DISABILITIES

Computers and information technology can be useful tools for inclusive education. Children with learning disabilities can find e-learning to be well suited to their specific academic learning levels; however, some children may face problems in understanding and using the computer interface. To overcome this, a tutorial system has been developed (Pieper, 2002) that can assist these students in achieving competence in the use of computer software for various applications. This is a platform-independent, HTML-based instructional program that can be studied offline or can be used in an Internet-based teaching environment. The tutorial system used Word for Windows as an example of a program to teach the use of computers to learning disabled students. The salient features of this system are:

- Clear and unique screen layout.
- Cleared up desktop organization.
- Neutral, eye-friendly colors of the background.
- Large fonts.
- Read-friendly, short text.
- Clear and practical sentences, no hypotactical sentence structure.
- No *termini technici* or other understanding barriers.

Learning-disabled children can access online training resources via Training with Animated Pedagogical Agents (TAPA). This is a multimodal interface that has animated characters that act like a lifelike virtual person to help access information over the Internet (Hammer, Haverkamp, Mohammed, Nöker, & Tebarth, 2002). TAPA is divided into two subsystems. The first subsystem is the "authoring subsystem" that combines the multimodal items to build up the story that is suitable for children and output as an XML file for every training unit. The second subsystem is the "runtime subsystem," which is Javascript based, and includes a XML training file, Extensible Stylesheet Language Transformations (XSLT) files, and a user/device profile. TAPA is a web-based system and can be evoked by using a standard web browser such as Internet Explorer. Another educational software is Step by Step 3, which can be adapted for use by children with learning disabilities (Niehaus & Prazak, 2002).

An adaptive web browser (AWB) to assist people who have a learning disability has also been developed (Chen, Chu, & Li, 2002). The toolbar of AWB consists of the most frequently used graphic icons, such as Forward, Backward, Refresh, Stop, Speak Out, and Home. The buttons and toolbars are provided with voice descriptors, which further assist people in navigating the Web. In addition, the contents of a web page can be synthesized as voice output and the user can listen to the content of the web page instead of reading it. AWB also has a huge database of 3,000 picture communication symbols that automatically pop up near the target word or phrase on the web page as the user moves the mouse over it.

## DEVELOPMENTAL DISABILITIES

People with developmental disabilities often find it difficult to find a job, even though many of them can learn complex work tasks provided that they are given systematic instructions. A palm top-based job aid system can assist such individuals to learn a new task and provides long-term support to maintain an acceptable level of performance (Cunha et al., 1999). For example, a worker with mild mental retardation could use a simplified palmtop computer that has a series of pictorial instructions guiding him or her through the steps in a task. If the worker becomes distracted from the task, a device similar to a commercial radio pager could then remind him or her to request the next instruction after a particular time period has elapsed. To monitor progress on a particular task, a supervisor could be provided with a similar device that sends an alert signal to the supervisor if the worker does not respond to a particular prompt.

Individuals with intellectual disabilities can also benefit from virtual reality to develop social and educational skills (Battersby, Lannen, & Standon, 2002). For example, a virtual environment can help these individuals learn how to shop or navigate in a new environment. An online gardening instructional resource has also been developed using the principles of virtual reality (Battersby, Brown, Kelly, & Powell, 2002). Such a device provides a useful teaching tool for learning horticultural skills, which may, in turn, provide these individuals with ongoing gainful employment. Furthermore, virtual reality can also be used to train children with autism on various daily tasks (Charitos, Karandanos, Koukouvinou, Martakos, Sereti, & Triantagillou, cited in Brooks & Rose, 2003).

A virtual learning environment developed by Brown, Lewis, Powell, and Shopland (2002) can assist in the travel training of people having various cognitive disabilities. By using this system, these individuals can learn independent travel skills. It also encourages independent use of public transportation and promotes self-esteem and motivation toward self-directed activities.

## DISCUSSION

The research and demonstration projects reviewed in this chapter show the various technological innovations that can be useful for people having a disability. Most of the work in this area is still in the research and development stage and commercially unavailable. There are, however, numerous assistive tech-

4. Computer Technology for People With Disability  81

nology devices that are currently available to people having a disability (Schneider, 1999). These are listed in Table 4.2. The major criticism of most devices that are currently on the market is their relatively high cost. One of the primary reasons for this is the relatively small number of businesses that manufacture these products, as well as the dearth of engineers and technology professionals in this area. In addition, most engineers and computer scientists are unfamiliar with system design and implementation, which has to be tailored to the specific needs of individuals with disabilities. To bridge this gap, it seems important for

### TABLE 4.2

An Overview of Assistive Technology Available for People Who Have a Disability

- Augmentative or alternative communication (AAC): Electronic and nonelectronic devices that provide a means for expressive and receptive communication for persons with limited or no faculty of speech.
- Computer access, alternative input interfaces: Special or modified keyboards, single and multiple switches, pointing device, voice recognition systems, alternative output interfaces, image magnification devices, special software and so on that enable persons with disabilities to use a computer.
- Environmental control systems: Primarily electronic systems that enable someone with limited mobility to control various appliances, electronic aids like automatic door openers or lighting control, security systems, and so on in their room, home, or other surroundings.
- Prosthetics and orthotics: Replacement, substitution or augmentation, of missing or malfunctioning body parts with artificial limbs or other orthotic aids (splints, braces, etc.). There are also prosthetics to assist with cognitive limitations or deficits, including audio tapes or pagers (that function as prompts or reminders).
- Seating and positioning: Accommodations to a wheelchair or other seating system to provide greater body stability, trunk/head support and an upright posture, and reduction of pressure on the skin surface (cushions, contour seats).
- Wheelchairs/mobility aids: Manual and electric wheelchairs, mobile bases for custom chairs, walkers, three-wheel scooters, lifting equipment, and other utility vehicles for increasing personal mobility.
- Vehicle modifications: Adaptive driving aids, hand controls, wheelchair and other lifts, modified vans, or other motor vehicles used for personal transportation.
- Aids for vision impaired: Aids for specific groups including magnifiers, Braille or speech output devices, large-print screens, closed-circuit television for magnifying documents, etc.
- Aids for hearing impaired: Aids for specific groups including assistive listening devices (infrared, FM loop systems), hearing aids, TTYs, visual and tactile alerting systems, etc.

*Note.* From Schneider (1999), with permission.

colleges and universities to offer courses in the field of engineering that teach the application of technology for the development of assistive technology options for people having a disability. Also, a collaborative effort between engineers, psychologists, special education teachers, and various rehabilitation professionals is necessary to help direct technological advancements to meet the specific needs of individuals with disabilities.

## REFERENCES

Al-Shibabi, T., DeLuca, J., Lengenfelder, J., Mourant, R. R., & Schultheis, M. T. (2002). Divided attention and driving: a pilot study using virtual reality technology. *Journal of Head Trauma Rehabilitation, 17,* 26–37.

Alafaci, M., Blenkhorn, P., Crombie, D., Evans, G., Gallagher, B., Ioannidis, G. T., King, N., Mager, A., O'Neill, A., Petrie, H., & Schlieder, C. (2002). TeDub: A system for presenting and exploring technical drawings for blind people. In J. Klaus, K. Miesenberger, & W. Zagler (Eds.), *Computers helping people with special needs* (pp. 537–539). New York: Springer.

Amaya, C., Civit, A., Jimenez, G., Rio, F. D., Rodriguez, M. A., & Sevillano, J. L. (2000). Analysis of tremor in handicapped people for design of computer interfaces. *Technology and Disability, 13,* 117–131.

Anderson, J., Bricout, J. C., & West, M. D. (2001). Telecommuting: Meeting the needs of businesses and employees with disabilities. *Technology and Disability, 16,* 97–104.

Arakane, S., Ikeuchi, H., Imado, K., Miyagawa, H., Ohnishi, K., & Saito, Y. (2002). The development of gait training system for computer-aided rehabilitation. In J. Klaus, K. Miesenberger, & W. Zagler (Eds.), *Computers helping people with special needs* (pp. 228–235). New York: Springer.

Archambault, D., Buaud, A., Burger, D., & Svensonn, H. (2002). Multimedia games for visually impaired children. In J. Klaus, K. Miesenberger, & W. Zagler (Eds.), *Computers helping people with special needs* (pp. 173–180). New York: Springer.

Archambault, D., Dutot, A., & Olivier, D. (2002). TL: A language to create computer games for visually impaired children. In J. Klaus, K. Miesenberger, & W. Zagler (Eds.), *Computers helping people with special needs* (pp. 193–195). New York: Springer.

Attree, E. A., Derwent, G., Enticknap, A., Harrison, A., & Rose, F. D. (2002). The role of virtual reality technology in assessment and training of inexperienced powered wheelchair users. *Disability and Rehabilitation, 24,* 599–606.

Bassano, J. C., Braunwarth, M., & Mekaouche, A. (1994, November). DIALECT 2: An information retrieval system based on distributed artificial intelligence tools. *1994 IEEE Proceedings of Tools with Artificial Intelligence,* pp. 800–803.

Battersby, S. J., Brown, D. J., Kelly, N., & Powell, H. M. (2002). Online gardening to promote social inclusion. In J. Klaus, K. Miesenberger, & W. Zagler (Eds.), *Computers helping people with special needs* (pp. 150–152). New York: Springer.

Battersby, S. J., Lannen, T. L., & Standen, P. J. (2002). Control of virtual environment for people with intellectual disabilities. In J. Klaus, K. Miesenberger, & W. Zagler (Eds.), *Computers helping people with special needs* (pp. 147–149). New York: Springer.

Bauer, D., Finke, M., & Plinge, A. (2002). Digital speech signal processing to compensate severe sensory hearing deficits: The /s, z, C, t/ transposer module in simulation—An overview and examples. In J. Klaus, K. Miesenberger, & W. Zagler (Eds.), *Computers helping people with special needs* (pp. 168–169). New York: Springer.

Beck, C., Mina, S., Panek, P., Seisenbacher, G., & Zagler, W. L. (2002). Technical assistance for motor- and multiple disabled children—Some long term experiences. In J. Klaus, K. Miesenberger, & W. Zagler (Eds.), *Computers helping people with special needs* (pp. 181–188). New York: Springer.

Bexten, E. M., & Jung, M. (2002). Visually impaired persons using Microsoft PowerPoint presentations. In J. Klaus, K. Miesenberger, & W. Zagler (Eds.), *Computers helping people with special needs* (pp. 463–468). New York: Springer.

Bledsoe, C., & Karshmer, A. I. (2002). Access to mathematics by blind students. In J. Klaus, K. Miesenberger, & W. Zagler (Eds.), *Computers helping people with special needs* (pp. 471–476). New York: Springer.

Bradley, N., & Poppen, W. (2003). Assistive technology, computers and Internet may decrease sense of isolation for homebound elderly and disabled persons. *Technology and Disability, 15,* 19–25.

Brooks, B. M., & Rose, F. D. (2003). The use of virtual reality in memory rehabilitation: current findings and future directions. *NeuroRehabilitation, 18,* 147–157.

Brown, D. J., Lewis, J., Powell, H. M., & Shopland, N. (2002). Virtual travel training for people with learning disabilities accessing employments including the introduction to the special thematic session "Virtual Reality." In J. Klaus, K. Miesenberger, & W. Zagler (Eds.), *Computers helping people with special needs* (pp 140–142). New York: Springer.

Chang, E., Chen, C. H., Chen, R., & Wu, F. G. (2003). Assistive drawing device design for cerebral palsy children. *Technology and Disability, 15,* 239–246.

Chen, M. C., Chu, N. C., & Li, T. Y. (2002). The design of an adaptive web browser for young children with reading difficulties. In J. Klaus, K. Miesenberger, & W. Zagler (Eds.), *Computers helping people with special needs* (pp. 189–190). New York: Springer.

Cheok, A. D., Kaynak, M. N., Ko, C. C., & Sengupta, K. (2001). Audio-visual modeling for bimodal speech recognition. *2001 IEEE Conference on Systems, Man and Cybernetics, 1,* 181–186.

Cook, A., Gu, J., Howery, K., & Meng, M. (2000). Robot enhanced interaction and learning for children with profound physical disabilities. *Technology and Disability, 13,* 1–8.

Cunha, B., Furniss, F., Lancioni, G., Morato, P., Rocha, N., Seedhouse, P., Waddel, N., & Ward, A. (1999). A palmtop-based job aid for workers with severe intellectual disabilities. *Technology and Disability, 10,* 53–67.

Curran, M., DiMatta, P. H., Gates, M., Gips, J., & Lees, D. (2002). Accessing Internet courses by eye movement and head movement. In J. Klaus, K. Miesenberger, & W. Zagler (Eds.), *Computers helping people with special needs* (pp 236–237). New York: Springer.

Dutton, G. (1994). Virtual reality: Perpetual pathway. *Popular Science, 245,* 34.

Fels, D., & Silverman, C. (2002). Emotive captioning in the digital world. In J. Klaus, K. Miesenberger, & W. Zagler (Eds.), *Computers helping people with special needs* (pp. 292–294). New York: Springer.

Floyd, S, McKinley, W., Reed, J., Sitter, P., & Tewksbury, M. A. (2004). Assistive technology and computer adaptations for individuals with spinal cord injury. *Neurorehabilitation, 19,* 141–146.

Fujioshi, M., Hara, S., Kawamitsu, R., Kusunoki, K., & Sato, H. (2002). Braille printing system. In J. Klaus, K. Miesenberger, & W. Zagler (Eds.), *Computers helping people with special needs* (pp. 594–601). New York: Springer.

Gaucher, P., & Leloup, J. (2002). HMPH—"Habitat Mobile pour Personnes Handicapées"—software for the design of an adapted living area. In J. Klaus, K.

Miesenberger, & W. Zagler (Eds.), *Computers helping people with special needs* (pp. 659–661). New York: Springer.

Gilden, D. (2002). Using MS Office features as low vision accessibility tools. In J. Klaus, K. Miesenberger, & W. Zagler (Eds.), *Computers helping people with special needs* (pp. 469–470). New York: Springer.

Guillet, V., Pinon, J., & Rumpler, B. (2002). Providing help for visually impaired people's navigation in an urban environment using GPS. In J. Klaus, K. Miesenberger, & W. Zagler (Eds.), *Computers helping people with special needs* (pp. 429–436). New York: Springer.

Hammer, S., Haverkamp, F., Mohammed, Y., Noker, M., & Tebarth, H. (2002). Evaluation study: Training with animated pedagogical agents. In J. Klaus, K. Miesenberger, & W. Zagler (Eds.), *Computers helping people with special needs* (pp. 117–124). New York: Springer.

Ishihara, Y., Kato, N., Minagawa, H., Murakami, H., & Naito, I. (2002). The user interface design for the sign language interpretation system. In J. Klaus, K. Miesenberger, & W. Zagler (Eds.), *Computers helping people with special needs* (pp. 164–165). New York: Springer.

Itoh, K., Oda, K., Osada, H., & Sudoh, Y. (1999). Development of a 3D laser printer to produce arbitrary tactile patterns. *Technology and Disability, 11*, 161–167.

Lazarro, J. J. (1993). *Adaptive technologies for learning & work environments.* Chicago: American Library Association.

Li, T., Meng, L., Wang, H., Wu, T., & Wu, W. (2002). Computer access assessment for persons with physical disabilities: A guide to assistive technology interventions. In J. Klaus, K. Miesenberger, & W. Zagler (Eds.), *Computers helping people with special needs* (pp. 204–211). New York: Springer.

McKenna, S. J., & Morrison, K. (2002). Automatic visual recognition of gestures made by motor-impaired computer users. *Technology and Disability, 14*, 197–203.

Modukuri, R., & Morris, R. J. M. (in press). Voice based web services—An assistive technology for visually impaired persons. *Technology and Disability, 16*(4), 195–200.

Niehaus, M., & Prazak, B. (2002). Usage of modern technologies—A chance for people with special needs?!—Pedagogically relevant criteria for the review of educational software exemplified by "Step by Step 3." In J. Klaus, K. Miesenberger, & W. Zagler (Eds.), *Computers helping people with special needs* (pp. 125–127). New York: Springer.

Nishioka, T. (2002). The see-through head mount display as the information offering device for the hearing impaired students. In J. Klaus, K. Miesenberger, & W. Zagler (Eds.), *Computers helping people with special needs* (pp. 166–167). New York: Springer.

Nozawa, M., & Sankai, Y. (2002). Control method of walking speed and step length for hybrid assistive leg. In J. Klaus, K. Miesenberger, & W. Zagler (Eds.), *Computers helping people with special needs* (pp. 220–227). New York: Springer.

Pieper, M. (2002). Tutorial systems to teach standard applications to the learning disabled. In J. Klaus, K. Miesenberger, & W. Zagler (Eds.), *Computers helping people with special needs* (pp. 83–89). New York: Springer.

Rassmus-Gröhn, K., & Sjöström, C. (1999). The sense of touch provides new computer interaction techniques for disabled people. *Technology and Disability, 10*, 45–52.

Schneider, M. (1999). Achieving greater independence through assistive technology, job accommodation and supported employments. *Journal of Vocational Rehabilitation, 12*, 159–164.

Wake, H. (1999). Tactile ATM controls for visually impaired users. *Technology and Disability, 11*, 133–141.

# 5

# Philosophical Congruence in Health Care

Tina Buck, Amos Sales, Charlene Kampfe, Leslie McAllan, and Cela Archembault

National surveys of the general population indicate that increasing numbers of consumers are using complementary and alternative medicine (CAM) in the United States. Eisenberg et al. (1993; 1998) conducted nationally representative surveys that revealed a rise in consumer CAM use from 33.8% in 1990 to 42.1% in 1997. In these surveys, researchers also found increased out-of-pocket expenditures from $14.6 billion in 1990 to $21.2 billion in 1997 (Eisenberg et al., 1998). Increased consumer use has been evident for some time; in 1991, the U.S. Congress mandated legislation in support of the National Institutes of Health Office of Alternative Medicine, later renamed the National Center on Complementary and Alternative Medicine (NCCAM). The NCCAM budget for fiscal year 2005 is $121 million, to be used for the purpose of conducting research, providing education, and disseminating authoritative information.

Further evidence that the mainstream medical culture is responding to increased consumer demand for CAM practices can be found in peer-reviewed journals and medical-school education. A review of CAM-related publications in the MEDLINE database was performed by Barnes, Abbot, Harkness, and Ernst (1999). This research revealed an increase in CAM-related articles of 2.1% between 1972 and 1986 to 10% between 1987 and 1996. Wetzel, Eisenberg, and Kaptchuk (1998) surveyed U.S. medical schools and found that 64% were offering one or more courses in CAM. Thirty-seven percent of these are offering two or more courses. Additionally, a survey by Pelletier and Astin (1998) revealed that insurance companies were reimbursing many health care practices that had previously been classified as CAM methods. These practices were described as "integrative" medicine due to their acceptance into the mainstream medical culture. The increased attention being given to CAM by consumers and mainstream medical culture indicated the beginning of a cultural shift toward integration of CAM and conventional medical practices.

The significance of CAM use, as it relates to persons with disabilities, is that research indicates a higher use of CAM in this population. Results of several studies (Astin, 1998; Eisenberg et al., 1993, 1998; Elder, Gilcrist, & Minz, 1997; Krauss, Godfrey, Kirk, & Eisenberg, 1998; Paramore, 1997; Wainapel, Thomas, & Kahan, 1998) indicated that persons with chronic pain were among the most likely to use CAM practices. Nayak, Matheis, Agostinelli, and Shiflett (2001) reported findings that 40% of people with spinal cord injuries were using CAM practices for treatment of chronic pain. Astin (1998) reported that individuals experiencing poorer health status were more likely to use CAM practices. Finally, in a national survey, Krauss et al. (1998) found that 57% of people with physical disabilities were using CAM therapies, a significantly greater proportion than in the general population.

Limited research has been conducted that investigates philosophical patterns and worldviews of CAM users. Astin (1998) found that CAM users versus non-CAM users had differences in philosophical beliefs, including health philosophy (health care approach to simultaneously treating the mind/body/spirit), and identification with subcultural values of commitment to environmentalism, feminism, and spiritual/personal growth. Results also indicated a change in "worldview"; however, the definition of worldview was not clearly defined. Differences in worldviews were determined by a positive, negative, or "not sure" response to the following statement: "I've had a transformational experience that causes me to see the world differently than before" (p. 1551).

Kroesen, Baldwin, Brooks, and Bell (2002) studied CAM use among veterans and also found that CAM users were not satisfied with the "medical system's lack of holism (inadequate information regarding diet, nutrition and exercise, and ignorance of social and spiritual dimensions)" (p. 57). Research regarding Pepperian worldviews indicates that individuals with more holistic "organismic" worldviews are more inclined toward CAM practices (Buck, 2002; Kagee & Dixon, 2000). These studies are reviewed in more depth later in the chapter.

In summary, this literature review shows that research indicates a high percentage of people with disabilities are using CAM practices. In addition, research reveals that individuals using CAM are likely to do so because of its holistic orientation. In this chapter, the authors provide an in-depth literature review of Pepperian worldviews and health care and discuss the relationship between worldviews and the potential benefit of assessing philosophical congruence for health care delivery.

# WORLDVIEWS

Intrinsic in the structure of worldviews are the meaning of time, nature, activity, human nature, and interpersonal relationships (Ibrahim & Kahn, 1987). These values provide a meaning of culture familiar to cultural anthropology. Often, family and the individual's extended culture are associated with the construction of core beliefs. Other terms that might be used to describe worldview are "construct" or "schema." These terms are used in psychology to describe individual fabric of beliefs and cognitive construction:

> An individual may gain awareness of events through experience. Knowledge is not possible: events are first construed, then constructs are tested by committed active involvement. Confirmation of a hypothesis is construed as consistency between the anticipated construction and the perceived event. (Anderson & Kirkland, 1990, p. 27)

This concept is broad, and explains how individuals construct meaning of life events based on reinforcing evidence. What it does not provide is the basis for personal philosophical beliefs on which explanations of events are organized—for example, the framework underlying how a person processes the interaction of events.

# PEPPERIAN WORLDVIEWS

Pepper (1942) described worldviews as "world hypotheses," or underlying assumptions about how a person explains the world and processes the interaction between events. Pepper (1942) originally described six worldviews, with two later being discarded. Pepper provided the boundaries of the four remaining hypotheses and described them through metaphoric representations. The first worldview he described was "formism." This worldview represents a categorical way of explaining events: either something is or it is not, it belongs to one category or another, is black or white, round or square. The formist uses structured categories to describe the world. The second worldview is labeled "mechanism." The basis of this worldview is that events can be explained by examining the cause and effect that parts have on each other. The metaphor for mechanism is a machine. One part causes another part to react. The third worldview is "contextualism." This worldview represents the recognition that the effects of cause and effect are dependent on the context in which they take place. The fourth worldview is "organicism." This worldview encompasses a wholistic viewpoint for explaining events. Events evolve in time with a multitude of varying influences. A metaphor for organicism is a puzzle. Without the larger whole, each part is dependent on the whole and has little meaning without the order implicit in the whole puzzle.

In 1974, Bethel created the World Hypotheses Scale (WHS) as a tool to measure worldview preference, and Germer, Efran, and Overton (1982) later developed the Organicism-Mechanistic Paradigm Inventory (OMPI), a dichotomous scale measuring Pepperian worldviews. The WHS and OMPI have been used in research spanning 30 years. Most of the research has been geared toward understanding how worldviews are compatible in different areas of life, including career preferences, friendships, alcoholism treatment preference, professional therapeutic orientation, and different aspects of health care. A review of the WHS and OMPI and research using these scales follows.

## World Hypotheses Scale (WHS)

The WHS consists of 12 descriptive statements that represent the 12 items for the scale. Under each item, there are four statements, each one reflecting one of the four worldviews. The scale has a total of 48 statements. Subjects rank the scores in order of their agreement with their perception of how each statement best described the descriptor: 1 for first choice, 2 for second choice, 3 for third choice, and 4 for fourth choice. Greater preference for each worldview yields lower scores, and less preference for each worldview yields higher scores. Scores are determined by summing the scores for each worldview across the 12 items. A potential high score of 12 and low score of 48 are obtainable for any of the four worldviews.

An example of a descriptor with statement response choices is as follows: David is taking a new job.

__A. David is taking a new job because he wants more creative, challenging work. Thus there is a specific reason for his taking a new job at this time.

__B. David is a real go-getter. He is always striving to get ahead. He's the kind of person who could be expected to get into new things.

__C. There are several ways to look at David's taking a new job. Monetarily David feels one way about it, and professionally he feels another way. There's more than one way David sees it.

__D. David's taking a new job is one stage in the development of his competence. This development began several years ago and passed through many stages before reaching its present phase.

The statements correspond with each of the worldviews as follows: "A" reflects mechanistic worldview, "B" reflects formistic worldview, "C" reflects contextualistic worldview, and "D" reflects organismic worldview.

Internal consistency reliability of the WHS was determined in studies by Bethel (1974), Burke (2000), and Buck (2002). Cronbach's alpha estimate of internal consistency reliability was used in these three studies to measure coefficients on each of the four subscales. Bethel (1974), originator of the scale, administered the 12-item scale to 554 college students, and found that the coefficients ranged from .76 (formism) to .83 (contextualism). Burke (2000) added one item to the 12-item scale, administered the scale to three hundred and thirty college students, and found coefficients ranging from .73 (formism) to .86 (contextualism). Buck (2002) studied 96 patients from a university hospital pain clinic and found the following scores: .81 (formism), .79 (mechanism), .87 (contextualism), and .82 (organicism). These studies revealed similar results indicating a high degree of internal consistency reliability.

## Organicism-Mechanism Paradigm Inventory (OMPI)

The OMPI, developed by Germer et al. (1982) (in Johnson, Germer, Efran, & Overton, 1988), is a dichotomous paradigm scale that combined Pepper's (1942) four worldviews, reducing them into two categories: mechanistic versus organismic worldviews. The questionnaire consists of 26 questions with forced-choice responses with scores ranging from 0 to 26, with higher scores representing organismic worldview and lower scores mechanistic worldview (Lyddon & Adamson, 1992). Good internal consistency is reported by Lyddon and Adamson (1992) with a Guttman split-half coefficient of .86 and .76 Cronbach's alpha coefficient.

## Career Preferences

Harris, Fontana, and Dowds (1977) used the WHS with college students as a tool to measure Pepperian worldviews in three separate studies regarding individual preference for vocational, friendship, and treatment preferences. Harris et al. (1977) studied 219 college students in order to assess their ideal occupation in relation to worldview preference. Students were asked to describe their ideal occupation without any restraints such as family influence or income. The authors organized occupations according to underlying orientation based on Pepper's worldview categories. Analysis revealed that student worldviews corresponded with underlying orientation of jobs. The authors suggested that job preference and ultimately job satisfaction might best be determined according to worldview rather than external influences. Results of preferences were listed by the authors (Harris et al., 1977):

1. Formism: "Librarian, laboratory technician, factory worker, repair person, accountant, athlete, actuary, secretary, file clerk."
2. Mechanism: "Physician, nurse, business person, scientist, manager, and social worker."
3. Contextualism: "Writer, entertainer, journalist, anthropologist, artist, and photographer."
4. Organicism: "Educator, clinical psychologist, community planner" (p. 541).

## Friendships

Another study reported by Harris et al. (1977) compared perceived satisfaction with friendships based on worldview. Ten college women were each invited to bring a woman they considered a good friend to attend a testing session. Several dimensions were used to determine success, or satisfaction, of friendships. The variables included "commonality of interests, likelihood that the pair would still be friends after 5 years, and likelihood that she would choose to work on an academic project with this particular friend" (Harris et al., 1977, p. 543). Results indicated that worldviews did play a part in satisfaction of friendships. Incompatible pairs reported discordant satisfaction with the dimensions measured. Not surprisingly, pairs reporting dissatisfaction on the dimensions had opposing worldviews. Five out of the 10 pairs reported dissatisfaction, and all five were paired with one friend endorsing mechanistic worldview and the other a contextualistic worldview preference. This indicated to the authors that there may be fascination between friends with different orientations, but that the initial intrigue may not last over time.

## Treatment

The final study to be reviewed from Harris et al. (1977) concerned preference for "therapy" for 47 males with alcoholism. Subjects were evaluated for worldview and treatment preference based on their participation and perceived benefit for group therapy or Alcoholics Anonymous (A.A.). Therapy and A.A. can have conflicting assumptions or orientations that may be represented by different worldview categories. One example provided by Harris et al. (1977) is the labeling of "alcoholic" used in A.A. and the attribution of behaviors based on the categorical label, whereas psychotherapy examines behaviors in relation to attitudes and life patterns.

In the study by Harris et al. (1977), therapists conducted 10 group sessions and evaluated patients on their participation, disputes of interpretation, and productive use of therapy. The results showed that when the worldview preference for counselor and patient were compatible, the patient attended more sessions than when the worldviews were incompatible and both patient and therapist rated the sessions as being more positive. Additionally, patients endorsing a mechanistic worldview were thought to be more argumentative when participating in the groups. For individuals attending A.A., there was a positive correlation between attendance and benefit; contextualistic worldview preference had a negative correlation with A.A. attendance and benefit.

## PHILOSOPHICAL CONGRUENCE

Several researchers used the WHS and OMPI to determine congruence between worldview and perceived benefit regarding several health care topics. Researchers hypothesized that clients would be more likely to relate to, and benefit most from, health care services that correlate with their underlying worldviews (Buck, 2002; Burke, 1999; Curtin, 1985; Johnson et al., 1988; Kagee & Dixon, 2000; Lyddon & Adamson, 1992). The results of these studies are reviewed next.

### Personality Traits

Johnson et al. (1988) studied personality traits of psychologists in relation to worldviews preference. Drawing from internationally recognized journals, the authors recruited subjects who were contributors and editorial staff for these journals for the study. The four groups of behavioral scientists used in the study represented four theoretical approaches to psychology: sociobiology, behaviorism, personality psychology, and human development. They used "self-report and peer ratings of personality, intellectual and interpersonal style, and occupation interests" (Johnson et al., 1988, p. 824) to determine the type of personality traits these individuals possessed and how these traits corresponded with their underlying worldviews. In addition, each subject completed the WHS, the OMPI, and various other psychological measures. The outcome of the study indicated consistency in personality traits as they differed between subjects endorsing opposing worldviews and theoretical models: mechanists preferred behavioral theoretical models and had personalities that were "orderly, stable, conventional, conforming, objective and realistic in their cognitive style, and interpersonally passive, dependent, and reactive" (Johnson et al., 1988, p. 833). On the other hand, those endorsing organismic worldview preferred the theoretical basis of a human development model and had personalities that were "fluid, changing, creative, and non-conforming ... participative and imaginative in their cognitive style ... active, purposive, autonomous, and individualistic" (Johnson et al., 1988, p. 833).

## Counseling Preference

Lyddon and Adamson (1992) studied worldview in relation to inclination toward counseling theoretical orientation. The subjects were 90 undergraduate students. Subjects were asked to listen to three prerecorded scripts in which representations of three counseling methods with differing orientations were described. The three counseling methods were: (a) behavioral—conditioning and environmental changes are brought about by a reinforcing behavior; (b) rationalist—irrational thinking determines emotions and behavior; and (c) constructivist—cognitive development transforms personal meanings. Subjects also completed the OMPI, used to measure worldview preference, and the Counseling Approach Evaluation Form (CAEF) that was used to measure preference for counseling approaches. Significant findings from the study demonstrated that subjects endorsing organismic worldview preferred constructivist counseling and those with mechanistic worldview preferred behavioral counseling. There was no significant difference in preference for rationalist counseling.

## Physician Compatibility and Patient Satisfaction

Curtin (1985) made use of the OMPI to measure physician compatibility with the biopsychosocial model of medicine in relation to higher preference for organismic worldview and better patient satisfaction. He hypothesized that physicians' ability to "apply the biopsychosocial model of medicine—attend to patients as persons and to strengthen affective bonds" (Curtin, 1985, p. xii), and to provide a more complex orientation toward patient health status, would correlate with physician organismic worldview preference. Curtin used qualitative research methods to study nine residents in family practice training programs while they interacted with a total of 40 patients. Questionnaires were used to evaluate patient perceptions of satisfaction.

Results of the Curtin study showed that resident physicians who had an organismic worldview preference demonstrated the following: (a) had better responses and reports of satisfaction from clients, (b) had more of a psychosocial interest in client care, and (c) demonstrated more multidimensional qualities than residents with a mechanistic worldview preference. Curtin concluded from this study that worldview was the primary factor associated with resident use of the biopsychosocial model of medicine.

## Health Promoting Behavior

Kagee and Dixon (2000) used the OMPI to study worldviews of 259 university students as predictors of consumer involvement in health promoting behavior. The investigators defined "health promoting behavior" as follows: "an expression of the human tendency to actualize and is directed at elevating the individual's level of well being, enhancing self-actualization, and maximizing personal fulfillment" (Kagee & Dixon, 2000, p. 167). Results showed that subjects preferring an organismic worldview displayed "greater willingness on the part of individuals to engage in health promoting behaviors more frequently with the aim of maintaining optimum health" (Kagee & Dixon, 2000, p. 177), more often than those with a mechanistic worldview. Subjects endorsing preference for organismic worldview were more likely than those with a mechanistic worldview to (a) engage in health promoting behavior, and (b) have willingness to receive services from alternative health care practitioners providing the following interventions: counseling psychology, homeopathy, reflexology, herbology, and aromatherapy. Subjects with an organismic worldview were *not* more willing to receive services from practitioners such as faith healers and acupuncturists. These results were notable because both faith healing and acupuncture can be categorized as having an underlying organismic worldview. A possible explanation for these results could be related to limitations of the Kagee study, including use of undergraduate students, who (a) might have had limited knowledge of the practices selected for the study and (b) did not represent a population most likely to use CAM practices. Additionally, the researchers reported that female subjects were more likely to endorse organismic worldview, therefore more health promoting behavior.

## Conventional and Alternative Medicine

Buck (2002) studied 96 patients with nonmalignant chronic pain at a teaching hospital outpatient pain clinic to determine inclination toward use of conventional or complementary and alternative (CAM) treatment methods and worldview preference. A Health Care Choice List was created through selection of an expert panel. Panel members were asked to rate 19 categories of pain interventions according to how effective each category was believed to be for chronic pain, and where methods were believed to fall on a continuum from "most" conventional to "most" CAM. From these 19 categories, 8 were chosen to represent the Health Care Choice List: (a) medical management; (b) physical or occupational therapy; (c) surgical procedures: minimally invasive; (d) surgical procedures: more invasive; (e) acupuncture, moxibustion, or cupping; (f) energy healing; (g) homeopathy; and (h) shiatsu or acupressure.

Subjects completed demographic information, the WHS, and a Health Care Choice List. Results of the study showed that older adults with formistic worldview preference were more likely to use conventional health care. There were borderline significant findings demonstrating preference for CAM use for subjects endorsing contextualistic and organismic worldviews. A fifth category emerged from the data, with 8 of the 96 subjects (7.3%) scoring equally in two worldview categories. This group was likely to use CAM methods, which is consistent with a more flexible approach to explaining events.

### Worldview Research Summary

In summary, 30 years of Pepperian worldview research demonstrates consistency between individual worldview preference and vocations, friendships, professional theoretical orientation, and philosophical congruence with mental and physical health care. In the following section a connection is made between philosophical congruence and health care, with hypothesized benefits for evaluating and referring patients to health care choices in order to maximize placebo effect. A description of the positive effects of placebo effect will assist with this understanding.

## PLACEBO EFFECT

The term *placebo effect* often brings up a negative connotation in health care due to its role in research and association with hypochondriasis. Positive results from use of placebo will "verify" beliefs that symptoms that "should" not exist truly are "all in a person's mind." Placebo effect, as defined by Shapiro (1961), follows

> any therapeutic procedure (or that component of any therapeutic procedure) which is given deliberately to have an effect, or unknowingly has an effect on a patient, symptom, syndrome, or disease, but is objectively without specific activity for the condition being treated. (Noon, 1999, p. 133)

Recruiting the positive benefits of placebo effect has been used in medicine throughout the centuries (Kapp, 1982; Straus & von Ammon Cavanaugh, 1996). Research by Schwartz, Soumerai, and Avorn (1989) revealed that among 110 physicians studied, 24% intentionally prescribed drugs for their placebo effect. This was not surprising due to research studies on placebo effect and pharmaceutical pain management that reveal some 30–40% of pain patients responded to placebo treatment and that 50–60% of pain symptom relief can be attributed to placebo effect (Noon, 1999). Additional research reveals that placebos are clinically beneficial in 60–90% of diseases (Benson & Friedman, 1996). Some characteristics of placebos that mimic active drug intervention are as follows: (a) direction of effect: a placebo will mimic an active treatment by increasing or decreasing the effect of the active treatment in the same direction; (b) equivalence of strength: the placebo will mimic the strength of the active treatment such as a mild analgesic versus a strong analgesic; (c) side effects: placebos have been found to mimic side effects of active treatments such as nausea, headaches, and so on; (d) time course: the length of time of active treatment effect will be mimicked by a placebo; and (e) "therapeutic window": with regard to dosage, the range of effectiveness will be mimicked by a placebo (Ross & Olsen, 1981). Additionally, research shows that placebo effectiveness can be found when the following components are presented: patient belief and expectancy in the placebo, practitioner belief and expectancy in the placebo, a good therapeutic alliance between the patient and practitioner (Benson & Friedman, 1996).

Noon (1999) described several theories that have been used to explain placebo effect. One theory is natural history that bases placebo effect on the naturally occurring ability of the body/mind to heal itself. An example of this is the body's natural ability to overcome a viral infection. Antibiotics are often prescribed for viral infections but have no actual clinical effect on viruses. An assumption about placebo effect in such situations is that the antibiotics might be believed to be the healing agent for the virus, when in fact it was the body's natural immune system that was able to overcome the virus. Another theory attributes placebo effect to anxiety reduction: the effects of reduced anxiety on symptom relief. Finally, expectancy theory explains placebo effect as the generation of beliefs that lead to expectations, and that it is the beliefs and expectations that contribute to the healing process.

Noon (1999) also indicated that when anxiety reduction and expectancy theories are combined, they can explain the gain of confidence in an intervention through expectation that in turn reduces anxiety, thus reducing symptoms. This combined theory can also be viewed in terms of the biopsychosocial model of medicine: that the central nervous system responds to cognitive processes and emotional responses that are guided by the cultural context in which they take place (Noon, 1999). Therefore, an important guiding force in the course of healing is the psychophysiological response to underlying beliefs. Pepper's world hypotheses represent worldviews that are the underlying beliefs and expectancies that drive cognitive processes in spite of the cultural context in which they take place.

It is evident that congruence with underlying world hypotheses can be beneficial to health care providers and the individuals who see them for care. When examining the benefits of accessing placebo effect, it is apparent that worldview research may be valuable if it were to be applied in practice. The point here is that health care practices are grounded in the philosophy underlying the *orientation of the practice*. Schwartz and Russek (1997) described the underlying philosophy of different health care practices.

## HEALTH CARE PHILOSOPHY

Schwartz and Russek (1997) described health care philosophy through worldviews:

1. Formistic: "All structures and functions exist as separate categories" (p. 9). "From a strict formistic perspective, health is the absence of disease" (p. 9).
2. Mechanistic: "All effects have causes that precede them" (p. 9). "Specific germs and specific viruses are envisioned as causing specific diseases, and specific drugs are interpreted as causing specific disorders to disappear. Similarly, specific psychosocial variables (for example, suppressed or repressed emotions) are envisioned as causing specific diseases, and specific psychosocial interventions (for example, biofeedback or muscle relaxation) are interpreted as causing specific disorders to disappear" (p. 10).
3. Contextual: "All structures and functions exist in context and are relative" (p. 9). "From a contextual perspective, a disease can be thought of as being caused by an outside agent or as being caused by the host. Certain diseases might require the presence of certain pathogens, but whether or not individuals are affected by the pathogen might depend on the presence of life stressors, the state of people's immune system at the time, and/or their diet" (p. 11).
4. Organismic: "All structures and functions reflect organizations of interactive relationships—parts interact and become whole systems" (p.

5. Philosophical Congruence in Health Care  97

9). "The organismic hypothesis enables us to study relationships of parts (forms) over time (mechanisms) from different perspectives (contexts), and then to integrate them. When people say that 'health is a combination of the capacity to heal and the capacity to function optimally,' they are implicitly adopting the organismic hypothesis" (p. 12).

These descriptions provide a framework for understanding how the worldviews might apply more directly to health care choices by consumers, theoretical models for practitioners, and a language base for communication between the patient and practitioner. These three aspects were discussed in the section on placebo effect and can represent accessing placebo effect through belief by the patient, the practitioner, and a good rapport between the two. In the last part of this chapter, we discuss the concept of accessing the positive aspects of placebo effect by providing health care participants with services that are philosophically congruent with their underlying belief structure.

## MEDICAL MODEL WORLDVIEW ORIENTATION

Pepper described use of metaphor in philosophy in a manner that is important to consider:

> Its explanatory function is to aid in conceptual clarification, comprehension, or insight regarding a mode of philosophical thought, a problem or an area of philosophical subject matter, or even a total philosophical system. (Pepper, 1982, p. 197)

When examining the philosophical underpinnings of U.S. conventional health care practices, it is evident that the first three worldviews are the preferred worldview represented. Cassidy (1994) described the cognitive process of evaluating reality:

> To the extent that human beings can grasp and talk about it, "reality" is itself a construct. Nothing can be "objectively" grasped, for the observer and his or her history and technology always affect the observed (the relativity principle in anthropology; the Heisenberg principle in physics). Thus, reality is socially constructed out of only partly understood components such as consciousness, body and self-awareness, culture, religion, history, physiology, genetics, and many other things. (p. 5)

## CONVENTIONAL OR COMPLEMENTARY AND ALTERNATIVE MEDICINE?

A review of literature on integrated medicine indicated that there are underlying philosophical differences between CAM and conventional medicine (Bell, Baldwin, Schwartz, & Russek, 1998; Cassidy, 1994; Dacher, 1995; Hewa & Hetherington, 1995; Micozzi, 1996, 1998; Ranjan, 1998; Schwartz & Russek, 1997; Weil, 1983). Cassidy (1994) provided metaphoric examples of conventional health care as compared to "holistic" health care. Cassidy described the aim of conventional medicine as the eradication of disease or correction of physical damage, whereas CAM methods aim more toward overall prevention and wellness. She described the metaphor for the conventional medical model as one that is reductionistic in nature: war. In a war, there is a winner and loser (categorical). One participant can cause harm to another participant (cause and effect). There is a beginning and ending. The metaphor is represented through linguistics used in the conventional medical model that describe the process by which a person relates to their disease. Researchers work to find a "magic bullet" while patients "fight" their disease. The final stage in the disease is when a patient dies, or the "battle is lost." The Pepperian worldviews that best correspond with the war metaphor are formism and mechanism.

In contrast, the metaphor Cassidy (1994) used to represent holistic medicine is that of a garden. The parts are seen as part of a greater whole and are nurtured by the process of nature. There is constant change of the system, as influenced by many factors, and the garden has the ability to self-regulate if provided with the proper nurturing. Parts are not removed without considering the effects on the rest of the garden. The Pepperian worldviews that best correspond with the garden metaphor are contextualism and organicism.

Cassidy (1994) also described the contrast in the philosophy underlying scientific research methods with philosophical underpinnings of some forms of complementary and alternative medicine, particularly energy medicine. Evidence from nonreductionistic methods is often dismissed in the absence of a cause and effect explanations for outcomes. Cassidy stated, "Reductionistic science says that seeing is believing; holistic science counters that believing is seeing" (Cassidy, 1994, p. 13). Furthermore, the relationship between practitioner and patient is contrary. In conventional practices, parts of the person are treated in a manner that is generally separate from the whole. Patients are provided with treatments used to remove symptoms and cures for disorders or diseases. These methods are given "to" or provided "for" patients, and "noncompliance" is commonplace when patients "refuse" to engage in recommendations. In many alternative practices, the patient is treated in a holistic manner. The practitioner recognizes the interrelatedness of the smaller pieces to the greater whole. The client is empowered to contribute to his or her own healing process by becoming aware of the interrelatedness of beliefs, thoughts, feelings, and the physical. Clients are provided with support in making choices to change those parts of the whole over which they have control.

Cassidy makes the point that limitations are present in each orientation. To summarize, in a reductionistic orientation the practitioner cannot "see the forest through the trees"; and in a holistic orientation the practitioner may fail to "see the trees through the forest." Either orientation is not complete in itself, and there is no philosophical basis that is superior to another. Each has its purpose in contributing to health. Regardless of benefits and limitations of each orientation, it is important to understand how philosophical congruence with health care can contribute to the healing process.

## CLOSING COMMENTS

In summary, individuals possess a personal philosophy ("metaphor"/"schema"/ "hypothesis"/"construct"), and it is ethically responsible to assist clients in using their own philosophy for positive health benefits. By doing so, clients contribute to their own healing process by accessing placebo effect. According to placebo research, components involved in accessing the positive aspects of placebo effect are for both clients and health care providers to expect and believe in the benefits of the health care practice. Finally, it is important to promote a good relationship between the two individuals. Research on Pepperian worldviews demonstrates the benefit of matching client and practitioner to practices that are congruent with their underlying worldview, and that the relationship between the client and practitioner may be strengthened through similar worldview orientations. Therefore, it is possible that philosophical congruence of health care practices may be a critical piece in the healing process.

During the past decade or more, there has been increased attention paid to providing rehabilitation services that are culturally sensitive. The authors would like to suggest that assessment of worldviews be included in a multicultural perspective of service delivery. When examining the underlying philosophy of conventional and complementary and alternative medicine, it is evident that roots of culture are not limited to ethnic and/or cultural barriers. Underlying worldviews are independent of culture; however, culture may have elements of philosophical underpinnings that are important to recognize in a thorough health care assessment. Perhaps more importantly, rehabilitation professionals can become aware of their own worldviews, examine the benefits and limitations of their underlying orientations, and learn to communicate within the larger perspective of an integrative health care system.

Finally, in order to make progress toward integrating health care practices used by persons with disabilities, it is important for rehabilitation professionals to be educated about all forms of health care practices. Rehabilitation educators will need to include information about CAM practices when teaching courses on medical aspects of disabilities. Rehabilitation counselors can learn about the many health care practices in their community that are being accessed by their clients; assess the legitimacy of these practices through research and education; and learn how to support clients in making appropriate health care choices based on efficacy, cost, and philosophical congruence, while conferring with and communicating about these health care decisions with their health care team.

## ACKNOWLEDGMENT

The described research in this chapter was supported, in part, by the David and Minnie Meyerson Foundation's Project on Research, Advocacy, and Policy Studies on Disability at the University of Arizona.

## REFERENCES

Anderson, R., & Kirkland, J. (1990). Constructs in context. *International Journal of Persona Construct Psychology, 3,* 21–29.

Astin, J. A. (1998). Why patients use alternative medicine. *Journal of the American Medical Association, 279*(21), 2303–2310.

Barnes, J., Abbot, N. C., Harkness, E. F., & Ernst, E. (1999). Articles on complementary medicine in the mainstream medical literature: An investigation of MEDLINE, 1966 through 1996. *Archives in Internal Medicine, 159*(9/23), 1721–1725.

Bell, I. R., Baldwin, C. M., Schwartz, G. E. R., & Russek, L. G. S. (1998). Integrating belief systems and therapies in medicine: Application of the eight world hypotheses to classical homeopathy. *Integrative Medicine, 1,* 95–105.

Benson, H., & Friedman, R. (1996). Harnessing the power of the placebo effect and renaming it "remembered wellness." *Annual Review in Medicine, 47,* 193–199.

Bethel, M. (1974). *The world hypotheses scale: A study of world organizing systems.* Unpublished doctoral dissertation, Clark University.

Buck, E. S. (2002). Worldviews and health care choices among people with chronic pain. *Dissertation Abstracts International, 63*(08G), 3685.

Burke, B. (1999). *World hypotheses: Properties & Correlates of a process approach to world views.* Unpublished master's thesis, University of Arizona, Tucson.

Cassidy, C. M. (1994). Unraveling the ball of string: Reality, paradigms, and the study of alternative medicine. *Advances, 10*(1), 5–31.

Curtin, S. (1985). *World view and the biopsychosocial model of medicine: Medical resident behavior and patient satisfaction.* Unpublished doctoral dissertation, Saybrook Institute, San Francisco, CA.

Dacher, E. S. (1995). A systems theory approach to an expanded medical model: A challenge for biomedicine. *Journal of Alternative and Complementary Medicine, 1*(2), 187–196.

Eisenberg, D. M., Kessler, R. C., Foster, C., Norlock, F. E., Calkins, D. R., & Delbanco, T. L. (1993). Unconventional medicine in the United States. *New England Journal of Medicine, 328*(4), 246–252.

Eisenberg, D. M., Davis, R. B., Ettner, S. L., Appel, S., Wilkey, S., Van Rompay, M., & Kessler, R. C. (1998). Trends in alternative medicine use in the United States, 1990–1997. *Journal of the American Medical Association, 280*(18), 1569–1575.

Elder, N. C., Gillcrist, A., & Minz, R. (1997). Use of alternative health care by family practice patients. *Archives in Family Medicine, 6,* 181–184.

Germer, C. K., Efran, J. S., & Overton, W. F. (1982, April). *The Organicism-Mechanism Paradigm Inventory: Toward the measurement of metaphysical assumptions.* Paper presented at the 53rd Annual Meeting of the Eastern Psychological Association, Baltimore, MD.

Harris, M., Fontana, A. F., & Dowds, B. N. (1977). The world hypotheses scale: Rationale, reliability and validity. *Journal of Personality Assessment, 41*(5), 537–547.

Hewa, S., & Hetherington, R. W. (1995). Specialists without spirit: Limitations of the mechanistic biomedical model. *Theoretical Medicine, 16,* 129–139.

Ibrahim, F. A., & Kahn, H. (1987). Assessment of world views. *Psychological Reports, 60,* 163–176.

Johnson, J. A., Germer, C. K., Efran, J. S., & Overton, W. F. (1988). Personality as the basis for theoretical predilections. *Journal of Personality and Social Psychology, 55*(5), 824–835.

Kagee, S. A., & Dixon, D. N. (2000). Worldview and health promoting behavior: A causal model. *Journal of Behavioral Medicine, 23*(2), 163–179.

Kapp, M. B. (1982). Placebo therapy and the law: Prescribe with care. *American Journal of Law and Medicine, 8*(4), 371–405.

Krauss, H. H., Godfrey, C., Kirk, J., & Eisenberg, D. M. (1998). Alternative health care: Its use by individuals with physical disabilities. *Archives in Physical Medicine and Rehabilitation, 79,* 1440–1447.

Kroesen, K., Baldwin, C. M., Brooks, A. J., & Bell, I. R. (2002). U.S. military veterans' perceptions of the conventional medical care system and their use of complementary and alternative medicine. *Journal of Family Practice, 19,* 57–64.

Lyddon, W. J., & Adamson, L. A. (1992). Worldview and counseling preference: An analogue study. *Journal of Counseling and Development, 71,* 41–47.

Micozzi, M. S. (1996). *Fundamentals of complementary and alternative medicine.* New York: Churchill Livingstone.

Nayak, S., Matheis, R. J., Agostinelli, S., & Shiflett, S. C. (2001). The use of complementary and alternative therapies for chronic pain following spinal cord injury: A pilot survey. *Journal of Spinal Cord Medicine, 24*(1), 54–62.

Noon, J. M. (1999). Placebo to credebo: he missing link in the healing process. *Pain Reviews, 6,* 133–142.

Paramore, L. C. (1997). Use of alternative therapies: Estimates from the 1994 Robert Wood Johnson Foundation National Access to Care Survey. *Journal of Pain and Symptom Management, 13*(2), 83–89.

Pelletier, K. R., & Astin, J. A. (1998, October). *Current trends in the integration and reimbursement of complementary and alternative medicine by managed care organizations*

(MCOs) *and insurance providers: 1998 update and cohort analysis.* In K. R. Pelletier, D. M. Eisenberg, & W. L. Haskell (Co-Chairs). Symposium conducted at the meeting of the First Annual Conference on Complementary and Alternative Medicine: Practical Applications and Evaluations, San Francisco, CA.

Pepper, S. C. (1942). *World hypotheses: A study in evidence.* Cambridge, England: Cambridge University Press. Reprinted 1961, University of California Press, Berkeley.

Pepper, S. (1982). Metaphor in philosophy. *Journal of Mind and Behavior, 3,* 197–205.

Ranjan. (1998). Magic or logic: Can "alternative" medicine be scientifically integrated into modern medical practice? *Advances in Mind-Body Medicine, 14,* 51–61.

Ross, M., & Olsen, J. M. (1981). An expectancy attribution model of the effects of placebos. *Psychological Reviews, 88,* 408–437.

Schwartz, G. E., & Russek, L. (1997). The challenge of one medicine: Theories of health and the eight "World Hypotheses." *Advances, 13,* 7–23.

Schwartz, R. K., Soumerai, S. B., & Avorn, J. (1989). Physician motivations for nonscientific drug prescribing. *Social Sciences in Medicine, 28*(6), 577–582.

Shapiro, A. K. (1961). Factors contributing to the placebo effect: Their implications for psychotherapy. *American Journal of Psychotherapy, 18,* 73–88.

Straus, J. L., & von Ammon Cavanaugh, S. (1996). Placebo effects: Issues for clinical practice in psychiatry and medicine. *Psychosomatics, 37*(4), 315–326.

Wainapel, S. F., Thomas, A. D., & Kahan, B. S. (1998). Use of alternative therapies in rehabilitation outpatients. *Archives in Physical Medicine and Rehabilitation, 79,* 1003–1005.

Weil, A. (1983). *Health and healing.* New York: Houghton Mifflin.

Wetzel, M. S., Eisenberg, D. M., & Kaptchuk, T. J. (1998). Courses involving complementary and alternative medicine at U.S. medical schools. *Journal of the American Medical Association, 280*(9), 784–787.

# Pictorial Illustrations, Visual Imagery, and Motor Activity: Their Instructional Implications for Native American Children With Learning Disabilities

Scott C. Marley and Joel R. Levin

The purpose of this chapter is threefold: (a) to provide an overview of the characteristics of Native American children with learning disabilities; (b) to review and discuss research findings related to the impact of activity- and imagery-based learning strategies on students' processing of written and verbal information; and (c) to relate these findings to a recent activity-based model of learning, while considering potential applications to learning-disabled Native American students.

## CHARACTERISTICS OF NATIVE AMERICAN CHILDREN WITH LEARNING DISABILITIES

Learning disabilities are generally characterized with respect to one or more of the following cognitive areas: receptive language, expressive language, basic reading skills, reading comprehension, written expression, mathematics calculations, and mathematical reasoning (Lyon, 1996). Identification of learning disabilities is commonly based on a discrepancy between a student's intelligence quotient (IQ) and his or her academic achievement. With this method of identification it is estimated that between 5% and 10% of the school-age population are eligible for special education services (Mather & Goldstein, 2002). These students are typically of normal or above average intelligence but have considerable difficulty in one or more academic domains (Kamphaus, 2000; Keogh & MacMillan, 1996). Causes of the IQ–achievement discrepancy exclude the effects of mental retardation, poverty, culture, and second-language acquisition.

Large numbers of Native American students are being identified as learning disabled according to the aforementioned criteria. Current estimates indicate that more than 18% of Native students served by Bureau of Indian Affairs (BIA) schools are eligible for special services. In the public schools, 10% of Native students are eligible for special services (Bureau of Indian Affairs, 2000; Pavel & Curtin, 1997). These students are predominantly second-language speakers who have fluency in their native language and who live in regions of high poverty. Some argue that with an IQ–achievement discrepancy formula, overidentification may be occurring in minority populations because such students are academically behind because of language, poverty and/or minority status (Zhang & Katsiyannis, 2002). To circumvent the problem of second-language learning, disabled students are often identified in school districts by comparing the student's academic advancement relative to the progress of other second-language learners served by the district (Gersten & Baker, 2003). If the student is not progressing at a rate comparable to similar background peers, he or she is then considered eligible for special education services.

Learning-disabled Native Americans are at risk for academic failure, with high numbers dropping out of school. Although national figures reflecting the prevalence of high school dropouts are difficult to obtain because of the small percentage of the population that is Native American, several states with large Native populations indicate a serious dropout problem. For example, in Arizona, a state with a very large Indian population, the 2001–2002 dropout rates are 17.6% and 14.7% for males and females, respectively. These figures are well above those for any other ethnic group represented by the state (Arizona Department of Education, 2002). Although no data exist regarding the percentage of dropouts who are learning disabled, it is safe to assume that many have experienced years of academic failure due to a learning disability.

### Indications That Native Americans Learn Differently

Several studies on Native American learning styles indicate an activity/physical learning preference (Berry, 1969; More, 1989; Shubert & Cropley, 1972). Participant observation research with Alaska natives has revealed that Kwakiutl children learn through observation, manipulation, and experimentation with physical objects in the home (Rohner, 1965). Research based on the Wechsler Intelligence Scale for Children (WISC), the WISC–R, the WISC–III, and the

Kaufman Assessment Battery with Native American students from various tribes consistently indicates that Native students' performance IQ scores are at or above the national norming group. However, the average Native child tends to score about one standard deviation below the national norms on verbal IQ (e.g., McCullough, Walker, & Diessner, 1985; McShane, 1980, McShane & Plas, 1984; Naglieri, 1984; Tanner-Halverson, Burden, & Sabers, 1993; Whorton & Morgan, 1990). Cultural biases of the tests, language acquisition, health issues, field dependence, and hemispheric dominance of the right brain are just a few of the explanations for the discrepancy between performance and verbal IQs. Based on these studies, it appears that Native Americans have inherent intellectual strengths for tasks with a visual/performance orientation. This suggests that teachers of Native children should exploit such children's strengths with instructional strategies that employ visual and "hands-on" activities. Yet when students are sent to public schools, instruction emphasizes learning through verbal and written modalities. The preference of teachers to use written and verbal instruction in all likelihood does not take full advantage of Native students' inherent cognitive strengths.

These findings lead to the conclusion that instructional interventions that capitalize on visual and motor modalities should be developed and systematically tested with Native American students. Currently in education it is commonly believed that hands-on activities are an effective means for attaining academic goals with all students. Much of this belief is based on the results of numerous carefully controlled experimental studies comparing instruction using visual imagery and motor activity with traditional instruction in a verbal modality. In those studies, a reliable improvement in cognitive performance has been achieved with both child and adult learners.

*A Caveat.* The experimental studies reviewed in this chapter have been conducted in populations other than learning-disabled Native American students. Thus, an initial assumption is that there is a modicum of generalizability of the research findings based on other populations to Native Americans. This assumption must be made because of the neglect of Native American students by educational researchers conducting experimental investigations of comparative learning strategies. Disregard for Native American learners and how they respond to standard learning strategies has resulted in a paucity of experimental literature on the topic. So, to begin with, we assume that Native students will respond similarly to other populations in which alternative learning modalities have been compared. A related assumption, which has been documented in the literature, is that matching of an individual student's cognitive style with his or her preferred instructional mode results in learning-strategy benefits (Riding &

Douglas, 1993; Riding & Mathias, 1991). Although it is possible that certain strategies will be more effective with Native students because of their alignment with such students' cognitive strengths, educational researchers should be aware of the following potential limitation described by Swisher (1991) regarding learning styles in native students:

> Diversity within cultural groups exists and reveals itself as differences among individuals in language use, child rearing, and formation of social networks. The degree to which members of a group absorb customs from the larger society ("macroculture") also determines diversity within the group. For this reason, assuming that a particular group will have a particular learning style is not a good idea. (p. 2)

Researchers and teachers should consider this caution before being overly broad in their generalizations regarding the efficacy of various instructional strategies in Native populations. Ideally, cross-cultural generalizations about learning strategies should not be made. It is important that empirical research be performed with a cross section of Native communities to confirm the efficacy of a learning strategy, especially when the consequences of misapplication of learning strategies can be so severe.

## ACTIVITY-AND IMAGERY-BASED COGNITIVE PROCESSES AND STRATEGIES

### Modes of Cognitive Representation

Piaget's (1962) constructivist theory of cognitive development suggests that children from ages 2 to 7 (preoperational stage) cannot produce internal visual representations in the absence of motor activity. In the context of comprehending a narrative passage, it would be posited that a young child is unable to understand fully the events that are taking place unless there is accompanying activity. This dependence on activity was evident in Piaget's findings that until around the age of 8 (the beginning of the concrete operational stage), children do not represent events internally and cannot reproduce an object's location from the perspective of another individual. That is, preoperational children depend on their body positions in relationship to the objects being manipulated.

Jerome Bruner (1964) later theorized that human beings make sense of their environment through three modalities, action, imagery, and language, which he labeled *enactive representation, iconic representation,* and *symbolic representation,* respectively. As with Piaget, Bruner found that young children were dependent primarily on enactive representations in their earliest years. As a child matures, he or she becomes less dependent on enactive learning and begins to produce iconic representations. These iconic representations are tied to "perceptual events." Later, when symbolic representations (such as words) are used for acquiring information, the binding of the modality to concrete representations is weakened. For example, the word "four" initially does not represent four objects any better than, say, the number "three." The meaning attached to the word, although commonly agreed on, is arbitrary. This raises the possibility that learning-disabled students are being asked to perform tasks in a more advanced mode (such as iconic or symbolic) prematurely. An example of this would be when students are required to read text or comprehend verbal instructions. Both text and verbal instructions require that the receiver is capable of binding the written or spoken words to concrete objects or concepts. When a child processes a story without iconic or enactive support, an inability to represent the interactions symbolically decreases his or her ability to comprehend the story.

## The Role of Motor Activity in Imaginal Representation

In two associative-learning experiments, Wolff and Levin (1972) provided evidence for the contentions that (a) motor activity and imagery can enhance young children's memory and (b) a direct connection exists between enactive and iconic representational modes. In Experiment 1, kindergartners and third graders were exposed to 16 toy pairs under one of four conditions: control (rote memorization), child-produced imagery (participants imagined the toy pairs interacting), child-produced motor activity (participants manipulated the toy pairs), and experimenter-produced motor activity (experimenter manipulated the toy pairs in a predetermined manner). With kindergartners, a positive memory effect was associated with both experimenter- and child-produced motor activity over imagery and control. In contrast, third graders' performance in the imagery condition approximated that in the two activity conditions, all of which were statistically superior to performance in the control condition. This finding, as anticipated from Piaget's and Bruner's work, suggests that the younger children were unable to generate facilitative internal iconic representations in the absence of motor activity.

To explore the existence and functioning of the enactive modality further, Wolff and Levin (1972) conducted a second experiment with presumed preoperational children (kindergartners and first graders), with toy pairs similar to those used in the first experiment. In one condition (imagery), the children held the toys in their hands behind a curtain and, without actually moving them, were asked to imagine the toys interacting. Children in a second condition (unseen motor activity + imagery) were given the same toys and instructed to play with the toys behind the curtain while imagining them interacting. Children in the second condition exceeded those in the first on the later memory measure. Because the only difference between the two conditions was the motor activity per se (i.e., with no visual feedback), it can be concluded that engaging the children's enactive modality helped foster internal imagery production.

A subsequent experiment by Varley, Levin, Severson, and Wolff (1974) found age-related differences similar to the ones described from the Wolff and Levin (1972) study. In this experiment, 80 kindergartners and 80 first graders were randomly assigned to receive imagery-strategy training under one of five conditions, which included an imagery-control condition and four different motor-activity variations. Participants in each condition were trained and practiced with eight toy pairs. After training, participants in all conditions studied 15 paired associates with instructions to think back to their previous training experience. That is, in the actual memory tests, all children were given imagery instructions in the absence of their specifically trained activity. Comparisons were made between the imagery-control condition (iconic representations) and the four activity conditions (enactive representations). With kindergartners, a statistically significant difference was found between the imagery-control and activity conditions, with the latter showing a marked benefit. This difference disappeared with first graders, where all five training variations were equally efficacious. Between kindergarten and first grade, the most dramatic increase in posttraining performance was associated with the imagery-control condition.

Because the posttraining conditions under which the participants studied were identical across conditions, the difference can be attributed to the previous training with the eight paired associates. With kindergartners unable to benefit from simple imagery instructions, this finding supports the contention that there is a relationship between the ability to produce dynamic internal visual representations (imagery) and age. However, this study shows that the relationship can be moderated by activity in previous learning experiences that capitalize on similar cognitive processes. This leads to the conclusion that effective educational strategies for preoperational children should include enactive representation either during or prior to learning tasks that involve iconic representations.

***Other Activity/Imagery Memory Research.*** Much research has also been conducted on the comparative efficacy of pictorial versus verbal modes in learning associated pairs. Because the visual modality is engaged during enactive learning, we include research documenting the facilitative effects of pictures (visual illustrations and visual imagery) as limited evidence supporting the importance of enactive learning strategies. Dilley and Paivio (1968) found that learning items as pictures frequently improves subsequent memory for those items, relative to that of items encoded solely as words. Multiple replications have found this to be one of the most robust scientific findings in cognitive psychology (Homzie, Noyes, & Lovelace, 1973; Levin, 1976; Paivio, 1971; Thompson & Paivio, 1994). Paivio (1971) offered a theoretical explanation for this finding in his "dual coding" theory, which essentially claims that items learned pictorially are encoded with both visual (as images) and verbal codes (as names or labels). Memory is enhanced in picture learning conditions because of the accessibility of two separate, yet interdependent, routes of retrieval (Paivio, 1971). Learning situations that require motor/visual activities take advantage of the nonverbal (iconic) and verbal (symbolic) representations that have been found to be successful in the dual-coding literature (see also Mayer, 2001; Mousavi, Low, & Sweller, 1995). In addition, motor/visual learning strategies add the effect of enactment, which has been found to be a salient form of encoding.

Beginning in the 1980s, an extensive amount of research was conducted to document what is called the *self-performed task* (SPT) effect. The SPT effect occurs when a person physically performs the actions directed by a sentence with his or her body in relation to imaginary or real objects (Cohen, 1981; Engelkamp & Zimmer, 1989; Kormi-Nouri, Nyberg, & Nillson, 1994; Saltz & Donnenwerth-Nolan, 1981). These studies, primarily with adult samples, compared SPTs with traditional verbal tasks (VTs), with variations to tease out the contributions of each modality. In these studies it has been consistently found that participants studying lists of phrases such as "wash the car" and "brush your teeth" remember considerably more phrases when they perform the action taking place during encoding than when only reading or hearing the phrases. This effect has also been observed in both paired-associate and free-recall tasks with 7- to 9-year-old children (Saltz & Dixon, 1982). As with the earlier studies by Levin, Wolff, and their colleagues, much effort has been made to disentangle the effects of different modalities. At the same time, from an applied viewpoint the specific mechanisms of influence are of lesser importance. Of greater import is that there is strong evidence that the physical interaction of a learner with his or her environment increases the likelihood of effectively encoding information for future successful retrieval. Recent research (Repp & Knoblich, 2004) similarly documented that people (in this case, skilled pianists) are much more adept at recognizing their own previously performed actions (piano playing) than those of others, even under conditions where minimal identification cues are present.

Such findings support the notion that powerful learning strategies can be developed that exploit multiple modalities. Evidence pointing to the effectiveness of visual and verbal modes has been supplied by dual-coding researchers and the effectiveness of activity-based learning is seen in the early findings of Levin and others, and more recently by SPT researchers. It stands to reason that a combination of the three forms of representation suggested by Bruner (enactive, iconic, and symbolic) will result in the most robust instructional strategies for learners with diverse cognitive styles.

## Learning-Strategy and Learner-Type Distinctions

Levin's (1972, p. 20) "imposed" versus "induced" distinction is a useful concept to include in the discussion of reading and listening comprehension strategies. An imposed strategy is an organizational structure that is provided by a teacher or experimenter. A teacher providing an outline prior to students' reading a text passage is an example of an imposed strategy. Induced strategies are organizational structures that learners themselves generate when facing cognitive tasks. In terms of the previous example, an induced strategy might be when students are requested to outline the passage as they read it. The distinction has implications for the use of multiple representational learning strategies in that providing a learner with physical props and explicit enactive cues during reading or listening to a passage is an imposed organizational strategy. If the same props are not provided but the learner is instructed to represent the passage internally in an analogous way that is meaningful to the learner, the strategy is induced. Reformulating the Wolff and Levin (1972) findings in terms of this distinction, young children around the ages of 6 and 7 (preoperational) are unable to generate memory-enhancing interactions when induced to do so, whereas older children have little difficulty. However, when interactions involving the items are experimenter imposed, even preoperational children experience success and performance differences between them and concrete operational children are considerably reduced.

Wiener and Cromer (1967) proposed that reading disabilities encompass different types of readers, including those labeled *deficit-poor* and *difference-poor*. Deficit-poor readers have trouble decoding unknown words and recognizing sight words, and have insufficient vocabularies. Difference-poor readers are able to decode adequately, recognize sight words, and have age-appropriate vocabularies. However, difference poor readers are unable to integrate individual word definitions into a unifying whole, which results in an inability to derive meaning from text and oral prose. In a subsequent study, Cromer (1970) found that a learning strategy that involves breaking sentences into meaningful phrases alleviated the disparity between difference poor readers and normal readers—an effect that was not found for deficit-poor readers. Levin (1973), hypothesizing that difference poor readers may have difficulty applying a relevant visual imagery strategy when reading or listening, tested the hypothesis with difference- and deficit-poor fourth-grade readers. Using an induced imagery strategy (instructions to generate integrative visual images while reading a text passage), Levin found support for the hypothesis by showing that difference-poor readers benefitted substantially from the imagery strategy (relative to normal reading instructions), whereas deficit-poor readers did not. Because it appears that difference-poor readers' comprehension improves when they generate facilitative organizational structures, further strategy research should investigate this learner type by treatment interaction.

According to Levin (1986), *understanding, remembering,* and *applying* are interrelated general cognitive outcomes desired of a learning strategy. Understanding refers to comprehending what is being learned when the material is present, remembering is being able to recall information when the learning material is no longer there, and applying is the transfer of previously learned material to novel situations. It is doubtful that a single strategy will serve as a "magic bullet" that effectively addresses all three cognitive outcomes. Teachers more than likely will find that the efficacy of various strategies is dependent on a unique combination of characteristics of the student, characteristics of the instructional materials, and the desired cognitive outcomes. Given these assumptions, a reasonable expectation is that a text-processing strategy will be more powerful when it is formulated at the appropriate developmental level (e.g., imposed vs. induced), targeted at specific learner characteristics (e.g., difference-poor vs. deficit-poor readers), and designed to enhance selected cognitive outcomes (remembering vs. understanding vs. applying). It is also hypothesized that Native American students will especially benefit from a multiple-modality strategy not only when the three aforementioned matches are made, but also when their performance IQs (i.e., their predominant physical/activity learning preferences) are engaged. As with the basic research discussed previously, the instructional strategies tested engage two or three of Bruner's representational modes for processing the information in written or oral text passages.

## PICTURES, ACTIVITY, AND STUDENTS' LEARNING FROM TEXT

The prototypical study of the effect of text-relevant pictures on students's text processing has combined iconic representations (visual illustrations and imagery) with symbolic representations (verbally or orally presented information). Pictures have been shown to improve students' understanding, remembering, and application of text information (see reviews by Carney & Levin, 2002;

Levin, Anglin, & Carney, 1987; Mandl & Levin, 1989; Peeck, 1993; and Pressley, 1977). In empirical research comparing the effectiveness of pictures and text with text alone, 41 of 51 comparisons were found to be statistically significant, favoring the former (Levie & Lentz, 1982). Facilitative effects of pictures are not guaranteed, as much is dependent on the type of learner and the alignment of the pictures with the text (Carney & Levin, 2002; Levin & Mayer, 1993). If the conditions are appropriate though, "moderate to substantial prose-learning gains can be expected" (Levin et al., 1987).

Mayer and Gallini (1990) provided evidence that the combination of text and illustration improves remembering and applying compared to text alone. In this set of experiments, college students were assigned to study various mechanical apparati using one of four methods: no illustrations, parts illustrations, steps illustrations, and parts and steps illustrations. With the same illustrations in each condition, the parts condition labeled the primary components of the mechanisms studied, the steps condition provided textual explanations of how various components interacted, and the parts and steps condition provided labeling of both the parts and steps. Three important findings resulted: (a) The parts and steps condition improved conceptual knowledge (remembering) relative to the other conditions, (b) the parts and steps condition improved problem solving (applying) relative to the other conditions, and (c) these two effects were differentially experienced, with low knowledge learners enjoying the largest gains.

In a study bearing directly on the particular theoretical position to be explicated here, Lesgold, Levin, Shimron, and Guttmann (1975) extended work with illustrations and text to include enactive representations. In Experiment 2a, 48 first graders were assigned to one of four conditions: picture after, where participants used plastic cutouts on a background to illustrate the story after listening to a passage; control after, where participants colored geometric patterns after the passage; picture during, where participants used the plastic cutouts and background to illustrate after each sentence in a passage; and control during, where participants colored geometric patterns after each sentence. Subsequent performance on free- and cued-recall outcomes was statistically superior in the two active illustration conditions. This finding suggests that having students physically manipulate iconic representations during or after listening to a passage increases remembering. In addition, the authors found that the children's picture construction in both illustrated conditions was generally appropriate, which implies that the students had an adequate understanding of the text passages while processing and constructing them.

Rubman and Waters (2000) recently performed a study very similar to that of Lesgold et al. (1975) using plastic cutout figures on a background storyboard.

The rationale for the study was that poor text-comprehending readers are deficient in proposition integration, and to test this theory, students read stories with inconsistencies embedded in the text. In the study, 192 students, half third graders and half sixth graders, were assigned to one of two conditions, storyboard or read only. Students in the storyboard condition, regardless of age, detected more proposition inconsistencies and recalled more critical propositions than did students in the read only condition. Consistent with the findings of Lesgold et al. (1975), analysis of the storyboards found very high levels of correctness, with 95% of the students in the storyboard condition constructing accurate representations.

Drawing while learning text from a science book engages enactive, iconic, and symbolic representations. Van Meter (2001) found that this combination increased students' free recall of key facts relative to students who were instructed only to read the passage. There were two variations of the drawing condition tested in that study: In one, students drew with a target illustration; in another, students drew without the illustration. It was discovered that in addition to higher performance, students who had the target illustration engaged in more self-monitoring behavior (e.g., self-questioning, looking back at the examples) than did students in the unaided drawing condition. This has implications for the application of activity with objects when learning new vocabulary, text, or directions—namely, that understanding and remembering of text can be enhanced when all of Bruner's hypothesized representations are engaged.

In summary, studies of applied text-processing strategies indicate that the inclusion of enactive and iconic representations increases measures of students' understanding, remembering, and applying. These studies further indicate that certain student characteristics moderate the efficacy of a strategy, with differential benefits in favor of lower ability (or lower prior knowledge) students often being observed. An intuitive conclusion is that readers and listeners with basic decoding and listening skills but who exhibit comprehension problems can be "induced" to comprehend by engaging their enactive and iconic modalities.

## GLENBERG'S ACTIVITY-BASED MODEL OF COMPREHENSION, LEARNING, AND MEMORY

With a considerable amount of pure and applied research implicating causal links between enactive–iconic representations and improved comprehension, learning, and memory performance, application of enactive and iconic encoding to real-world educational situations should be explored. Can the previously reviewed findings be extended to situations that better represent the needs of teachers and students? Do the research outcomes suggesting that individuals learn word pairs and sentences better when imagery and motor activity are invoked extend to reading passages, vocabulary learning, and complex instructions? Can the external support be faded so that eventually the strategy becomes a useful metacognitive tool? And more importantly for the present focus, if activity enhances information encoding and later retrieval, will learning-disabled Native American students benefit? These are questions that have not been thoroughly addressed by the literature.

Glenberg's (e.g., Glenberg, 1997; Glenberg & Robertson, 1999, 2000) activity-based model of cognitive performance is one such attempt to address the preceding questions, and it has offered encouraging preliminary results. The model posits that language comprehension is embodied and that there is a connection between modalities and the act of language comprehension. The associated indexical hypothesis proposes a three-component process comprised of indexing objects to symbols, deriving affordances, and the meshing of affordances.

The first part of the process requires the indexing of objects to symbolic representations. This consists of a learner first generating an enactive or iconic representation of the object and then linking it to a symbolic representation, such as a word. An example of this would be the object commonly known as a ladle. If a teacher were to say "ladle" to a second-language learner, he or she might respond in a puzzled manner. The teacher in turn might describe the ladle as an object with a big bowl attached to a shaft for dipping soup. After hearing this explanation, the learner might say, "Oh, you mean a big spoon?" However, the learner might not know what a "shaft" and/or a "bowl" are. What if all the symbolic representations used to define what a ladle is are unknown to the learner? This results in what is known as a *symbol grounding* problem, where the meaning of the symbol cannot be conveyed with other symbols (Harnad, 1990). Because the symbolic representations of the objects are amodal and arbitrary, the teacher might quickly end up in a quandary if the only way to define the word is through symbolic representation. Unless an object is presented in a form that looks similar enough (or is a *ladle*, for that matter), the teacher will never be able to help the student associate the word "ladle" with the physical object known as a *ladle*. This is to say, the symbolic representation requires grounding in a perceptual symbol, be it experiential or visual.

The second part of the process is the generation of affordances, as derived from certain Gibsonian concepts (e.g., Gibson, 1979). Affordances are possible/potential actions that can be performed with objects. A ladle has many potential uses beyond dishing out soup and for some individuals, dishing out soup is not a potential usage. For example, the affordances of a ladle available to a baby are quite different from those available to an adult. An adult can work in a soup kitchen serving individuals with the ladle or stand at a sink and wash the ladle, whereas a baby physically cannot. On the other hand, a baby may be very content to put parts of the ladle in his or her mouth for hours, which would be an unusual (although possible) action for an adult. Awareness of affordances contributes to more efficient text processing in that the learner becomes more aware of the realm of possible actions.

The third part of the process is the meshing of affordances. Meshing is the syntax-guided combination of affordances. When a child reads or listens to a passage, syntax limits the infinite number of affordances available to those that are context relevant. Without the limitations imposed by meshing, a potential for an explosion of affordances exists. In the *ladle* example, the affordances derived are quite different for an infant than an adult. A competent reader or listener who is aware of these affordances will quickly determine the particular affordances described in a passage by how the affordances are meshed. If the learner is unaware of available affordances and the syntax directs unknown possibilities, comprehension of the story will be disrupted. An example of poor meshing of affordances and syntax may be found in the previously described Rubman and Waters (2000) study, in which storyboards were used by children to detect inconsistencies in text. One story's syntax described a strainer that holds water and allows spaghetti to pour through it onto a plate. An affordance-aware reader would quickly notice that the syntax of the story is guiding the affordances into impossible combinations. Studies by Glenberg and his colleagues have yielded supportive results, further indicating that individuals taught with activity-based learning strategies understand and remember better than those taught exclusively using symbolic (verbal) representations. These studies are discussed in the remainder of this chapter.

## Experimental Studies Supporting Activity, Imagery, and Indexing Propositions

A number of recent experimental investigations have attempted to test aspects of Glenberg's activity-based learning model, interpreting the results within an embodied cognition framework. Each study is presented here in order of its perceived importance (less to more, relative to this chapter's theme) for providing evidence that activity-based learning strategies can improve students' understanding, remembering, and application of text information.

***Adults' Cognitive Performance.*** Glenberg and Robertson (1999) tested the efficacy of indexing symbolic representations to iconic representations. In that study, 95 women with no prior knowledge of using compasses for navigation were taught how to use a compass in four conditions: listening to a script (L), listening to and reading a script (LR), listening with pictures (LP), and listening and indexing (LI). In the LI condition, participants viewed a videotape that showed an actor's hands interacting with a compass and map components described by the script. According to the Glenberg model, by showing the interaction of the actor with the object, improved indexing of perceptual symbols to symbolic representations should occur. Statistical differences were found among conditions on a performance task that required participants to record bearings of various landmarks in a room, with LR and LI both showing improved performance relative to the other conditions. However, when the number of times that participants referred to the script (presumably to remind themselves of the compass and map components) was assessed, a statistical difference between LI participants and LR participants emerged, with the former needing to refer to the script on average only about half as many times as the latter. A reasonable interpretation of these results is that more efficient indexing was exhibited by LI participants, which in turn improved their ability to apply previously learned material in a novel context. This suggests that indexing while learning provides useful information that might not be accessed as well (or at all) by listening and reading alone—which in turn lends support to the notion that the enactive/iconic learning component of the indexical hypothesis has the potential to improve students' processing of text passages.

Seasoned actors often state that they remember dialogue from scripts better when they act out the script during practice. Noice and Noice (2001) investigated this phenomenon with college students who had entry-level acting training. In Experiment 1, 23 beginning acting students were randomly assigned to one of three conditions: bodily movement with verbal communication (movement), verbal communication (verbal), and memorization (control). Upon completion of the scripts in each condition, participants were tested on three outcomes: verbatim recall, near verbatim recall, and acceptable verbatim recall. Each outcome assessed degree of recall, from almost 100% to better than 50%. Subsequent analysis of students' performance indicated that on all three measures students in the movement condition recalled relatively more aspects of the script compared with students in the two other conditions. In Experiment 2, 54 inexperienced acting students from the general college population were assigned to the same three conditions as in Experiment 1. Type of learning strategy was found to be statistically significant in favor of the movement condition, thereby replicating the results of the first experiment. An interaction between learning strategy and type of speech (a within-subjects factor) was also found to be significant, with participants in the movement condition better remembering speech that was enacted relative to speech that was not enacted.

***Children's Recall of Narrative Texts.*** The best recent evidence for activity-based learning propositions is provided in a series of three experiments with children, using farm and house scenarios that could depict the objects and actions described in short text passages (Glenberg, Gutierrez, Levin, Japuntich, & Kaschak, 2004). The conditions in this study closely resembled actual reading situations in educational environments. Individuals who work in contexts of special education classrooms, where students are provided with intensive one-on-one tutoring or small group instruction, should readily see the relevant applications.

In Experiment 1 of this study, 32 first graders were randomly assigned to one of three conditions, two of which are described here: children's visual and physical interaction with toys represented in the stories during reading (manipulation), and children's observation of static toys represented in the stories during reading (read). Immediate assessment of free and cued recall of targeted sentences resulted in large statistically significant differences favoring the manipulation condition over the read condition. When activity/visual support was removed (i.e., when all conditions were the same), differences between conditions vanished. This suggests that a manipulation learning strategy may require more intensive, more prolonged support (in the form of training, practice, and metacognitive monitoring and feedback) if internalized strategy maintenance is the objective (e.g., Ghatala, Levin, Pressley, & Goodwin, 1986).

In Experiment 2, 28 children were randomly assigned to conditions that were similar to those described for Experiment 1. A large recall difference was found favoring the manipulation condition over a condition where were the children were provided with a second opportunity to read each sentence (reread)—for the latter condition's rationale, see Levin, Bender, and Lesgold (1977). In addition, participants were evaluated on a spatial relations and associated justification outcome, which respectively assessed location of various objects mentioned in the text and the children's reasoning behind their answers. Statistical analyses found superior performance on both measures, favoring the manipulation condition over the reread condition. As in Experiment 1, a statistically significant strategy maintenance effect was not evident when the manipulatives were removed.

Experiment 3 was performed with 25 second-semester first- and second-grade children, to investigate further the previous findings from Experiments 1 and 2, where maintenance of the manipulation strategy was not evident when the physical props were removed. This experiment was very similar to the previous ones, with the exception that children's actual manipulation of the toys (the previous manipulation condition) was replaced with instruction in and practice with children's imagining the toys interacting (imagined manipulation). Children in the reread condition were again asked to read each sentence of the passage a second time. In addition, half the children in the imagined manipulation condition were given a specific reminder to imagine during the maintenance session. In the initial experimental session, children in the imagined manipulation condition recalled more sentences, correctly answered more spatial inference questions, and were better able to justify their answers to spatial inference questions when compared with children in the reread condition. Benefits of imagined manipulation were still present in the maintenance session, with no main effects or interactions associated with the reminder instruction.

*Native American Learning-Disabled Students' Learning From Text.* The results of the Glenberg et al. (2004) study suggest that (a) indexing (through physical manipulation) of objects to symbols enhances memory for text, (b) indexing of objects improves application of information on spatial inference tasks, and (c) physical manipulation can be replaced by imagined manipulation after training. The study also outlines a practical procedure that might be applicable to teachers of Native American special education students. With this procedure, students practice reading stories and manipulating the objects in the stories; in time they are taught to imagine the objects interacting with each other during manipulation; and eventually the objects are removed altogether, with the students instructed to imagine the objects interacting.

To test these speculations experimentally, a study was recently conducted by Marley, Levin, and Glenberg (2005) in a southwestern Native American community, with third- through sixth-grade learning-disabled students listening to narrative passages accompanied by toy scenarios similar to those of Glenberg et al. (2004). In that study, 45 students were randomly assigned in equal numbers to receive one of three text-processing conditions: manipulation, where students manipulated toys corresponding to the content of 12-sentence orally presented passages; visual, where students viewed the results of experimenter manipulations but performed no manipulations themselves; and free study, where students listened to the story without visual support and were provided additional time to think about each sentence of the passage as it was presented. Compared to students in the free-study condition, those in the two visual-support conditions performed considerably better on both free- and cued-recall measures. Such findings are consistent with earlier cited findings from the "pictorial representations of text" literature (e.g., Carney & Levin, 2002; Levin et al., 1987; Peeck, 1993). At the same time, that there were no statistical differences between the manipulation and visual conditions is somewhat problematic for predictions derived from Glenberg's (1997) activity-based model, which consequently may necessitate a reconsideration and reformulation of certain propositions associated with that model. Finally, in the Marley et al. (2005) study and in contrast to the findings of Glenberg et al. (2004, Experiment 3), when external visual support was removed for children in the manipulation and visual conditions on a subsequent imagined-manipulation maintenance passage, no statistical differences among the three conditions were detected—again suggesting that more focused and more extensive efforts may be required for internalized pictorial benefits to materialize in this specially targeted population of learners.

## SUMMARY AND CONCLUSIONS

Recent estimates of the number of Native American students with learning disabilities range between 10% and 18%. These students are at high risk for academic failure. Regional dropout rates indicate that many Native students are not completing high school. An assertion can be made with little hesitation or uncertainty: A large percentage of the students dropping out prior to completion of an educational program are learning disabled. Observational studies indicate that Native American students may have a preference for activity/physically oriented learning tasks. Psychometric studies provide converging evidence for the observational studies, with Native children scoring at or above the national norms on performance elements of IQ tests.

Such findings indicate that Native American students may derive substantial benefits from learning strategies that engage multiple representations—enactive and iconic representations, in particular. In general, learning-strategy researchers have neglected Native American special needs populations. A dearth of research on how Native students respond to various learning strategies may be partially responsible for high academic failure rates in those populations. Numerous theoretical perspectives have been pursued in attempts to explain the consistent improvement that occurs in non-Native students' associative learning and text processing when multiple modalities are engaged. This research provides a long history of evidence indicating the efficacy of the strategies, regardless of the specific theoretical perspective taken.

What is more important from an applied standpoint is the universality of a promising strategy's utility. Empirical studies show that proper matching of individual characteristics and desired outcomes with the learning strategy has the most powerful results. This indicates that a student's developmental stage and reading proficiency, along with the level of external support provided and whether understanding, remembering, or applying are the desired outcomes, should be considered when matching an strategy and a learner. When the match is appropriately made, pronounced strategy benefits can be expected.

With Native special needs students we expect undiscovered effects of this kind to emerge, specifically with multiple-modality learning strategies. Little empirical evidence confirming this expectation appears to exist, due to the neglect of this population by educational researchers.

Glenberg's (1997) indexical hypothesis can help to explain why the results from multiple theoretical perspectives converge. The processes of indexing objects to symbolic representations and manipulating the affordances of these symbolic representations within meshed syntax offer multiple points of study. Future research embodying Glenberg's indexical hypothesis as a unifying theoretical framework will provide multiple directions of inquiry. If fruitful, that sort of inquiry should result in powerful methods for improving learning-disabled children's comprehension of oral and written text. With such carefully controlled programmatic investigations, it is hoped that learning-strategy researchers adopting this theoretical perspective will not continue to neglect the educational needs of America's first people.

## ACKNOWLEDGMENTS

We are grateful to the University of Arizona's Meyerson Disability Research Project for supporting this work and to Arthur Glenberg for his helpful feedback on an early draft of this chapter.

## REFERENCES

Arizona Department of Education. (2002). *Dropout rate study: 2001–2002 Annual dropout rates*. Retrieved from http:/www.ade.az.gov/researchpolicy/dropoutinfo/2001-2002DORreport.pdf

Berry, J. (1969). Ecology and socialization as factors in figural assimilation and the resolution of binocular rivalry. *International Journal of Psychology, 4*, 270–280.

Bruner, J. S. (1964). The course of cognitive growth. *American Psychologist, 19*, 1–15.

Bureau of Indian Affairs, Division of School Program Support and Improvement. (2000). *Special education eligibility document, PL 105-17*. Washington, DC: U.S. Department of the Interior.

Carney, R. N., & Levin, J. R. (2002). Pictorial illustrations still improve student's learning from text. *Educational Psychology Review, 4*, 5–26.

Cohen, R. (1981). On the generality of some memory laws. *Scandinavian Journal of Psychology, 22*, 267–281.

Cromer, W. (1970). The difference model: A new explanation for some reading difficulties. *Journal of Educational Psychology, 61*, 471–483.

Dilley, M., & Paivio, A. (1968). Pictures and words as stimulus and response items in paired-associate learning of young children. *Journal of Experimental Child Psychology, 6*, 231–240.

Engelkamp, J., & Zimmer, H. D. (1989). Memory for action events: A new field of research. *Psychological Research, 51,* 153–157.

Gersten, R., & Baker, S. (2003). English-language learners with learning disabilities. In H. L. Swanson, K. R. Harris, & S. Graham (Eds.), *Handbook of learning disabilities* (pp. 94–109). New York: Guilford.

Ghatala, E. S., Levin, J. R., Pressley, M., & Goodwin, D. (1986). A componential analysis of the effects of derived and supplied strategy utility information on children's strategy selections. *Journal of Experimental Child Psychology, 41,* 76–92.

Gibson, J. J. (1979). *The ecological approach to visual perception.* New York: Houghton Mifflin.

Glenberg, A. M. (1997). What memory is for. *Behavioral and Brain Sciences, 20,* 1–55.

Glenberg, A. M., Gutierrez, T., Levin, J. R., Japuntich, S., & Kaschak, M. (2004). Activity and imagined activity can enhance young readers' reading comprehension. *Journal of Educational Psychology, 96,* 424–436.

Glenberg, A. M., & Robertson, D. (1999). Indexical understanding of instructions. *Discourse Processes, 18,* 1–26.

Glenberg, A. M., & Robertson, D. A. (2000). Symbol grounding and meaning: A comparison of high-dimensional and embodied theories of meaning. *Journal of Memory & Language, 43,* 379–401.

Harnad, S. (1990). The symbol grounding problem. *Physica D, 42,* 335–346.

Homzie, M., Noyes, E., & Lovelace, E. (1973). Children's memory for picture versus word responses in paired associates: Recall and recognition tasks. *American Journal of Psychology, 14,* 567–577.

Kamphaus, R. (2000). Learning disabilities. In A. E. Kazdin (Ed.), *Encyclopedia of psychology* (pp. 280–283). Washington, DC, and New York: American Psychological Association and Oxford University Press.

Keogh, B., & MacMillan, D. (1996). Exceptionality. In D. C. Berliner & R. C. Calfee (Eds.), *Handbook of educational psychology* (pp. 311–330). New York: Macmillian.

Kormi-Nouri, R., Nyberg, L., & Nilsson, L. G. (1994). The effect of retrieval enactment on recall of subject-performed tasks and verbal tasks. *Memory & Cognition, 22,* 723–728.

Lesgold, A. M., Levin, J. R., Shimron, J., & Guttmann, J. (1975). Pictures and young children's learning from oral prose. *Journal of Educational Psychology, 67,* 636–642.

Levie, W. H., & Lentz, R. (1982). The effects of text illustration. *Educational Communication and Technology Journal, 30,* 195–232.

Levin, J. R. (1972). Comprehending what we read: An outsider looks in. *Journal of Reading Behavior, 4,* 18–28.

Levin, J. R. (1973). Inducing comprehension in poor readers: A test of a recent model. *Journal of Educational Psychology, 65*(1), 19–24.

Levin, J. R. (1976). What have we learned about maximizing what children learn? In J. R. Levin & V. L. Allen (Eds.), *Cognitive learning in children: Theories and strategies* (pp. 105–134). New York: Academic Press.

Levin, J. R. (1986). Four cognitive principles of learning-strategy instruction. *Educational Psychologist, 21,* 3–17.

Levin, J. R., Anglin, G. J., & Carney, R. N. (1987). On empirically validating functions of picture in prose. In D. M. Willows & H. A. Houghton (Eds.), *The psychology of illustration: I. Basic research* (pp. 51–85). New York: Springer-Verlag.

Levin, J. R., Bender, B. G., & Lesgold, A. M. (1977). Pictures, repetition, and young children's oral prose learning. *AV Communication Review, 24,* 367–380.

Levin, J. R., & Mayer, R. E. (1993). Understanding illustrations in text. In B. K. Britton, A. Woodward, & M. Binkley (Eds.), *Learning from textbooks* (pp. 95–113). Hillsdale, NJ: Lawrence Erlbaum Associates.

Lyon, G. R. (1996). Learning disabilities. *The Future of Children: Special education for students with disabilities* [Special issue], *6,* 54–76.

Mandl, H., & Levin, J. R. (Eds). (1989). *Knowledge acquisition from text and pictures.* Amsterdam: Elsevier.

Marley, S. C., Levin, J. R., & Glenberg, A. M. (2005, April). *Can text-relevant motor activity improve the recall of learning-disabled Native American children?* Paper presented at the annual meeting of the American Educational Research Association, Montreal.

Mather, N., & Goldstein, S. (2002). *Learning disabilities and challenging behaviors: A guide to intervention and classroom management.* Baltimore, MD: Brooks.

Mayer, R. E. (2001). *Multimedia learning.* New York: Cambridge University Press.

Mayer, R. E., & Gallini, J. K. (1990). When is an illustration worth ten thousand words? *Journal of Educational Psychology, 82,* 715–726.

McCullough, C., Walker, J., & Diessner, R. (1985). The use of Wechsler scales in the assessment of Native Americans of the Columbia River Basin. *Psychology in the Schools, 22,* 23–28.

McShane, D. (1980). A review of the scores of American Indian children on the Wechsler intelligence scales. *White Cloud Journal, 1*(4), 3–10.

McShane, D., & Plas, J. (1984). The cognitive functioning of American Indian children: Moving from the WISC to the WISC-R. *School Psychology Review, 13,* 61–73.

More, A. J. (1989). Native Indian learning styles: A review for researchers and teachers. *Journal of American Indian Education, 28*(4), 15–28.

Mousavi, S. Y., Low, R., & Sweller, J. (1995). Reducing cognitive load by mixing auditory and visual presentation modes. *Journal of Educational Psychology, 87,* 319–334.

Naglieri, J. (1984). Concurrent and predictive validity of the Kaufman Assessment Battery for Children with a Navajo Sample. *Journal of School Psychology, 22,* 373–380.

Noice, H., & Noice, T. (2001). Learning dialogue with and without movement. *Memory & Cognition, 29,* 820–827.

Paivio, A. (1971). *Imagery and verbal processes.* New York: Holt.

Pavel, D., & Curtin, T. (1997). *Characteristics of American Indian and Alaskan Native Education: Results from the 1990–91 and 1993–94 schools and staffing surveys.* Washington, DC: NCES.

Peeck, J. (1993). Increasing picture effects in learning from illustrated text. *Learning and Instruction, 3,* 227–238.

Piaget, J. (1962). *Play, dreams, and imitation in childhood.* New York: Norton.

Pressley, M. (1977). Imagery and children's learning: putting the picture in developmental perspective. *Review of Educational Research, 47,* 585–622.

Repp, B. H., & Knoblich, G. (2004). Perceiving action identity: How pianists recognize their own performances. *Psychological Science, 15,* 604–609.

Riding, R. J., & Douglas, G. (1993). The effect of cognitive style and mode of presentation on learning performance. *British Journal of Educational Psychology, 63,* 297–307.

Riding, R. J., & Mathias, D. (1991). Cognitive style and preferred learning mode, reading attainment and cognitive ability in 11-year-old children. *Educational Psychology, 11,* 383–393.

Rohner, R. (1965). Factors Influencing the academic performance of Kwakiutl children in Canada. *Comparative Education Review, 9,* 331–340.

Rubman, C. N., & Waters, H. S. (2000). A, B seeing: The role of constructive processes in children's comprehension monitoring. *Journal of Educational Psychology, 92,* 503–514.

Saltz, E., & Dixon, D. (1982). Let's pretend: The role of motoric imagery in memory for sentences and words. *Journal of Experimental Child Psychology, 34,* 77–92.

Saltz, E., & Donnenwerth-Nolan, S. (1981). Does motoric imagery facilitate memory for sentences? A selective interference test. *Journal of Verbal Learning and Verbal Behavior, 20,* 322–332.

Shubert, J., & Cropley, A. (1972). Verbal regulation of behavior and IQ in Canadian Indian and white children. *Developmental Psychology, 7,* 295–301.

Swisher, K. (1991). *American Indian/Alaskan native learning styles: Research and practice.* Charleston WV: ERIC Clearinghouse on Rural Education and Small Schools (No. ED335175). Retrieved Oct. 1, 2004 from http://www.ericfacility.net/ericdigests/ed335175.html

Tanner-Talverson, P., Bruden, T., & Sabers, D. (1993). WISC–III normative data for Tohono O'Odham Native-American children. *Journal of Psychoeducational Assessment Monograph Series: Advances in Psychoeducational Assessment, Wechsler Intelligence Scale for Children* (3rd ed.), 125–133.

Thompson, V., & Paivio, A. (1994). Memory for pictures and sounds: Independence of auditory and visual codes. *Canadian Journal of Experimental Psychology, 48,* 380–398.

Van Meter, P. (2001). Drawing construction as a strategy for learning from text. *Journal of Educational Psychology, 93,* 129–40.

Varley, W. H., Levin, J. R., Severson, R. A., & Wolff, P. (1974). Training imagery production in young children through motor involvement. *Journal of Educational Psychology, 66,* 262–266.

Whorton, J., & Morgan, R. (1990). Comparison of the test of nonverbal intelligence and the Wechsler Intelligence Scale for Children–Revised in rural Native American and White children. *Perceptual and Motor Skills, 70,* 12–14.

Wiener, M., & Cromer, W. (1967). Reading and reading difficulty: A conceptual analysis. *Harvard Educational Review, 37,* 620–643.

Wolff, P., & Levin, J. R. (1972). The role of overt activity in children's imagery production. *Child Development, 43,* 537–547.

Zhang, D., & Katsiyannis, A. (2002). Minority representation in special education: A persistent challenge. *Remedial and Special Education, 23,* 180–187.

# Cognitive and Behavioral Effects of Children's Exposure to Pesticides: Critical Issues and Research Trends

Patricia Sánchez Lizardi, Richard J. Morris, and Mary Kay O'Rourke

Organophosphate (OP) pesticides are one group of insecticides commonly used for agricultural purposes. They are also used inside the homes and in yards in smaller quantities to control pests and are currently the most commonly used household insecticides (Kamrin, 1997). These pesticides are also regularly used in others settings such as hospitals and schools with the purpose of controlling for pests (U.S. General Accounting Office [GAO], 1999). They are known to be highly toxic, but their presence in the environment is shorter than that of other types of pesticides (e.g., DDT; Wigle, 2003). Acute poisonings associated with pesticides can occur in spite of extensive control measures. They occur because of misuse, failure of control measures, and/or accidental spills and exposure. These types of incidents are more common than expected. For example, O'Malley (1997) reported that the latest estimates from the World Health Organization (WHO, 1986) indicate that 1 million serious accidental poisonings and 2 million suicide attempts involving pesticides occur each year worldwide. In the United States, it is estimated that there are approximately 10,000 cases per year of poisonings by organophosphate (OP) pesticides (Steenland et al., 1994). In 1990, OP pesticides accounted for 33% of all pesticide poisoning reports in the United States. Diazinon and chlorpyrifos led the list, accounting for more than 50% of the reports (Kamrin, 1997).

Most of the agricultural fields growing the vegetables and fruits that people consume in the United States use OP pesticides to control pests. Therefore, most of the produce people place on their tables every day can potentially have, and some do have, a residue of these chemicals (Food and Drug Administration [FDA], 2004). In spite of this, only limited knowledge exists about the effects of exposure to OP pesticides on human health. Most research has focused on the carcinogenic effects of these chemicals on humans (U.S. Environmental Protection Agency [EPA], 1998), particularly on adults exposed to pesticides in occupational settings.

A vast array of pesticides exists, and they affect human health in various ways. For example, pesticides have been associated with the development of cancer, respiratory diseases, and liver and renal injuries. In addition, the U.S. Environmental Protection Agency (1998) reported that children develop leukemia three to nine times more often when pesticides are used around their respective homes, and that brain tumors and other cancers in children have been linked to insecticides exposure. Moreover, the U.S. EPA reported that as much as 75% of all household pesticide use occurs inside the home and 22% occurs in yards and gardens surrounding the home. Although many household pesticides could have various health effects, OP pesticides are the specific type of pesticides that most commonly cause systemic illnesses (O'Malley, 1997).

Although this research is certainly important and deserves the scientific community's attention, it tends to be overlooked given that most people nowadays are not farm workers or pesticide applicators. At this time, several questions remain unanswered: What is the effect of OP pesticide nonoccupational exposure in human health? What is a "safe" exposure? Are people safe eating the produce of fields treated with these chemicals? What are the long-term effects of OP pesticide exposure? Most importantly, what happens when developing children are exposed to these toxics? What happens to the developing child if the pregnant mother is exposed to pesticides? What are the health effects of OP pesticide exposure on children of farm workers, who are exposed to OP pesticides through their parents' occupation? Much research is needed to begin answering these questions, and each one of these deserves close attention. In a humble attempt to make a contribution to this area, this chapter reviews the literature available regarding the effects of OP pesticide exposure on the cognitive and behavioral functioning of children.

Research with adults who have been acutely exposed to OP pesticides has shown that some of the sequelae are seen in such areas as memory, comprehension, coordination, increased anxiety, abstraction in and flexibility of thinking, verbal attention, visual attention, visual-motor speed, sequencing and problem solving, and motor steadiness. Contrary to these results, some findings have indicated that OP pesticide exposure actually enhances performance in some neurological measures. Research on the cognitive and behavioral functioning of exposed children has been scarce.

Typically, information is inferred from the adult literature. Because of the prevalence of OP pesticides and the seriousness of the type of systemic illness that such pesticides can produce, it seems logical to examine what might be the cognitive and behavioral effects of exposure to or poisoning by OP pesticides. With this in mind, this chapter focuses on research conducted in the area of OP pesticides exposure, particularly with respect to its effects on cognitive and behavioral functioning. Although the target population for this chapter is children, it is important to note that most research has involved adult farm workers who are occupationally exposed to pesticides and animals in experimental studies (O'Brien, 1990). It is only in recent years that the effects of OP pesticides on children's health have begun to be documented (Eskenazi, Bradman, & Castorina, 1999; Leiss & Savitz, 1995; McConnell et al., 1999; Sánchez Lizardi, 2003; Weiss, 1997).

In this chapter, the authors review the fairly limited literature concerning exposure to OP pesticides and its effects on cognitive and behavioral functioning. A rationale for further studies in this area is developed. To date there has been only one study evaluating the effects of OP pesticide exposure on children's growth and development, and its findings suggest that OP pesticides do have an adverse effect on children's development. To conclude, a discussion of research and methodological issues is presented, which is followed by recommendations for future areas of investigation.

## OVERVIEW OF THE EFFECTS OF OP PESTICIDES

OP pesticides are one type of insecticides commonly used for agricultural purposes. They are also used inside homes and yards in smaller quantities to control pests and are currently the most commonly used household insecticides (Kamrin, 1997). The restricted use of organochlorine pesticides (e g., DDT) has resulted in an increased use of OP pesticides in the United States (Ecobichon, 2000). Although OP pesticides have been found to remain in the environment for less time than the organochlorine pesticides, they have also been found to acutely poison the people who use them or who come into contact with them (Human Toxic Chemical Exposure, 1998).

The major symptoms or signs of poisoning by OP pesticides appear within 12 h of exposure. They include dizziness, anxiety, restlessness, muscle twitching, weakness, tremor, incoordination, hypersecretion, miosis, and pulmonary edema. Toxic psychosis can also occur (Morgan, 1989). Repeated exposure to OP pesticides can also cause anorexia, weakness, and malaise. Depression of respiration and pulmonary edema are the usual causes of death from OP pesticides poisoning (O'Malley, 1997).

Once the OP pesticides enter the body, they are metabolized (processed by the body) and almost entirely excreted within 24 h of absorption as OP pesticide metabolites, with a half-life of 2 to 10 h in a urine sample (Krieger, 1999). Walker and Nidiry (2002) reported that the OP pesticide metabolites can often be detected in urine up to 48 h after exposure. These OP pesticide metabolites are known as dialkylphosphates and are urinary metabolites. These metabolites are dimethylphosphate (DMP), dimethylphosphorothioate (DMTP), dimethylphosphorodithioate (DMDTP), diethylphosphate (DEP), diethylphosphorothioate (DETP), and diethylphosphorodithioate (DEDTP). The detection of these metabolites in urine has been used as an indication of exposure. This, however, can be only related to events or exposures that took place within the previous 24 to 48 h of the urine sample collection.

OP pesticides poison the nervous system by inhibiting the acetylcholinesterase enzyme (AchE) at the nerve endings. The enzyme is critical for the normal control of nerve impulse transmission from nerve fibers to muscle and gland cells and also to other nerve cells in the autonomic ganglia and in the brain. A fair amount of the tissue enzyme mass must be inactivated before symptoms and signs of poisoning are manifested. When there is a sufficient dosage, the loss of AchE enzyme function allows accumulation of the acetylcholine neurotransmitter at neuroeffector junctions (muscarinic effects), at skeletal nerve–muscle junctions and autonomic ganglia (nicotinic effects), and in the brain (Morgan, 1989; O'Malley, 1997; Steenland et al., 1994).

High acetylcholine concentrations cause muscle contraction and secretion at the cholinergic nerve junctions with smooth muscle and gland cells. At the skeletal muscle junctions, a high level of acetylcholine may be excitatory, which causes muscle twitching, but may also weaken or paralyze the cell by depolarizing the endplate. In the brain, excess of acetylcholine causes sensory and behavioral disturbances, incoordination, and motor function. Recovery depends ultimately on generation of new AchE enzyme in all critical tissues. Within 1 to 2 days of initial AchE inhibition, some reactivation can occur by the administration of the antidote pralidoxime (Morgan, 1989; Steenland et al., 1994).

Some OP pesticides have also been associated with a different type of neurotoxicity consisting of damage to the axons of peripheral and central nerves associated with inhibition of "neurotoxic esterase." Main symptoms are weakness or paralysis and paresthesia of extremities, predominantly the legs, persistent for weeks to years. Many of these occurrences have taken place 8 to 21 days following an acute poisoning episode of the acetylcholinesterase type; however, some of these symptoms have also been reported by researchers in which no prior exposure was evident. Only a few of the OP pesticides used have been implicated as causes of delayed neuropathy in humans (Morgan, 1989).

Although the acute effects of OP pesticides poisoning are well known and established in the literature, the chronic effects of exposure have not been well researched, and the available data are mainly from studies carried out with adult populations (Ames, Steenland, Jenkins, Chrislip, & Russo, 1995; Rosenstock, Daniell, Barnhart, Schwartz, & Demers, 1990). For example, Whyatt (1989) noted that there were few studies conducted to determine the effects on neurological development of low-level exposure to OP pesticides during infancy. "In fact, federal regulations currently do not require that *any* pesticide be evaluated for the effects of low-level of exposure on behavior, including such processes as learning ability, activity level and memory, or on emotion, sight, and hearing" (Whyatt, 1989, p. 9). Consistent with Whyatt's comments, there are few studies concerning chronic toxicity in children (National Research Council, 1993), with no studies published yet on the neurotoxic effects of low levels of children's exposure to OP pesticides (Aprea, Strambi, Novelli, Lunghini, & Bozzi, 2000), and there is only one study that has assessed the developmental differences in children exposed to OP pesticides (Guillette, Meza, Aquilar, Soto, & Garcia, 1998).

## IMPACT OF OP PESTICIDES ON COGNITIVE AND BEHAVIORAL FUNCTIONING

Because the current knowledge about the effects OP pesticide exposure on the cognitive and behavioral functioning has been mainly based on studies dealing with adult populations, this section first examines and discusses the research findings in regard to this group. The limited research available with children is then presented.

The increased use of OP pesticides in the last four decades has been accompanied by a considerable amount of poisonings in adults (Morgan, 1989). The symptoms for acute poisoning have been documented in the literature (e.g., Rosenstock et al., 1990), and relate to the neuropsychological sequelae of OP pesticide poisoning. The neuropsychological sequelae are explained in terms of memory deficits and comprehension, mood changes, and increased anxiety. Most of this research has investigated the effects of poisoning by (or exposure to) OP pesticides of those people whose work involves the handling of pesticides, such as pest control applicators or farm workers. For example, Maizlish, Schenker, Weisskopf, Seiber, and Samuels (1987) conducted a study to evaluate the neurobehavioral effects of short-term, low-level exposure to diazinon among pest control workers. They had two groups of adult participants, the diazinon applicators and the nonapplicators. All of them completed seven computerized behavioral tests, among other types of measures such as medical history, neurological screenings, and urine analysis for OP metabolites. Participants were tested twice in one day, first in the morning before they started their working shift and then after their shift, when they had finished using diazinon. The researchers reported that the only significant differences between exposed and nonexposed groups were shown, after the working shift, in Symbol-Digit speed and Pattern Memory accuracy, where the exposed group had a poorer performance. Although this study represents an attempt at evaluating short-term and low-level exposure to OP pesticides, the use of the same measures twice during the same day is questionable because performance might have been affected by practice effects, fatigue, or other factors that may not be directly related to the use of diazinon.

Another study was conducted by Savage et al. (1988) to evaluate the neuropsychological effects of OP pesticide poisoning in individuals who had been poisoned versus those who had not. The researchers tested 100 adults in each of the "poisoned" and "control" groups using various dependent measures. They also conducted physical examinations, neurological evaluations, electroencephalograph (EEG) examinations, and neuropsychological testing. Differences were found in the neurological examination, where the "poisoned" group performed significantly worse on measures of memory, abstraction, and mood. In addition, significant differences were found in the neuropsychological testing. The differences occurred on tests of varying abilities such as intellectual functioning (WAIS Full Scale IQ), academic skills, astraction and flexibility of thinking, speed (digit symbol, tapping) and coordination, and dexterity. Poisoned subjects performed worse on these measures than did their nonpoisoned counterparts. In a similar study, Rosenstock, Keifer, Daniell, McConnell, and Claypoole (1991) studied the chronic neuropsychological dysfunctions that acute intoxication with OP pesticides produce. They had two groups, with 36 adult participants in each group. The "exposed" group was tested 2 years after the acute poisoning had occurred and was compared with the "matched control" group. The exposed group performed significantly worse than did the control group on most of the neuropsychological tests that assessed verbal and visual attention (sustained attention), visual memory, visuomotor speed (digit symbol), sequencing and problem solving, and motor steadiness (pursuit aiming) and dexterity. These findings were consistent with those of Savage et al. (1988).

Steenland et al. (1994) also conducted a study to determine if there were chronic neurological effects as a result of acute OP pesticide poisoning among males. They studied 128 poisoned and 90 nonpoisoned male participants, and tested them with various measures including nerve conduction tests, vibrotactile sensitivity tests, a test of postural sway, neurological and physical examinations, and neurobehavioral tests. For the neurobehavioral tests, the researchers used a computerized program that assessed mood, motor speed, sustained visual attention, visuomotor accuracy, visuomotor speed, symbol digit, pattern memory, and serial digit learning. In addition, they used two noncomputerized tests of psychomotor function. Steenland et al. found that the performance of poisoned males was significantly worse than that of the nonpoisoned males on the test of sustained visual attention (continuous performance) and on the tension and confusion measures in the mood scales. No other significant differences were found. When the researchers differentiated between subjects who had a documented cholinesterase inhibition and those who had been hospitalized as a consequence of OP pesticides poisoning, they found that the group that had cholinesterase inhibition performed worse in the measure of vibrotactile sensitivity for finger and toe. In addition, they found that the group of hospitalized subjects performed worse in the sustained attention and symbol digit tests. These results are consistent with the findings of Savage et al. (1988) in the areas of tapping and symbol digit, and with Rosenstock et al. (1991) in the areas of sustained attention and symbol digit. Consistent with the findings of Savage et al. (1988), the neurological examination did not show overall significant differences between the poisoned and nonpoisoned groups; however, when the type of pesticides to which subjects were exposed was considered in the analysis, significant differences were observed in nerve conduction velocity.

In another study, Ames et al. (1995) examined the effects of OP pesticides poisoning in agricultural workers and included a measure of cholinesterase to determine the inhibition of the acetylcholinesterase enzyme (AchE) in all the participants. They hypothesized that chronic neurological sequelae are associated with cholinesterase depression that is just below the level of OP pesticide poisoning. The researchers used a series of neurological and neuropsychological tests to compare the performance of 45 adult males who had a history of moderate cholinesterase inhibition with that of 90 adult males who did not have a history of cholinesterase inhibition or of current pesticide exposure. The results showed that the serial digit measure was the only test that significantly differentiated the two groups. This significant difference, however, was in the opposite direction than hypothesized by the researchers, indicating that having prior cholinesterase inhibition was associated with enhanced neurologic performance. The findings therefore suggested that there was not a significant relationship between cholinesterase inhibition history due to OP pesticides poisoning and long-term detrimental neuropsychological sequelae. This finding contradicts previous studies, which reported significant differences between poisoned and control groups in neuropsychological measures, with exposed (or poisoned) participants performing worse in the measures used.

In a similar study, Stephens et al. (1995) evaluated the neuropsychological effects of long-term exposure to OP pesticides in sheep farmers. They formed two groups, 146 farmers who had been exposed to OP pesticides in the course of sheep dipping (submerging sheep) and 143 nonexposed farmers. Similar to other studies, they used a variety of neuropsychological measures to evaluate the effects of OP pesticides. The results showed that the performance of participants in the exposed farmers group was significantly slower than the performance of the control group participants on three tests: simple reaction time, symbol-digit substitution, and syntactic reasoning. The researchers also found that the chance of exposed farmers being regarded as vulnerable to psychiatric disorders was 50% greater than that of controls and that farmers with the greatest exposure to OP pesticides showed the most pronounced effects on the syntactic reasoning test. Although the results of this study are also consistent with many earlier research findings, these findings should be interpreted with caution since the participants' level and duration of exposure were not established.

## Children and Adolescent Studies

Historically, various chemical substances have had serious consequences for children's health and development. For example, in the 1950s, the drug thalidomide was commonly used to treat morning sickness in pregnant women and was used as a sedative. It was found to have caused an epidemic of 15,000 babies born worldwide with missing limbs (Lenz, 1988). Later, it was also discovered that thalidomide caused other developmental disabilities, including mental retardation and autism (Miller & Strömland, 1993; Rodier, Ingram, Tisdale, & Croog, 1997). Currently, there is an understanding that chemicals in the environment have the potential to cause a wide range of developmental disabilities in children and that anatomic malformations are only the most obvious types of these disabilities (Stein, Schettler, Wallinga, & Valenti, 2002; Weiss & Landrigan, 2000). For instance, elevated blood lead levels and lead poisoning have been found to adversely affect the cognitive development of nearly 1 million children in the United States (Centers for Disease Control and Prevention, 1997), and prenatal exposure even at low levels has been found to result in lifelong reductions of intellectual functioning and in learning and behavior disorders (Needleman & Gatsonis, 1990; Needleman, Riess, Tobin, Biesecker, & Greenhouse, 1996; Needleman, Schell, Bellinger, Leviton, & Allred, 1990; Wasserman, Staghezza-Jaramillo, Shrout, Popovac, & Graziano, 1998). Other chemicals known for their harmful effects to the environment and human and animal health are the polychlorinated biphenyls (PCBs), which are widely distributed in the environment. PCBs can cross the placenta to cause in utero injury to the developing brain (Jacobson & Jacobson, 1996; Patandin et al., 1999). Recently, OP pesticides have also been documented to induce prenatal brain injury in rodents and to cause functional deficits in animals (Eskenazi et al., 1999; Weiss, 1997).

As noted, many of these chemicals have been documented to have adverse effects on the environment and on human health. However, the question about the effect of OP pesticides on children's cognitive and behavior functioning remains unanswered. Stein et al. (2002) indicated that despite the current state of knowledge regarding pesticides, only 12 of approximately 80,000 commercially used pesticides have been tested for their effects in brain development in accordance to U.S. EPA standards. These researchers added that, in fact, of the 3000 chemicals currently produced in large volume (over 1 million lb/yr), public records show very little or no toxicological data regarding the effects of these chemicals on the developing nervous system. They finalize by stating that there are no current requirements for the testing of chemicals for their possible effects on brain development.

Regarding children's neurodevelopment and chemicals in the environment (e.g., lead, PCBs, organic mercury compounds, and certain pesticides), Weiss and Landrigan (2000) suggested that it is possible that some neurodevelopmental disabilities might be related to these chemicals, given that fewer than 25% of neurodevelopmental disabilities that affect children have a known cause.

The effects of OP pesticides on children's neurodevelopment, growth, and symptoms of respiratory illnesses were only recently explored (Eskenazi et al., 1999). Data exclusively about children's cognitive and behavioral functioning are not yet available. Some studies focusing on the effects of children's behavior as a potential factor for exposure have been published. For example, videotaping children's activities has been useful to quantify hand-to-mouth behavior of young children and to use this information in exposure modeling to determine if this is an important pathway of young children's exposure (Reed, Jimenez, Freeman, & Lioy, 1999; Zartarian, Ferguson, & Leckie, 1997). However, the assessment of cognitive and behavioral functions of these children has yet to be explored.

To date, the only published study investigating the effects of OP pesticides in children's growth and development was conducted by Guillette et al. (1998). These researchers evaluated preschool children in Mexico. They selected children who were exposed to pesticides based on living in proximity to areas where OP pesticides were used. They evaluated a group of 34 children who lived close to the areas where pesticides were used for agriculture (valley) and compared them to a group of 17 children who lived in areas where pesticides where not used on a regular basis (foothills). All children were of Yaqui Indian background (Sonora, Mexico). Researchers developed the Rapid Assessment Tool for Preschool Children (RATPC) to measure growth and development based on the Bayley Developmental Scales, the Battelle Developmental Inventory, and the McCarthy Scales. The evaluation included measures of physical growth, motor coordination (catching a ball, sense of balance), physical endurance (length of jumping time), perception abilities (drawing a person), short-term memory (number repetition), long-term memory (recalling a direction that was given at the beginning of the evaluation at the end of it), and fine eye–hand motor coordination (dropping raisins in a bottle cap). In addition, physical body measurements were obtained for all children. Researchers did not find a significant difference in physical growth pattern, but they did find that children from the valley had significantly lower physical endurance, worse ability to catch a ball, worse fine eye–hand motor coordination, and worse long-term memory. The most striking difference was observed in the drawing of a person, in that children from agricultural areas drew an average of 1.6 body parts, versus 4.4 body parts drawn by children from the nonagricultural areas. Although standardization of the RATPC has not been reported, the results of this study illustrate that children living in areas where pesticides are used perform worse on certain psychodevelopmental tests than their counterparts who live in nontreated areas.

Another study now available was conducted as the doctoral dissertation of this chapter's first author. She investigated the effects of OP pesticides on the cognitive and behavioral functioning of Hispanic children in agricultural areas. The author formed two groups of children of farm workers based on their exposure data obtained by the Children's Pesticide Survey in Arizona (O'Rourke et al., 2000). Both groups, Exposed ($n = 25$) and Non-Exposed ($n = 23$), were assessed with cognitive and behavior measures. Children also provided a urine sample the day of cognitive assessment for analysis of OP pesticides metabolites. Results indicated that the Exposed group did not perform significantly differently from the Non-Exposed group in most of the measures. However, some significant differences were found in the length of time taken to complete one of the cognitive measures (Trail Making Test B [TMTB]). When groups were subdivided by school grade and exposure condition, exposed younger children made a greater number of errors in the TMTB. These results suggested that exposure to OP pesticides might have only an adverse effect on the cognitive functions measured by the TMTB, such as speed of attention, sequencing, mental flexibility, and motor functioning in younger children. Additional significant correlations were found between the OP pesticide metabolite concentration on the day of cognitive assessment and some measures of the Wisconsin Card Sorting Test (Sánchez Lizardi, 2003).

## IMPLICATIONS OF EXPOSURE TO OP PESTICIDES ON CHILDREN'S CLASSROOM FUNCTIONING

Schools across the country are regularly treated with pesticides to control for the presence of roaches, rats, termites, ants, and other pests. In a report by the U.S. General Accounting Office (1999), it was stated that comprehensive nationwide information about the amount of pesticides used in the public schools is not available. Although the Federal Insecticide, Fungicide, and Rodent Act (FIRFA) regulates the used of pesticides and requires that certified applicators of restricted pesticides (the ones that are particularly toxic) maintain records that include the name, amounts, date, and location of application, the records are to be maintained for only 2 years and there is no requirement for these applicators to report their applications to EPA.

The U.S. GAO (1999) reported that according to the U.S. EPA, by 1999 there were eight states that had been identified as collecting information about the use of pesticides, but only two had collected information regarding the use of pesticides in schools. In addition, it was reported that 18 states require that signs be posted in areas where pesticides will be or have been used, and 9 states require that parents be directly notified that pesticides will be used. Consistent with what has been presented in this chapter; the U.S. GAO (1999) also reported that information regarding the effects of pesticide exposure in human health continues to be very limited. The fact that pesticides are so routinely used in the schools despite the limited knowledge about their effects poses a serious concern. In spite of some empirical literature suggesting that human exposure to pesticides is likely to cause neurobehavioral harm as well as respiratory diseases even at low levels of exposure (Eskenazi et al., 1999; Weiss, 1997; Leiss & Savitz, 1995), these pesticides continue to be applied in settings such as schools, where children spend a considerable amount of their time (Wigle, 2003).

Because OP pesticides are designed as neurotoxins to poison the nervous systems of unwanted insects, they can also potentially affect the nervous system of humans. For example, Kurtz (as cited in O'Brien, 1990) conducted a study where rats exposed to malathion (an OP pesticide) exhibited decreased shock avoidance behavior 60 min after a dose of 50 mg/kg was injected. This did not cause significant effects on red blood cell, plasma, or brain cholinesterase activity. Motor activity, however, was depressed at a lower dose level of 25 mg/kg, suggesting that it is necessary to use more than one dependent measure in the assessment of behavioral activity. According to these data, "it appears that malathion may disrupt rat behavior without producing significant inhibition of either blood or brain activity" (O'Brien, 1990, p. 6).

Given this evidence, one may speculate that low-level chronic exposure to OP pesticides may adversely affect children's nervous systems, resulting in lower cognitive functioning (e.g., memory, attention), behavioral problems (e.g., irritability, mood change), and other subtle neurological difficulties. Studies also show that exposure to OP pesticides disrupts the area of the nervous system that regulates the motor functioning of the lungs. This has led some researchers to hypothesize that these pesticides are among the preventable causes of asthma in children (Eskenazi et al., 1999)—an illness that is one of the most common reasons for school absenteeism (Curtis & Fiorello, 1998) and related children's learning problems.

Some researchers have also stated that pesticides can be more harmful to children than to adults because children breathe more air and consume more food and beverage per pound of body weight than do adults (e.g., Hubal, Sheldon, Burke, et al., 2000). Compared to adults, 1-year-old infants consume (per unit bodyweight per day) twice as much tap water, total vegetables, and total citrus fruits, and 10 to 12 times as many pears, apples, and total diary products; children aged 3 to 5 years consume 2 to 3 times as much tap water, total vegetables, and total citrus fruits and 7 to 8 times as many apples and total diary products (Wigle, 2003). Children are also more likely to place toys and their fingers in their mouths than do adults. In addition, because the nervous system undergoes rapid growth and development in the first years of life, children are more likely to have neurological problems based on OP pesticides exposure (Landrigan et al., 1999). For example, during this period, structures are developing and vital connections are being established and a child's developing nervous system is not well equipped to repair any structural damaged caused by environmental toxins. Thus, if chemicals destroy cells in the developing brain, there is a risk that a resulting dysfunction would appear, which would be irreversible (e.g., loss of intelligence; National Research Council, 1993).

## METHODOLOGICAL AND CONCEPTUAL ISSUES IN RESEARCH

Some of the methodological issues related to this type of research refer to the difficulty in obtaining accurate exposure assessment data, with exposure assessment being a necessary endeavor. In most of the research conducted so far, children's exposure is assumed, either because children live very closely to agricultural fields or because they are the children of farm workers. To date, assessment of OP pesticide exposure using urinary biomarkers seems to be the best method available. However, this method has the limitation of only providing information about the exposure occurring 24 to 48 h prior to the collection of the urine sample (Krieger, 1999; O'Rourke et al., 2000). Researchers depend on the use of this kind of biological marker for quantifying children's OP pesticide exposure. Issues regarding accurate characterization of children's exposure to pesticides are currently being addressed by research in the area of children's exposure assessment (e.g., Needham & Sexton, 2000; Hubal, Sheldon, Zufall, Burke, & Thomas, 2000; Fenske et al., 2000).

Another important methodological issue refers to the number of participants available for this type of research. To date, there is only one published study assessing development in children that have been exposed to pesticides, and the sample size is considerably small for making general statements ($n = 54$) (Guillette et al., 1998). This indicates that research in this area is just beginning and that more studies are necessary to build a comprehensive understanding of the effects of pesticide exposure on children's cognitive development and behavior as well as their overall health.

## SUMMARY

According to the literature reviewed, concerns for children's exposure to environmental contaminants have gained more attention in recent years, although it continues to be relatively limited. One of these contaminants is organophosphate (OP) pesticides, which are widely used in agriculture, homes, and schools, among other settings, for the treatment of unwanted plagues.

OP pesticides have the potential of harming children's neurodevelopment because they are specifically designed to kill insects by interfering with the neurotransmitter acetylcholinesterase, which is critical for proper nerve conduction. Research investigating the effects of OP pesticides with acutely exposed adults has indicated deficits in such cognitive areas as memory, attention, comprehension, abstract reasoning, intellectual functioning, academic skills, abstraction and flexibility of thinking, verbal attention, visual attention, visual-motor speed, sequencing and problem solving, and motor steadiness (e.g., Rosenstock et al., 1991; Savage et al., 1988; Steenland et al., 1994). In the behavioral areas, effects have also been reported involving increased anxiety, changes in mood, and attention problems (e. g., Ames et al., 1995; Maizlish et al., 1987; Rosenstock, et al., 1990, 1991; Savage et al., 1988; Steenland et al., 1994; Stephens et al., 1995). Very little research, however, has been conducted with children who have been acutely exposed to OP pesticides or to long-term exposure to low levels of OP pesticides. Results of this early research indicate that a similar type of effect in children has been found. Children who have had a detectable trace of OP metabolites tend to perform more poorly in tests of speed of attention, mental flexibility, visual search, memory, and eye–hand motor coordination. These initial results are encouraging and suggest the need to further investigate the effects of OP pesticides on children's cognitive and behavioral functioning, as well as on their overall health.

## REFERENCES

Ames, R. G., Steenland, K., Jenkins, B., Chrislip, D., & Russo, J. (1995). Chronic neurologic sequelae to cholinesterase inhibition among agricultural pesticide applicators. *Archives of Environmental Health, 50,* 440–444.

Aprea, C., Strambi, M., Novelli, M. T., Lunghini, L., & Bozzi, N. (2000). Biologic monitoring of exposure to organophosphorus pesticides in 195 Italian children. *Environmental Health Perspectives, 108,* 521–525.

Centers for Disease Control and Prevention. (1997). *Screening young children for lead poisoning: Guidance for state and local public health officials.* Atlanta, GA: Author.

Curtis, S. E., & Fiorello, C. A. (1998). Asthma in children. In A. Canter & S. Carroll (Eds.), *Helping children at home and school: Handouts from your school psychologist* (pp. 361–364). Bethesda, MD: NASP.

Ecobichon, D. J. (2000). Our changing perspectives on benefits and risks of pesticides: A historical overview. *NeuroToxicology, 21,* 211–218.

Eskenazi, B., Bradman, A., & Castorina, R. (1999). Exposure of children to organophosphate pesticides and their potential adverse health effects. *Environmental Health Perspectives, 107*(suppl. 3), 409–419.

Fenske, R. A., Lu, C., Simcox, N. J., Loewenherz, C., Touchstone, J., Moate, T. F., Allen, E. H., & Kissel, J. C. (2000). Strategies for assessing children's organophosphorus pesticide exposures in agricultural communities. *Journal of Exposure Analysis and Environmental Epidemiology, 10,* 662–671.

Food and Drug Administration. (2004). *Pesticide program residue monitoring 2002* [Electronic version]. Rockville MD: Author. Retrieved from http://www.fda.gov

Guillette, E. A., Meza, M. M., Aquilar, M. G., Soto, A. D., & Garcia, I. E. (1998). An Anthropological approach to the evaluation of preschool children exposed to pesticides in Mexico. *Environmental Health Perspectives, 106,* 347–353.

Hubal, E. A. C., Sheldon, L. S., Burke, J. M., McCurdy, T. R., Berry, M. R., Rigas, M. L., Zartarian, V. G., & Freeman, N. C. (2000). Children's exposure assessment: A review of factors influencing children's exposure, and the data available to characterize and assess that exposure. *Environmental Health Perspectives, 108,* 475–486.

Hubal, E. A. C., Sheldon, L. S., Zufall, M. J., Burke, J. M., & Thomas, K. W. (2000). The challenge of assessing children's residential exposure to pesticides. *Journal of Exposure Analysis and Environmental Epidemiology, 10,* 638–649.

Human Toxic Chemical Exposure. (1998). *Bulletin of Pacific Toxicology Laboratories, 1*(6), Section B.

Jacobson, J. L., & Jacobson, S. W. (1996). Intellectual impairment in children exposed to polychlorinated biphenyls in utero. *New England Journal of Medicine, 335,* 783–789.

Kamrin, M. A. (Ed.). (1997). *Pesticide profiles: Toxicity, environmental impact, and fate.* Boca Raton, FL: CRC Press.

Krieger, R. I. (1999). Biomonitoring human pesticide exposures. In D. J. Ecobichon (Ed.), *Occupational hazards of pesticide exposure: Sampling, monitoring, measuring* (pp. 187–208). Philadelphia: Taylor & Francis.

Landrigan, P. L., Claudio, L., Markowitz, S. B., Berkowitz, G. S., Brenner, B. L., Romero, H., Wetmur, J. C., Matte, T. D., Gore, A. C., Godbold, J. H., & Wolff, M. S. (1999). Pesticides and inner-city children: Exposures, risks, and prevention. *Environmental Health Perspectives, 107*(suppl. 3), 431–497.

Lenz, W. A. (1988). A short history of the thalidomide embryopathy. *Teratology, 38,* 203–215.

Leiss, J. K., & Savitz, D. A. (1995). Home pesticide use and childhood cancer: A case-control study. *American Journal of Public Health, 85,* 249–252.

Maizlish, N., Schenker, M., Weisskopf, C., Seiber, J., & Samuels, S. (1987). A behavioral evaluation of pest control workers with short-term, low-level exposure to the organophosphate diazinon. *American Journal of Industrial Medicine, 12,* 153–172.

McConnell, R., Pacheco, F., Wahlberg, K., Klein, O., Malespin, O., Magnotti, R., Akerblom, M., & Murray, D. (1999). Subclinical health effects of environmental pesticide contamination in a developing country: Cholinesterase depression in children. *Environmental Research, 81,* 87–91.

Miller, M. T., & Strömland, K. (1993). Thalidomide embryopathy: an insight into autism? *Teratology, 47,* 387–388.

Morgan, D. P. (1989). *Recognition and management of pesticide poisonings.* Washington, DC: U.S. Environmental Protection Agency.

National Research Council. (1993). *Pesticides in the diets of infants and children.* Washington, DC: National Academy Press.

Needham, L. L., & Sexton, K. (2000). Assessing children's exposure to hazardous environmental chemicals: An overview of selected research challenges and complexities. *Journal of Exposure Analysis and Environmental Epidemiology, 10,* 611–629.

Needleman, H. L., & Gatsonis, C. A. (1990). Low-level lead exposure and the IQ of children. *Journal of the American Medical Association, 263,* 673–678.

Needleman, H. L., Riess, J. A., Tobin, M. J., Biesecker, G. E., & Greenhouse, J. B. (1996). Bone lead levels and delinquent behavior. *Journal of the American Medical Association, 275,* 363–369.

Needleman, H. L., Schell, A., Bellinger, D., Leviton, A., & Allred, E. N. (1990). The long-term effects of exposure to low doses of lead in childhood: An 11-year follow-up report. *New England Journal of Medicine, 322,* 83–88.

O'Brien, M. (1990). Are pesticides taking away the ability of our children? *Journal of Pesticide Reform, 10,* 4–8.

O'Malley, M. (1997). Clinical evaluation of pesticide exposure and poisonings. *Lancet, 349,* 1161–1166.

O'Rourke, M. K., Sánchez Lizardi, P., Rogan, S. P., Freeman, N. C., Aguirre, A., & Saint, C. G. (2000). Pesticide exposure and creatinine variation among young children. *Journal of Exposure Analysis and Environmental Epidemiology, 10,* 672–681.

Patandin, S., Lanting, C. I., Mulder, P. G., Boersam, E. R., Sauer, P. J., & Weisglas-Kuperus, N. (1999). Effects of environmental exposure to polychlorinated biphenyls and dioxins on cognitive abilities in Dutch children at 42 months of age. *Journal of Pediatrics, 134,* 33–41.

Reed, J. K., Jimenez, M., Freeman, N. C. G., & Lioy, P. J. (1999). Quantification of children's hand and mouthing activities through a videotaping methodology. *Journal of Exposure Analysis and Environmental Epidemiology, 9,* 513–520.

Rodier, P. M., Ingram, J. L., Tisdale, B., & Croog, V. J. (1997). Linking ethiologies in humans and animal models: Studies of autism. *Reproductive Toxicology, 11,* 417–422.

Rosenstock, L., Daniell, W., Barnhart, S., Schwartz, D., & Demers, P. (1990). Chronic neurological sequelae of occupational exposure to organophosphate insecticides. *American Journal of Industrial Medicine, 18,* 321–325.

Rosenstock, L., Keifer, M., Daniell, W. E., McConnell, R., & Claypoole, K. (1991). Chronic central nervous system effects of acute organophosphate pesticide intoxication. *Lancet, 338,* 223–227.

Sánchez Lizardi, P. (2003). *Effects of pesticides on the cognitive and behavioral functioning of Hispanic children in agricultural areas.* Unpublished doctoral dissertation, University of Arizona, Tucson.

Savage, E. P., Keefe, T. J., Mounce, L. M., Heaton, R. K., Lewis, J. A., & Burcar, P. J. (1988). Chronic neurological sequelae of acute organophosphate pesticide poisoning. *Archives of Environmental Health, 43,* 38–45.

Steenland, K., Jenkins, B., Ames, R. G., O'Malley, M., Chrislip, D., & Russo, J. (1994). Chronic neurological sequelae to organophosphate pesticide poisoning. *American Journal of Public Health, 84,* 731–736.

Stein, J., Schettler, T., Wallinga, D., & Valenti, M. (2002). In harm's way: Toxic threats to child development. *Journal of Developmental and Behavioral Pediatrics, 23*(1S), S13–S22.

Stephens, R., Spurgeon, A., Calvert, I. A., Beach, J., Levy, L. S., Berry, H., & Harrington, J. M. (1995). Neuropsychological effects of long-term exposure to organophosphates in sheep dip. *Lancet, 345,* 1135–1139.

U.S. Environmental Protection Agency. (1998). *The EPA children's environmental health yearbook.* Washington, DC: Author.

U.S. General Accounting Office. (1999). *Pesticides: Use, effects and alternatives to pesticides in schools.* Washington, DC: Author.

Walker, B., Jr., & Nidiry, J. (2002). Current concepts: Organophosphate toxicity. *Inhalation Toxicology, 14,* 975–990.

Wasserman, G. A., Staghezza-Jaramillo, B., Shrout, P., Popovac, D., & Graziano, J. (1998). The effect of lead exposure on behavior problems in preschool children. *American Journal of Public Health, 88,* 481–486.

Weiss, B. (1997). Pesticides as a source of developmental disabilities. *Mental Retardation and Developmental Disabilities, 3,* 246–256.

Weiss, B., & Landrigan, P. L. (2000). The developing brain and the environment: An introduction. *Environmental Health Perspectives, 108*(suppl. 3), 373–374.

Whyatt, R. (1989). Intolerable risk: The physiological susceptibility of children to pesticides. *Journal of Pesticide Reform, 9,* 5–9.

Wigle, D. T. (2003). *Child health and the environment.* New York: Oxford University Press.

World Health Organization. (1986). Environmental health criteria 63. In *Organophosphorus insecticides: A general introduction.* Geneva: Author.

Zartarian, V. G., Ferguson, A. C., & Leckie, J. O. (1997). Quantified dermal activity data from a four-child pilot field study. *Journal of Exposure Analysis and Environmental Epidemiology, 7,* 543–552.

# 8

# Disability and Juvenile Delinquency

Kimberly A. Morris, Gretchen Schoenfield, Priscilla Bade-White, Deepti Joshi, and Richard J. Morris

The juvenile justice system was established in 1899 in the state of Illinois. The role and function of this system have been discussed extensively in the literature (e.g., Sheperd, 1999). However, there is a paucity of research examining the relationship between juvenile delinquency and the presence of learning disabilities, emotional and behavior disorders, and/or mental retardation in these youths. This chapter reviews the literature on juveniles with disabilities, beginning with a brief overview of the history of the juvenile justice system, followed by a discussion of definitional issues regarding disability and the law, prevalence and incidence rates of disabilities among juvenile delinquents, types of services provided to these youths, and issues unique to female juvenile offenders. In addition, preliminary results from a large scale research project on disability and juvenile delinquency is presented.

## HISTORY

The juvenile justice system was first established for the purpose of rehabilitating juvenile offenders. This approach was assumed to protect youth and the community at large. Delinquent youth, once rehabilitated, were then reintroduced into society when they were no longer deemed a threat (Rothman, 1980). Judges within the juvenile system had considerable discretion and were encouraged to "act in the best interests of the child" (Marcotte, 1990, p. 61). In fact, during the first 60 years of this justice system, defense counsel, trial by jury, and rules of evidence were deemed unnecessary. This approach shifted, however, in the late 1960s and soon became one of punishment and retribution, with the general public believing that the leniency placed on youths within the juvenile justice system led to the victimization of the public (Moon, Sundt, Cullen, &

Wright, 2000). Studies conducted after the 1970s revealed a continuing upsurge in juvenile crime, in addition to an increase in recidivism. Research findings also suggested that there was an increase in juvenile violent crime arrests between the 1980s and the mid-1990s. Specifically, a 26% increase was discovered in the number of juvenile cases processed within the justice system (Sickmund, 2000), with approximately 1,471,000 cases being processed in 1992 and increasing to 1.8 million cases in 1997 (Sickmund, 2000).

This shift in emphasis of the juvenile courts during the 1960s and 1970s led to several court cases resulting in the implementation of due process protections for juveniles. For example, a 1966 Supreme Court Case (*Kent v. United States*) limited juvenile court judges' discretion with respect to transferring juvenile cases to adult court. The 1967 case of *In re Gault* guaranteed juveniles the right to counsel, notice of charges, privilege against self-incrimination, and a right to cross-examine witnesses (Marcotte, 1990). However, in 1971 the Supreme Court held in *McKeiver v. Pennsylvania* that the constitutional right to a jury does not extend to state juvenile delinquency proceedings. Despite the granted rights in *In re Gault* (1967), a study conducted by Feld (1988) revealed that many juveniles do not receive representation by counsel. Feld's research suggested that approximately 50% of juveniles who faced court proceedings in Minnesota, North Dakota, and Nebraska were not represented by counsel.

Today, there is much discussion regarding the juvenile court's role in society, with the focus of such discussions varying from the role and function of the court to the types of support services that should or should not be provided juveniles and to the nature of the connection between the juvenile court system and the adult criminal system. According to Woolard, Fondacaro, and Slobogin (2001), there are three reasons the juvenile justice system must remain a separate institution from the adult criminal system: (a) Children are more treatable than adults, (b) children are less culpable, and (c) children are less easily deterred. Although Woolard et al. (2001) acknowledged the lack of evidence supporting these assumptions, they also asserted that sending a youth to adult prison is not productive, nor does it protect society in any way. The assumption on which the adult criminal justice system is based is that if an individual is incarcerated for a period of time, he or she will be less likely to commit crimes in the future. Moreover, within the adult system support services are rarely available; therefore, if children are more treatable, they may be better served in the juvenile system, where more programs are in place for rehabilitation (Woolard et al., 2001). With respect to the contribution of a youth's disability in the decision making of judges and/or other juvenile court personnel, very little literature exists. However, the research literature does suggest that a large proportion of juvenile delinquents may be classified as having a disability and in need of educational and/or mental health services (McGarvey & Waite, 2000; Morgan, 1979; Podboy & Mallory, 1979; Rutherford, Nelson, & Wolford, 1985).

## DEFINITIONAL ISSUES

There are several issues to consider when examining the concept of "disability" within the juvenile justice system. The first issue is related to an individual's right to receive educational services in accordance with federal and state laws. For example, states must provide a person with a free education until he or she reaches 18 years-of-age, although in many states juveniles have the right to refuse educational services at 16 years-of-age. (Council of Chief State School Officers, 2000). In this regard, juveniles diagnosed or determined to have a "disability" and who require special education services are entitled to a free and appropriate education in the least restrictive environment until the age of 22 (Individuals with Disabilities Education Act [IDEA, 1990, 1997, 2004], Burrell & Warboys, 2000). Related to this issue is what constitutes a "disability" in juveniles. Youth in the general school population who have been diagnosed or otherwise determined to have a disability are typically defined as such according to the criteria established under the Individuals with Disabilities Education Act (IDEA, 1990, 1997, 2004). In 1975, Public Law 94-142 (Education for All Handicapped Children Act [EHCA], 1975) mandated comprehensive educational services for all children with disabilities. The EHCA was amended in 1990 and became IDEA. IDEA was amended again in 1997, and required that children with disabilities have access to educational services that were critical to promoting their cognitive, social, emotional, and physical development and communication skills. IDEA decreed that each state develop "its own set of rules and procedures that provide at least as much protection as the federal laws and regulations governing special education" (Block, 2000).

IDEA (1997, 2004) defines disability within 13 categories. These categories are autism, deaf–blindness, blindness, hearing impairment, mental retardation, multiple disabilities, orthopedic impairment, serious emotional disturbance (SED), specific learning disability, speech or language impairment, traumatic brain injury, visual impairment, and other health impairment. The potential exists for some interpretation within certain categories. For example, "other health impairment" is a broad category that may include disabilities that do not fall into the other 12 categories. An individual having SED could also be diagnosed as having a behavioral-emotional disability, as being severely emotionally disturbed, or haing a behavior disorder (National Council on Disability, 2003).

A difficulty with IDEA's definition of disability concerns the possibility that state juvenile justice jurisdictions may not utilize the categories in a consistent manner (Dahle, 2003). For example, Warboys and Schauffer (1986) indicated that the definition of "orthopedic impairment," under P.L. 94-142, is "a severe orthopedic impairment which adversely affects the child's educational performance" and includes "impairments caused by congenital anomaly ... impairments caused by disease ... and impairments from other causes." However, Warboys and Schauffer (1986) noted that an Oregon state statute permitted the inclusion of impairments not detailed in the federal regulations, including "a disability which has been diagnosed by a physician licensed by the Board of Medical Examiners for the State of Oregon as permanent or which is expected to extend over a 2-month period" (p. 36). Rutherford, Bullis, Anderson, and Griller-Clark (2002) also addressed the issue of varying definitions across states. They reported that the possibility exists for an individual to have different diagnoses in different states, or to meet special education placement criteria in one state but not in another state. These issues regarding disability definitions led the National Council on Disability (2003) to acknowledge the difficulty in comparing and summarizing research within and across disability categories and/or handicapping conditions.

Section 504 of the 1973 Rehabilitation Act is a non-discrimination statute that protects individuals with disability status. Section 504 requires that reasonable accommodations be in place to allow individuals with disabilities to access public facilities or programs that receive federal assistance (*Rehabilitation Act*, 1973). Section 504 protects individuals who have a physical or mental impairment which substantially limits one or more major life activities (e.g., caring for oneself, performing manual tasks, walking, seeing, hearing, breathing, learning, working, and attending school). Impairment is defined in Section 504 as "(A) any physiological disorder or condition, cosmetic disfigurement, or anatomical loss affecting one or more of the following body systems: neurological; musculoskeletal; special sense organs; respiratory, including speech organs; cardiovascular; reproductive, digestive, genito-urinary; hemic and lymphatic; skin; and endocrine; or (B) any mental or psychological disorder, such as mental retardation, organic brain syndrome, emotional or mental illness, and specific learning disabilities" (*Rehabilitation Act*, 1973, 104.3[2]). Students who are not entitled to special education services as defined by IDEA may be eligible for services under the provisions of Section 504.

The *Diagnostic and Statistical Manual of Mental Disorders* (*DSM*; American Psychiatric Association [APA], 1980, 1987, 1994, 2000) utilizes a multiaxial system to diagnose mental illness using criteria that do not change from state to state. The *DSM* defines the term *mental disorder* as "a clinically significant behavioral or psychological syndrome or pattern that occurs in an individual and that is associated with present stress (e.g., a painful symptom) or disability (i.e., impairment in one or more areas of functioning) or with a significantly increased risk of suffering death, pain, disability, or important loss of freedom" (*DSM–IV–TR*, APA; 2000, p. xxxi). The application of this system in a clinical setting generally requires that the person making a *DSM* diagnosis be a licensed mental health provider (e.g., psychiatrist, psychologist, or psychiatric social worker; Dahle, 2003). A *DSM* psychiatric diagnosis, unlike IDEA and 504 classifications, does not require behaviors to interfere with educational performance. Therefore, an individual with a psychiatric diagnosis such as attention deficit hyperactivity disorder (ADHD) is not automatically eligible to receive special education services under IDEA. However, he or she may be eligible for such services under Section 504 if it can be demonstrated that the child's disorder interferes with his or her ability to learn (Dahle, 2003).

## PREVALENCE AND INCIDENCE DATA

The prevalence and incidence rates of juveniles having disabilities within the juvenile justice system vary considerably in the research literature. This variability may be attributed to screening and assessment differences between public school districts and the juvenile justice system, issues related to a juvenile's school not providing the student's complete educational records (including psychological evaluations) to the courts and/or correctional facility, and differing definitions and measures of "disability" (Rutherford et al., 2002). In addition, it is difficult to compare various studies because the prevalence and incidence rates reported may not take into account whether the participants in the study were incarcerated, were a combined group of incarcerated and not incarcerated juveniles, or were adjudicated and not adjudicated juveniles.

Nonetheless, researchers suggest that 30% to 60% of juveniles within the juvenile justice system have a "disability" (Morgan, 1979; Murphy, 1986; Rutherford et al., 1985). For example, Morgan (1979) studied 204 juvenile offenders in state correctional facilities and discovered that approximately 42% had some type of disability. Another study revealed that more than 40% of juveniles within Virginia's Department of Juvenile Justice met special education criteria (McGarvey & Waite, 2000). Rutherford and his associates (1985) provided a lower estimate, with 28% ($n = 9,443$) of incarcerated juveniles having a disability. Morgan (1979) reported that 100% of the incarcerated juveniles had a disability in three of the states surveyed. Despite the great variability of disability prevalence and incidence rates within the literature, these values are higher than the reported 11.48% of the approximate 5.5 million students who were receiving special education services in the public school systems across the

United States in 2000–2001 under the IDEA classification system (U.S. Department of Education, 2002).

Similarly, Sanger (1999) found that 22% of the juvenile offenders that they tested on the Clinical Evaluation of Language Fundamentals-3 (CELF-3) "performed poorly" and were considered candidates for language and/or communication services. This is in contrast with estimates suggesting that only 5% of children in the general population need language and/or communication services.

## Learning Disability, Emotional Disorder, and Mental Retardation

The prevalence and incidence percentages for three specific disability categories—learning disability, emotional disorder, and mental retardation—have been examined in more detail than other disability categories (Robinson & Rappaport, 1999). For example, a study by Snyder and Sickmund (1995) revealed that 50% of incarcerated juveniles had a specific learning disability. This estimate is much higher than the estimated 5.44% of school-age youth reported to have a specific learning disability during the 1995–1996 school year (U.S. Department of Education, 1997). An earlier study reported similar prevalence rates with nearly half of the juveniles in a detention facility having a learning disability (Podboy & Mallory, 1979). In another study, Morgan (1979) determined that nearly all of the 129 incarcerated juveniles assessed had significant learning problems. However, there are definitional problems with these studies. For example, researchers did not utilize a consistent set of criteria to define "learning disability" such as those under P.L. 94-142 or IDEA. Notwithstanding this definitional issue, it does appear that the percentage of learning disability in the juvenile delinquency population is appreciably higher than the estimated 5.74% prevalence of learning disabilities in the general school-age population for the 2000–2001 school year (U.S. Department of Education, 2002).

Researchers suggest four hypotheses that address the nature of the relationship between learning disabilities and delinquency: (a) the "susceptibility hypothesis," (b) the "differential treatment hypothesis," (c) the "school failure hypothesis," and (d) the "metacognitive hypothesis" (e.g., Brier, 1989; Keilitz & Miller, 1980; Lane, 1980; Larson, 1988; Larson & Turner, 2002; Malmgren, Abbott, & Hawkins, 1999; National Council on Disability, 2003; Waldie & Spreen, 1993). The susceptibility hypothesis suggests that various intellectual and neurological difficulties associated with a learning disability act as factors contributing to a child's antisocial behavior (Brier, 1998; Malmgren et al., 1999). This hypothesis assumes that juvenile delinquents have low social skills, which may lead to antisocial behavior (Lane, 1980; Larson, 1988; Waldie &

Spreen, 1993). The differential treatment hypothesis proposes that those juvenile delinquents having a disability engage in the same frequency and severity of antisocial behaviors as their non-disabled peers; however, the police, social service workers, and other officials treat youth with disabilities differently, which may result in increased rates of delinquency (Keilitz, Zaremba, & Broder, 1979; Larson, 1988; Malmgren et al., 1999). The school failure hypothesis suggests that poor performance coupled with learning disabilities is the first step in a sequence of events that leads to delinquency (Brier, 1989; Larson, 1988). It is hypothesized that this step is followed by peer rejection, negative self-image, and frustration, among other disappointments, that lead to suspensions, dropout, and delinquency (Brier, 1989; Keilitz & Miller, 1980; Lane, 1980; Malmgren et al., 1999; Waldie & Spreen, 1993). The metacognitve hypothesis indicates that as a result of the disability, juveniles lack the necessary interpersonal skills to build relationships with their peers, and in order to gain social status, these juveniles engage in behaviors, some of which are delinquent, to impress their peers (Larson & Turner, 2002). These hypotheses provide insight into the possible nature of the relationship between learning disability and delinquency.

With respect to emotional and/or behavior disorders, Bullock and McArthur (1994) found prevalence values ranging from 0% to 48% for juveniles incarcerated in state correctional facilities across the United States, with the average national prevalence being 10%. These percentages differ from the 60% prevalence value identified by Snyder and Sickmund (1995) in their study of incarcerated juveniles having emotional behavior disorders. Noteworthy is the fact that these percentages are appreciably higher than the 0.94% prevalence value reported for all school-age youth classified under IDEA as having an emotional disturbance during the 2000–2001 school year, or the 0.91% value reported in the 1995–1996 school year (U.S. Department of Education, 1997, 2002).

The prevalence values for mental retardation have also been shown to have much variability. For example, Bullock and McArthur (1994) reported that 2% of juvenile delinquents residing in detention centers were diagnosed as having mental retardation, whereas Snyder and Sickmund (1995) reported 10% of incarcerated juveniles were classified as having mental retardation. Additionally, Casey and Keilitz (1990) found that the overall weighted prevalence for juvenile delinquents having mental retardation was 12.6%. These latter percentage values are appreciably higher than the estimate of approximately 1% of all school-age children meeting the IDEA criteria for mental retardation during the 1995–1996 and 2000–2001 school years (U.S. Department of Education, 1997, 2002).

When comparing the estimated prevalence for learning disability, emotional and behavior disorder, and mental retardation within the juvenile delinquency population with those of nondelinquent school-age youth, the disproportionality becomes apparent. This finding led Rutherford et al. (2001) to conclude that although the existence of learning disabilities, mental retardation, or emotional disturbance does not predispose an individual to delinquency, the relationship between disabilities and delinquency is apparent. Unfortunately, little research has been published on those factors that may be contributing to this disproportional prevalence.

Some research indicates that police officers, attorneys, judges, corrections staff, and probation officers are unaware of the characteristics associated with someone who has a disability, such as mental retardation, learning disability, or emotional disturbance (Keilitz & Dunivant, 1986). This lack of understanding may lead to misinterpretation of a youth's disability. For example, police officers may misinterpret a youth with a mental illness to be inebriated. Research also suggests that youth having mental retardation may be more vulnerable to involvement in the juvenile correctional system as a result of poor reasoning ability, inappropriate affect, and inattentiveness, which, in turn, may be misinterpreted by juvenile justice personnel as being a lack of compliance or even hostility (Quinn, Rutherford, & Leone, 2001). Once within the juvenile correctional system, youth classified as having mental retardation have been reported as having difficulties complying with and responding to the rules and regulations associated with the correctional system (Leone, Meisel, & Drakeford, 2002). In addition, it has been suggested that these youths may not understand their legal rights, may confess to charges that they did not commit, and may have difficulty communicating with lawyers and court officials (Leone, Rutherford, & Nelson, 1991). This, in turn, may lead to an increased likelihood that these individuals will plead guilty and be incarcerated at an earlier age and for a longer duration than their peers without mental retardation (Leone et al., 1991; Santamour & West, 1982, as cited in Murphy, 1986).

## EDUCATIONAL SERVICES

Given that education is central to the socialization of children and adolescents in the United States, the logical question is, "What are the types and quality of educational services provided to incarcerated and nonincarcerated juvenile delinquents?" According to Foley (2001), the types of educational services available to juvenile delinquents range from instruction in elementary and middle school curricula through high school and postsecondary school educational services until the juvenile reaches 18 years of age. However, if a particular youth is diagnosed as having a disability under the provisions of IDEA, he or she is eligible for special education services until she or he graduates from high school or reaches 22 years of age. If the youth does not meet the disability criteria under IDEA but meets the definition of disability under Section 504 of the 1973 Rehabilitation Act, then the individual is entitled to an accommodation in his or her education services in order to minimize the possibility of the disability interfering with his or her ability to learn. The educational services provided to these juveniles have been reported by Foley (2001) as contributing to the successful transition of these youths. This may be due to the juvenile's realization that these educational services are one of the last opportunities to acquire necessary academic and/or vocational skills to successfully function in society, because the literature suggests that many of these youths never return to school once they are released from detention or incarceration (Foley, 2001).

Rutherford et al. (1985) estimated that 23% of all incarcerated juveniles receive special education and related services. However, if the actual percentage of incarcerated youth who have a disability is appreciably higher than 23%, as some research has suggested, then there are many children and adolescents within the juvenile justice system who are not receiving the special education services to which they are entitled. In this regard, a case study of a state's Department of Juvenile Services found that there were undue delays within the system in providing special education and related services to eligible youths, the system lacked a procedure for referral for children who needed to be evaluated for a disability, and there was no effective mechanism and/or protocol for retrieving the school records of those youths placed in the system (Leone, 1994).

The question also arises of whether youths transferred to the adult correctional system receive the special education and related services to which they are entitled, particularly if they have not graduated from high school. For example, in a national survey, Quinn et al. (2001) found that only 29% of juveniles in adult correctional facilities were receiving educational services. Findings such as these led Eggleston (1996) to state that there are many individuals under 22 years of age within adult correctional facilities who are not receiving special education or related services, despite the fact that IDEA entitled them to such services.

## MENTAL HEALTH SERVICES

The social policy literature suggests that many juvenile delinquents may be eligible for mental health services in addition to special education services (e.g., Lyons, Barger, Quigley, Erlich, & Griffin, 2001). In this regard, Timmons-Mitchell et al. (1997) found that 27% of male and 84% of female juvenile delinquents within the state of Ohio were diagnosed as having a mental disorder. However, these percentages may vary across states because Johnson-Reid, Williams, and Webster (2001) found that state and county agencies may use different criteria to determine a youth's eligibility for mental health services.

IDEA and Section 504 of the 1973 Rehabilitation Act mandate the provision of educational and mental health services to eligible youths, though some researchers argue that a chasm exists between such mandates and the actual services states provide (Shum, 2002). Additionally, incarcerated youths may need and be eligible for these services, yet may have limited access to them by virtue of their residential placement within the juvenile justice system. Moreover, cultural, ethnic, gender, and socioeconomic factors, language barriers, and/or juvenile justice history may further limit access to these services (Rogers, Powell, & Strock, 1998). Researchers also suggest that the decision regarding whether these youths receive mental health services may be based solely on risk factors such as preexisting mental health diagnoses, history of aggression and/or violent behavior, or risk of suicide (Leone, 1994; Lyons et al., 2001). In this regard, although Rogers et al. (1998) found that 97% of their sample of detained juvenile offenders ($n = 244$, representing 8% of all detained youths within the facility) met the criteria for a *DSM–IV* diagnosis, they reported that the juvenile detention facility did not conduct a formal psychological or psychiatric evaluation either at intake or during the time period in which the youths were housed in the juvenile detention center.

Some researchers suggest that the lack of community-based and preventive mental health services for youths, particularly within rural and inner-city areas, may result in escalation of behavior disorders to the point of warranting juvenile justice system involvement (e.g., Pumariega et al., 1999). In this regard, Pumariega et al. (1999) indicated that increased provision of outpatient mental health services may prevent at-risk youths from being referred to the juvenile justice system.

## FEMALES WITHIN THE JUVENILE JUSTICE SYSTEM

Although the number of crimes committed by females is increasing (Sanger, Creswell, Schaffar, Engelbert, & Opfer, 2000; Morton, 1998), the juvenile justice system has primarily focused on the male juvenile offender (Calhoun, 2001; Morton, 1998), with relatively little research devoted to those factors contributing to female juvenile delinquency and whether existing diversion and prevention programs are successful for the female population (MacDonald & Chesney-Lind, 2001; Morton, 1998). There has been even less research conducted that focuses on female juvenile delinquents having a disability, despite data suggesting a higher occurrence of disabilities among juvenile offenders than in mainstream youths. According to Morton (1998), individuals interacting with female delinquents within the juvenile justice system have expressed frustration about the lack of information regarding the special needs of this population. Additionally, incarcerated youths with disabilities have greater social, emotional, and learning needs than their peers without disabilities, resulting in an increased demand for transition services within the community (Pollard, Pollard, & Meers, 1994).

According to statistics reported by the U.S. Department of Justice, Office of Juvenile Justice and Delinquency Prevention (OJJDP) (1996), 20% of the delinquency cases handled in 1993 within juvenile courts were those involving females. Moreover, between 1989 and 1993, the number of juvenile court cases involving females increased by 31%, whereas the number of cases involving males increased by only 21%. Nearly one quarter (23%) of the delinquency cases processed in 1997 involved a female offender, compared to 19% in 1988. Further, between 1988 and 1997, the number of delinquency cases involving females increased by 83% (U.S. Department of Justice, OJJDP, 2000) and arrest rates in 1999 for females under the age of 16 increased by 89%, whereas those involving detention of females increased by 57% versus 35% for males. In addition, Morton (1998) reported that females comprised approximately 25% of all juvenile arrests and 6% and 10%, respectively, of those incarcerated within jail versus state or federal facilities.

Morton (1998) also indicated that increases in arrests have been greater for female juveniles than for male juveniles in most offense categories. With regard to the type of offense, in 1996 females were most likely detained for person offenses (e.g., assault, sex offenses, harassment, threatening, robbery) and public order offenses (e.g., disorderly conduct, carrying concealed weapon), and were involved in 41% of status offense (e.g., truancy and runaway cases), although they were only charged in 23% of the formally processed delinquency cases (U.S. Department of Justice, OJJDP, 1996). Females were also responsible for 17% of the growth in juvenile arrests for the Violent Crime Index offenses between 1989 and 1993, which yielded an increase of 23% compared to an 11% increase in male juvenile arrests (U.S. Department of Justice, OJJDP, 1996). Lane (2003) indicated that female arrests were due to prostitution or other commercialized vice offenses. Lane (2003) also reported that the most common offense committed by females is running away, which constituted 59% of arrests in 1999 for this population.

Research has also suggested that males and females charged with similar offenses are treated unequally within the juvenile justice system (MacDonald & Chesney-Lind, 2001). For example, females referred for status offenses are more likely than males to receive a formal court hearing. Research from the U.S.

Department of Justice, OJJDP (1999) also suggests that females are more likely to be detained for status offenses. However, other OJJDP findings have revealed that delinquency cases involving female youths received less severe outcomes than cases involving males at all stages of juvenile court processing. For example, females referred to juvenile court were less likely than males to be formally processed with the filing of a delinquency petition.

With respect to disability, Fejes-Mendoza and Rutherford (1987) found that 53% of their interviewed female juvenile offenders were retained at least one grade, and 27% met the criteria for having a learning disability and being eligible for special education services within the public schools.

In a later study, Feyez-Mendoza (1995) reported that the educational records of female juvenile offenders placed in 8th to 12th grades in the states of Iowa, Montana, and Arizona showed scholastic failure as well as a high percentage who had received special education services. Feyez-Mendoza also found a grade retention rate of 43% within Iowa and Montana and a 53% retention rate of female juvenile offenders within Arizona. Moreover, the majority of the students within the sample were found to be performing at least one grade level behind their actual grade placement. Additionally, Feyez-Mendoza (1995) commented on the relatively high incidence of special education needs within the sample, namely, 27% in Arizona, and 33% each in Iowa and Montana. Another study by Hugo and Rutherford (1992) found that 24% of those female juvenile offenders interviewed had a disability. In a more recent study conducted by Sanger et al. (2000), it was reported that 42% of female juvenile offenders had received special education services, whereas Lenssen, Doreleijers, Van Dijk, and Hartman (2000) reported that 48% of females within their sample received special education services at some time. This latter study also found a disparity in IQ scores between female and male juveniles, with 37% of the females scoring below an IQ of 80 in contrast to 15% of the male sample.

## PRELIMINARY FINDINGS OF ARIZONA STUDY ON THE RELATIONSHIP BETWEEN DISABILITY AND JUVENILE DELINQUENCY

As one might surmise from the preceding research summary, despite the increased number of male and female offenders entering the juvenile justice system, as well as our knowledge of the disproportional numbers of youths having a disability within the system, little systematic research has been conducted on those factors that may be contributing to this increased prevalence. In order to address possible contributing factors, a large-scale epidemiological study is being conducted that examines disability within the juvenile justice system in a large county in the state of Arizona. Specifically, the case files of disabled versus non-disabled juvenile delinquents referred to juvenile court are being reviewed to determine the nature of the relationship between type of disability and gender, ethnicity, age of first referral, number of referrals, and type of referral.

## Participants

The current study has examined to date 2,076 randomly selected cases from the entire population of juvenile delinquency case files ($n = 81,125$) on record between 1976 and 2002 in a county in Arizona, which encompasses a large geographical area and includes approximately one million people.

## Procedure

Each case file was reviewed by a member of the research team to determine the presence/absence of a disability diagnosis based on the criteria listed in either IDEA or in the third or fourth edition of the DSM (American Psychiatric Association, 1980, 1987, 1994). A "disability diagnosis" was therefore defined as the presence of an IDEA or DSM diagnosis in the psychological or psychiatric report(s), school records, or individual education plan (IEP) of a juvenile's case file. Specifically, one or more of the following diagnoses from IDEA or the DSM constituted a "disability diagnosis": (a) IDEA diagnoses—emotional disturbance, specific learning disability, mental retardation, speech or language disability, autism, deaf–blindness, visual impairment including blindness, deafness, hearing impairment, multiple disabilities, orthopedic impairment, other health impairment, and traumatic brain injury; (b) DSM diagnoses—an Axis I diagnosis or an Axis II diagnosis.

Each member of the research team was independently trained to a 100% errorless criterion level in the structured review format for a case file, as well as in identifying IDEA and DSM disability diagnoses. Data collected for each juvenile also included the following: (a) number of referrals, (b) age of first referral, (c) type of offense(s), (d) whether the juvenile was "adjudicated" (defined as the juvenile having a formal hearing in front of a judge for the alleged offense and being found guilty), (e) gender, and (f) ethnicity. All data were coded according to each juvenile's case file number. Identifying information such as name and address was never recorded on any research document.

## PRELIMINARY RESULTS

Of the 2,076 case files reviewed, 427 juvenile delinquents (20.60%) were found to have an IDEA or *DSM* diagnosis. Preliminary data revealed that youths with a disability diagnosis were more frequently adjudicated than their non-disabled peers (84.5% and 39.1%, respectively; see Table 8.1). Youths with disabilities also were found to recidivate more frequently than their non-disabled peers (77.0% and 43.6%, respectively; see Table 8.2).

Consistent with the research, females were found to account for lower incidence rates within all types of offenses compared to males in each of the sample groups (disability vs. non-disability), with the exception of status offenses (i.e., truancy, runaway).

### TABLE 8.1

Adjudicated vs. Nonadjudicated by Gender and Presence of a Disability: Preliminary Findings

|  | *Adjudicated* | *Not Adjudicated* | n |
|---|---|---|---|
| Cases without disabilities | 645 (39.1%) | 1,004 (60.9%) | 1,649 |
| Males | 46.3% | 53.7% | 1,030 |
| Females | 27.1% | 72.9% | 619 |
| Cases found to have a disability | 361 (84.5%) | 66 (15.5%) | 427 |
| Males | 85.1% | 14.9% | 309 |
| Females | 83.1% | 16.9% | 118 |

### TABLE 8.2

Recidivism by Presence/Absence of a Disability and by Gender: Preliminary Findings

|  | *Repeat Offenses* | | |
|---|---|---|---|
|  | Yes | No | n |
| Cases without disabilities | 43.6% | 56.4% | 1,649 |
| Males | 54.4% | 45.6% | 1,030 |
| Females | 40.2% | 59.8% | 619 |
| Cases found to have a disability | 77.0% | 23.0% | 427 |
| Males | 76.7% | 23.3% | 309 |
| Females | 78% | 22% | 118 |

According to preliminary data, there was a higher percentage of youths under 11 years of age found in the disabled vs. non-disabled sample (47.1% and 33.2%, respectively; see Table 8.3). In addition, of the cases reviewed within the study, juveniles of Hispanic descent accounted for the highest percentage (46.0%) of youths with disabilities. Table 8.4 represents the breakdown of ethnicity within the entire sample and within the sample of youths with a disability diagnosis.

## DISCUSSION AND LIMITATIONS OF THE STUDY

In summary, preliminary findings have suggested that juveniles with a disability are more likely to be adjudicated than their non-disabled peers, to have higher recidivism rates than non-disabled juvenile delinquents, and to enter the system at a younger age. Analysis of final collected data will include testing

**TABLE 8.3**

Age of First Referral by Gender in the Disabled vs. Non-Disabled Samples: Preliminary Findings

|                   | Disabled |        | Non-Disabled |        |
|-------------------|----------|--------|--------------|--------|
| Age Range (years) | Male     | Female | Male         | Female |
| <11               | 46.6%    | 30.5%  | 41.7%        | 19.2%  |
| 12–17             | 53.4%    | 69.5%  | 58.3%        | 80.8%  |
| n                 | 309      | 118    | 1,030        | 619    |

**TABLE 8.4**

Ethnicity by Cases in Entire Sample and Cases Found to Have a Disability: Preliminary Findings

|                              | African American | Asian | Caucasian | Hispanic | Native American | Other |
|------------------------------|------------------|-------|-----------|----------|-----------------|-------|
| Random sample (n = 2076)     | 7.8%             | 0.8%  | 41.1%     | 44.7%    | 4.2%            | 0.3%  |
| Disability sample (n = 427)  | 10.1%            | 1.2%  | 39.3%     | 45.0%    | 4.2%            | 0.2%  |
| Non-disability sample (n = 1649) | 7.2%         | 0.7%  | 41.5%     | 44.7%    | 4.2%            | 0.3%  |

whether there is a significant relationship between disability and adjudication as well as between disability and recidivism. Additionally, chi-square analyses will be performed on the final data set to determine whether significant relationships exist between juvenile delinquency and other variables such as gender, ethnicity, age, type of offense, and disability category.

Limitations of the study include the fact that educational records and/or psychological and medical evaluations were often not included in cases with single referrals, particularly when not adjudicated. Because of this lack of information, it is difficult to determine with certainty the occurrence of disability within youths who enter the juvenile court system. Additionally, the sample is limited to a large county in Arizona, which may not reflect characteristics of children from other geographic regions.

Trends over time regarding disability could not be evaluated within this sample due to the lack of availability of archived files. Additionally, cases were reviewed within the confines of the county juvenile court, which did not include individuals whose cases were transferred to criminal court.

## DIRECTIONS FOR FUTURE RESEARCH

There is a paucity of research that addresses not only the relationship between type of disability and juvenile delinquency but also the contribution of type of disability to the sentencing decision-making by judges. Despite the increased number of youths entering the juvenile justice system, as well as the research literature indicating the disproportional numbers of youths having a disability within the system, little systematic research has been conducted with adjudicated youths on the relationship between disability and type of offense committed as well as length and type of sentence. In addition, little information is available in the literature on disability in those youths transferred to the adult criminal court system.

Another area that may warrant further study relates to specific differences among youths within the population of juvenile delinquents with disabilities. Specific differences could include types of disability, age, gender, grade level, ethnicity, type of offenses, number of referrals, and whether the juvenile received special education services in inclusive, mainstreamed, resource, or self-contained classroom settings prior to incarceration. Awareness of these factors may impact teaching methodologies and strategies. Ultimately, research would be beneficial on the strategies that facilitate long-term success of this population within mainstream society.

Further study should also include those youths transferred to adult criminal court. Collecting demographic data, information regarding the presence or absence of a disability, and data on the kinds of services provided to these youths would yield more accurate estimates of the characteristics of juvenile delinquency. Moreover, research needs to be conducted examining incarcerated versus non-incarcerated youth to determine how many are receiving special education services, as well as the type of services, in addition to or independent of their regular educational services. Evaluating the efficacy of mental health treatment within the juvenile justice system also warrants further study. At present, little systematic research has been published in this area (Meyers, Webb, Frantz, & Randall, 2003).

## REFERENCES

American Psychiatric Association. (1980). *Diagnostic and statistical manual of mental disorders* (3rd ed.). Washington, DC: Author.

American Psychiatric Association. (1987). *Diagnostic and statistical manual of mental disorders* (3rd ed., rev.). Washington, DC: Author.

American Psychiatric Association. (1994). *Diagnostic and statistical manual of mental disorders* (4th ed.). Washington, DC: Author.

American Psychiatric Association. (2000). *Diagnostic and statistical manual of mental disorders* (4th ed., Text Revision). Washington, DC: Author.

Block, A. K. (2000). *Special education law and delinquent children: An overview.* Juvenile Justice Fact Sheet. Charlottesville, VA: Institute of Law, Psychiatry, & Public Policy, University of Virginia. Retrieved April 30, 2004, from http://www.ilppp.virginia.edu/Juvenile_Forensic_Fact_Sheets/SpecEdLaw.html

Brier, N. (1989). The relationship between learning disability and delinquency: A review and reappraisal. *Journal of Learning Disabilities, 22,* 546–553.

Bullock, L. M., & McArthur, P. (1994). Correctional special education: Disability prevalence estimates and teachers' preparation programs. *Education and Treatment of Children, 17,* 347–355.

Burrell, S., & Warboys, L. (2000). *Special education and the juvenile justice system.* Washington, DC: Office of Juvenile Justice and Delinquency Prevention.

Calhoun, G. B. (2001). Differences between male and female juvenile offenders as measured by the BASC. *Journal of Offender Rehabilitation, 33,* 87–96.

Casey, K., & Keilitz, I. (1990). Estimating the prevalence of learning disabled and mentally retarded juvenile offenders: A meta-analysis. In P. E. Leone (Ed.), *Understanding troubled and troubling youth* (pp. 82–101). Newbury Park, CA: Sage.

Council of Chief State School Officers. (2000). *Key state education policies on K–12 education: 2000.* Washington, DC: Council of Chief State School Officers.

*Education for All Handicapped Children Act.* (1975). P.L. 94-142.

Dahle, K. B. (2003). The clinical and educational systems: Differences and similarities. *Focus on Autism and Other Developmental Disabilities, 18,* 238–246.

Eggleston, C. R. (1996). The justice system. In S. C. Cramer & W. Ellis (Eds.), *Learning disabilities: Lifelong issues* (pp. 197–202). Baltimore, MD: Paul H. Brookes.

Fejes-Mendoza, K. E. (1995). Portraits of dysfunction: Criminal, educational, and family profiles of juvenile female offenders. *Education & Treatment of Children, 18,* 309–412.

Fejes-Mendoza, K. E., & Rutherford, R. B. (1987). Learning handicapped and non-learning handicapped female juvenile offenders: Educational and criminal profiles. *Journal of Correctional Education, 38,* 148–153.

Feld, B. (1988). In re Gault revisited: A cross-state comparison of the right to counsel in juvenile court. *Crime & Delinquency, 34,* 393–424.

Foley, R. M. (2001). Academic characteristics of incarcerated youth and correctional educational programs. *Journal of Emotional & Behavioral Disorders, 9,* 248–260.

Hugo, K. E., & Rutherford, R. B. (1992). Issues in identifying educational disabilities among female juvenile offenders. *Journal of Correctional Education, 43,* 124–127.

In re Gault, 387 U.S. 1 (1967).

Individuals With Disabilities Education Act. (1990). P.L. 101-476.

Individuals With Disabilities Education Act. (1997). P.L. 105-17.

Individuals With Disabilities Education Act. (2004). P.L. 108-446.

Jonson-Reid, M., Williams, J. H., & Webster, D. (2001). Severe emotional disturbance and violent offending among incarcerated adolescents. *Social Work Research, 25,* 213–222.

Keilitz, I., & Dunivant, N. (1986). The relationship between learning disability and juvenile delinquency: Current state of knowledge. *Remedial and Special Education, 7,* 18–26.

Keilitz, I., & Miller, S. L. (1980). Handicapped adolescents and young adults in the justice system. *Exceptional Education Quarterly, 1,* 117–126.

Keilitz, I., Zaremba, B. A., & Broder, P. K. (1979). The link between learning disabilities and juvenile delinquency: Some issues and answers. *Learning Disabilities Quarterly, 2,* 2–11.

Kent v. United States, 383 U.S. 541 (1966).

Lane, B. A. (1980). The relationship of learning disabilities to juvenile delinquency: Current status. *Journal of Learning Disabilities, 13,* 20–29.

Lane, E. C. (2003). Correlates of female juvenile delinquency. *International Journal of Sociology and Social Policy, 23,* 114.

Larson, K. A. (1988). A research review and alternative hypothesis explaining the link between learning disability and delinquency. *Journal of Learning Disabilities, 21,* 357–363.

Larson, K. A., & Turner, K. D. (2002). *Best practices for serving court involved youth with learning, attention, and behavioral disabilities. Monograph series on education, disability, and juvenile justice.* Washington DC: American Institutes for Research, Center for Effective Collaboration and Practice; College Park, MD: National Center on Education, Disability, and Juvenile Justice.

Lenssen, S. A. M., Doreleijers, T. A. H., Van Dijk, M. E., & Hartman, C. A. (2000). Girls in detention: What are their characteristics? A project to explore and document the character of this target group and the significant ways in which it differs from one consisting of boys. *Journal of Adolescence, 23,* 287–303.

Leone, P. E., Rutherford, R. M., & Nelson, C. M. (1991). *Special education in juvenile corrections.* Reston, VA: The Council for Exceptional Children.

Leone, P. E. (1994). Education services for youth with disabilities in a state-operated juvenile correctional system: Case study and analysis. *The Journal of Special Education, 28,* 43–58.

Leone, P. E., Meisel, S. M., & Drakeford, W. (2002). Special education programs for youth with disabilities in juvenile corrections. *Journal of Correctional Education, 53,* 46–50.

Lyons, J. S., Baerger, D. R., Quigley, P., Erlich, J., & Griffin, E. (2001). Mental health service needs of juvenile offenders: A comparison of detention, incarceration, and treatment settings. *Children's Services: Social, Policy, Research, and Practice, 4,* 69–85.

MacDonald, J. M., & Chesney-Lind, M. (2001). Gender bias and juvenile justice revisited: A multiyear analysis. *Crime & Delinquency, 7,* 173–195.

Malmgren, K., Abbott, R. D., & Hawkins, J. D. (1999). LD and delinquency: Rethinking the "link." *Journal of Learning Disabilities, 32,* 194–200.

Marcotte, P. (1990). Criminal kids. *ABA Journal, 76,* 61–65.

McGarvey, E. L., & Waite, D. (2000). Mental health needs among adolescents committed to the Virginia Department of Juvenile Justice. *Developments in Mental Health Law, 20,* 1–12.

*McKeiver v. Pennsylvania,* 403 U.S. 528 (1971).

Meyers, K., Webb, A., Frantz, J., & Randall, A. (2003). What does it take to retain substance-abusing adolescents in research protocols? Delineation of effort required, strategies undertaken, costs incurred, and 6-month post-treatment differences by retention difficulty. *Drug & Alcohol Dependence, 69,* 73–86.

Moon, M. M., Sundt, J. L., Cullen, F. T., & Wright, J. P. (2000). Is child saving dead? Public support for juvenile rehabilitation. *Crime & Delinquency, 46,* 38–60.

Morgan, D. I. (1979). Prevalence and types of handicapping conditions found in juvenile correctional institutions: A national survey. *Journal of Special Education, 13,* 283–295.

Morton, J. B. (1998). *Complex challenges, collaborative solutions: Programming for adult and juvenile female offenders.* Lanham, MD: American Correctional Association.

Murphy, D. M. (1986). The prevalence of handicapping conditions among juvenile delinquents. *Remedial and Special Education, 7,* 7–17.

National Council on Disability. (2003). *Addressing the needs of youth with disabilities in the juvenile justice system: The current status of evidence-based research.* Washington DC: National Council on Disability. Accessed online at http://www.ncd.gov/newsroom/publications/pdf/juvenile.pdf (December 13, 2003).

Podboy, J., & Mallory, W. (1979). Learning handicap: The underdiagnosed disability. *Juvenile and Family Court Journal, 29,* 13–16.

Pollard, R. R., Pollard, C. J., & Meers, G. (1994). Determining effective transition strategies for adjudicated youth with disabilities: A national delphi study. *Journal of Correctional Education, 45,* 190–195.

Pumariega, A. J., Atkins, D. L., Rogers, K., Montgomery, L., Nybro, C., Caesar, R., & Millus, D. (1999). Mental health and incarcerated youth. II: Service utilization. *Journal of Child and Family Studies, 8,* 205–215.

Quinn, M. M., Rutherford, R. B., & Leone, P. E. (2001). *Students with disabilities in correctional facilities.* ERIC Clearinghouse on Disabilities and Gifted Education. Arlington, VA: ERIC.

Rehabilitation Act. (1973). P.L. 93-112.

Robinson, T. R., & Rapport, M. K. (1999). Providing special education in the juvenile justice system. *Remedial and Special Education, 20,* 19–26.

Rogers, K., Powell, E. & Strock, M. (1998). The characteristics of youth referred for mental health evaluation in the juvenile justice system. In Chapter 7, *Child Welfare and Juvenile Justice, Proceedings of the Annual Research Conference, a System of Care for Children's Mental Health: Expanding the Research Base:* 10th Tampa, FL, February 23–26, 1997.

Rothman, D. (1980). *Conscience and convenience: The asylum and its alternatives in progressive America.* Boston: Little, Brown.

Rutherford, R. B., Jr., Bullis, M., Anderson, C. W., & Griller-Clark, H. M. (2002). *Youth with disabilities in the correctional system: Prevalence rates and identification issues.* Washington, DC: Office of Juvenile Justice and Delinquency Prevention.

Rutherford, R. B., Jr., Griller-Clark, H. M., & Anderson, C. W. (2001). Treating offenders with educational disabilities. In J. B. Ashford, B. D. Sales, & W. H. Reid (Eds.), *Treating adult and juvenile offenders with special needs* (pp. 221–245). Washington, DC: American Psychological Association.

Rutherford, R. B., Nelson, C. M., & Wolford, B. I. (1985). Special education in the most restrictive environment: Correctional/special education. *Journal of Special Education, 19*, 59–71.

Sanger, D. (1999). The communication skills of female juvenile delinquents: A selected review. *Journal of Correctional Education, 50*, 90–94.

Sanger, D., Creswell, J., Schaffart, B., Engelbert, K., & Opfer, T. (2000). Understanding the meanings of female delinquents' communication behaviors. *Journal of Correctional Education, 51*, 300–305.

Shepherd, R. E., Jr. (1999). The juvenile court at 100 years: A look back. *Office of Juvenile Justice and Delinquency Prevention, 6*, 16–24.

Shum, L. (2002). Educationally related mental health services for children with serious emotional disturbance: Addressing barriers to access through the idea. *Journal of Health Care Law & Policy, 5*, 233–258.

Sickmund, M. (2000). *Offenders in juvenile court, 1997*. Washington, DC: Office of Juvenile Justice and Delinquency Prevention.

Snyder, H. N., & Sickmund, M. (1995). *Juvenile offenders and victims: A national report*. Washington, DC: Office of Juvenile Justice and Delinquency Prevention.

Timmons-Mitchell, J., Brown, C., Schulz, S. C., Webster, S. E., Underwood, L. A., & Semple, W. E. (1997). Comparing the mental health needs of female and male incarcerated juvenile delinquents. *Behavioral Sciences and the Law, 15*, 195–202.

U.S. Department of Education. (1997). *To assure the free appropriate public education of all children with disabilities: Nineteenth annual report to Congress on the implementation of the Individuals with Disabilities Education Act*. Accessed online at http://www.ed.gov/offices/OSERS/OSEP/Research/OSEP97AnlRpt/index.html (March 28, 2004).

U.S. Department of Education. (2002). *To assure the free appropriate public education of all children with disabilities: Twenty-fourth annual report to Congress on the implementation of the Individuals with Disabilities Education Act*. Jessup, MD: Education Publications Center. Accessed online at http://www.ed.gov/about/reports/annual/osep/2002/index.html (December 14, 2003).

U.S. Department of Justice, Office of Juvenile Justice and Delinquency Prevention. (1996). *Female offenders in the juvenile justice system*. Washington, DC: U.S. Government Printing Office.

U.S. Department of Justice, Office of Juvenile Justice and Delinquency Prevention. (1999). *Juvenile offenders and victims: 1999 National report*. Washington, DC: U.S. Government Printing Office.

U.S. Department of Justice, Office of Juvenile Justice and Delinquency Prevention. (2000). *Female Delinquency Cases, 1997*. Washington D.C.: U.S. Government Printing Office.

U.S. Department of Justice, Office of Juvenile Justice and Delinquency Prevention. (2003). *Juveniles in Court*. Washington DC: U.S. Government Printing Office.

Waldie, K., & Spreen, O. (1993). The relationship between learning disabilities and persisting delinquency. *Journal of Learning Disabilities, 26*, 417–423.

Warboys, L. M., & Shauffer, C. B. (1986). Legal issues in providing special educational services to handicapped inmates. *Remedial and Special Education, 7,* 34–40.

Woolard, J. L., Fondacaro, M. R., & Slobogin, C. (2001). Informing juvenile justice policy: Directions for behavioral science research. *Law & Human Behavior, 25,* 13–24.

# 9

# Fears and Related Anxieties in Children Having a Disability: A Synthesis of Research Findings From 1937 to 2004

Huijun Li and Richard J. Morris

Research findings have suggested that individuals with a disability tend to manifest a higher prevalence of psychopathology (e.g., Kim, Szatmari, Bryson, Streiner, & Wilson, 2000; Ollendick, Matson, & Helsel, 1985; Wenar, 1992). More specifically, people who have learning disabilities, mental retardation, physical handicaps, health impairments, and other disabilities are more prone to develop depression, anxiety, withdrawal, and poor self-image. The greater prevalence of psychopathology is usually related to these individual's handicapping condition and lack of social acceptance and social contact outside home settings (Weimer & Kratochwill, 1991). Moreover, it has been reported that families with a handicapped child experience more stress and frustration than do families with no handicapped children (Lee, Lieh-Mak, Hung, & Luk, 1983).

To date, numerous studies have been conducted on fears and related anxieties in "typical" non-disabled children, adolescents, and young adults (e.g., Dong, Yang, & Ollendick, 1994; King & Ollendick, 1989; Morris & Kratochwill, 1998). These studies have many valuable findings regarding the nature, prevalence, intensity, and developmental aspects in regard to fears and related anxieties in regular population. For example, children of elementary school age are reportedly fearful of supernatural beings, bodily injury, and loud noises. In addition, they are increasingly sensitive to and fearful of failure in social and academic performance. As children enter middle school and high school, social, academic, and health-related fears become predominant, and these fears may continue to exist into adulthood (Barrios & Hartman, 1997; Morris & Kratochwill, 1983, 1998). Furthermore, some fears tend to be transitory in nature, and when children grow older, their fears may decrease in number (Morris & Kratochwill, 1983; Wenar, 1990).

Gender differences in reported fears and related anxieties seem to have become a norm and pattern in the regular population, with females reporting higher prevalence and intensity of fears and anxiety than males (American Psychiatric Association, 1994; Beidel, Turner, Hamlin, & Morris, 2000; Dong et al., 1994; Ollendick & King, 1991; Ollendick et al., 1985b).

Only a few studies, however, have been conducted with children and adolescents having a disability. Too often, educators and researchers focus their attention on the external aspects of a disability. For example, an orthopedically impaired child is made sure that he or she is equipped to get access to school facilities. Their emotional needs, however, are often given minor attention. The major purpose of this chapter is to synthesize the research studies conducted on fears and related anxieties in children having a disability, and to inform mental health professionals, educators, and parents of the emotional stress, fears, and related anxieties, in particular, that these children experience on a daily basis. The literature review does not seek to critique the studies that have been conducted.

## LITERATURE REVIEW

The studies reviewed in this chapter were selected using the following steps. First, a thorough computer search was conducted using various online databases and search engines. Articles on fear and/or anxieties in children and adolescents with a disability were identified. For each identified article, the reference section was carefully examined to locate additional studies to be reviewed. At the time when this chapter was in preparation, there were 30 studies published on fears and related anxieties in children and adolescents having a disability. Among the 27 studies, 2 were on hearing impairment, 6 on visual impairment, 3 on health impairment, 2 on autism, 8 on mental retardation, 6 on children having learning disabilities (LD), and 3 studies compared fears and related anxieties across different disability groups. Table 9.1 presents studies by disability, name of authors, year of publication, number of studies in each disability category, assessment instruments used, and participant age information. The literature is reviewed according to the nature of disability, in the order of hearing impairment (HI), visual impairment (VI), health impairment, autism, mental retardation (MR), learning disabilities (LD), and studies involving comparison of different disability groups.

TABLE 9.1
Publications on Fears and Related Anxieties in Children Having a Disability

| Disability | Name(s) of Author(s) and Year of Publication (from most recent) | Instruments | Sample Size | Age of Participants (years) |
|---|---|---|---|---|
| HI | Pintner & Brunschwig (1937) | Fear-arousing words and short phrases of things or objects | 145 vs. 345 | |
| | King, Mulhall, & Gullone (1989) | Fear Survey Schedule for Children–Revised (FSSC–R) | 138 vs. 134 | 8–16 |
| Subtotal | 2 | | | |
| VI | Wiemer & Kratochwill (1991) | Fear Survey for Children with and without Mental Retardation (FSCMR) | 42 | 5–18 |
| | King, Gullone, & Stafford (1990) | FSSC–R | 129 vs.129 | 8–16 |
| | Wilhelm (1989) | Children's Fear Survey Schedule–Revised (CFSS–R) | 139 | 6–16 |
| | Matson, Manikam, Heinze, & Kapperman (1986) | Children's Manifest Anxiety Scale, Fear Survey Schedule, State-Trait Anxiety Inventory (STAIC) | 75 | 9–12 |

(continued)

TABLE 9.1 (*continued*)

| Disability | Name(s) of Author(s) and Year of Publication (from most recent) | Instruments | Sample Size | Age of Participants (years) |
|---|---|---|---|---|
| | Ollendick, Matson, & Helsel, (1985b) | FSSC–R | 176 vs.106 | 10–18 |
| | Hardy, R. E. (1968) | | | |
| Subtotal | 6 | | | |
| Health impairment | King, Gullone, & Ollendick (1990) | FSSC–R | 73 | 7–18 |
| | Lee, Lieh-Mak, Hung, & Luk (1983) | Children's Apperception Test (CAT) | | 6–10 |
| | Spinetta, Rigler, & Karon (1973) | Pictures (PIX), Hospital Anxiety and Home Anxiety, storytelling about a three-dimensional model of a hospital room | 50 | |
| Subtotal | 3 | | | |
| Autism | Kim, Szatmari, Bryson, Streiner, & Wilson (2000) | | 40 with autism, 19 with Asperger syndrome | 9–14 |
| | Matson & Love (1990) | FSSC–R | 14 vs. 14 | 2.5–17 |
| Subtotal | 2 | | | |

| | | | | |
|---|---|---|---|---|
| MR | Ramirez & Kratochwill (1997) | Fear Survey Schedule for Children and Adolescents (FSSC–II) | 187 vs. 372 | 7–18 |
| | Gullone, Cummins, & King (1996) | FSSC, RCMAS, State-Trait Anxiety Inventory for Children, Vineland Adaptive Behavior Scales | 51 | 7–18 |
| | Cullone, Cummins, & King (1995) | | | |
| | King, Josephs, Gullone, Madden, & Ollendick (1994) | | | |
| | Vandenberg (1993) | | 42 vs. 112 | 4–12 |
| | Knapp, Barrett, Groden, & Groden (1992). | FSSC–R | 28 | 9–21 |
| | Duff, La Rocca, Lizzet, Martin, Pearce, Williams, & Peck (1981) | Fear Survey Schedule, Peabody Picture Vocabulary Test | 20 | No age data reported |
| | Derevensky (1979) | Individual interview on "What are the things to be afraid of?" | 133 | 7–18 |
| | Guarnaccia & Weiss (1974) | Louisville Fear Survey for Children | 102 | 6–21 |
| Subtotal | 8 | | | |

*(continued)*

TABLE 9.1 (continued)

| Disability | Name(s) of Author(s) and Year of Publication (from most recent) | Instruments | Sample Size | Age of Participants (years) |
|---|---|---|---|---|
| LD | Fisher, Allen, & Kose (1996) | STAIC, Means-Ends Problem Solving Procedure (MEPS) | 55 boys | 9–11 |
| | Rodriguez & Routh (1989) | RCMAS, the Anxiety-Withdrawal subscale of the Revised Behavior Problem Checklist (RBPC) | | |
| | Stein & Hoover (1989) | RCMAS | 30 vs. 30 | 4th to 6th grade |
| | Margalit & Raviv (1984) | A list of words of minor somatic complaint | | 1st to 7th grade |
| | Paget & Reynolds (1984) | RCMAS | 106 | 6–17 |
| | Pattern (1983) | Self-Esteem Inventory and the General Anxiety Scale for Children, Mathematics, Reading Recognition, and General Information, Peabody Individual Achievement Test | 88 | K–6th grade |
| Subtotal | 6 | | | |

| | | | | |
|---|---|---|---|---|
| Cross-disability comparison | Li (2004) | FSSC–R, RCMAS | 74 With mild mental retardation, 135 with LD | 7–19 |
| | Newcomer & Barenbaum (1995) | Depression and Anxiety in Youth Scale | 87 With conduct disorder, 85 with LD | 7–18 |
| | King, Josephs, Gullone, & Madden (1994) | FSSC–R | 302 With intellectual disabilities, 192 with visual disabilities, 218 with hearing disabilities vs. control 30 | 27–18 |
| Subtotal | 3 | | | |

## Hearing Impairment

Pintner and Brunschwig (1937) were the first researchers to examine fears and related anxieties among deaf children, and they were also the pioneers to study fears in individuals with a disability in general. In their study, Pintner and Brunschwig administered a fear test composed of 39 fear-arousing words and short phrases of things or objects to 159 deaf students and 345 hearing students. Among the student participants in similar grades, deaf boys were at an average 2 years older than hearing boys and deaf girls were 3 years older than hearing girls. This age discrepancy was reportedly deliberate because deaf students were believed to be delayed in their language development and academic performance for 2 to 3 years (Pintner & Brunschwig, 1937). The two researchers seemed to be the first to report gender differences in terms of fears and related anxieties. They found that girls in both the deaf and hearing groups reported more fears than deaf and hearing boys. Moreover, deaf girls expressed a significantly larger number of fears than hearing girls. An important finding reported by Pintner and Brunschwig is that students who were deaf since birth or early childhood had more fears than those who lost their hearing at a later age.

Lastly, socioeconomic status (SES) was reportedly a significant factor that influenced fear contents. Student participants of this study were urban school children from average to low SES. Six fears among the 10 most common were related to personal safety and environmental hazards—"war," "death," "bad man," "robbers," "snake," and "fire"—most of which are encountered in their daily life. This finding seems to find support in Graziano's assumption that the type of fears is influenced by the environment people live in (1975).

The second study that examined fearfulness in hearing-impaired individuals was conducted by King, Mulhall, and Gullone (1989). They administered Fear Survey Schedule for Children–Revised (FSSC–R; Ollendick, 1983) to prelingually deaf children aged between 8 and 16 years, and a group of matched age controls without a hearing impairment. King et al. found that children with hearing impairment reported significantly more fears of the unknown and small animals, whereas children without a disability reported more fears of social evaluation, such as fear of criticism and parent quarrel. This finding may indicate that fears of children with hearing impairment are more like those of younger non-disabled children. The study also revealed that females in both groups reported significantly more fears, although the differences between males and females in the non-disabled group were greater. King et al. explained that it could be that the gender role for children and adolescents with hearing impairment may be less polarized than for the non-disabled population.

Both of these studies indicate gender differences where females reported more fears than males. However, inconsistency is observed regarding within-group differences. In the Pintner and Brunschwig study, it was indicated that gender differences were greater in the hearing impairment group, whereas the second study reported greater gender differences in the nondisabled group. More studies are needed to further explore gender differences in this population.

Individuals with hearing impairment experience more stress in daily social and academic functioning, perceive the world as more intimidating and frightening, and may be more at risk of developing psychological problems (King et al., 1989). However, this is one of the least researched area in comparison with studies on other disability groups, because there have been only two published studies and they were conducted with more than 50 years apart, with no studies for the past 15 years. This creates a huge gap in terms of information on the emotional well-being of this group children. Thus, it is essential that professionals and researchers examine the patterns of emotion—fears and related anxieties in particular—in children and adolescents with hearing impairment, so that we are able to better understand the development and emotional needs of this population and more effectively assist them.

## Visual Impairment

Loss of vision has been regarded as only secondary to loss of life. Individuals with visual impairment have to face developmental tasks that are more challenging for them to handle relative to sighted persons, and that they have to face possible rejection and derision from peers and other people, all of which may lead to emotional stress and psychosocial problems (Ollendick et al., 1985b; Wiemer & Krotochwill, 1991).

There are six studies on fears and related anxieties in children and adolescents with visual impairment. Hardy (1968) was among the first to examine anxiety in visually handicapped children. His study showed that older children with visual impairment exhibited more anxiety than younger ones. However, Matson, Manikam, Heinze, and Kapperman (1986) found least anxiety in the oldest group (17 to 22 years of age). This inconsistent finding needs further exploration by future studies.

Ollendick et al. (1985b) found no age differences between children with visual impairment and those with normal sight in self-reported fears, which was supported by Wiemer and Krotochwill's study (1991), where they found considerable similarity in the most common fears between the 5- to 11-year-olds and 12- to 18-year-olds. The fact that the last two studies using the same instruments yielded similar results may indicate some validity of the instrument and reliability of results. These findings, however, deserve some attention in that they are not consistent with the normative data regarding developmental patterns and differences of fears in children and adolescents. One explanation may be that fears in children and adolescents with visual impairment are more stable, and they may also lack strategies to deal with them even when they get older, due to overprotection by family members and other people.

As to the content of fears, there again appeared inconsistent findings, Ollendick et al. (1985b) found in their American study that children with visual impairment reported more total fears and fears of physical harm, whereas those normally sighted reported more psychological fears which are social evaluative in nature. Using the same assessment instrument, King et al. (1989) in their Australian participants found a different result in that normally sighted children reported more danger related fears than those with visual impairment. Certain cultural factors may be partially responsible for such differences.

Although there are some inconsistent findings regarding to gender difference, most research studies seem to be in agreement that females reported significantly more fears than males (King et al., 1989; Matson et al. 1986; Ollendick et al., 1985b; Wiemer & Kratochwill, 1991).

Studies involving children with visual impairment seemed to suggest some inconsistent findings in terms of disability, age, and gender. Children with visual impairment reported more fears of failure and criticism in one study; more studies seem to suggest that they report experiencing more fears of physical harm and danger to life. These fears, as suggested by Gullone (1996) and Morris and Kratochwill (1983, 1998), may serve as survival mechanisms for these children and be adaptive to the environment in nature. Findings related to specific fears and related anxieties in different age groups may suggest that the age differences in reported fears of children with visual impairment may not be as apparent as those in normally sighted children, that is there is a decrease in the number of fears as children grow into adolescents, and that children with visual impairment tend to report more fears than normally sighted children, regardless of developmental differences. Matson et al. (1986), however, did report decreased anxiety levels in older children.

## Health Impairment

People with health impairment and chronic medical conditions are likely to have a higher prevalence of psychological disturbances compared to non-health-impaired people (King, Gullone, & Ollendick, 1990). Blum (1992) discussed problems faced by adolescents with chronic illness and indicated that overprotection from parents, in addition to self-rejection and depression associated with puberty, can lead to lowered self-esteem and increased anxiety.

Only three studies, however, have explored the types of fears and related anxieties in this population. Spinetta, Rigler, and Karon (1973) compared anxiety levels in 25 hospitalized children with a diagnosis of leukemia and 25 children with chronic but nonfatal illness. The two groups of children were matched for age, seriousness of illness condition, and amount of intervention.

In comparison with the control group of chronically ill children, Spinetta et al. (1973) found that stories told by children with leukemia both at initial hospital entry and at subsequent readmissions indicated significantly greater concern and preoccupation with threats to body and physical functioning. Furthermore, children with leukemia manifested a significantly greater anxiety in both hospital-related and non-hospital-related questions. Spinetta et al. suggested that young children with fatal illness may not have the cognitive ability to overtly express the concept of death, but it may be conveyed and expressed through their fears and anxieties.

Using different assessment instruments, Lee and his colleagues (1983) examined the anxiety pattern in Chinese children with leukemia and those with orthopedic disorder. Consistent with the findings of Spinetta et al., Lee and his colleagues reported that children with leukemia exhibited twice as many fears and anxiety responses as children having orthopedic disorder. Moreover, they found that some of the children with leukemia were so overwhelmed by their own anxieties that they were not able to complete their stories. Those children with orthopedic disorder, however, appeared to express anxieties in a more comprehensible manner, and their stories often had happy endings.

In another study, King, Gullone, and Ollendick (1990) investigated fears in children 7 to 18 years of age who had different health impairments, including cerebral palsy, peripheral musculoskeletal anomalies, spine bifida, muscular dystrophy, and asthma. These health conditions either were congenital or developed in the child's early years of life. Their findings showed that children with health impairments reported significantly greater number of fears than the control children. Moreover, similar to the findings of King et al. (1989) on children with hearing impairment, their fears were more related to the unknown, injury, and small animals, which are more prevalent in younger non-disabled children. Consistent with the normative data of fears and related anxieties, older children with health impairment reported significantly fewer fears than younger ones, and females reported a significantly greater number of fears than males.

Across the three studies, significantly more fears were reported in children with health impairment in comparison with healthy children, and significantly more fears and anxieties in fatally ill children. What's more, their fears are directly related to their worry about their health. This information should be very critical for medical professionals and parents to be aware of in the treatment procedures; such heightened levels of anxiety may negatively affect treatment effect, so strategies should be developed to decrease children's anxiety levels as a way to improve physical health status.

## Autism

Matson and Love (1990) examined fears in autistic children using a modified version of Ollendick's FSSC–R. Results showed that the 10 most common fears for children with autism were often associated with the characteristics of their diagnosis. Specifically, their fears included fear of noises, fear of the dark, and fear of being with people. These fears are characteristic of younger normal children, indicating a suppressed cognitive functioning in this group of autistic children and adolescents.

The second study involving children and adolescents with autism and Asperger syndrome (AS) was conducted by Kim et al. (2000). Kim and his colleagues examined the prevalence and correlates of anxiety and mood problems in 9- to 14-year-old children and adolescents. In comparison with a community control sample, they found that children with AS and autism manifested greater anxiety problems, with no difference in the number of anxiety problems between AS and autistic children. The authors suggested that AS and high-functioning autistic children and adolescents may be at a greater risk for developing anxiety problems.

The students just described are the only two studies that examined fears and related anxieties in children with autism and Asperger syndrome. The findings indicate that these children may experience more fears and anxieties, like the children with health impairment, hearing, and visual impairment. Furthermore, the fears are related to the diagnostic features, such as fear of loud noise. However, no age- and gender-related findings are available to examine within-group differences in this group of children.

## Mental Retardation

There are eight studies on fears and related anxieties in children and adolescents with mental retardation. In addition to the studies reviewed by Gullone (1996), three studies that focused on fears and related anxieties in mentally retarded people are reviewed here. Duff et al. (1981) compared fears of mildly retarded adults with those of non-retarded adult controls and children matched with the retarded adult's mental age. An integrated fear survey schedule compiled from four different fear survey schedules was used to measure fears in these participants. Duff et al. found that retarded adults reported significantly more fears and greater intensity of fears than non-retarded adults, but less overall fear than the non-retarded children. The types of fears reported by retarded adults were found to be similar to those of the matched children, which include fear of thunder, lightning, and being kidnapped. These fears are mostly in the unknown factor, which may indicate low cognitive functioning in these participants.

In a preliminary investigation of the nature and prevalence of fears in developmentally disabled children and adolescents 9 to 22 years of age, Knapp, Barrett, Groden, and Groden (1992) found that the FSSC–R elicited significantly more fears than spontaneous recall using a structured interview procedure. Among the 10 most prominent fears reported by the participants, 7 are shared by developmentally non-handicapped participants of similar age as reported by Ollendick et al. (1985b). Nevertheless, those fears not shared by the developmentally non-handicapped participants are noteworthy. Specifically, participants with developmental disabilities were fearful of animals and objects or events that endanger physical well-being, whereas the developmentally non-handicapped group was more afraid of such abstract concerns as criticism and failure (Knapp et al., 1992).

A third study by Vanderberg (1993) compared 112 normal children between 4 and 12 years of age and 42 educationally mentally retarded children 7 to 12 years of age. He found significant age and gender differences in the types of fears reported by the two groups of children. Specifically, older normal children reported less fear of imaginary or unknown things and more fear of "human agency" and events in the physical world, suggesting that with the development and increase of knowledge and experience, older children's fears and anxieties become more realistic (the author did not further specify what the imaginary things and human agency and events refer to). Consistent with the two previous studies and those studies reviewed by Gullone (1996), children with mental retardation exhibited patterns of fears similar to those of younger normal children—that is, retarded children were more afraid of imaginary things.

## Learning Disabilities

Students with learning disabilities (LD), due to their cognitive and social communicative difficulties, often experience distress and failure in academic and social activities. These failures often lead to derision and rejection from peers, which may contribute to their feelings of anxieties and lowered self-esteem.

La Greca and Stone (1990) compared peer ratings of liking and disliking of children with learning disabilities and low achievers. Findings suggest that children with LD were less accepted and less well liked, and they also perceived lower self-worth and social acceptance. Pattern (1983) examined the relationships between self-esteem, anxiety, and academic performance in children with learning disabilities from kindergarten through sixth grade. Pattern found a negative correlation between general anxiety and general information achievement scores for the total group. That is, students reported higher level of anxiety obtained lower information achievement scores.

Furthermore, this feeling of anxiety may be accompanied by psychophysiological changes in students with LD and may lead to "imprisoned intelligence" (Margalit & Raviv, 1984; Orenstein, 2000; Thomas, 1979). Margalit and Raviv (1984) were among the first to examine the psychophysiological aspects of fears and related anxieties in persons with disabilities. In their study, they looked into minor somatic complaints (MSCs) in three groups of students: LD, regular students, and students with educable mental retardation (EMR). The results show that students with LD, in comparison with regular and EMR students, demonstrate a significantly higher frequency of MSCs, especially fatigue, headache, and stomachaches. Furthermore, upon such complaints, significantly fewer students with LD are allowed to leave class or stay at home than are regular students. A consequence of this is that students with LD have to confront such difficulties with passive and avoidance behavior, "the accompanying emotions being anxiety and helplessness" (Margalit & Raviv, 1984, p. 227). Thus, the authors caution teachers and even nurses that they should be aware of such complaints and their implications and possible emotional distress accompanied in students with LD (Margalit & Raviv, 1984).

In recent years, mainstreaming students with LD has become a trend. It was designed to improve the self-concept and emotional well-being of these students. Two studies were conducted to investigate if there is any difference in anxiety manifestation as a function of time that students with LD spend in special education classes. Stein and Hoover (1989), using RCMAS, compared manifest anxiety in students placed in part-time resources rooms, full-time LD classrooms, and regular classrooms. The results show that students receiving part-time special education services scored significantly higher than the LD students attending regular classrooms on the Total Anxiety and the Worry/Oversensitivity cluster. These results support the findings of Paget and Reynolds (1984). This may suggest that children receiving resource services may often miss regular classroom instruction, and they have difficulty in catching up what they have missed. In addition, going to the resource room itself may cause derision from peers and anxiety in these students.

Both studies also found significantly higher Lie scale scores among students with LD receiving full-time special education relative to the students in the other two groups. This suggests that these LD students may be trying to present themselves favorably to adults. The fact that both studies using the same instrument yielded similar results enhances validity of RCMAS with children having a disability (Stein & Hoover, 1989).

Rodriguez and Routh (1989) examined the influence of time factor on manifested anxiety in three groups of students: students recently placed in LD class, students in LD service for more than 1 year, and a non-LD control group (mean age = 11 years). Besides instruments used to measure children's attributional styles and depression, the authors used RCMAS and the Anxiety-Withdrawal subscale of the Revised Behavior Problem Checklist (RBPC). Results showed that both groups of students with LD reported significantly more anxiety on the RCMAS than the control group. Moreover, the experienced group reported higher mean anxiety scores than the control group and the new LD students, whereas recently placed LD students differed significantly from the control group only in the Anxiety-Withdrawal subscale of the RBPC. This result may indicate that experienced students have started to realize the nature of service they are receiving, and why they need such service and many of their peers do not.

Students with LD, due to their high levels of anxiety, are also reported to be less adapted than non-disabled peers to social interactions and academic problem-solving activities (Fisher, Allen, & Kose, 1996). In order to examine this explanation, Fisher et al. (1996) studied the relationship between anxiety and problem solving skills in boys with and without LD (9 to 11 years of age). They found that boys with LD reported greater pretest anxiety than non-LD boys on all STAIC measures. It was also found that the state anxiety of these boys was elevated during the social problem-solving activities, as measured by Means-Ends Problem Solving Procedures (MEPS), an untimed test for a person to use different strategies to solve daily social problems.

Students with LD take up 65% of the population with different types of disabilities; the studies just reviewed indicate these students may manifest heightened level of anxiety than non-disabled peers and low achievers. Their anxiety level may be related to the length and other time factors of services.

## Comparative Studies Across Disability Groups

Newcomer and Barenbaum (1995) in their study included not only students with LD but also students with conduct disorder (CD). These students were administered the Depression and Anxiety in Youth Scale (DAYS). The results showed that students with CD reported the highest self-ratings in both depression and anxiety. The teachers of these students also rated them similarly. In addition, it was found that LD students did not rate themselves as more anxious than non-LD children, but teachers did. Newcomer and Barenbaum (1995) also reported a significant gender effect, with female students rating themselves higher than male students in anxiety and depression. Within the LD groups, difference in anxiety level was reported, with mainstreamed LD students reporting lower anxiety as compared to students in self-contained classes.

In addition to Newcomer and Barenbaum's study that included students with LD and CD, King, Josephs, Gullone, Madden, and Ollendick (1994) compared fears in adolescent and youth (13 to 18 years of age) having either a visual impairment, or a hearing impairment, or an intellectual disability. FSSC–R was administered with various modifications to adapt to the needs of the students. The results showed that children with intellectual disability had the highest mean total fear score and they had the greatest number of intense fears. In addition, the content of their fears was found to be qualitatively different from the regular and other groups. The most discriminating fears included thunderstorms, dark places, and ghosts, which belong to Factor 2, "the unknown." Fear of small animals and injury was found in these students. King et al also found that females and younger children reported significantly more fears and with greater intensity then males and older children. These findings are also consistent with those of Duff et al. (1981) and Knapp et al. (1992).

A recent study conducted by Li (2004) examined fears and related anxieties in two disability groups—LD and mild mental retardation (MIMR)—using FSSR–C and RCMAS. Results show that students in the LD group reported a significantly higher level of total fear score than students in the MIMR group. In addition, the LD group reported significantly higher levels of fear on two of the five fear factors—fear of danger and death and fear of failure and criticism. In comparison with the MIMR group, the LD group also reported significantly higher total anxiety score and higher levels of anxiety in all the three subscale scores of RCMAS: worry/oversensitivity, physiological anxiety, and concentration anxiety. The findings regarding the anxiety measures are consistent with those of Margalit and Raviv (1984) and Rodriguez and Routh (1989). As pointed out by Margalit and Raviv (1984), the anxiety of LD students could be in the form of a vicious cycle. Specifically, anxiety in students with LD may be manifested as physiological complaints. Teachers, however, usually think that these students are trying to avoid work, and do not allow them to see nurses or go to restrooms when they request to do so. With the physical complaints being neglected, students with LD tend to become more anxious and less attentive to class activities. Consequently, their grades and academic performance may be negatively affected, which makes them more worried and sensitive to others' opinion about their performance.

Consistent with previous findings regarding gender difference, Li found that female students as a whole reported significantly higher total fear scores and higher intensity of fears than did male students. Li's study also indicated that girls in the LD group reported significantly higher total fear score, higher intensity of fears, and higher levels of fear on all the five factors than did their male counterparts in the same group. These findings are consistent with those obtained from studies involved non-disabled population (e.g., Ollendick, Yang, King, Dong, & Akande, 1996). Male students in the MIMR group, however, reported significantly higher level of fears on fear of the unknown and fear of failure and criticism. These findings suggest that male students with MIMR may be subject to more derision from peers but less protection from adults due to their male status. They may be more sensitive to others' opinions about them.

Li's results also revealed that younger children with LD reported a higher level of fear of unknown and medical fear, as well as higher level of total anxiety, than did the older children with LD. These results are supported by the normative data and previous findings by Matson et al. (1986). Specifically, Matson et al. reported that greater anxiety was observed in the youngest age group and least anxiety in the oldest group (17 to 22 years of age), indicating that younger children with a disability are more likely to become anxious and worrisome in specific environmental events. Results of Li's study showed that students in the MIMR group who are above age 10 reported higher total fear score, higher levels of fear intensity, higher levels of fear of the unknown, fear of failure and criticism, and fear of danger and death, than students who are at or below 10 years of age. The finding on fear of failure and criticism is consistent with the normative data for older children and adolescents, although other previous studies suggest children with intellectual disabilities tend to report fears similar to those of younger non-disabled population. Further studies are warranted to explore this aspect of fears in children and adolescents with intellectual disabilities.

## SUMMARY AND DIRECTIONS FOR FUTURE RESEARCH

A review of the literature on fears and related anxieties in children and youth having a disability draws the following major findings.

First, children having a disability reportedly experience more specific fears and higher anxiety level than their controlled counterparts. The contents of their fears are mostly related to physical well-being, the unknown things and phenomena, and small animals. What is more, their fears are often indicative of their disability. For example, children with autism were found to be afraid of noise, the dark, and being with people. One interesting finding is that students with hearing impairment reported fear of "thunder" (Pintner & Brunschwig, 1937). However, the authors did not further discuss whether those children were congenitally deaf students or students who were deaf at a later age. It is important to make this distinction in that it helps to explain the origin of such fears—for example, if congenitally deaf students report such fear, but they have never heard the sound of thunder, how and where have they acquired this fear without being exposed to it? Children with LD reported more fears of failure and criticism, danger and death, and overall anxiety. Professionals and educators who work with this population put a great deal of effort into assisting these children in achieving their academic potential. However, they should also be aware of the emotional well-being of these students and realize that a heightened level of anxiety may adversely affect the academic performance of these students.

Second, findings from the reviewed studies show that young children, except children with MR, reported more fears and a higher level of anxiety than older children. These findings are consistent with the normative data. However, educators, paraprofessionals, and parents should be aware that children with a disability may realize from an early age that they are somewhat different from their peers and even siblings in such a way that they need extra attention both at home and at school. The way they act and respond to adults may lead to teasing and derision from peers. These may make them very sensitive and vulnerable to others' attitudes and opinions about them. Their high anxiety and fear level may hold these children back from socialization and interaction with peers and from participating in classroom activities from an early age. Thus, parents, school psychologists, and educators should monitor the interactions of these children with their peers and encourage their involvement in daily home and school activities. When they grow older, they may more or less adapt to others' attitudes toward them. In the meantime, they may be more mature in coping with their fears and anxiety. One explanation of why older children with MR reported more fears and anxiety may be that the cognitive level of younger children (at age 10 or under) with MIMR may have delayed their cognitive processing of imaginary things, concept of danger and death, and teasing from others, suggesting that they may not worry about what they do not comprehend.

Li's (2004) results indicate that older male students with MIMR and male students with MIMR may experience more specific fears than their female and younger counterparts in the same group. Due to their limited cognitive functioning, these students may find it hard not only to understand their environment but also to express their emotions and feelings even if they experience a lot of fears and have a lot of worries. Teachers, paraprofessionals, and parents should try to help these students understand some abstract concepts using different ways and help them identify their emotions and express them properly.

Third, there are gender differences in the reported fears and related anxieties. The studies reviewed almost uniformly reported that girls had more fears and higher intensity of fears and anxiety. The unknown and minor injury and small animals are the two major factors that girls are mostly afraid of. These findings are consistent with those obtained from studies involving "regular" children both within the United States and across the borders. One explanation for this result may be that girls are more protected by adults than their male counterparts, and that it is more acceptable for girls to express and show their fears and anxieties. Boys are expected to be brave, eventually they may have fewer fears and feel reluctant to openly express or report them.

With this confirming result, more effort should be made to see what educators and parents should do to not overprotect girls with a disability, and what professionals and parents should do to help them overcome their fears and anxieties.

Fourth, the most common fears in children having a disability were found to be mostly in the fear of danger and death factor and the unknown factor. To compare with non-disabled children, children having a disability did not report fear of failing a test, having parents argue, and getting poor grades. These items are all in the fear of failure and criticism factor. More exploration should be conducted to examine the role of lacking fear of failure and criticism in children having a disability in their motivation to overcome their disability and achieve their potential.

Fifth, with the review of the literature, it is noted that different accommodations as well as formats were used in administering the assessment instruments to students having a disability. Some studies administered the instruments in group formats and some in individual formats. Furthermore, some studies indicated variations of administration whereas others did not. There is a great lack of uniformity in administration procedures; the different procedures/standards of administration may make result comparison and generalization very difficult. Thus, more effort should be made to standardize the administration process to the handicapped population. Interrater agreement can be examined among parents, teachers, and children using the same survey instruments.

Sixth, one thing observed in the methodology section is the description of participants, especially in studies involving children and adolescents with mental retardation. Some studies provided cognitive functioning level of participants and others did not. This may raise the issues of whether the participants had the cognitive ability to fully understand what they were asked about and whether they could choose their answers in a valid and reliable manner, which could directly affect the validity of research findings. In addition, many studies did not specify the different subtypes of a disability. Take learning disability as an example: Authors did not differentiate reading, writing, or math disabilities. For studies with hearing and visual impairment, few studies have specified the degree of impairment. Furthermore, studies on children with mental retardation have used different terms for their participants, for example, "mental retardation," "developmental disability," "intellectual disability," and "mild mental retardation." Readers may get confused by such variations. Thus, a more uniform name for this group of children and adolescents is preferred.

Few studies provided information on the comparability of participants in terms of age, gender, and disability and control groups. Because the participants were not randomly selected, it is deemed crucial to provide such necessary information to inform readers potential errors and biases in the results.

Seventh, almost all the studies reviewed in this article employed self-report measures of fears and related anxieties, even in children as young as 2.5 years of age. Self-report is a subjective and indirect way to determine the existence of fears and related anxieties. It requires the individual to reflect back on his or her inner world—his or her experience, thoughts, and expectations. A child's ability to read and understand the items directly affects the validity of the responses. Furthermore, young children having a disability, especially mental retardation and autism, may have a difficult time reflecting back on their inner world—their experience, thoughts, expectations, and fears and related anxieties. This may adversely affect the validity of responses. An abstract concept, such as "worry," may be hard for younger handicapped children to understand. In responding to the questionnaires, children and youths are more likely to underestimate/underreport anxiety in order to present a more favorable evaluation of themselves. Moreover, when an adult helps the child to read and explains the items, the adult's expectation of the child may set up a bias that will influence the validity of the result. Gullone (1996) recommended observational method as an alternative, although she indicated a great lack of research given the difficulty of observing fears for a wide range of stimuli. Thus, instruments that can examine fears and related anxieties in children in a more concrete and valid manner should be investigated.

Next, very few studies have focused their attention on fears and related anxieties in preschool children. Literature suggests that younger children tend to manifest their fears and anxieties as behavior problems, and parents, educators, and mental health professionals also tend to treat overt problems as behavior problems and seldom explore the underlying anxieties. More studies should be done in preschool children for early intervention and prevention purposes.

Finally, if we say that there is a serious shortage in the number of studies assessing fears and related anxieties in individuals having a disability, there is even a greater paucity of research on the intervention part. A search of the literature found very few research articles on treatment of fears and anxieties in children with a disability, with two thirds of them conducted in England mainly using psychoanalytical strategies, which may not be very practical for schoolchildren.

## REFERENCES

American Psychiatric Association. (1994). *Diagnostic and statistical manual of mental disorders* (4th ed.). Washington, DC: Author.

Barrios, B. A., & Hartman, D. P. (1997). Fears and anxieties. In E. J. Mash & L. G. Terdal (Eds.), *Assessment of childhood disorders* (pp. 230–237). New York: Guilford.

Beidel, D. C., Turner, S. M., Hamlin, K., & Morris, T. L. (2000). The Social Phobia and Anxiety Inventory for Children (SPAI–C): External and discriminative validity. *Behavior Therapy, 31*, 75–87.

Blum, R. W. (1992). Chronic illness and disability in adolescence. *Journal of Adolescent Health, 13*, 364–368.

Derevensky, J. L. (1979). Children's fears: A developmental comparison of normal and exceptional children. *The Journal of Genetic Psychology, 135*, 11–21.

Dong, Q., Yang, B., & Ollendick, T. H. (1994). Fears in Chinese children and adolescents and their relations to anxiety and depression. *Journal of Child Psychology & Psychiatry, 35*, 351–362.

Duff, R., La Rocca, J., Lizzet, A., Martin, P., Pearce, L., Williams, M., & Peck, C. (1981). A comparison of the fears of mildly retarded adults with children of their mental age and chronological age matched controls. *Journal of Behavioral Therapy and Experimental Psychiatry, 12*, 121–124.

Fisher, B. L., Allen, R., & Kose, G. (1996). The relationship between anxiety and problem-solving skills in children with and without learning disabilities. *Journal of Learning Disabilities, 29*, 439–446.

Graziano, A. M. (1975). Reduction of children's fears. In A. M. Graziano (Ed.), *Behavior therapy with children, Vol. 2* (pp. 283–290). Chicago: Aldine.

Guarnaccia, V. J., & Weiss, R. L. (1974). Factor structure of fears in the mentally retarded. *Journal of Clinical Psychology, 30*, 540–544.

Gullone, E. (1996). Normal fears in people with a physical or intellectual disability. *Clinical Psychology Review, 16*, 689–706.

Gullone, E., Cummins, R. A., & King, N. J. (1995). Adaptive behaviour in children and adolescents with and without an intellectual disability: Relationship with fear and anxiety. *Behaviour Change, 12*, 227–237.

Gullone, E., Cummins, R. A., & King, N. J. (1996). Self-reported fears: A comparison study of youths with and without an intellectual disability. *Journal of Intellectual Disability Research, 40*, 227–240.

Hardy, R. E. (1968). A study of manifest anxiety among blind residential school students. *New Outlook for the Blind, 62,* 173–180.

Kim, J. A., Szatmari, P., Bryson, S. E., Streiner, D. L., & Wilson, F. J. (2000). The prevalence of anxiety and mood problems among children with autism and Asperger syndrome. *Autism, 4,* 117–132.

King, J. J., Gullone, E., & Ollendick, T. H. (1990). Fears in children and adolescents with chronic medical conditions. *Journal of Clinical Child Psychology, 19,* 173–177.

King, J. J., Gullone, E., & Stafford, C. (1990). Fears in visually impaired and normally-sighted children and adolescents. *Journal of School Psychology, 28,* 225–231.

King, N. J., Josephs, A., Gullone, E., Madden, C., & Ollendick, T. H. (1994). Assessing the fears of children with disability using the Revised Fear Survey Schedule for Children: A comparative study. *British Journal of Medical Psychology, 67,* 377–386.

King, N. J., Mulhall, J., & Gullone, E. (1989). Fears in hearing impaired and normally hearing children and adolescent fears. *Behaviour Research and Therapy, 27,* 577–580.

King, J. J., & Ollendick, T. H. (1989). Children's anxiety and phobic disorders in school settings: Classification, assessment, and intervention issues. *Review of Educational Research, 59,* 431–470.

Knapp, L. G., Barrett, R. P., Groden, G., & Groden, J. (1992). The nature and prevalence of fears in developmentally disabled children and adolescents: A preliminary investigation. *Journal of Developmental and Physical Disabilities, 4,* 195–203.

La Greca, A. M., & Stone, W. L (1990). LD status and achievement: Confounding variables in the study of children's social status, self-esteem, and behavioral functioning. *Journal of Learning Disabilities, 23,* 483–490.

Lee, P. W. H., Lieh-Mak, F., Hung, B. K. M., & Luk, S. L. (1983). Death anxiety in leukemic Chinese children. *International Journal of Psychiatry in Medicine, 13,* 281–289.

Li, H. (2004). Fears and related anxieties in children having a disability. *Dissertation Abstracts International Section A: Humanities Social Science, 64,* 3190.

Margalit, M., & Raviv, A. (1984). LD's expressions of anxiety in terms of minor somatic complaints. *Journal of Learning Disabilities, 17,* 226–228.

Matson, J. L., & Love, S. R. (1990). A comparison of parent-reported fear for autistic and nonhandicapped age-matched children and youth. *Australia and New Zealand Journal of Developmental Disabilities, 16,* 349–357.

Matson, J. L., Manikam, R., Heinze, A., & Kapperman, G. (1986). Anxiety in visually handicapped children and youth. *Journal of Clinical Child Psychology, 15,* 356–359.

Morris, R. J., & Kratochwill, T. R. (1983). *Treating children's fears and phobias: A behavioral approach.* New York: Pergamon Press.

Morris, R. J., & Kratochwill, T. R. (1998). Childhood fears and phobias. In R. J. Morris & T. R. Kratochwill (Eds.), *The practice of child therapy* (3rd ed., pp. 91–131). Boston: Allyn & Bacon.

Newcomer, P. L., & Barenbaum, E. (1995). Depression and anxiety in children and adolescents with learning disabilities, conduct disorders, and no disabilities. *Journal of Emotional & Behavioral Disorders, 3,* 27–49.

Ollendick, T. H. (1983). Reliability and validity of the Revised Fear Survey Schedule for Children (FSSC–R). *Behavioral Research Therapy, 21,* 685–692.

Ollendick, T. H., & King, N. J. (1991). Origins of childhood fears: An evaluation of Rachman's theory of fear acquisition. *Behaviour Research & Therapy, 29,* 117–123.

Ollendick, T. H., Matson, J. L., & Helsel, W. J. (1985a). Fears in children and adolescents: Normative data. *Behavior Research Therapy, 23,* 465–467.

Ollendick, T. H., Matson, J. L., & Helsel, W. J. (1985b). Fears in visually-impaired and normally-sighted youths. *Behavioural Research and Therapy, 23,* 375–378.

Ollendick, T. H., Yang, B., King, N. J., Dong, Q., & Akande, A. (1996). Fears in American, Australian, Chinese, and Nigerian children and adolescents: A cross-cultural study. *Journal of Child Psychology and Psychiatry, 37,* 213–220.

Orenstein, M. (2000). *Smart but stuck: What every therapist needs to know about learning disabilities and imprisoned intelligence.* Binghamton, NY: Haworth Press.

Paget, K. D., & Reynolds, C. R. (1984). Dimensions, levels and reliabilities on the revised children's manifest anxiety scale with learning disabled children. *Journal of Learning Disabilities, 17,* 137–141.

Pattern, M. D. (1983). Relationships between self-esteem, anxiety, and achievement in young learning disabled students. *Journal of Learning Disabilities, 16,* 43–45.

Pintner, R., & Brunschwig, L. (1937). A study of certain fears and wishes among deaf and hearing children. *The Journal of Educational Psychology,* 259–270.

Ramirez, S. Z., & Kratochwill, T. R. (1997). Self-reported fears in children with and without mental retardation. *Mental Retardation, 35,* 83–92.

Rodriguez, C. M., & Routh, D. K. (1989). Depression, anxiety, and attributional style in learning-disabled and non-learning-disabled children. *Journal of Clinical Child Psychology, 18,* 299–304.

Spinetta, J. J., Rigler, D., & Karon, M. (1973). Anxiety in the dying child. *Pediatrics, 52,* 841–845.

Stein, P. A., & Hoover, J. H. (1989). Manifest anxiety in children with learning disabilities. *Journal of Learning Disabilities, 22,* 66, 71.

Thomas, A. (1979). Learned helplessness and expectance factors: Implications for research in learning disabilities. *Review of Educational Research, 49,* 208–221.

Vandenberg, B. (1993). Fears of normal and retarded children. *Psychological Reports, 72,* 473–474.

Wenar, C. (1990). Childhood fears and phobias, In M. Lewis & S. Miller (Eds.), *Handbook of developmental psychopathology* (pp. 281–292). New York: Plenum.

Wiemer, S. A., & Kratochwill, T. R. (1991). *Fears of visually impaired children. Journal of Visual Impairment & Blindness, 85,* 118–124.

Wilhelm, J. G. (1989). Fear and anxiety in low vision and totally blind children. *Education of the Visually Handicapped, 20,* 163–172.

# 10

# School Bullying and Victimization of Children With Disabilities

Árni Víkingur Sveinsson and Richard J. Morris

School aggression and violence is a documented problem in many countries around the world (e.g., Goldstein, 1996; Pellegrini, Bartini, & Brooks, 1999; Smith & Morita, 1999). The problem appears particularly serious in the United States, where extensive accounts of school violence have been documented over the last decade (e.g., DeVoe et al., 2003; Gable, Hendrickson, & Sasso, 1995; Goldstein, 1994; Goldstein, Harootunian, & Conoley, 1994).

School violence has traditionally been defined as acts of assault, theft, and vandalism (Batsche & Knoff, 1994; Morrison, Furlong, & Morrison, 1997). These behaviors are easily observed and documented, and directly responded to with disciplinary actions at the school level or referrals to the juridical system. Preventive efforts have involved strict weapon policies, metal detectors, and presence of law enforcement on school campuses (Bemark & Keys, 2000). Less obvious forms of student aggression have for the most part received little attention from educators and policymakers (e.g., Goldstein et al., 1994; Morrison et al., 1997) until very recently where 15 states have now passed laws addressing bullying and/or harassment in public schools (Limber & Small, 2003). Emerging research on childhood aggression and victimization has indicated that such "softer" forms of student aggression have serious negative impact on children's development and social adjustment (e.g., Boulton & Underwood, 1992; Kochenderfer & Ladd, 1996, 1997, 2001; Kupersmidt & Coie, 1990; Perry, Kusel, & Perry, 1988; Swearer, Song, Cary, Eagle, & Mickelson, 2001), and are a risk factor for future criminal behavior of the perpetrators (e.g., Olweus, 1991; Patterson, Reid, & Dishion, 1992; Walker, Colvin, & Ramsey, 1995).

Bullying, which is a subcategory of aggressive behavior (Dodge & Coie, 1987; Smith & Morita, 1999), is one such form of aggression that occurs frequently in the school setting (Hoover, Oliver, & Hazler, 1992; Nansel et al., 2001; Olweus, 1992). It has been described in historical accounts and literary work dating back to the 18th century (Ross, 2003), and the word has been used freely in popular publications, where its common meaning appears to be well understood by the general public. However, there appears to be no one standard definition of bullying in either the research literature (e.g., Arora, 1996; Farrington, 1993; Harachi, Catalano, & Hawkins, 1999) or emerging legislations on school bullying (Limber & Small, 2003). The most commonly used definition appears to be that of Olweus (1999b), who defines bullying as a repeated exposure to negative acts by one or more students, consisting of intentional aggression repeated over time (as opposed to one incident) and within a context of a disproportionate power relationship. Bullying can therefore be a particularly vicious form of aggression because the behavior is directed repeatedly toward a particular victim. Research findings do indeed indicate that aggressive children selectively target a minority of victimized children while leaving other children alone (e.g., Dodge, Coie, Pettit, & Price, 1990; Olweus, 1978; Perry et al., 1988).

In this chapter we discuss school bullying as it relates to victimization of children who have disabilities. Specifically, we briefly review school bullying research, explore current models that attempt to explain bullying behavior, and discuss current knowledge regarding bullying in disabled populations of school children.

## REVIEW OF SCHOOL BULLYING LITERATURE

Although literary works and historical accounts indicate school bullying to have been in our schools for centuries (e.g., Ross, 2003), it is only in the last 30 years that bullying has been subjected to systematic study. The main body of research originates in Sweden and Norway, where Olweus (1978, 1991, 1993) conducted several studies addressing prevalence and various characteristics of bullying, as well as efficacy of interventions for school bullying. The results and following publications generated interest in the study of bullying, and, together with an European conference on the issue in Norway in 1987 (Smith & Brain, 2000), stimulated discussion and research on bullying in a number of different countries in the late 1980s and early 1990s (e.g., Bentley & Li, 1995; Boulton & Underwood, 1992; Genta, Menesini, Fonzi, Costabile, & Smith, 1996; Hoover et al., 1992; Rigby & Slee, 1991). However, it is only within the last few years that interest in the study of bullying has become prevalent in the United States, where the majority of research studies were published after 1998.

Emerging international research has documented bullying to be a substantial problem within different school systems and seemingly independent of country or culture. Although most studies report prevalence rates between 15% and 30%, there has been considerable variation between different countries, with rates of bullying (i.e., being victimized by bullies) ranging from 8% in Norway (Olweus, 1993) to 77% to 78% in the United States (Crockett, 2003; Hoover et al., 1992). Cultural, linguistic, and environmental variables are likely to account for some of this large variance (see, e.g., Smith, Cowie, Ólafsson, & Liefooghe, 2002); however, a range of up to 70% is likely to indicate inconsistency in conceptualization and assessment methods in bullying research. Such concerns have indeed been raised in the literature, in particular regarding definitions (e.g., Arora, 1996; Ross, 2003) and lack of care with assessment and psychometric principles (Farrington, 1993; Sveinsson & Morris, in press).

The vast majority of bullying research has used self-reports to establish prevalence and to explore other demographics of bullying. The most commonly used self-report has been a translated and/or adopted versions of the *Olweus Bully/Victim Questionnaire* (e.g., Genta et al, 1996; O'Moore, Kirkham, & Smith, 1997; Tomás de Almeida, 1999; Whitney & Smith, 1993). There appears to be little published data regarding established reliability or validity of this instrument, where available information appears limited to the Norwegian version of the *Olweus Bully/Victim Questionnaire* (Olweus, 1991; Solberg & Olweus, 2003) For example, studies translating and modifying the Olweus's *Bully/Victim Questionnaire* for first-time use generally do not report any reliability procedures for the modified version (e.g., Borg, 1999; Genta et al., 1996; Olafsen & Viemerö, 2000; Tomás de Almeida, 1999). Hence, the majority of the available data on bullying appears to be based on an instrument for which basic psychometric properties may be lacking in its respective application (i.e., assessment outside of Norway).

In summary, much of bullying research appears to have overlooked the importance of methodological issues, rendering comparison between studies difficult, and generating spuriously high variance in prevalence rates. Furthermore, in spite of recent increase of interest in bullying and proliferation of new publications on the topic, attention to conceptual and methodological issues has remained negligible. For example, in an introductory article to a recent issue of *School Psychology Review* dedicated to bullying, Espelage and Swearer (2003) provided a review of the literature and ideas for future directions, but without addressing apparent inconsistencies in regards to prevalence, or the methodological problems in current methods of assessment (see, e.g., Farrington, 1993; Sveinsson & Morris, in press).

## Theoretical Frameworks Regarding Bullying

Consistent with shaping the groundwork in bullying research, Olweus's conceptual framework has guided much of the literature to date. The initial model (Olweus, 1978) postulated special individual characteristics that predisposed students to become bullies or victims, which would then be shaped by their family environment, group climate (i.e., reactions and behaviors in the peer group), and the school setting (i.e., class composition, school size, teacher's approach). Olweus (1984) has since increased the importance of personality traits or individual differences in his model, where bullies were "characterized by an aggressive personality pattern, with a tendency to react aggressively in many different situations, with fairly weak controls or inhibitions against aggressive tendencies, and with a positive attitude to violence" (p. 67).

Similarly, victims were postulated to have certain characteristics that contributed to peer rejection, which in turn would make them vulnerable to bullying. Specifically, these characteristics included sensitivity and anxiousness, lack of assertiveness, insecurity, low self-esteem, and isolation among peers, which were often in combination with relative physical weakness (Olweus, 1978, 1984, 1999b). However, situational factors were acknowledged to have a role in determining if a child would become a victim, such as whether the peer group included a potential bully or not. Furthermore, the data from the Swedish studies showed incidents of other students than bullies taking part in bullying, and Olweus has acknowledged that "social psychological mechanisms" are also relevant. Since then, two decades of research have indeed confirmed that bullying is not always a dyad between a bully and a victim, but often a group process (e.g., Grotpeter & Crick, 1996; Lagerspetz, Björkqvist, Berts, & King, 1982; Ólafsson, Ólafsson, & Björnsson, 1999; O'Moore et al., 1997; Salmivalli, Huttunen, & Lagerspetz, 1997; Smith & Shu, 2000).

While acknowledging Olweus's model as a strong foundation for understanding bullying, Craig and Pepler (1997) held that perspectives limited to personality and social-interactional frameworks cannot fully explain bullying behavior. In other words, they argued that bullying is too complex to be explained by individual personality traits, even when some children may indeed have developed a behavioral style consistent with bullies or victims. Rather, bullying must also be considered within an ecological perspective, taking into account the larger peer group and the school social system. Similarly, Swearer and Doll (2001) applied such an ecological perspective to bullying, emphasizing the contributions of peers, teachers, physical characteristics of the school grounds, family factors, and cultural characteristics in addition to the individual characteristics of the child who bullies. Within this ecological framework, both Swearer and Doll (2001) and Craig and Pepler (1997) applied social learning theory to explain peer contributions to bullying. Specifically, Craig and Pepler adopted three contextual processes that have been identified to increase the likelihood of aggression, namely, observing aggression, receiving aggression, and reinforcement of aggression, and postulated that peers are likely to play a role in all three processes during bullying. That is, peers may serve as instigators, models for aggression, and may join in a bullying episode. They may further reinforce the interactions by serving as "an audience for the theatre of bullying" (p. 43). Testing this hypothesis, Craig and Pepler reported that peers were involved in 85% of the bullying episodes observed on the playground, and coded as reinforcing the bullying in 81% of the episodes.

In their follow-up work, O'Connell, Pepler, and Craig (1999) took a more theoretical approach to study the peer processes observed in bullying, adopting a social learning perspective of modeling and reinforcement. Citing Bandura's social learning theory (Bandura, 1977) as the basis of their conceptualization regarding bullying, O'Connell et al. posited that the following conditions are often present during bullying: The model is observed to be powerful, to receive rewards for the behavior, and to share similar characteristics Specifically, the bully represents a powerful figure to peers when observed tormenting a victim, and his or her behavior may often go unpunished. Hence, O'Connell et al. hypothesized that given these modeling conditions, peers may be influenced to actively participate in bullying. In turn, the aggressive behaviors of the bully may be actively or passively reinforced by the peer group's attention and engagement. The role of the peer group as a reinforcing agent has indeed been documented in recent studies that have addressed the larger social context of bullying (e.g., O'Connell et al., 1999; Salmivalli et al., 1997; Salmivalli, Lagerspetz, Björkqvist, Österman, & Kaukiainen, 1996; Sutton & Smith, 1999). In contrast, very little attention has been given to the role of the children who serve as the targets of peers' aggressive acts (Crick & Grotpeter, 1996; Perry et al., 1988). Although the theoretical formulations reviewed here attempt to explain the behavior of the bully and the peer group, there is much less emphasis on explaining victimization: why certain children get repeatedly targeted by bullies.

**Victimization of Children With Disabilities**

Childhood aggression has been the subject of extensive study over the past 30 years (see for reviews Crick & Dodge, 1994; Farrington, 1993; Goldstein & Conoley, 1997), where research findings indicate that aggressive children selectively target a minority of children while leaving other children alone (e.g., Dodge et al., 1990; Olweus, 1978; Perry et al., 1988). At the same time, however, relatively little research is available on children who have been the targets of peer aggression. Furthermore, as discussed in the previous section, attempts to explain bullying and childhood aggression have generally focused on the aggressor. Although this has been the case in Olweus's research and discussions (Olweus, 1978, 1984, 1993, 1999a), he has also reported on the general characteristics of victims. Specifically, Olweus (1999b) described victims as more anxious and insecure than other students, and as generally reacting to aggression by crying and withdrawal. The literature on peer victimization reported similar observations, where children who are repeatedly targeted by peers tend to be submissive and exhibit emotional reactions (e.g., Perry, Williard, & Perry, 1990; Schwartz, Dodge, & Coie, 1993). However, Olweus (1978) noted in his pioneering research in Sweden that victims were not a homogeneous group, and that a small proportion were actively irritating and hot-tempered. Further research has confirmed this distinction, where a minority of victims are now referred to as "aggressive" or "provocative" (e.g., Olweus, 1993, 1996, 1999b; Pellegrini et al., 1999; Schwartz, Dodge, Pettit, & Bates, 1997; Schwartz, Proctor, & Chien, 2001).

Regardless of whether victims react to bullying by submissive or aggressive behaviors, the literature indicates that these children are often socially isolated or have few friends (Perry, Hodges, & Egan, 2001; Olweus, 1999a), even are rejected (Smith, 1999; Wilton, Craig, & Pepler, 2000), and are therefore "easy targets" posing less risk of social consequences for their attackers. In fact, based on their review of the literature on peer relations of victimized children, Hodges and Perry (1999) hypothesized that lack of friends and peer rejection would contribute to victimization over time. Their findings did indeed confirm significant contribution of interpersonal factors (i.e., rejection) to peer victimization, but also highlighted the importance of personal attributes, such as submissive and anxious behaviors, as well as physical weakness.

There is some indication that children with disabilities may be at higher risk for being bullied than their peers. Circumstances or manifestations associated with their disability may involve some of the characteristics that have been identified as risk factors for victimization, such as physical weakness or impaired social relations. For example, a meta-analysis of studies on children with learning disabilities (LD) and social skill deficits (Kavale & Forness, 1996) indicated that almost 80% of students with LD appeared to be rejected by their peers. Furthermore, peer ratings showed LD students had lower social status and were less popular, not as competent in communication, and not as cooperative. Similarly, in a study addressing attitudes and behavior of children toward peers with disabilities, Roberts and Smith (1999) reported that 47% of non-disabled children indicated they spent no time at all with classmates with disabilities, a finding the authors stated was "not uncommon in the inclusion literature" (p. 43). Placement in self-contained classes is furthermore likely to result in lack of opportunities for socialization with the general student population, and thus further increase the risk of social isolation.

The visibility of a disability may also present different risk factors, such as stereotypical generalizations and "stigma." For example, based on a series of international studies on children's views and social preference toward peers with visible physical differences, Harper (1999) reported that physical or observable differences appeared to be a factor in social acceptance. Specifically, the more limiting the disability, the more peers tended to avoid interaction with children who had those disabilities.

With respect to the relationship between children having disabilities and being victims of bullying, a small body of research has been emerging from the United Kingdom (e.g., Marini, Fairbairn, & Zuber, 2001; Mishna, 2003). For example, Whitney, Smith, and Thompson (1994) interviewed 186 children from eight schools, of whom 93 had special needs based on mild or moderate learning disabilities, hearing impairments, visual impairments, or physical disabilities. The two groups were matched in terms of age, gender, ethnicity and grade, where 37 pairs were drawn from primary schools and 56 pairs from secondary schools. The authors found a significant difference between the two groups, where almost two-thirds of the children with special needs reported being bullied, compared to roughly a quarter of the children from the general student population. The difference was greater for secondary schools, where the prevalence of victimization in the general population dropped significantly from primary (46%) to secondary schools (16%), while prevalence rates remained similar (around 60%) for students with special needs across primary and secondary schools. Children with special needs also reported bullying others more frequently; however, most reported that they were also bullied by others. The rate of reported victimization varied considerably based on disability, where students with hearing impairments and moderate learning disabilities reported higher rates than, for example, students with visual impairments or physical disabilities.

A component of a longitudinal survey of health and behavior of children and adolescents in Scottish schools compared rates of bullying and/or teasing in a sample of 2,586 primary school children with an average age of about 11 years (Sweeting & West, 2001). The study reported that children with disabilities, as well as those with conditions of serious or more limiting illness, were significantly more likely to experience frequent victimization. Specifically, 39% of children with speech difficulties and 30% of those with reading difficulties were teased/bullied weekly or more often, compared to around 15% of the general population. The rate was lower for students with hearing difficulties (22.4%) and not significantly different from that of the general population, which shows lack of correspondence with the findings of Whitney et al. (1994) above.

Doren, Bullis, and Benz (1996) explored predictors of victimization among high school students with disabilities that included learning disabilities, mental retardation, serious emotional disturbance, speech–language impairments, hearing impairments, visual impairments, orthopedic impairments, and other health impairments. The findings indicated that 54% of the sample ($n = 408$) had experienced victimization at one time or another during their school years. Further analysis of risk factors revealed that students with serious emotional disturbance were more likely to experience victimization than any other disability group, in particular if they demonstrated low interpersonal skills.

Dawkins (1996) compared a group of children ($n = 46$) with visible physical disabilities (e.g., cerebral palsy, spina bifida, muscular dystrophy) with a control group ($n = 57$) having nonvisible health conditions (e.g., asthma, abdominal pains, headaches). Participants completed the Olweus Bully/Victim Questionnaire, where 30% of the physically disabled children reported being bullied "sometimes or more often" compared to 14% of the controls. In a similar vein, comparison of children with hemiplegia to matched controls in primary schools in the United Kingdom indicated that these children were three times as likely to be victimized (Yude, Goodman, & McConachie, 1998).

Nabuzoka and Smith (1993) studied bullying and victimization among 179 primary school children in the United Kingdom, of whom 36 had been diagnosed with learning disabilities (LD). Each child was individually administered a peer nomination measure, where significantly more children with LD (33.3%) were nominated as victims of bullying when compared to their non-LD peers (7.7%). Sabornie (1994) reported similar findings for students with learning disabilities in the United States, where a sample of 38 LD students was matched with non-LD controls in grades 6 and 7, and responded to two questions addressing victimization. Comparison of the two groups revealed that LD students reported significantly more victimization than their controls. Likewise, a survey of high school students' experiences of school violence and feelings of safety (Morrison, Furlong, & Smith, 1994) found that students in a special day class (all identified as having a severe learning disability) experienced bullying at a higher rate than any of the other comparison groups (i.e., regular education, opportunity, or leadership classes).

However, using peer nominations to identify victims and bullies in a sample of children with learning disabilities ($n = 28$) and children in regular education ($n = 113$) from fifth grade in two Finnish schools, Kaukiainen et al. (2002) did not confirm their hypothesis of more frequent victimization among the children with learning disabilities, but found significantly more bullies in this group. Nabuzoka (2003) reported similar trends, where teacher ratings of 121 primary school children in the United Kingdom identified children with learning disabilities more often as bullies, but at the same time, also as victims. However, when teacher and peer nominations were combined, children with LD were measured as victims of bullying significantly more often than non-LD children.

There appears to be only one published study that has directly addressed bullying in the context of children with speech/language impairments (SLI). Knox and Conti-Ramsden (2003) compared two groups of SLI students receiving varying levels of special services ($n = 48$; $n = 46$) with a group of non-special education students ($n = 50$) in primary schools in the United Kingdom. Victimization was assessed by a self-report, where 36% of students with SLI perceived themselves to be at risk of being bullied compared to 12% of the non-disabled students. Student placement (i.e., level of service) did not seem to affect the risk of being bullied, where comparison of victimization for the two SLI groups did not yield statistical significance.

In summary, the research that has been published in this area indicates a higher risk of victimization for children who have a disability when compared to their non-disabled peers. However, the degree to which having a disability increases the risk of victimization remains unclear, as reported rates of victimization tend to vary from one study to another. In addition, little is known in regard to whether children having a particular disability have a higher likelihood of being bullied. In fact, of the relatively few published studies addressing victimization across several disability categories (e.g., Doren, Bullis, & Benz, 1996; Sweeting & West, 2001; Whitney et al., 1994), findings were inconsistent in regard to which children's disability presented the highest risk for victimization. These discrepancies appear to be the result of the use of different study designs, where studies varied by type of disability being investigated, sample size, and age of the participating children. In addition, assessment methods varied by informant source, with some studies using self-reports (e.g., Dawkins, 1996; Knox & Conti-Ramsden, 2003), whereas others used structured interviews (e.g., Whitney et al., 1994), or peer nominations (e.g., Kaukiainen et al., 2002; Nabuzoka, 2003), where most of these methods involved nonvalidated assessment instruments.

## CONCLUSIONS AND FUTURE DIRECTIONS FOR RESEARCH

There has been a tremendous increase over the past 20 years, in bullying related research and related scholarship, which have documented school bullying to be a substantial problem regardless of countries or cultures. However, research findings have not been consistent, in particular regarding prevalence rates, where it appears that much of bullying research has not devoted adequate attention to methodological concerns (Sveinsson & Morris, in press).

The research on bullying has for the most part been guided by the framework of Olweus (1978, 1984, 1999b), who postulated that special personality traits predisposed individuals to become bullies, and that victims had certain characteristics that increased their risk of being bullied. It is only with the increasing research in recent years that alternative viewpoints have begun to emerge, where, for example, researchers have applied ecological perspectives (e.g., Craig & Pepler, 1997; Swearer & Doll, 2001) to explain bullying behavior. Specifically, these frameworks emphasize the contributions of the larger peer group and the school social system, applying social learning theory to explain the role of peers as participants and reinforcers of bullying behavior. However, these frameworks do not specifically address why bullies selectively and repeatedly target certain children while leaving other children alone.

Studies that have addressed bullying in the context of children's disabilities generally indicate that a child who has a disability is more likely to be a target of school bullying than his or her non-disabled peers. However, a few studies have reported inconsistent findings (e.g., Kaukiainen et al., 2002), and current research in this area remains limited to about dozen studies from only three countries. In addition, studies on bullying and disability show considerable variation in regards to methodology used and disability under study, making comparisons between these studies difficult. Hence, there appear to be a number of areas regarding bullying and disability that call for further research. First, more comparison studies are needed to confirm whether children with disabilities are indeed more likely to be victimized by school bullies, and to explore whether such risk factors are consistent across countries and cultures.

Second, similar to the general bullying literature, this area of research seems to have devoted limited attention to methodological and psychometric issues. Future research in this area should select psychometrically sound assessment instruments, and use study designs that maximize the replicability of the research findings.

Only a handful of studies have specifically addressed whether any given disability places children at a higher risk for bullying. Furthermore, the findings from these studies have been inconsistent where the risk of victimization associated with different disabilities varies from one study to another (e.g., Sweeting & West, 2001; Whitney et al., 1994). The first author is currently conducting a study that specifically addresses this question in a population of Hispanic students in the southwestern United States. Specifically, self-reported levels of victimization are being compared between students with specific learning disabilities, speech-language impairments, emotional disabilities, mild mental retardation, hearing impairments, orthopedic impairments, and students who do not have a disability. This appears to be the first study in the United States attempting to compare rates of bullying across various disability categories, indicating a critical need for additional research in this area.

Although there has been a considerable increase in bullying research over the past several years, our knowledge regarding victimization of children with disabilities appears to be limited to about dozen studies, most of which were conducted outside the United States. There is thus a tremendous opportunity for future research in this area, which, in the light of recent proliferation of bullying research, is likely to flourish and continue to advance our understanding regarding bullying and victimization in populations of children with disabilities.

## REFERENCES

Arora, C. M. J. (1996). Defining bullying: Towards a clearer general understanding an more effective intervention strategies. *School Psychology International, 17,* 317–329.

Bandura, A. (1977). *Social learning theory.* Englewood Cliffs, NJ: Prentice Hall.

Batsche, G. M., & Knoff, H. M. (1994). Bullies and their victims: Understanding a pervasive problem in the schools. *School Psychology Review, 23,* 165–174.

Bemark, F., & Keys, S. (2000). *Violent and aggressive youth: Intervention and prevention strategies for changing times.* Thousand Oaks, CA: Corwin Press.

Bentley, K. M., & Li, A. K. F. (1995). Bully and victim problems in elementary schools and students' beliefs about aggression. *Canadian Journal of School Psychology, 11,* 153–165.

Borg, M. G. (1999). The extent and nature of bullying among primary and secondary schoolchildren. *Educational Research, 41,* 137–153.

Boulton, M. J., & Underwood, K. (1992). Bully/victim problems among middle school children. *British Journal of Educational Psychology, 62,* 73–87.

Craig, W. M., & Pepler, D. J. (1997). Observations of bullying and victimization on the school yard. *Canadian Journal of School Psychology, 2,* 41–60.

Crick, N. R., & Dodge, K. A. (1994). A review and reformulation of social information-processing mechanisms in children's social adjustment. *Psychological Bulletin, 115,* 74–101.

Crick, N. R., & Grotpeter, J. K. (1996). Children's treatment by peers: Victims of relational and overt aggression. *Development and Psychopathology, 8,* 367–380.

Crockett, D. (2003). Critical issues children face in the 2000s. *School Psychology Quarterly, 18,* 446–453.

Dawkins, J. L. (1996). Bullying, physical disability, and the pediatric patient. *Developmental Medicine and Child Neurology, 38,* 603–612.

DeVoe, J. F., Peter, K., Kaufman, P., Rudy, S. A., Miller, A. K., Planty, M., Snyder, T. D., & Rand, M. R. (2003). *Indicators of school crime and safety.* Washington DC: Departments of Education and Justice.

Dodge, K. A., & Coie, J. D. (1987). Social-information-processing factors in reactive and proactive aggression in children's peer groups. *Journal of Personality and Social Psychology, 53,* 1146–1158.

Dodge, K. A., Coie, J. D., Pettit, G. S., & Price, J. M. (1990). Peer status and aggression in boys' groups: Developmental and contextual analyses. *Child Development, 61,* 1289–1309.

Doren, B., Bullis, M., & Benz, M. R. (1996). Predictors of victimization experiences of adolescents with disabilities in transition. *Exceptional Children, 63,* 7–18.

Espelage, D. L., & Swearer, S. M. (2003). Research on school bullying and victimization: What we have learned and where do we go from here? *School Psychology Review, 32,* 365–383.

Farrington, D. P. (1993). Understanding and preventing bullying. In M. Tonry (Vol. Ed.), *Crime and justice: Vol. 17. A review of research* (pp. 381–458). Chicago: The University of Chicago Press.

Gable, R. A., Hendrickson, J. M., & Sasso, G. M. (1995). Toward a more functional analysis of aggression. *Education and Treatment of Children, 18,* 226–242.

Genta, M. L., Menesini, E., Fonzi, A., Costabile, A., & Smith, P. K. (1996). Bullies and victims in schools in central and southern Italy. *European Journal of Psychology of Education, 11,* 97–110.

Goldstein, A. P. (1994). *The ecology of aggression.* New York: Plenum Press.

Goldstein, A. P. (1996). *Violence in America: Lessons on understanding the aggression in our lives.* Palo Alto, CA: Davies-Black.

Goldstein, A. P., & Conoley, J. C. (Eds.). (1997). *School violence intervention: A practical handbook* (pp. 236–264). New York: Guilford Press.

Goldstein, A. P., Harootunian, B., & Conoley, J. C. (1994). *Student aggression: Prevention, management, and replacement training.* New York: Guilford Press.

Grotpeter, J. K., & Crick, N. R. (1996). Relational aggression, overt aggression, and friendship. *Child Development, 67,* 2328–2338.

Harachi, T. W., Catalano, R. F., & Hawkins, J. D. (1999). United States. In P. K. Smith, Y. Morita, J. Junger-Tas, D. Olweus, R. Catalano, & P. Slee (Eds.), *The nature of school bullying: A cross-national perspective* (pp. 279–295). New York: Routledge.

Harper, D. C. (1999). Social psychology of difference: Stigma, spread, and stereotypes in childhood. *Rehabilitation Psychology, 44,* 131–144.

Hodges, E. V. E., & Perry, D. G. (1999). Personal and interpersonal antecedents and consequences of victimization by peers. *Journal of Personality and Social Psychology, 76,* 677–695.

Hoover, J. H., Oliver, R., & Hazler, R. J. (1992). Bullying: Perceptions of adolescent victims in the Midwestern USA. *School Psychology International, 13,* 5–16.

Kaukiainen, A., Salmivalli, C., Lagerspetz, K., Tamminen, M., Vauras, M., Mäki, H., & Poskiparta, E. (2002). Learning difficulties, social intelligence, and self-concept: Connections to bully-victim problems. *Scandinavian Journal of Psychology, 43,* 269–278.

Kavale, K. A., & Forness, S. R. (1996). Social skill deficits and learning disabilities: A meta-analysis. *Journal of Learning Disabilities, 29,* 226–237.

Knox, E., & Conti-Ramsden, G. (2003). Bullying risks of 11-year-old children with specific language impairment (SLI): Does school placement matter? *International Journal of Language and Communication Disorders, 38,* 1–12.

Kochenderfer, B. J., & Ladd, G. W. (1996). Peer victimization: Manifestations and relations to school adjustment in Kindergarten. *Journal of School Psychology, 34,* 267–283.

Kochenderfer, B. J., & Ladd, G. W. (1997). Victimized children's responses to peers' aggression: Behaviors associated with reduced versus continued victimization. *Development and Psychopathology, 9,* 59–73.

Kochenderfer Ladd, B., & Ladd, G. W. (2001). Variation in peer victimization: Relations to children's maladjustment. In J. Juvonen, & S. Graham (Eds.), *Peer harassment in school: The plight of the vulnerable and victimized* (pp. 25–48). New York: The Guilford Press.

Kupersmidt, J. B., & Coie, J. D. (1990). Preadolescent peer status, aggression, and school adjustment as predictors of externalizing problems in adolescence. *Child Development, 61,* 1350–1362.

Lagerspetz, K. M., Björkqvist, K., Berts, M., & King, E. (1982). Group aggression among school children in three schools. *Scandinavian Journal of Psychology, 23,* 45–52.

Limber, S. P., & Small, M. A. (2003). State laws and policies to address bullying in schools. *School Psychology Review, 32,* 445–455.

Marini, Z., Fairbairn, L., & Zuber, R. (2001). Peer harassment in individuals with developmental disabilities: Towards the development of a multidimensional bullying identification model. *Developmental Disabilities Bulletin, 29,* 170–195.

Mishna, F. (2003). Learning disabilities and bullying: Double jeopardy. *Journal of Learning Disabilities, 36,* 336–347.

Morrison, G. M., Furlong, M. J., & Smith, G. (1994). Factors associated with the experience of school violence among general education, leadership class, opportunity class, and special day class pupils. *Education and Treatment of Children, 17,* 356–369.

Morrison, G. M., Furlong, M. J., & Morrison, R. L. (1997). The safe school: Moving beyond crime prevention to school empowerment. In A. P. Goldstein & J. C. Conoley (Eds.), *School violence intervention: A practical handbook* (pp. 236–264). New York: Guilford Press.

Nabuzoka, D. (2003). Teacher ratings and peer nominations of bullying and other behaviour of children with and without learning difficulties. *Educational Psychology, 23,* 307–321.

Nabuzoka, D., & Smith, P. K. (1993). Sociometric status and social behaviour of children with and without learning difficulties. *Journal of Child Psychology and Psychiatry and Allied Disciplines 34,* 1435–1448.

Nansel, T. R., Overpeck, M., Pilla, R. S., Ruan, W. J., Simons-Morton, B., & Scheidt, P. (2001). Bullying behaviors among U.S. youth: Prevalence and association with psychosocial adjustment. *Journal of the American Medical Association, 285,* 2094–2100.

O'Connell, P., Pepler, D., & Craig, W. (1999). Peer involvement in bullying: Insights and challenges for intervention. *Journal of Adolescence, 22,* 437–452.

Olafsen, R. N., & Viemerö, V. (2000). Bully/victim problems and coping with stress in school among 10- to 12-year-old pupils in Åland, Finland. *Aggressive Behavior, 26,* 57–65.

Ólafsson, R. F., Ólafsson, R. P., & Björnsson, J. K. (1999). *Umfang og eðli eineltis í íslenskum grunnskólum* [Prevalence and nature of bullying in Icelandic elementary schools]. Available from Rannsóknarstofnun Uppeldis-og Menntamála, Suðurgata 39, 101 Reykjavík, Iceland.

Olweus, D. (1978). *Aggression in the schools: Bullies and whipping boys.* Washington, DC: Hemisphere.

Olweus, D. (1984). Aggressors and their victims: Bullying at school. In N. Frude & H. Gault (Eds.), *Disruptive behavior in schools* (pp. 57–76). New York: John Wiley & Sons.

Olweus, D. (1991). Bully/victim problems among school children: Basic facts and effects of a school based intervention program. In D. J. Pepler & K. H. Rubin (Eds.), *The development and treatment of childhood aggression* (pp. 411–448). Hillsdale, NJ: Lawrence Erlbaum Associates.

Olweus, D. (1992). Bullying among school children: Intervention and prevention. In R. D. Peters, R. J. McMahon, & V. L. Quinsey (Eds.), *Aggression and violence throughout the lifespan* (pp. 100–125). Newburry Park, CA: Sage.

Olweus, D. (1993). *Bullying at school: What we know and what we can do.* Oxford, UK: Blackwell.

Olweus, D. (1996). Bully/victim problems at school: Facts and effective intervention. *Journal of Emotional and Behavioral Problems, 5,* 15–22.

Olweus, D. (1999a). Norway. In P. K. Smith, Y. Morita, J. Junger-Tas, D. Olweus, R. Catalano, & P. Slee (Eds.), *The nature of school bullying: A cross-national perspective* (pp. 28–48). New York: Routledge.

Olweus, D. (1999b). Sweden. In P. K. Smith, Y. Morita, J. Junger-Tas, D. Olweus, R. Catalano, & P. Slee (Eds.), *The nature of school bullying: A cross-national perspective* (pp. 7–27). New York: Routledge.

O'Moore, A. M., Kirkham, C., & Smith, M. (1997). Bullying behavior in Irish schools: A nationwide study. *Irish Journal of Psychology, 18,* 141–169.

Patterson, G. R., Reid, J. B., & Dishion, T. J. (1992). *A social interactional approach: Vol. 4. Antisocial boys.* Eugene, OR: Castalia.

Pellegrini, A. D., Bartini, M., & Brooks, F. (1999). School bullies, victims, and aggressive victims: Factors relating to group affiliation and victimization in early adolescence. *Journal of Educational Psychology, 91,* 216–224.

Perry, D. G., Hodges, E. V. E., & Egan, S. K. (2001). Determinants of chronic victimization by peers: A review and new model of family influence. In J. Juvonen & S. Graham (Eds.), *Peer harassment in school: The plight of the vulnerable and victimized* (pp. 73–104). New York: Guilford Press.

Perry, D. G., Kusel, S. J., & Perry, L. C. (1988). Victims of peer aggression. *Developmental Psychology, 24,* 807–814.

Perry, D. G., Williard, J. C., & Perry, L. C. (1990). Peers' perception of the consequences that victimized children provide aggressors. *Child Development, 61,* 1310–1325.

Rigby, K., & Slee, P. T. (1991). Bullying among Australian school children: Reported behavior and attitudes toward victims. *The Journal of Social Psychology, 131,* 615–627.

Roberts, C. M., & Smith, P. R. (1999). Attitudes and behaviour of children toward peers with disabilities. *International Journal of Disability, Development, and Education, 46,* 35–50.

Ross, D. M. (2003). *Childhood bullying, teasing, and violence: What school personnel, other professionals, and parents can do* (2nd ed.). Alexandria, VA: American Counseling Association.

Sabornie, E. J. (1994). Social-affective characteristics in early adolescents identified as learning disabled and nondisabled. *Learning Disability Quarterly, 17,* 268–279.

Salmivalli, C., Huttunen, A., & Lagerspetz, K. M. (1997). Peer networks and bullying in schools. *Scandinavian Journal of Psychology, 38,* 305–312.

Salmivalli, C., Lagerspetz, K. Björkqvist, K. Österman, K., & Kaukiainen, A. (1996). Bullying as a group process: Participant roles and their relations to social status within the group. *Aggressive Behavior, 22,* 1–15.

Schwartz, D., Dodge, K. A., & Coie, J. D. (1993). The emergence of chronic peer victimization in boys' playgroups. *Child Development, 64,* 1755–1772.

Schwartz, D., Dodge, K. A., Pettit, G. S., & Bates, J. E. (1997). The early socialization of aggressive victims of bullying. *Child Development, 68,* 665–675.

Schwartz, D., Proctor, L. J., & Chien, D. H. (2001). The aggressive victim of bullying: Emotional and behavioral dysregulation as a pathway to victimization by peers. In J. Juvonen & S. Graham (Eds.), *Peer harassment in school: The plight of the vulnerable and victimized* (pp. 147–174). New York: Routledge.

Smith, P. K. (1999). England and Wales. In P. K. Smith, Y. Morita, J. Junger-Tas, D. Olweus, R. Catalano, & P. Slee (Eds.), *The nature of school bullying: A cross-national perspective* (pp. 68–90). New York: Routledge.

Smith, P. K., & Brain, P. (2000). Bullying in schools: Lessons from two decades of research. *Aggressive Behavior, 26,* 1–9.

Smith, P. K., Cowie, H., Ólafsson, R. F., & Liefooghe, A. P. D. (2002). Definitions of bullying: A comparison of terms used, and age and gender differences, in a fourteen-country international comparison. *Child Development, 73,* 1119–1133.

Smith, P. K., & Morita, Y. (1999). Introduction. In P. K. Smith, Y. Morita, J. Junger-Tas, D. Olweus, R. Catalano, & P. Slee (Eds.), *The nature of school bullying: A cross-national perspective* (pp. 1–4). New York: Routledge.

Smith, P. K., & Shu, S. (2000). What good schools can do about bullying: Findings from a survey in English schools after a decade of research and action. *Childhood, 7,* 193–212.

Solberg, M. E., & Olweus, D. (2003). Prevalence estimation of school bullying with the Olweus bully/victim questionnaire. *Aggressive Behavior, 29,* 239–268.

Sutton, J., & Smith, P. K. (1999). Bullying as a group process: An adaptation of the participant role approach. *Aggressive Behavior, 25,* 97–111.

Sveinsson, A. V., & Morris, R. J. (in press). Conceptual and methodological issues in assessment and intervention with school bullies. In M. J. Elias, J. E. Zins, & C. A. Maher (Eds.), *Handbook of prevention and intervention in peer harassment, victimization, and bullying.* New York: Haworth Press, Inc.

Swearer, S. M., & Doll, B. (2001). Bullying in schools: An ecological framework. In R. A. Geffner, M. Loring, & C. Young (Eds.), *Bullying behavior: Current issues, research and interventions* (pp. 7–23). Binghampton NY: The Haworth Press, Inc.

Swearer, S. M., Song, S. Y., Cary, P. T., Eagle, J. W., & Mickelson, W. T. (2001). Psychosocial correlates in bullying and victimization: The relationship between depression, anxiety, and bully/victim status. In R. A. Geffner, M. Loring, & C. Young (Eds.), *Bullying behavior: Current issues, research and interventions* (pp. 95–121). Binghampton, NY: Haworth Press.

Sweeting, H., & West, P. (2001). Being different: Correlates of the experience of teasing and bullying at age 11. *Research Papers in Education, 16,* 225–246.

Tomás de Almeida, A. M. (1999). Portugal. In P. K. Smith, Y. Morita, J. Junger-Tas, D. Olweus, R. Catalano, & P. Slee (Eds.), *The nature of school bullying: A cross-national perspective* (pp. 174–186). New York: Routledge.

Walker, H. M., Colvin, G., & Ramsey, E. (1995). *Antisocial behavior in school: Strategies and best practices.* San Francisco: Brooks/Cole.

Whitney, I., & Smith, P. K. (1993). A survey of the nature and extent of bullying in junior/middle and secondary schools. *Educational Research, 35,* 3–25.

Whitney, I., Smith, P. K., & Thompson, D. (1994). Bullying and children with special educational needs. In P. K. Smith & S. Sharp (Eds.), *School bullying: Insights and perspectives* (pp. 213–240). New York: Routledge.

Wilton, M. M. M., Craig, W. M., & Pepler, D. J. (2000). Emotional regulation and display in classroom victims of bullying: Characteristic expressions of affect, coping styles and relevant contextual factors. *Social Development, 9,* 226–245.

Yude, C., Goodman, R., & McConachie, H. (1998). Peer problems of children with hemiplegia in mainstream primary schools. *Journal of Child Psychology and Psychiatry, 39,* 533–541.

# III

# Disability Policy Areas

# ❧ 11 ❧

# Mental Retardation and the Death Penalty: Current Issues for Attorneys and Psychologists

Julie C. Duvall and Richard J. Morris

Society has long struggled with the question of whether there should be a death penalty in the United States. Public opinion on this issue changes frequently, with support of the death penalty waxing and waning over the years (Death Penalty Information Center, "History of the Death Penalty"). In the United States, the death penalty has long been approved by the U.S. Supreme Court as an appropriate sentence for certain defendants. The Eighth Amendment of the U.S. Constitution protects individuals against "cruel and unusual punishments." The Supreme Court determines whether a particular punishment is cruel and unusual, usually through an examination of the prevailing societal mores.

In 1972, the Supreme Court decided the *Furman v. Georgia* cases, which set forth the circumstances under which a punishment could be "cruel and unusual." Those circumstances were: (a) if the punishment was too severe for the crime, (b) if the punishment was arbitrary, (c) if the punishment offended society's sense of justice, or (d) if the punishment was less effective than a less severe penalty. The *Furman* decision was written by all nine justices, who each wrote a separate opinion. Nine separate opinions illustrates a lack of agreement among the justices; however, by a one-vote margin, 5 to 4, the court held that Georgia's death penalty statute, which gave the jury complete sentencing discretion, could result in arbitrary sentencing. The punishment then was therefore "cruel and unusual" and violated the Eighth Amendment. Although Justices Brennan and Blackmun wrote opinions that reflected their beliefs that the death penalty itself was unconstitutional, the majority of the court merely had a problem with Georgia's statute and not the underlying penalty. Thus, the *Furman* decision paved the way for all the states to amend and craft legislation that would satisfy the court's concerns regarding the arbitrariness of the imposition of the death penalty.

Although the *Furman* court held that the death penalty was constitutional, considerable disagreement existed about whether certain types of people could always avoid death sentences, for example, mentally ill defendants, juvenile defendants, and defendants with mental retardation. These questions resulted in many court decisions that clarified the parameters of the types of individuals eligible for the death penalty. In one of those clarifying decisions in 1989, the U.S. Supreme Court held that the Eighth Amendment to the U.S. Constitution did not prohibit as "cruel and unusual punishment" the execution of people with mental retardation. (*Penry v. Lynaugh*, 1989, p. 330). The majority opinion, again with a one-vote margin, was written by Justice O'Connor. The opinion noted that the Eighth Amendment barred historically prohibited punishments, as well as those that run counter to "evolving standards of decency that mark the progress of a maturing society" (*Penry v. Lynaugh*, 1989, p. 330). After an examination of both federal and state legislation, Justice O'Connor determined that there was not "sufficient evidence at present of a national consensus" against the execution of defendants with mental retardation. The opinion also stated that there was insufficient evidence that all people with mental retardation lack the capacity to act with the degree of culpability associated with the imposition of the death penalty.

Justice Brennan filed a dissenting opinion in the *Penry* case in which he strongly disagreed with O'Connor's conclusion on the broader question of executing persons with mental retardation. Justice Brennan stated that all people with mental retardation have, by definition, significant limitations on their intellectual abilities and therefore are functioning lower in society. He argued that neither the goal of retribution nor that of deterrence was furthered by executing mentally retarded defendants because they did not understand how to weigh different courses of actions. He also argued that the death penalty was disproportionate to the relative culpability of mentally retarded defendants. As a result, he concluded, "the execution of mentally retarded individuals is nothing more than the purposeless and needless imposition of pain and suffering"(*Penry v. Lynaugh*, 1989, p. 348).

In 1989, when the *Penry* decision was decided, only two states barred the execution of persons with mental retardation. In 2002, 18 states and the federal government barred the execution of mentally retarded persons, in addition to 12 states that prohibited capital punishment altogether (*Atkins v. Virginia*, 2002;

18 U.S.C. Section 3596). As the Eighth Amendment mandates an examination of evolving standards of decency, in 2002 the U.S. Supreme Court decided to review the issue in the case of *Atkins v. Virginia*. Justice Stevens wrote the majority opinion in *Atkins*. He examined the growing number of national and state legislative actions to halt the execution of defendants with mental retardation and concluded:

> Given the well-known fact that anti-crime legislation is far more popular than legislation providing protections for persons guilty of violent crime, the large number of States prohibiting the execution of mentally retarded persons (and the complete absence of States passing legislation reinstating the power to conduct such executions) provides powerful evidence that today our society views mentally retarded offenders as categorically less culpable than the average criminal. (*Atkins v. Virginia*, 2002, pp. 315–316)

Justice Stevens, like Justice Brennan before him, further stated that because neither of the goals of deterrence and retribution would be furthered by the execution of mentally retarded individuals, the Eighth Amendment indeed forbids such executions. In terms of guidance to the states in terms of which defendants are mentally retarded, Justice Stevens stated:

> To the extent there is serious disagreement about the execution of mentally retarded offenders, it is in determining which offenders are in fact retarded .... Not all people who claim to be mentally retarded will be so impaired as to fall within the range of mentally retarded offenders about whom there is a national consensus. As was our approach in *Ford v. Wainwright*, with regard to insanity, "we leave to the States the task of developing appropriate ways to enforce the constitutional restriction upon its execution of sentences." (*Atkins v. Virginia*, 2002, p. 317)

The *Atkins* decision therefore held that mentally retarded individuals could not be executed for capital crimes if they were so impaired as to fall within the range of mentally retarded offenders about whom there is a national consensus. This decision, however, did not specify objective criteria that delimit that "range of mentally retarded offenders" nor the judicial procedure for determining whether a given defendant meets the objective criteria.

Since the Supreme Court decided *Atkins* opinion in 2002, individual states have worked to pass new laws and procedures that prohibit the execution of mentally retarded offenders to comply with the *Atkins* ban. Although 10 states have enacted statutes, others were unable to agree on definitions and/or procedures ("Legislature failed," 2003; Lilienthal, 2003; Maggi, 2003). Statutes enacted both before and after the *Atkins* decision commonly deal with identical sets of problems, namely: (a) What is the definition of "mental retardation"; (b) what procedure must be used to determine whether a person meets the definition; and (c) who makes that ultimate determination of the presence of mental retardation (van Dulmen-Krantz, 2002)? The legal questions also arise of whether the definition and associated determination applies retroactively to those people sentenced to death before *Atkins* was decided and whether the equal protection clause of the U.S. Constitution protects defendants in some states from being treated differently than defendants in other states (Entzeroth, 2002).

## DEFINITIONS

### Clinical Definitions of Mental Retardation

The *Atkins* opinion quotes two widely recognized clinical definitions of mental retardation: (a) the 1992 definition published by the American Association on Mental Retardation (AAMR) and (b) the 2000 definition published by the American Psychiatric Association (APA) in the *Diagnostic and Statistical Manual of Mental Disorders*, 4th ed. (*DSM–IV*; APA, 2000). *Atkins* noted that the 1992 AAMR formulation is:

> Mental retardation refers to substantial limitations in present functioning. It is characterized by significantly subaverage intellectual functioning, existing concurrently with related limitations in two or more of the following applicable adaptive skill areas: communication, self-care, home living, social skills, community use, self-direction, health and safety, functional academics, leisure and work. Mental retardation manifests before age 18. (*Atkins v. Virginia*, 2002, p. 308, n. 3)

The APA *DSM–IV* formulation is:

> The essential feature of mental retardation is significantly subaverage general intellectual functioning (Criterion A) that is accompanied by significant limitations in adaptive functioning in at least two of the following skill areas: communication, self-care, home living, social/interpersonal skills, use of community resources, self-direction, functional academic skills, work, leisure, health, and safety (Criterion B). The onset must occur before age 18 years (Criterion C). (APA, 2000, p. 41)

Under both definitions, psychologists and psychiatrists typically use the term *mild mental retardation* to describe the condition of people who have a Full Scale IQ level of between 50 to 55 and approximately 70 (APA, 2000).

The AAMR slightly revised its formulation in 2002 (AAMR, 2002). The change was minor and focused on refining the description of the adaptive skills component. The adaptive behavior requirement is expressed as conceptual, social, and practical adaptive skills (Kanaya, Scullin, & Ceci, 2003). This formulation was preceded by a less elaborate but largely identical formulation published in 1983 by the AAMR, which defines mental retardation as "significantly subaverage general intellectual functioning existing concurrently with deficits in adaptive behavior and manifested during the developmental period" (Ellis, 2002, p. 5). All of the definitions require that all three prongs of the definition be met. Unless all three requirements are present, a person does not fall within the definition of mental retardation.

The first of the three requirements is subaverage intellectual functioning. Limitations in "intellectual functioning" in mental retardation are generally assessed through the use of standardized individually administered IQ tests (Morris, Morris, & Bade, in press). Scores on those standardized tests that fall two standard deviations or more below the mean for the specific assessment instrument used, taking into consideration the assessment instrument's standard error of measurement (SEM), as well as the instrument's strengths and limitations, are viewed as falling into the mentally retarded range (Luckasson et al., 2002). Because most IQ tests have a mean of 100, a standard deviation of 15, and an SEM of 5, the requisite IQ score for a diagnosis of mental retardation is generally 70 or lower. With the inclusion of the SEM criterion, the ceiling IQ score for mental retardation is raised to 75, with IQ being reported as a confidence band (e.g., 65 to 75) rather than a finite score (Luckasson et al., 2002). Therefore, although a Full Scale IQ score below 70 virtually always indicates subaverage intellectual functioning, due to variations in the circumstances of a test administration a person may score up to 75 on an IQ test and still be found to have subaverage intellectual functioning (APA, 2000). This phenomenon is recognized in the most recent definition from the AAMR (2002), which states:

> Mental retardation is characterized by significantly subaverage intellectual capabilities or "low intelligence." If the IQ score is valid, this will generally result in a score of approximately 70 to 75 or below. This upper boundary of IQs for use in classification of mental retardation is flexible to reflect the statistical variance inherent in all intelligence tests and the need for clinical judgment by a qualified psychological examiner. (Luckasson et al., 2002, p. 1)

Similarly, the *DSM–IV* states, "Thus it is possible to diagnose mental retardation in individuals with IQs between 70 and 75 who exhibit significant deficits in adaptive behavior" (APA, 2000, pp. 41–42).

The second requirement is an adaptive behavior limitation. Adaptive behavior is defined by the AAMR as the conceptual, social, and practical skills that people use in order to function in their daily lives (Luckasson et al., 2002). Conceptual skills include communication skills, money and calculation skills, and self-direction. Social skills include interpersonal skills and the ability to understand and follow rules and laws. Practical skills may include skills in personal activities, such as eating or food preparation, as well as some occupational skills (Luckasson et al., 2002). This requirement ensures that the person is truly impaired and not just a poor test-taker. This added requirement also guards against malingered claims of mental retardation (Lustig, 2003).

The third requirement is that the impairment be manifested before age 18. This requirement also protects against malingered claims and differentiates mental retardation from other types of brain damage that may occur later in life, such as types of dementia due to disease. (APA, 2000). The issue of malingering, which has received considerable attention in the mental illness arena, has not proven to be a practical problem in the assessment of individuals who may have mental retardation (Lustig, 2003). As Ellis (2002) stated:

> Any concerns that an individual could somehow manage to feign cognitive impairment, undetected by clinical evaluators, should be dispelled by the fact that such deception would have had to begin during an individual's childhood. There are no reports in the clinical literature indicating that this is a practical problem in the assessment of individuals who are thought to have mental retardation. (Ellis, 2002, p. 10)

Thus, the most widely recognized and used definitions require all three prongs be met in order to make the diagnosis of mental retardation. Because the *Atkins* case left the matter of determining the definitions and procedures up to the individual states, the question arises whether the states have actually followed the mandates set forth by the AAMR and the *DSM–IV*.

## Statutory Definitions of "Mental Retardation"

Thirty-eight states and the federal government presently allow the execution of defendants found guilty of certain crimes: Alabama, Arizona, Arkansas, California, Colorado, Connecticut, Delaware, Florida, Georgia, Idaho, Illinois, Indiana, Kansas, Kentucky, Louisiana, Maryland, Mississippi, Missouri, Montana, Nebraska, Nevada, New Hampshire, New Jersey, New Mexico, New York, North Carolina, Ohio, Oklahoma, Oregon, Pennsylvania, South Carolina, South Dakota, Tennessee, Texas, Utah, Virginia, Washington, and Wyoming. Prior to the *Atkins* decision, 18 states, including Arkansas, Arizona, Colorado,

Connecticut, Florida, Georgia, Indiana, Kansas, Kentucky, Maryland, Missouri, Nebraska, New Mexico, New York, North Carolina, South Dakota, Tennessee, and Washington, and the federal government had enacted statutes prohibiting the execution of persons meeting a statutory definition of "mentally retarded" (Atkins, 2002, pp. 314–315).[1] After the Atkins decision was handed down, an additional seven states enacted such statutes: California, Delaware, Idaho, Illinois, Nevada, Utah, and Virginia. As of March 2004, 13 of the states that allow the death penalty lack any type of bar to the execution of a mentally retarded person: Alabama, Louisiana, Mississippi, Montana, New Hampshire, New Jersey, Ohio, Oklahoma, Oregon, Pennsylvania, South Carolina, Texas, and Wyoming. In those jurisdictions, it remains an open question as to what the definitions and procedures will be.

In 2004, the Texas Criminal Court of Appeals addressed the issue of how to decide whether someone had mental retardation in the *Ex Parte Briseno* case (*Ex Parte Briseno*, 2004). In that case, death-row inmate Jose Briseno appealed his conviction, stating he was retarded and thus could not have received the death penalty as a constitutional sentence. In the absence of legislation, the Criminal Appeals Court noted:

> We, however, must define that level and degree of mental retardation at which a national consensus of Texas citizens would agree that a person should be exempted from the death penalty. Most Texas citizens would agree that Steinbeck's Lennie should, by reason of his lack of reasoning ability and adaptive skills, be exempt.... Is there a national or Texas consensus that all of those persons whom the mental health profession might diagnose as meeting the criteria for mental retardation are automatically less morally culpable than those who just barely miss meeting those criteria? Is there, and should there be, a "mental retardation" bright line exemption from our state's maximum statutory punishment? (*Ex Parte Briseno*, 2004, p. 1)

The court goes on to use the 1992 AAMR definition, but notes that the adaptive behavior criteria are "exceedingly subjective, and undoubtedly experts will be found to offer opinions on both sides of the issue in most cases" (*Ex Parte Briseno*, 2004, p. 3). The court goes through the three-day hearing examining the testimony of both defense and state experts to show that both sides examine the same behavior and reach different conclusions. For example, both sides examined Briseno's conduct in prison to answer the adaptive functioning criteria.

---

[1] Although the Atkins decision lists 19 states that had pre-Atkins prohibitions against the execution of people with mental retardation and included Texas in this list, Texas actually did not have such a statute. The Texas legislature had brought forward a bill to disallow those executions and the governor vetoed the bill (*Ex Parte Briseno*, 2004, p. 1).

The prosecutor called four officers from the Texas prison system, who testified that his behavior in prison seemed "normal" and "appropriate" and that he could read magazines and fill out order forms for commissary goods. The chief deputy stated that he had 10 different dealings with Briseno and that he was "intelligent, shrewd and very cunning" (*Ex Parte Briseno*, 2004, p. 18). The defense expert, on the other hand, testified that his IQ was 72 and that he lacked adaptive behavior skills in prison by noting that he had numerous prison disciplinary reports for refusing to work and arriving to work late. To the defense expert, this was consistent with deficits in adaptive skills around vocational and career areas. To the state's expert, this was just an example of Briseno's aversion to working and generally antisocial behavior (*Ex Parte Briseno*, 2004, p. 18). The court concluded by agreeing with the trial court judge that although there is evidence to support the mental retardation claim, there is also evidence to dispute it, and therefore denied relief to Briseno.

The Appeals Court decision in the *Briseno* case illustrates some of the problems that courts will encounter when they have to make decisions in the absence of guidance. The court, rather than focusing on the requirements and criteria listed in the AAMR definition and literature, instead focused on an examination of Briseno's extensive criminal background to conclude that he does not have mental retardation. Although Texas does not have a statute, other states do, and thus, an examination of those statutes is necessary to determine whether the other states have some of the same problems that the *Briseno* case illustrates.

***Ten States Have a Standard Clinical Definition Without Modification.*** The statutes in 10 states—California, Georgia, Indiana, Kansas, Missouri, Nevada, New York, Pennsylvania, Tennessee, and Washington—employ virtually verbatim a standard clinical formulation, specifically the 1983 or 1992 AAMR formulation [Cal. Pen. Code § 1376(a); Ga. Code Ann. § 17-7-131 (a)(3); Ind. Code § 35-36-9-2; Kan. Stat. Ann. §§ 21-4623(e) and 76-12b01; Mo. Rev. Stat. § 565.030(6); Nev. Rev. Stat. § 174.098(7); New York Crim. Proc. Law § 400.27 (12)(e); Pa. Consol. Stat. Ann. tit. 50, § 4102; Tenn. Code Ann. § 39-13-203(a); Wash. Rev. Code § 10.95.030(2)]. Illinois slightly changed the definitions by defining mental retardation as a "low IQ," along with the deficits in the other two areas [Ill. Comp. Stat. ch. 725, § 5/144-15(d)]. However, Illinois does not define "low IQ."

***Twelve States Have Restrictive Modifications, Specifying a "Cutoff" Score.*** The most common modification to the standard clinical formulation is one that makes the "subaverage intellectual functioning requirement" more restrictive. In

12 states the statutes enacted modifications that impose a strict numerical upper limit of "70" (or two standard deviations below the statistical mean of 100) on the qualifying IQ score. Among those 12 states, Connecticut strictly defines "significantly subaverage intellectual functioning" as an IQ score of more than two standard deviations below the mean [Conn. Gen. Stat. § 1-1g(a) and (b)]. Florida and Virginia strictly define "significantly subaverage intellectual functioning" as an IQ score of two or more standard deviations below the mean [Fla. Stat. § 921.137(1); Va. Code. Ann. § 19.2-264.3:1.1(A)]. Arizona, Delaware, Idaho, Kentucky, Maryland, Nebraska, New Mexico, North Carolina, and Tennessee also require a score of 70 or below to indicate significant subaverage intellectual functioning [Ariz. Rev. Stat. § 13-703.02(K)(2) and (4); Del. Code Ann. tit. 11, § 4209(d)(3); Idaho Code § 19-2515A(1)(a) and (b); Ky. Rev. Stat. Ann. § 532.130(2); Md. Crim. Code Ann. § 2-202(b)(1)(I); Neb. Rev Stat. § 28-105.01(3); N.M. Stat. Ann. § 31-20A-2.1(A); N.C. Gen. Stat. § 15A-2005(a)(2); Tenn. Code Ann. § 39-13-203(a)(1)].

The cutoff scores in these state statutes directly conflict with clinical guidelines that permit clinicians to accept scores of 70 to 75, or even higher, as indicative of sufficiently subaverage intellectual functioning. As Mossman (2003) indicated:

> The modifier "approximately" in the APA's diagnostic criteria reminds mental health professionals that using seventy as a cut-off score reflects a statistical convention rather than a natural boundary between two distinctive groups of individuals. When conscientious mental health professionals interpret IQ scores and plan treatment interventions, they keep in mind that someone who scores 71, and that two persons with an IQ score of say, 67 and 73 have much more in common with each other than with a person who scores 88 .... Using such precise cut-offs mistakenly suggests that a one-point difference in two persons' scores reflects a significant difference in their cognitive capacity. (p. 268)

**Six States Have Modified the "Adaptive Behavior Limitation" Requirement.** No state statute appears to have modified significantly the "adaptive behavior limitation" requirement in the standard clinical formulation, but three states appear to have added minor additional restrictions by requiring, for example, that the adaptive behavior deficits have been "continuous" [Mo. Rev. Stat. § 565.030(5) and (6)], or "significant" [Ark. Code § 5-4-618(a)(1)(A)], or "documented" [Colo. Rev. Stat. § 18-1.3-1101(2)].

Three other states add their own unique interpretation of this prong. The Connecticut statute recognizes the cultural context of the individual by defining adaptive behavior as "the effectiveness of degree with which an individual meets the standards of personal independence and social responsibility expected for the individual's age and cultural group" [Conn. Gen. Stat. § 1-1g(a) and (b)]. Utah adds the requirement that the difficulties in adaptive functioning "exist primarily in reasoning or impulse control, or both of these areas" [Utah Code Ann. §77-15a-102(1) and (2)]. Finally, Virginia uses the 2002 AAMR formulation, which calls for difficulties in adaptive behavior as expressed in conceptual, social, and practical adaptive skills [Va. Code Ann. § 19.2-264.3:1.1(A)] (AAMR, 2002). Virginia also provides the following guidance to the practitioner:

> [The assessment of adaptive behavior] shall be based on multiple sources of information, including clinical interview, psychological testing and educational, correctional and vocational records. The assessment shall include at least one standardized measure generally accepted by the field of psychological testing for assessing adaptive behavior and appropriate for administration to the particular defendant being assessed, unless not feasible. In reaching a clinical judgment regarding whether the defendant exhibits significant limitations in adaptive behavior, the examiner shall give performance on standardized measures whatever weight is clinically appropriate in light of the defendant's history and characteristics and the context of the assessment. [Va. Code Ann. § 19.2-264.3:1.1(B)(2)]

***Three States Extended the "Age of Onset" Requirement.*** Although the standard clinical formulations and related scholarly literature indicate that the age of onset of mental retardation must be before 18 years of age, the statutes in three states—Indiana, Maryland, and Utah—have enacted modifications that make the requirement less restrictive by extending the age of onset to 22 years of age [Ind. Code § 35-36-9-2; Md. Crim. Law Code Ann. § 2-202(b)(1)(ii); Utah Code Ann. § 77-15a-102(2)].

***Three States Have Modifications That Have No Relationship to the Standard Clinical Definitions.*** The statutes of three states include special provisions that are wholly unrelated to the three-prong requirements recognized in the standard clinical definitions. The Kansas statute adds a requirement that the mental retardation "substantially impair one's capacity to appreciate the criminality of one's conduct or to conform one's conduct to the requirements of the law" [Kan. Stat. Ann. § 21-1623(e)]. Utah's statute provides that before the prosecution can use any mentally retarded defendant's confession, it must show that the confession is independently corroborated by other evidence [Utah Code Ann. § 77-15a-101(2)]. The New York statute provides that any mentally retarded defendant serving prison time on a homicide charge who commits another murder can be executed [New York Crim. Proc. Law § 400.27(12)(d)].

## PROCEDURES

### Criminal Procedures Mandated to Determine Whether a Person Has Mental Retardation

Just as the individual states were allowed to create their own definitions of mental retardation, they were also allowed to set forth how the determination would take place, including how many evaluations were allowed, what tests should be used, and who could perform the evaluations. Only four states, though, specifically set forth the procedures to be followed in the psychological assessment, namely, Arizona, California, Nevada, and Virginia. In all the other states, the judge makes the determination in each capital case.

Although Arizona is unique in mandating the administration of either three or four IQ tests in approximately 65 days, the statutes of a few other states also require that a defendant be evaluated more than once. For example, the Colorado statute provides that the court may order "one or more evaluations of the defendant," whereas Utah provides for "at least" two evaluations [Colo. Rev. Stat. § 18-1.3-1104(1); Utah Code Ann. § 77-15a-104(3)]. Florida and Kansas provide for two evaluations [Fla. Stat. § 921.137(4); Kan. Stat. Ann. § 21-4623(b)]. The New York, Nevada, and South Dakota statutes all provide that a defendant who raises a mental retardation claim must undergo an examination by an expert selected by the prosecution [Nev. Rev. Stat. § 174.098(3)(b); S.D. Codified Laws § 23A-27A-26.5; N.Y. Crim. Proc. Law § 400.27(13)(c)]. No state statute addresses the primary language of the defendant, or whether the defendant is appropriately represented in the standardization group. Moreover, no state statute mandates communication between the evaluators.

In Virginia, the court appoints only one qualified mental health expert to assess whether the defendant is mentally retarded and to assist the defense in the preparation and presentation of information concerning the defendant's mental retardation [Va. Code Ann. § 19.2-264.3:1.2(A)].

## DECISION MAKERS

### Burden of Proof

Any question that ends up in any court is inherently controversial. Because that controversy must be resolved, the fact finder in the case, whether that be a judge or a jury, must resort to a comparison of probabilities to resolve the issue. In some cases, the evidence may be one-sided. Usually, however, the evidence points to different conclusions. In those cases, the fact finder must know the following: "who must prove what and how persuasive that proof must be" (Fishman, 1992). In cases where persons having mental retardation may face the death penalty, there remains for consideration which party has the burden to establish the claim that the defendant has mental retardation, and to what level of certainty that fact has to be proven. In all states with statutes on the subject, the defense team has the burden to establish that a client has mental retardation. This is logical because the defense is in a unique position to obtain all necessary records and to have the defendant tested. The area that individual states differ on, however, is on the level of certainty of that proof. For example, in Arkansas, Arizona, California, Nebraska, Nevada, Idaho, Illinois, South Dakota, Tennessee, New Mexico, New York, Maryland, and Washington, the defense must prove its claim by a "preponderance of the evidence." The preponderance of evidence standard is usually defined as being met "if the fact finder is satisfied that the fact is more likely true than not true" (Fishman, 1992; Strong, 1999). On the other hand, Colorado, Delaware, Florida, Indiana, and North Carolina require that the defendant prove his or her mental retardation by "clear and convincing" evidence. To meet the clear and convincing standard the defendant must "persuade the jury that the proposition is highly probable, or must produce in the mind of the fact finder a firm belief or conviction that the allegations in question are true" (Fishman, 1992).

## Who Makes the Findings

There are two possible fact finders in any judicial proceeding: the judge or the jury. Most statutes call for the judge to make the finding [see, e.g., Ark. Code § 5-4-618(d)(2); Del. Code Ann. tit. 11, § 4209(d)(3)(c); Fla. Stat. § 921.137(4); Ga. Code Ann. § 17-7-131(b)(2); Idaho Code § 19-2515A(2); Ill. Comp. Stat. ch. 725, § 5/114-15(b); Ind. Code § 35-36-9-4; Kan. Stat. Ann. § 21-1623(b); Ky. Rev. Stat. Ann. § 532.135(2); Neb. Rev. Stat. § 28-105.01(5); Nev. Rev. Stat. § 174.098(6); N.M. Stat. Ann.§ 31-20A-2.1(c); New York Code 400.27; N.C. Gen. Stat. § 15A-2005(c); S.D. Codified Laws § 23A-27A-26.3; Tenn. Code Ann. § 39-13-203(c); Utah Code Ann. § 77-15a-104(12)(a); Wash. Rev. Code § 10.95.030(2)]. Only three states require the jury to make the finding [Conn. Gen. Stat. § 53a-46a(h); Mo. Rev. Stat. § 565.030(5); Va. Code Ann. § 19.2-264.3:1.1(c)].

A major legal problem, however, may arise in the states that have a judge versus a jury determine whether a defendant has mental retardation. In 2002, the Supreme Court ruled in *Ring v. Arizona*, 536 U.S. 584, that Arizona's sentencing procedure in capital cases whereby the judge, and not the jury, made sentencing decisions was unconstitutional. The court held that a jury, and not a judge, had to make the findings of "aggravating circumstances" in capital cases. The question arises then of whether the *Ring* decision invalidates those states' procedures which call for a judge to be the decision maker. Most legal commentators agree that a jury, and not a judge, must make these findings (Fagan, 2003; Seiden, 2003).

## Retroactivity of Atkins Decision and Equal Protection Claims

Two additional legal problems arise out of the concept of fairness. First, what happens to all the convicted people who have mental retardation and are already on death row? And what kind of relief, if any, will the *Atkins* case have on these people who were sentenced to death before *Atkins* was decided? Although three states, Nebraska, Nevada, and Virginia, built in procedures for defendants previously sentenced to death to come forward with mental retardation claims, most did not. The nationwide population of death row inmates, as of October 2003, was approximately 3,504 (Death Penalty Information Center, n.d.). The exact number of these defendants who have mental retardation is not known (Hall, 2002). However, some studies estimate that between 5 and 10 % of the people on death row have mental retardation and an additional 25% are classified in the borderline area (van Dulmen-Krantz, 2002, p. 213). Legal commentators have argued that *Atkins* must apply retroactively, considering previous rulings by the Supreme Court (Entzeroth, 2002).

Another issue relates to whether different states can/should treat people differently who have identical diagnoses of mental retardation. Rational thought should lead to the view that it is fundamentally unfair that two defendants with the same IQ and diagnoses, who are guilty of the same crime, under the same circumstances but in different states, have different sentencing outcomes—namely, one escapes death and the other does not. In this regard, one group of authors compared two cases in Indiana involving similar crimes and defendants with similar mental capacities: One was found mentally retarded and exempted from the death penalty, and the other was not (Note: Implementing Atkins, 2003). According to the authors, the different outcomes depended almost entirely on the quality and thoroughness of the psychiatric evaluations performed on each defendant. The authors also explained that in the case where no mental retardation diagnosis was found, the court and experts seemed to have a number of misconceptions about people who had mental retardation.

## SUMMARY AND CONCLUSIONS

The Supreme Court decision in *Atkins v. Virginia* reversed previous Supreme Court case rulings allowing the execution of people having mental retardation. The decision in *Atkins* mirrored changing societal mores about the acceptability of executing people with mental retardation. Although the decision is a positive one for people with disabilities who have been charged with or convicted of capital crimes, the lack of guidance in the *Atkins* opinion to the states is troubling. An extensive review of the statutes nationwide that preexisted the Atkins decision, or attempt to implement *Atkins*, has revealed a complete lack of uniformity among the states: Definitions are different, procedures are different, and ultimately the outcomes of similar people in different states will also be different. The U.S. Supreme Court trusted the individual states to make fair laws and procedures to make the determination of which defendants had mental retardation. That trust seems to be misplaced, as there is little or no consistency between and among the states. The question of fairness then will have to be litigated in the courts, a lengthy and cumbersome process for all the parties involved.

## REFERENCES

American Association on Mental Retardation. (2002). *Definitions*. Retrieved January 10, 2004, from http://www.aamr.org/policies/faq_mental_retardation.shtml

American Psychiatric Association. (2000). *Diagnostic and statistical manual of mental disorders* (4th ed.). Washington, DC: Author.

Arizona Revised Statutes § 13-703.02.

Arkansas Code Annotated. § 5-4-618.

*Atkins v. Virginia*, 536 U.S. 304 (2002).

California Penal Code § 1376.

Colorado Revised Statutes §§ 18-1.3-1101 through 18-1.3-1105.

Connecticut General Statutes §§ 1-1g and 53a-46a.

Death Penalty Information Center. (n.d.). *History of the death penalty*. Retrieved January 10, 2004, from http://www.deathpenaltyinfo.org

Delaware Code Annotated, title 11, § 4209.

Ellis, J. W. (2002). *Mental retardation and the death penalty: A guide to state legislative issues*. Retrieved October 10, 2003, from http://www.deathpenaltyinfo.org/MREllisLeg.pdf

Entzeroth, L. (2002). 2001–2002 Supreme Court review: Constitutional prohibition on the execution of the mentally retarded criminal defendant. *Tulsa Law Review, 38*, 299–328.

Ex Parte Briseno, 135 S.W.3d 1 (2004).

Fagan, J. (2003). *Atkins*, adolescence, and the maturity heuristic: Rationales for a categorical exemption for juveniles from capital punishment. *New Mexico Law Review, 33*, 207–254.

11. Mental Retardation and the Death Penalty  219

Fishman, C. S. (1992). *Jones on evidence: Civil and criminal* (7th ed., pp. 229–239). Eagan, MN: Lawyers Cooperative.
Florida Statutes § 921.137.
*Furman v. Georgia*, 408 U.S. 238 (1972).
Georgia Code Annotated § 17-7-131.
Hall, T. S. (2002). Legal fictions and moral reasoning: Capital punishment and the mentally retarded defendant after *Penry v. Johnson*. *Akron Law Review, 35,* 327–370.
Idaho Code § 19-2515A.
Illinois Compiled Statutes, chapter 725, § 5/114-15.
Indiana Code § 35-36-9-1 through 35-36-9-7.
Kanaya, T., Scullin, M. H., & Ceci, S. J. (2003). The Flynn effect and U.S. policies: The impact of rising IQ scores on American society via mental retardation diagnoses. *American Psychologist, 58,* 778–790.
Kansas Statutes Annotated §§ 21-4623 and 76-12b01.
Kentucky Revised Statutes Annotated §§ 532.130 and 532.135.
Legislature failed to make needed death penalty reforms. (2003, May 31). *Houston Chronicle,* p. A38.
Lilienthal, C. (2003, August 25). Criminal practice Harrisburg judge finds capital defendant mentally retarded; First death penalty case to head to the state high court after U.S. justices' decision. *Pennsylvania Law Weekly, 26*(34), 3.
Luckasson, R., Borthwick-Duffy, S., Buntinx, W. H. E., Coulter, D. L., Craig, E. M., Reeve, A., et al. (2002). *Mental retardation: Definition, classification, and systems of supports* (10th ed.). Washington, DC: AAMR.
Lustig, S. (2003, December 22). An unlikely feat; No need to worry that capital defendants will fake mental retardation to avoid execution; more important task is to identify the truly disabled. *New Jersey Law Journal.*
Maggi, L. (2003, May 29). Death penalty bill advances; Mentally challenged could be spared. *Times-Picayune (New Orleans, LA),* p. National-4.
Maryland Criminal Law Code Annotated § 2-202.
Missouri Revised Statutes § 565.030.
Morris, R. J., Morris, Y. P., & Bade, P. B. (in press). Developmental disabilities. In H. H. Zaretsky, M. G. Eisenberg, & E. F. Richter (Eds.), *Medical aspects of disability: A handbook for the rehabilitation professional* (3rd ed.). New York Springer.
Mossman, D. (2003). *Atkins v. Virginia*: A psychiatric can of worms. *New Mexico Law Review, 33,* 255–291.
Nebraska Revised Statutes § 28-105.01.
Nevada Revised Statutes § 174.098.
New Mexico Statutes Annotated § 31-20A-2.1.
New York Criminal Procedure Law § 400.27.
North Carolina General Statutes § 15A-2005.
Note: Implementing *Atkins*. (2003). *Harvard Law Review, 116,* 2565–2587.
Oklahoma Statutes, Title 22, § 1175.3.
Pennsylvania Consolidated Statutes Annotated, Title 50, § 4102.
*Penry v. Lynaugh*, 492 U.S. 302 (1989).
*Ring v. Arizona*, 536 U.S. 584 (2002).
Seiden, J. (2003). Case note: U.S. Court of Appeals for the Fourth Circuit: *Walker v. True. Capital Defense Journal, 16,* 233–244.
South Dakota Codified Laws §§ 23A-27A-26.1 through 23A-27A-26.7.

Strong, J. W. (1999). *McCormick on evidence* (5th ed., pp. 421–428). St. Paul, MN: West Group.
Tennessee Code Annotated § 39-13-203.
18 United States Code § 3596.
Utah Code §§ 77-15a-101 through 77-15a-106.
van Dulmen-Krantz, J. J. (2002). The changing face of the death penalty in America: The strengths and weaknesses of *Atkins v. Virginia* and policy considerations for states reacting to the Supreme Court's Eighth Amendment interpretation. *Hamline Journal of Public Law & Policy, 24,* 185–223.
Virginia Code Annotated § 19.2-264.3:1.1.
Washington Revised Code § 10.95.030.

# 12

# ADHD and the Law: Students' Rights, Schools' Responsibilities, and Educational Issues

Susan Arnpriester and Richard J. Morris

Attention deficit hyperactivity disorder (ADHD) is among the most frequently diagnosed childhood behavior disorders in the United States. Since its inclusion in the third edition of the American Psychiatric Association *Diagnostic and Statistical Manual of Mental Disorders* in 1980, there has been a steady increase in the frequency of this diagnosis in children and adolescents (Morris & Morris, 2000; Safer & Krager, 1988). By the early 1990s, it was estimated that between 3% and 5% of the school-age population in the United States had this diagnosis, with boys outnumbering girls by a ratio of 3:1 (Kauffman, 1993). Estimates for 2000 were that 15% of all U.S. children (approximately 7.5 million children) would be diagnosed as having ADHD (Panksepp, 1998).

Like other childhood psychiatric disorders, what is known today as ADHD has had a long and varied history. For example, in 1902 the British physician George Still first described a series of behavioral symptoms in 20 children who were seen in his clinical practice. These symptoms, including aggressiveness, defiance, and resistance to discipline, constituted the first conceptualization of this type of childhood behavior disorder (Armstrong, 1995). Since that time, children with symptoms now associated with ADHD have been labeled as having such disorders as "restlessness syndrome," "minimal brain damage," "hyperactive child syndrome," "hyperkinetic reaction of childhood," and "developmental hyperactivity," (Morris & Morris, 2000). Although physicians and mental health professionals in the United States are now fairly consistent in using the label ADHD to describe symptoms outlined in the fourth edition of the *Diagnostic and Statistical Manual of Mental Disorders* (DSM–IV; American Psychiatric Association, 1994), the World Health Organization International

Classification of Disease (ICD) also lists hyperkinetic disorder (HKD) as a subgroup of ADHD (Taylor, 1998). Differences in definitions have therefore led to some confusion in international research on ADHD, as research in the United States uses one set of criteria for its definition (i.e., *DSM–IV*), whereas research from European countries may use the *DSM–IV* or ICD criteria (i.e., ICD, Gingerich, Turnock, Litfin, & Rosen, 1998).

## ADHD AND EDUCATIONAL SERVICES ISSUES UNDER CURRENT FEDERAL LAWS

The American Psychiatric Association (APA) maintains that ADHD is an enduring mental disorder that includes the characteristics of hyperactivity, impulsivity, and inattention. According to the *DSM–IV* (APA, 1994), *hyperactivity* includes behaviors such as fidgeting, inappropriate wandering, inappropriate running or climbing, difficulty playing quietly, excessive talking, and constant movement. *Impulsivity* includes blurting out answers before questions are given, difficulty waiting turns and waiting in line, and interrupting and intruding on others. *Inattention* includes behaviors such as making careless mistakes, failing to sustain attention, not listening, not following through on instructions, failing to finish projects, difficulty organizing tasks, avoiding tasks that require sustained mental effort, losing things necessary for completion of tasks, becoming easily distracted, and forgetting things necessary for daily activities (APA, 1994).

In order to make a clinical diagnosis of ADHD using *DSM–IV* guidelines, certain additional criteria must be met. First, the identifying behaviors must have been present for at least 6 months. Second, some behaviors must have been present before 7 years of age. Third, impairment must be present in at least two situations (e.g., home and school and/or work). Fourth, social, academic, or occupational functioning must be impaired. Finally, symptoms must not be attributable to or better accounted for by another disorder. Specifically, the identifying behaviors cannot be the result of a pervasive developmental disorder or any psychotic disorder such as schizophrenia, and the behaviors can not be explained by a mood disorder, anxiety disorder, dissociative disorder, or personality disorder (APA, 1994).

### Federal Law and Educational Services

Traditionally, there has been a schism between the use of psychiatric diagnostic systems (e.g., *DSM–III* and *DSM–IV*) and the application of special education definitions and eligibility criteria for special education services for those children having attentional, impulsive control, and/or hyperactive behavior problems. Specifically, because a psychiatric diagnosis is not mandated in laws pertaining to the education of students having disabilities, and because such a diagnosis does not necessarily guarantee that a student will receive a special education placement, many school districts have not utilized the psychiatric definition for ADHD. Instead, school psychologists and school administrators have often relied on state and federal disability definitions to guide them in the identification and placement procedures for students with attention, impulse control, and/or hyperactivity problems (Atkins & Pelham, 1992; McConaughy & Achenbach, 1990).

In school settings, one of the most widely used definitions of disability is found in the U.S. government's Individuals With Disabilities Education Act (IDEA). This act, originally called the Education of All Handicapped Children Act (Public Law 94-142, 1974), was renamed to its current title in 1990, and reauthorized by the U.S. Congress in 1997. To be eligible for services under IDEA, a child must meet the requirements of a two-part test. First, the child must have a disability that fits within one of the categories of eligibility. Those categories include *mental retardation, deafness or hearing impairments, speech or language impairments, blindness or visual impairments, serious emotional disturbance, orthopedic impairments, autism, traumatic brain injury, other health impairments, specific learning disabilities, deaf-blindness,* and *other multiple disabilities.* Second, the child's disability must be such that "special education" and "related services" are needed. In IDEA, *special education* refers to free special instruction specifically designed to meet the unique needs of the child who has a disability. *Related services* refers to those services required to assist the child in order for him or her to benefit from the special education services. Such related services include, but are not limited to, physical or occupational therapy, counseling, speech-language therapy, and transportation (20 U.S.C. 1401).

In spite of intense lobbying by advocates for children with ADHD, Congress declined to add ADHD to the list of disabilities in the 1997 reauthorization of IDEA; however, in certain cases, a child with ADHD can qualify for services under IDEA. For example, if a child with ADHD meets the requirements under the category of "learning disabilities" or the category of "seriously emotionally disturbed," then that child may receive services under IDEA (Office of Special Education Programs, 1994). Additionally, a child with ADHD might meet the requirements of the category "other health impaired." *Other health impaired* is defined as "having limited strength, vitality, or alertness, including heightened alertness to environmental stimuli that results in limited alertness with respect to the educational environment" (20 U.S.C. 1401). The application of this definition has been interpreted to mean that a child having either acute or chronic

ADHD who (a) has had experiences that limit his or her alertness due to the presence of ADHD, (b) has academic difficulties as a result of the ADHD, and (c) would benefit from special services is eligible for such services under IDEA (Office of Special Education Programs, 1998a).

If a child having ADHD does not qualify for special education services, it is possible that he or she might be eligible for services under Section 504 of the U.S. Government's Rehabilitation Act of 1973. The Rehabilitation Act is not an education act but a civil rights law, which prevents any institution that receives federal monies from discriminating against persons with disabilities. According to Section 504 of this act, any individual who has, has had, or is perceived to have a physical or mental impairment that limits a major life activity (such as learning) qualifies for protection under civil rights discrimination [34 CFR 104.3(j)(2)(ii)]. Unlike the definition of disability utilized in IDEA, the definition of physical or mental impairment under the Rehabilitation Act is not limited to specific categories; physical or mental impairment is simply defined as any physiological, mental, or psychological disorder [34 CFR 104.3(j)(2)(I)].

Given the disparate definitions of "disability" under IDEA and the Rehabilitation Act, it is understandable that public schools could be confused concerning which law accommodates which students having ADHD. After Congress decided not to include ADHD in the original IDEA legislation, uncertainty among professionals led the U.S. Department of Education to issue a memorandum concerning the eligibility of ADHD students under IDEA and Section 504 (U.S. Department of Education, 1991). The memorandum specified the requirements for inclusion under IDEA and outlined Section 504's broader definition of disability, but it also seemed to raise as many questions as it answered (Zirkel & Gluckman, 1997).

Since 1991, however, court rulings and clarifications from the U.S. Office of Special Education Programs (OSEP) and the U.S. Office for Civil Rights (OCR) have offered some guidance but have failed to completely elucidate the situation. For example, although it is clear that children identified as having ADHD under either IDEA or Section 504 are guaranteed any necessary adaptations in their regular education programs (U.S. Department of Education, 1991), it is unclear what the role and function are of special education services for ADHD students under Section 504. Over the past 25 to 30 years, special education services (i.e., specifically designed educational instruction subsidized by federal monies) have been viewed as being appropriate for only those children identified under IDEA; however, OCR publications relevant to Section 504 (e.g., OCR, 1993a, 1993b) clearly stated that children who qualify under 504 may also receive special education services. Few, if any, research studies, however, have been published that have critically evaluated whether ADHD children receiving services under IDEA should be educated in the same or different manner as those ADHD children receiving services under Section 504.

In addition to the lack of systematic research comparing special education services to ADHD children under IDEA versus Section 504, federal dollars for such services are only available for school districts to spend on those students identified under IDEA. No federal dollars are available for special education services for those students identified under Section 504. Many state education procedures, therefore, may prohibit offering special education services to children not identified under IDEA (Gammel, 1992). Because of the costs associated with education services and because Congress has not provided additional funding for children identified under Section 504, it may be hypothesized that school districts will be reluctant to identify children with ADHD.

According to IDEA, the obligation to evaluate a child starts when the school suspects the child has one of the 12 aforementioned disability categories (see Bartow County School District, 1995). Under Section 504 of the Rehabilitation Act, the obligation of the school district begins when school personnel or others maintain that a child could benefit from special services because his or her disability is interfering with his or her ability to receive a fair education (Zirkel, 1996). Under both laws, if a parent expresses concern and requests an evaluation of his or her child, the school must either oblige or inform the parents of his or her due process rights (Office of Special Education Programs, 1993). The type of evaluation conducted and the specific timeline requirements differ between IDEA and Section 504—with the evaluation protocol of IDEA being more narrow than that of Section 504. Some legal experts (e.g., Hakola, 1992), however, have recommended that schools, in order to best serve children and avoid lawsuits, adopt the IDEA protocol to use with all referred students, regardless of the particular federal law that applies. This would involve the assembly of a multidisciplinary team to determine the needs of each referred child by using a variety of assessment tools via qualified personnel and in the child's native language (34 CFR 300.533). In the case of ADHD, the case law has suggested that assessment tools must be specifically designed to identify problems related to ADHD (e.g., Columbia County School District, 1991). The evaluation team would then make recommendations and set classroom intervention and curricular guidelines for the child's appropriate education, and specify those guidelines in an individualized education program (IEP) for the child. In 1992, it was estimated that the cost of this type of IDEA multidisciplinary evaluation was approximately $3,000 (Gammel, 1992).

The cost and effort associated with providing a psychoeducational evaluation and special education services may lead some school districts to impose an unspoken "don't identify, don't tell" rule on teachers and staff, especially in cases of ADHD that might fall under Section 504. Because schools cannot be found in violation of Section 504 if they did not know or did not have reason to know of a child's disability (see, e.g., South Harrison Community School Corp., 1993), this unspoken rule could assist school district personnel in avoiding the provision of particular services that they feel the district can not afford. Although this might help the school navigate around the letter of the law, it certainly is not in concordance with the spirit of the law. School districts, whether they choose to follow the IDEA evaluation protocol for ADHD or their own Section 504 evaluation procedures, have an obligation under these laws to identify, evaluate, and provide the necessary educational services to all students who are disabled by ADHD.

## Assessment Issues

Even when school districts have an acceptable evaluation protocol in place, financial constraints, time, and personnel limitations may prohibit school psychologists and other diagnostic personnel from using thorough and scientifically sound procedures in their assessment (Balinky, 1985). Ideally, to ensure the validity of a diagnosis, multiple measures should be used when making diagnostic decisions regarding ADHD (see, e.g., Atkins & Pelham, 1992; Barkley, 1990; Reid & Maag, 1994; Schaughency & Rothlind, 1991). Moreover, according to recent rulings of the federal Office of Civil Rights (OCR), to ensure students' rights in matters of educational placement, multiple measures must be used when making placement decisions regarding ADHD (34 CFR 104.35c; 34 CFR 300.533). In this regard, the most common measures used for assessing ADHD include behavior checklists and rating scales, structured diagnostic interviews, and direct observations of behavior (see, e.g., DuPaul & Barkley, 1998; Morris & Collier, 1987; Morris & Morris, 2000).

Behavior checklists and rating scales are often utilized as a way to objectively quantify a child's behavior in comparison to the behaviors of the population. According to Power and Ikeda (1996), many of the behavior checklists and rating scales that are used to evaluate children are psychometrically sound, norm-referenced, and ecologically valid. Although these authors suggested that behavior checklists and rating scales should be an integral part of the diagnostic assessment of ADHD, Reid and Maag (1994) indicated a different view. Specifically, they stated that although behavior checklists and rating scales are valuable in identifying ADHD for *research purposes*, using such scales for the purpose of making an individual diagnosis of a child can yield imprecise results. They gave several reasons for their view. First, interobserver or interrater agreement levels are often lacking in ADHD behavior checklists and rating scales. Because the behavior items listed on such checklists and rating scales are often not operationally defined, independent observers or raters (e.g., teachers, parents, etc.) may differ appreciably in their respective interpretation of such behavior items. Second, Reid and Maag indicated that reliability and validity data of many behavior checklists and rating scales are often lacking. Finally, these authors suggested that although most scales claim to be norm-referenced, such norm groups are often not representative of the child being evaluated in a particular clinic or school setting.

Consistent with this notion, Stoner and Carey (1992) suggested that the psychometric properties and norms of any behavior checklist or rating scale should be scrutinized by those individuals who will be using the instruments prior to its use. Similarly, Salvia and Ysseldyke (1991) recommended that for diagnostic decision-making purposes all assessment instruments should have a minimum test–retest reliability coefficient of .90. In addition, they advised that clinicians look beyond the norm group size when judging the representative adequacy of a particular behavior checklist or rating scale. Although a large norm group is desirable, other characteristics in the standardization process should include the proportional representation of ethnicity, age, socioeconomic status, and geographic location. Moreover, Du Paul (1991) indicated that separate norm tables for gender should be associated with these assessment instruments, especially in light of gender differences in behaviors related to ADHD. Barkley (1997) also mentioned that the inclusion of a structured interview, as well as direct observational recording in the child's natural environment, further contributes to the reliability and validity of the diagnostic procedure.

Platzman et al. (1992) reviewed the research literature to determine the kinds of direct observational measures that have been found to be useful in identifying children having ADHD. They found that observations in natural settings—especially the classroom—were helpful in providing diagnostic information. They also reported, however, that such observational procedures are not routinely included in a particular child's assessment protocol because of the difficulty and expense in training reliable observers, the time-consuming nature of such observations, the tendency for insurance companies not to reimburse private clinicians for such out-of-office assessment and diagnostic services, and the time involved in scheduling such observations, as well as coding observational sessions in a reliable fashion (Barkley, 1997).

## Developmental Issues Related to Diagnosis

The diagnosis of ADHD has traditionally been limited to school-age children (see, e.g., Barkley, 1990, 1997; Du Paul & Barkley, 1998). Although precursors of ADHD such as excessive activity and poor sleeping habits can, retrospectively, be traced to infancy (Barkley, 1997), and although teachers' retrospective comments about the restlessness, inattention, and/or oppositional behaviors of subsequently diagnosed children with ADHD often start as young as preschool (Campbell, 1990), the diagnosis of ADHD before age 4 is difficult. For example, according to Tynan and Nearing (1994), "normal" toddlers often exhibit high activity levels, disobedience, and destructiveness—behaviors that drop sharply between 3 and 4 years of age. Moreover, in a study that followed children with "difficult-to-manage" behaviors from preschool to school age, only half of the children who were reported as being problematic as preschoolers exhibited significant clinical problems at 6 years of age (Campbell, 1987).

These findings could create a dilemma for school districts that are mandated by federal and state law to provide educational services to preschool children with disabilities. For example, based on results like those of Campbell (1987), school personnel may feel it is unnecessary to provide services to young children with ADHD, because these children are likely to spontaneously improve by the time they reach elementary school. School personnel may be reluctant to engage in psychological assessment services of ADHD in young children whose behaviors may be representative of behaviors also found in non-ADHD children. On the other hand, under IDEA, school districts are required to provide preschool services to children with disabilities starting at 3 years of age regardless of the possibility of spontaneous improvement of the child and/or the difficulty of the diagnostic assessment (34 CFR 300.300). Similarly, under Section 504, preschools that benefit from federal financial assistance are obligated to provide accommodations to those children having disabilities; therefore, if a public school offers preschool services to non-disabled children, the school district is required to abide by the official regulations of Section 504, subpart D. This subpart requires schools, and preschools, to do the following: identify children whose disabilities interfere with their learning, notify parents of their legal rights, and provide the identified children with a free and appropriate public education regardless of the nature or severity of their disability.

Similarly, older adolescents and young adults with ADHD have a right to a free and appropriate education if their disability interferes with their ability to learn. Although as children grow older they may outgrow the symptoms of ADHD—or gain substantial coping strategies that diminish the severity and frequency of many of the symptomatic behaviors associated with this disorder

(Barkley, 1997)—research suggests that a number of children with ADHD also continue to exhibit symptoms into adulthood (Weiss & Hechtman, 1993). Secondary and postsecondary school personnel should, therefore, be receptive to making accommodations for adolescents and young adults with ADHD. There is also legal protection for the education of these persons who continue to seek an education and who meet the criteria for ADHD. For example, individuals with ADHD who have a disability as defined under IDEA are guaranteed services until they reach their 22nd birthday. Moreover, one of the provisions contained in IDEA requires that school districts provide transition services to all children with disabilities starting at 16 years of age and in some instances beginning at 14 years of age (20 USC 1401a). These transition services must involve a written plan designed to successfully move students with disabilities from a secondary school setting to a postschool venue. Postschool settings include colleges and universities, vocational training programs, and places of employment (Hakola, 1996). Consistent with IDEA, Section 504 indicates that students with disabilities, regardless of age, who meet the academic or technical requirements for admission to a postsecondary institution or vocational program may not be discriminated against. Under these latter conditions, although an educational institution or vocational training setting is no longer required to monitor people having disabilities, such venues must make the necessary accommodations to ensure that students with ADHD (or other disabilities) are not discriminated against on the basis of their disability. Accommodations such as extended time to meet degree requirements, substitution of courses, and/or auxiliary aids are appropriate as long as they do not jeopardize the essential academic requirements of the program of instruction and/or training (34 CFR 104.44).

## Minority Students Issues

Another issue facing school districts involves the potentiality of the over-identification of ADHD in minority students. Although current epidemiological data on the prevalence of ADHD among minorities are lacking (Gingerich et al., 1998), some of the research literature suggests the possibility that school personnel may be biased in identifying attention problems in these children (e.g., Stevens, 1981). For example, Stevens (1981) found children of lower socioeconomic status (SES) and ethnic minorities (e.g., African American and Mexican American) were rated as more hyperactive than similarly behaving higher SES Anglo American children.

Even if assessment bias among school professionals could be controlled, the literature still suggests caution when interpreting the results of behavior rating scales and checklists with culturally different children (Shapiro & Kratochwill, 2000). Although behavior checklists and rating scales are among the more commonly used assessment instruments to evaluate the presence of ADHD in school populations (DuPaul & Barkley, 1998), a review of the literature regarding cross-cultural assessment differences suggests three problems (Reid, 1995). First, cultural minorities are not adequately represented in the standardization groups of many behavior checklists and rating scales. Second, too few studies have attempted to ascertain the cross-cultural and content validity of such checklists and scales. Finally, from the few studies that have provided data on the use of these assessment instruments with culturally different groups, there is evidence of overidentification of ADHD in students from cultural minorities (Reid, 1995).

Protecting against overidentification of minorities is a priority for both the OSEP (the overseeing office of IDEA) and the OCR (the overseeing office for Section 504). For example, in 1998, following a 2-year study that found disproportionate numbers of African American and Hispanic children in special education in New York City, the OCR stepped in to require the city to reduce this inequity (Office of Special Education Programs, 1998b). Correspondingly, one of the duties of OSEP is to make certain schools abide by the nondiscrimination regulations set forth in IDEA. Specifically, assessments used to determine IDEA eligibility must not be racially or culturally discriminatory (see Office of Special Education Programs, 1996) and must be administered in the child's native language or other mode of communication (Burnette, 1998).

## Classroom Issues

School districts may also be hesitant to identify and serve children having with ADHD because of issues surrounding the behavior of these children in the classes. Although all students, with or without disabilities, are guaranteed certain rights of due process in matters of discipline (*Goss v. Lopez*, 1975), there are additional legal protections for students with disabilities. Specifically, under both IDEA and Section 504, a child with a disability has certain rights of protection that may disallow particular school or classroom disciplinary practices for those behaviors associated with the disability (Zirkel, 1996). In addition, schools are restricted from removing a student with a disability from his or her current placement (i.e., suspending the student for an extended period of time or expelling the student). Under IDEA, students cannot be suspended for more than 10 days at a time without alternative educational provisions [20 U.S.C. 1415(k)]. Moreover, patterns of repeated suspensions that amount to an accumulation of more than 10 days in a school year are generally not permitted under the law (see, e.g., Cobb County School District, 1993). This 10-day limit, however, may be extended to 45 days in instances where a child carries a weapon to school or knowingly possesses, sells, or solicits the sale of illegal drugs at school (20 U.S.C. 1415). Although IDEA explicitly delineates these rights, the OCR generally applies the same standards to students identified under Section 504 (Dayton & Arnau, 1999).

The issue for schools is twofold. First, in matters concerning ADHD, it is difficult to determine which inappropriate or maladaptive behaviors are linked to a student's disability. Because, by definition, children with ADHD exhibit impulsive, hyperactive, and/or inattentive behaviors, and because these behaviors are often linked to various disciplinary actions in the regular education student population, it is reasonable to conclude that school officials might be reluctant to discipline students with ADHD. It should be pointed out, however, that because a school is not permitted to unilaterally remove a student for behavior problems related to ADHD, this does not necessarily mean that there are no corrective behavior management options available to school personnel. For example, in *Honig v. Doe* (1988), the court ruled that behavior-correcting procedures such as "study carrels, timeouts, detention, or the restriction of privileges" could be used to discipline students with disabilities, as long as such procedures do not result in a change of school placement. These behavior management techniques are consistent with the literature on preventing and managing behavioral problems in children with ADHD (see e.g., Barkley, 1990, 1997; Du Paul & Barkley, 1998). In addition, according to Rief (1993), Morris (1985), and Morris and Kratochwill (1998) timeouts, incremental consequences, increased structure, and positive reinforcement are all effective methods for preventing and dealing with children's disruptive behaviors.

The second part of the dilemma involves the "worst-case scenario" of an extremely disruptive, dangerous student. It could be argued that school personnel may be hesitant to classify such students as "disabled" out of concern that they will be not be permitted to legally discipline these students. Moreover, if an extremely disruptive student already qualifies as disabled under IDEA or Section 504, school personnel may feel that they cannot adequately discipline such a student. It should be noted, however, that although removing or suspending a student with disabilities from a classroom is difficult, it is not without precedent (Dayton & Arnau, 1999). For example, school personnel may ask a hearing officer to place a dangerous student in an alternative educational setting for up to 45 days. School personnel may also seek a preliminary court injunction to remove a student who is clearly dangerous to himself/herself or others as long as the school continues to provide a free, appropriate, public education to that student (Zirkel, 1996).

## CONCLUSIONS AND RECOMMENDATIONS

Research and policy literature suggests that school districts should consider developing procedures for monitoring whether accommodations need to be made in the educational curricula of those children diagnosed as having ADHD. Schools can make these accommodations in several ways. First, at least one person on staff at a school should be knowledgeable in the rules and procedures outlined in both IDEA and Section 504 and be available to consult with others at the school. This person should also keep all school personnel current in the changing laws based on information provided from the local office of the school superintendent and the state's Department of Education. Second, schools should consider investing teacher training funds in sponsoring workshops on classroom and behavior management procedures with children having ADHD (see, e.g., Barkley, 1990; DuPaul & Barkley, 1998). It is important that such training be offered to both regular education and special education teachers because the majority of children with ADHD are served under Section 504 in the regular education setting. University teacher education programs should also consider emphasizing methods for teaching children with ADHD (see, e.g., Bos & Nahmias, 1997). Such courses would supplement the already existing courses on exceptional children, as well as those on teaching children with learning and emotional disabilities. Third, educational institutions should be proactive in responding to public pressure that suggests it is unfair to non-disabled students to make accommodations for students with hidden disabilities such as ADHD. By mounting a public awareness campaign regarding ADHD, schools could increase the public's knowledge of ADHD and thus increase the potential for these children receiving the best available education.

School personnel should also share with parents and other concerned persons all current information regarding the rights of children and adults who have ADHD. Parents should also be informed that they have the right to ask questions if they do not understand the information provided them, and that they may contact child and parent advocacy centers (e.g., the Center for Disability Law and the Center for Law in the Public Interest) for additional assistance.

As people become more aware of the rights of individuals with ADHD as well as in providing them with an appropriate education, a balance is more likely to develop between meeting the needs of these individuals and those of the educational and/or vocational setting.

# REFERENCES

American Psychiatric Association. (1980). *Diagnostic and statistical manual of mental disorders* (3rd ed.). Washington, DC: Author.
American Psychiatric Association. (1994). *Diagnostic and statistical manual of mental disorders* (4th ed.). Washington, DC: Author.
Armstrong, T. (1995). *The myth of the A.D.D. child.* New York: Dutton.
Atkins, M. S., & Pelham, W. E. (1992). School-based assessment of attention-deficit hyperactivity disorder. *Journal of Learning Disabilities, 24,* 197–204.
Balinky, J. L. (1985). *Maintaining professional psychological identity and integrity in school practice.* Paper presented at the Annual Conference of the American Psychological Association, Los Angeles, CA. (ERIC Document Reproduction Service No. ED263495)
Barkley, R. A. (1990). *Attention deficit hyperactivity disorder: A handbook for diagnosis and treatment.* New York: Guilford Press.
Barkley, R. A. (1997). Attention-deficit/hyperactivity disorder. In E. J. Mash & L. G. Terdal (Eds.), *Assessment of childhood disorders* (3rd ed., pp. 71–129). New York: Guilford Press.
Bartow County (GA) School District. (1995). *OCR Rulings.* 22 IDELR 508.
Bos, C. S., & Nahmias, M. L. (1997). Implementing interactive professional development in a workshop course on educating students with ADHD. *Teacher Education and Special Education, 20,* 132–145.
Burnette, J. (1998). Reducing the disproportionate representation of minority students in special education. *Eric OSEP Digest, 4,* 3–4.
Campbell, S. B. (1987). Parent referred problem three year olds: Developmental changes in symptoms. *Journal of Child Psychology and Psychiatry, 28,* 835–846.
Campbell, S. B. (1990). *Behavior problems in preschool children: Clinical and developmental issues.* New York: Guilford Press.
Cobb County (GA) School District. (1993). *OCR Rulings.* 20 IDELR 1171.
Columbia County (GA) School District. (1991). *OCR Rulings.* 17 EHLR 586.
Dayton, J., & Arnau, L. M. (1999). *Special education law: A review and analysis. FOCUS on Legal Issues for School Administrators* (pp. 1–20). Arlington, VA: Educational Research Service.
DuPaul, G. J. (1991). Parent and teacher ratings of ADHD symptoms: Psychometric properties in a community-based sample. *Journal of Clinical Child Psychology, 20,* 245–253.
DuPaul, G. J., & Barkley, R. A. (1998). Attention-deficit hyperactivity disorder. In R. J. Morris & T. R. Kratochwil (Eds.), *The practice of child therapy* (3rd ed., pp. 167–198). Needleham Heights, MA: Allyn & Bacon.
Gammel, D. L. (1992). Comments on legal rights of students with attention deficit disorder. *School Psychology Quarterly, 7,* 298–301.
Gingerich, K. J., Turnock, P., Litfin, J. K., & Rosen, L. A. (1998). Diversity and attention deficit hyperactivity disorder. *Journal of Clinical Psychology, 54,* 415–426.
*Goss v. Lopez.* 419 U.S. 565 (1975).
Hakola, S. R. (1992). Legal rights of students with attention deficit disorder. *School Psychology Quarterly, 7,* 285–297.
Hakola, S. (1996). *Transitioning students: your guide to successful strategies.* Individuals with Disabilities Education Law Report, Special Report 16.

Honig v. Doe. 484 U.S. 305 (1988).
Individuals With Disabilities Education Act of 1990, 34 CFR 300 et seq.
Individuals With Disabilities Education Act of 1990, 20 USC 1400 et seq.
Kauffman, J. M. (1993). *Characteristics of emotional and behavioral disorders of children and youth* (5th ed.). New York: Merrill.
McConaughy, S. H., & Achenbach, T. M. (1990). Contributions of developmental pscyhopathology to school services. In T. B. Gutkin & C. R. Reynolds (Eds.), *The handbook of school psychology* (2nd ed., pp. 244–268). New York: Wiley.
Morris, R. J. (1985). *Behavior modification with exceptional children: Principles and practices.* Glenview: IL: Scott, Foresman.
Morris, R. J., & Collier, S. (1987). Attention deficit disorder and hyperactivity. In C. L. Frame & J. L. Matson (Eds.), *Handbook of assessment in childhood psychopathology: Applied issues in differential diagnosis and treatment evaluation.* New York: Plenum.
Morris, R. J., & Kratochwill, T. R. (1998). *The practice of child therapy* (3rd ed.). Boston: Allyn & Bacon.
Morris, R. J., & Morris, Y. P. (2000). Practice guidelines regarding the conduct of psychotherapy with children and adolescents. In G. Stricker, W. Troy, & S. Shueman (Eds.), *Handbook of quality management in behavioral health* (pp. 237–264). New York: Plenum.
Office of Civil Rights. (1993a). *Memorandum.* 19 IDELR 876 (OCR 1993).
Office of Civil Rights. (1993b). *Response to Zirkel.* 20 IDELR 134.
Office of Special Education Programs. (1993). *Response to Williams.* 20 IDELR 1210.
Office of Special Education Programs. (1994). *Letter to Williams.* 21 IDELR 73.
Office of Special Education Programs. (1996). *Letter to Copenhaver.* 25 IDELR 640.
Office of Special Education Programs. (1998a). *Letter to Sawyer.* 30 IDELR 540.
Office of Special Education Programs. (1998b). *Letter to Anonymous.* 30 IDELR 706.
Panksepp, J. (1998). Attention deficit hyperactivity disorders, psychostimulants, and intolerance of childhood playfulness: A tragedy in the making? *Current Directions in Psychological Science, 7,* 91–98.
Platzman, K. A., Stoy, M. R., Brown, R. T., Coles, C. D., Smith, I. E., & Falek, A. (1992). Review of observational methods inattention deficit hyperactivity disorder (ADHD): Implications for diagnosis. *School Psychology Quarterly, 7,* 155–177.
Power, T. J., & Ikeda, M. J. (1996). The clinical utility of behavior rating scales: Comments on the diagnostic assessment of ADHD. *Journal of School Psychology, 34,* 379–385.
Rehabilitation Act of 1973, 34 CFR 104 et seq.
Reid, R. (1995). Assessment of ADHD with culturally different groups: The use of behavioral rating scales. *School Psychology Review, 24,* 537–560.
Reid, R., & Maag, J. W. (1994). How many fidgets in a pretty much: A critique of behavior rating scales for identifying students with ADHD. *Journal of School Psychology, 32,* 339–354.
Reif, S. F. (1993). *How to reach and teach ADD/ADHD children.* West Nyack, NY: Center of Applied Research in Education.
Safer, D. J., & Krager, J. M. (1988). A survey of medication treatment for hyperactive/inattentive students. *Journal of the American Medical Association, 260,* 2256–2258.
Salvia, J., & Ysseldyke, J. E. (1991). *Assessment* (5th ed.). New York: Houghton Mifflin.
Schaughency, E. A., & Rothlind, J. (1991). Assessment and classification of attention deficit hyperactivity disorders. *School Psychology Review, 20,* 187–202.

Shapiro, E. S., & Kratochwill, T. R. (2000). *Behavioral assessment in schools: Theory, research, and clinical foundations* (2nd ed). New York: Guilford.
South Harrison (IN) Community School Corp. (1993). *OCR Rulings.* 20 IDELR 1360.
Stoner, G., & Carey, S. P. (1992). Serving students diagnosed with ADD: Avoiding deficits in professional attention. *School Psychology Quarterly, 7,* 302–307.
Taylor, E. (1998). Clinical foundations of hyperactivity research. *Behavioral Brain Research, 94,* 11–24.
Stevens, G. (1981). Bias in the attribution of hyperkinetic behavior as a function of ethnic identification and socioeconomic status. *Psychology in the Schools, 18,* 99–106.
Tynan, W. D., & Nearing, J. (1994). The diagnosis of attention deficit hyperactivity disorder in young children. *Infants and Young Children, 6,* 13–20.
U.S. Department of Education. (1991). *Joint Policy Memorandum.* 18 IDELR 116.
Weiss, G., & Hechtman, L. (1993). *Hyperactive children grown up: ADHD in children, adolescents, and adults.* New York: Guilford.
Zirkel, P. A. (Ed.). (1996). *Practical primer of education law.* Horsham, PA: LRP.
Zirkel, P. A., & Gluckman, I. B. (1997). ADD/ADHD students and Section 504. *Principal, 76,* 47–48.

# 13

# Access to E-Texts for Disabled Students: A Practical Reality or Just a Myth

Michael S. Somsan

Each year, a focus group of disabled students gathers with the director and counselors of a university's disability resource center to brainstorm solutions to any present accessibility problems. New construction continues to be a problem, but campus planners are making a better effort to solicit advice from disabled students on questions of accessibility. For example, in the past several years, the University of Arizona's central mall area and the surrounding campus have been torn down in order to create more room for newer facilities. The numerous construction sites on campus prevented some disabled students from attending classes and reaching critical buildings. With the coordination of campus planning and the Disability Resource Center, an electronic map of safe accessible routes was created and e-mail messages were sent to students to keep them apprised of any changes. Because of the tremendous efforts of campus planning and the Disability Resource Center to incorporate the disabled student community into the planning process, problems of inaccessibility were minimized, and no injuries were reported. Without the proactive efforts of all involved, accessibility concerns for disabled students would have been neglected.

A blind student raises a perplexing question about how one obtains electronic textbooks so information can be accessed more efficiently through a computer. An electronic formatted textbook can be as simple as a text file created by any word processing program or may include a more elaborate production process of a book in a multimedia format that displays text, graphics, and sounds. Members of the focus group recommend getting the textbooks from the publishers; however, some blind students attest that this task is not that simple.

Publishers are unwilling to give electronic versions of their textbooks due to copyright concerns, and many requests are not honored in a timely manner. Further, publishers are hesitant to give textbooks to students because logistically many textbooks are not available by mere electronic text.

A counselor makes the suggestion that students can use a variety of scanners to read and create their own electronic textbooks. Although this suggestion represents a viable solution, other concerns about using staff resources and the cumbersome nature of such processes are raised. What may appear to be a simple request for accommodations is actually a complicated task of identifying the responsibilities of all parties, deciphering the relevant laws to impose such obligations, and deriving practical solutions to provide the broadest access possible for students with disabilities. The purpose of this chapter is to provide the reader with both legal strategies and practical solutions to assist blind or visually impaired students in their pursuit to acquire electronic textbook versions for their college education.

This chapter addresses access to electronic textbooks. To accomplish this task, certain laws are implicated. The legal analysis focuses on Title II and Title III of the Americans with Disabilities Act (ADA) and relevant state laws.[1] Title II protects the rights of the disabled in the areas of public services by local and state governments. Title III is concerned with the role of private entities (any nongovernmental entity), regardless of size, in providing equal access to goods and services to individuals with disabilities. Although Title III is mainly used for publishers in this research, it can also be used to bring private universities into the coverage of the ADA [42 U.S.C. § 12181(7)(J)].

The first section of this chapter examines the role of public universities under Title II of the ADA to provide disabled students with electronic versions of their textbooks. In the next section, arguments are made on Title III grounds to persuade publishers to produce the electronic textbooks requested by disabled students.

Recently, there has been a proliferation of state laws addressing the issue of accessibility to electronic textbooks. Although these state laws are less compre-

---

[1]Requiring certain institutions to take responsibility for providing electronic textbooks for disabled students must be justifiable under the law. The most comprehensive law to protect the rights of the disabled, which was passed in 1990, is the Americans With Disabilities Act (ADA) [see Public Law 101-336 (S 933)]. Title II of the ADA, 42 U.S.C. § 12131–12150, covers such responsibilities for public universities. Title III, under 42 U.S.C. § 12181–12189, may be used to bring publishers within the coverage of the ADA. Another federal law that may be implicated is the Rehabilitation Act of 1973, 29 U.S.C. § 794. However, because of the similarity between the Rehabilitation Act and Title II of the ADA, all arguments made concerning the ADA are equally applicable to the Rehabilitation Act. The topic of education is so tied to state's rights that it became apparent that any research in this area implicates some state law. The presence and scope of any such laws will vary from state to state. How state laws differ from the ADA and its impact on accessibility will be discussed later in the chapter (see final section).

13. Access to E-Texts for Disabled Students  239

hensive than their federal counterparts, these laws do provide supporting evidence that this new electronic medium is recognized as a valuable tool in the education of disabled students. Finally, the strength of our laws is measured by their ability to create positive social change and whether such laws can be implemented in a practical setting. These issues are further explored in the final section of this chapter.

## THE SCOPE OF TITLE II

### Threshold Issue Under Title II

A public university is a covered entity with an obligation to provide reasonable accommodations. Under Title II of the ADA, a public entity is "any department, agency, special purpose district, or other instrumentality of a State or States or local government." A public university is not specifically mentioned in Title II; however, it is clearly an instrumentality of the state. Public funds are allocated to support such public institutions. The requisite nexus can also be established through the Rehabilitation Act of 1973 (which is the precursor legislation to the ADA if the public educational institution receives any federal funding) [42 U.S.C. § 12131(1)(B)].

Additionally, a public entity shall furnish appropriate auxiliary aids and services ("accommodations") where necessary to afford an individual with a disability an equal opportunity to participate in and enjoy the benefits of a service, program, or activity provided by a public entity.[2] The problem under Title II is not establishing that a public university is a covered entity; it clearly is. Rather, the difficulty under Title II is in defining the scope of the public university's responsibility to provide reasonable accommodations in the form of electronic formatted textbooks.

### Are Electronic Formatted Textbooks Considered Reasonable Accommodations?

Under the ADA, reasonable accommodations may include "job restructuring, acquisition or modification of equipment or devices, appropriate adjustment or

---

[2]No disabled individuals should be excluded from participation or be denied any benefits offered by a public entity. See 42 U.S.C. § 12132. It is important to note that reasonable accommodations are not specifically defined under Title II. To interpret this term, many courts have adopted the meaning of reasonable accommodations from Section 504 of the Rehabilitation Act of 1973 and its case law. "Title II of the ADA was expressly modeled after Section 504 of the Rehabilitation Act [29 U.S.C. § 794], and is to be interpreted consistently with that provision" [*Wong v. The Regents of the University of California*, 192 F.3d 807, 816 (9th Cir. 1999), quoting *Theriault v. Flynn*, 162 F.3d 46, 48 n. 3 (1st Cir.1998)].

modifications of examinations, training materials or policies, the provision of qualified readers or interpreters, and other similar accommodations for individuals with disabilities."[3] Nowhere are electronic texts explicitly mentioned. However, the list of accommodations is not exhaustive and serves only to illustrate the potential possibilities of available accommodations.[4] The term "other similar accommodations" in the statute may reasonably encompass electronic formatted textbooks, given the appropriate set of facts to support a student's request.

When reviewed in the courts, reasonable accommodations are analyzed using the totality of the circumstances (*Hurley-Bardige*, 1995; *Johnsen*, 1995; *Jones*, 1998; *Zukle*, 1999). Three fundamental considerations often arise in such a factual analysis: (a) The individual's request must be examined in relation to the needs of that person's disability; (b) The purpose of such accommodations in light of other reasonable available alternatives; and (c) The ability of a covered entity to provide those services. (One problem that arises, however, is that the answer to such an inquiry is limited to each particular situation, and failure to conduct an individualized inquiry runs counter to the ADA's requirements [*PGA Tour*, 2001]). Accommodations deemed reasonable in one particular situation might be considered unreasonable when imported to another set of facts.

In determining what accommodations (auxiliary aid or service) are reasonable or necessary, a public entity shall give primary consideration to the requests of the disabled individual. This requirement recognizes that not all disabilities are the same and that accommodations should reflect those distinct needs. This is consistent with the Department of Justice (DOJ) interpretive guidelines on accommodations, which state that deference to the request of the individual with a disability is desirable because of the range of disabilities, the variety of auxiliary aids and services, and different circumstances requiring effective communication (DOJ, 1992). Despite the deference given to a student's request for

---

[3] 42 U.S.C. § 12111 (9). This provision is actually found in Title I, the employment provision of the ADA. Caution needs to be exercised because no cases could be found that imported the definitional language of reasonable accommodations from Title I into a Title II action. Requesting electronic textbooks from a public university is clearly a Title II action and not a Title I (employment related) cause of action. Nonetheless, under Title II, the statute mentions the need of public entities to provide reasonable modifications for qualified disabled individuals. See 42 U.S.C. § 12131. The modifications language under Title II specifically states, "A public entity must reasonably modify its policies, its practices, or procedures to avoid discrimination." "If the public entity can demonstrate, however, that the modifications would fundamentally alter the nature of its service, program, or activity, it is not required to make the modification." See also DOJ (1992, II-3.6100).

[4] *Wooten v. ACME Steel Co.* (1997). See also ADA Title I EEOC interpretive guidance Section 1630.2 (o), which states that "there are a number of other specific accommodations that may be appropriate for a particular situation but are not specifically mentioned in this listing" and "this listing is not intended to be exhaustive of accommodation possibilities."

accommodations, however, the request itself is not conclusive evidence that the accommodations are reasonable.[5] Moreover, under Title II, accommodations must also be analyzed in light of their purpose and the availability of other reasonable alternatives. The use of electronic textbooks may be deemed reasonable for one course of study, but this may not be the case for another course of study.

A final critical dimension in determining the reasonableness of an accommodation is the educational institution's ability to provide such services. Within any university, a disability resource center of some type and size exists. The daunting task of providing accommodations may lie in the hands of one individual or a staff of disability specialists. The size of the disabled student population will often dictate what staffing requirements and services are available, and individual requests for accommodations must be weighed against the public entity's ability to meet such needs with the available resources.

Presently, no published court case exists on the issue of accessibility to electronic textbooks. The limited precedent that does exist has largely come from administrative decisions rendered by the Office of Civil Rights (OCR). In a 1994 OCR action, a disabled community college student alleged disability discrimination against a school district in California for its failure to provide adequate access to written materials for students with visual impairments, and failure to make its computer laboratory, library, physical education courses, and employment services accessible. During the course of the OCR investigation, the college agreed to a voluntary resolution plan.[6] Even though no opinion on the reasonableness of the request was made, the letter of resolution is instructive for several reasons. The OCR noted that under Title II of the ADA, "a public entity shall take appropriate steps to ensure that communications with applicants, participants, and members of the public with disabilities are as effective as communications with others." Furthermore, printed materials fall within the meaning of "communication." Effective communication in the context of

---

[5]Although primary consideration is afforded to the individual's request, the public entity must also consider other factors that may render the request unreasonable. An example provided by DOJ *Technical Assistance Manual* (DOJ, 1992) illustrates this point. A blind individual voting in local elections wanted a Braille ballot because having a reader assist him would destroy the secrecy of the balloting. A Braille ballot, however, poses a burden to the public entity because it has to be counted separately and will be readily identifiable. Anonymity is thus not protected. Further, because the county can demonstrate that its system with readers is effective in providing the blind with an equal opportunity to vote, the public entity need not provide the ballots in Braille.

[6]The voluntary resolution plan was a recognition by the Los Rios Community College system that something had to be done. A problem of inaccessibility did exist. Because the merits of the case were not specifically addressed, we can only speculate whether the complainant would have prevailed. Certainly a settlement eliminates the costs of litigation and spares the reputation of the educational institution from being perceived as non-accommodating to a disabled student.

Title II, as defined by DOE, is the transfer of information with three basic components: (a) timeliness of delivery; (b) accuracy of the translation; and (c) provision in a manner and medium appropriate to the significance of the message and the abilities of the individual with the disability.[7] If the requested medium is contrary to the medium chosen by the public entity, the educational institution may not categorically refuse to provide the accommodation. According to the *National Disability Law Reporter* (NDLR), "The post-secondary institution must be prepared to timely offer access to its printed materials in all three mediums [auditory, tactile (Braille), and enlarged print] with the particular medium used for the student's request dependent on a case by case analysis" (NDLR, 1994, p. 423 [case #09-93-2214-I]). The OCR further noted in the California case that "if the student with the visual impairment prefers, and the public entity is willing to provide, access through 'E-text' (electronic text in a digital format read by computer), such method may be used in lieu of access through another medium." Accordingly, the OCR opinion in the California case suggests that electronic texts are reasonable accommodations under Title II and the Rehabilitation Act of 1973.

In contrast to the California case, another OCR decision involving the University of Alaska at Anchorage found electronic textbooks to be unreasonable based on the particular facts in that case (NDLR, 1999, p. 251 [case #10992002]). In the 1999 Alaska case, the complainant alleged that the university failed to make textbook materials available to him in a format that accommodated for his particular combination of physical and mental impairments associated with his cerebral palsy. The complainant wanted the university to transfer his textbooks onto computer disks so that he could have electronic access to these materials. The complainant claimed that the University of Alaska violated Section 504 and Title II by failing to make printed materials accessible to him in a manner that would accommodate his combination of disabilities. The student also alleged that the university denied him effective access to its writing lab and refused to provide access, by way of an alternative location, as an accommodation. The first charge was adjudicated in favor of the university; the second charge was not addressed because it was not filed within a timely manner with the agency. During the course of the OCR investigation, the agency found the student's requests to be unreasonable and ruled against the disabled student.

---

[7]U.S. Department of Education, Office of Civil Rights, Letter of Resolution, Docket No. 09-97-2002 (Apr. 7, 1997) (cited in Waddell, 1999), noting that entities covered under both ADA Title II and III must meet the "effective communication" requirement. If the requested medium is contrary to the medium chosen by the public entity, the educational institution may not categorically refuse to provide the accommodation.

In reaching its conclusion, the OCR did not reject entirely the idea that electronic formatted textbooks could be considered reasonable accommodations. The agency did not declare that electronic texts were per se unreasonable. It recognized that the complainant had access to all of this technology and could have produced his own accommodations. However, the agency never addressed the efficiency of such processes except to note that the complainant could not proofread all of the mistakes produced by scanning his textbooks. It was unclear whether the university made an attempt to assist the complainant to scan his textbooks. In the end, no firm obligation to do so was established. However, in this particular case the complainant lacked the supporting documentation to explain why or how such accommodations could help him and they were thus deemed to be unreasonable.[8] The agency simply did not view the complainant's request as truly necessary. For instance, without the requested accommodations the complainant still managed to achieve a grade point average of 3.0 through the use of audiocassettes and enlarged print copies of his textbooks provided by the university. If a university is making a good faith effort to work with the student and to provide some accommodations, regardless of whether it is entirely effective, it will be entitled to academic deference on that decision (*Wong*, 1999). The implication of the decision is that a disabled student is entitled to reasonable accommodations but not necessarily to the best accommodations (*Beck*, 1996; *Dyer*, 1995; *Hall*, 2001; *Singer*, 1999).

The question of electronic formatted textbooks as reasonable accommodations under Title II of the ADA is far from settled. Questions of reasonableness based on the facts will surely shape the outcome of each case. However, a common thread does exist. The individual's needs and the purposes underlying such requests will be weighed against the available alternatives for accommodations and whether the public entity can meet those needs. Given the rapid change in computer technology and the increasing accessibility to that technology by disabled individuals, electronic textbooks will become more possible and, therefore, more reasonable in the near future. For example, Bulkeley (1998) wrote, "Speech recognition on powerful PCs is as much as 98% accurate today with continuous speech by a familiar voice. Within three to five years, that level of speech recognition will be available in battery-powered devices the size of a pocket tape recorder" (p. R4).

---

[8]The agency decided that the complainant's request for the electronic texts lacked the medical justification or clinical basis necessary to approve it. The complainant's audiologist did provide a note attesting to those needs, but perhaps some sort of testing from a learning specialist indicating the complainant's needs for such accommodations would have been more credible. An established and successful learning pattern built around electronic texts is ample evidence to justify such accommodations.

# THE SCOPE OF TITLE III OF THE ADA

## The General Rule

As a general rule, Title III of the ADA prohibits discrimination on the basis of disability "in the full and equal enjoyment of goods, services, facilities, privileges, advantages or accommodations of any place of public accommodation" [42 U.S.C. § 12182(a)]. The general rule of "full and equal" access is the cornerstone of Title III. However, conflicting interpretations of the general rule have led to many problems in defining the scope of accessibility under Title III.

In seeking access to an electronic formatted text under Title III, the students (plaintiffs) would bring a cause of action against the publishers (defendants), a private entity. Whether a publisher has an obligation to provide electronic formatted textbooks as a reasonable accommodation, will depend on how Title III is interpreted.

Title III is perhaps the broadest Title under the ADA. In fact, it even covers individuals who are not disabled but who are perceived as disabled or who are treated as such because of their relationship with someone who is considered disabled [42 U.S.C. § 12182(b)(1)(e)]. Despite Title III's broad statutory scheme, however, claimants seeking its protections must still be able to withstand judicial scrutiny and meet the required burdens of a prima facie ADA case. Several threshold steps are required to meet those burdens. The most significant is whether a publisher is even considered a public accommodation and thus a covered entity under the statute. For a publisher to be considered a covered entity under Title III, it must fall within the categories of listed public accommodations [ADA, 42 U.S.C. § 12181(7)]. It must also fall within the definition of a private entity under 42 U.S.C. § 12181(6), and it must also affect commerce, as defined under 42 U.S.C. § 12181(1)(a) and (2)(b). Moreover, even if a court finds that a publisher is a covered entity, the plaintiff must then establish that an electronically formatted text is a reasonable accommodation. Additionally, a plaintiff still may not prevail if the defendant can show that providing such an accommodation would create an undue hardship [ADA, 42 U.S.C. § 12182(b)(2)(a)(ii)].

## Public Accommodation

In order for publishers and their services to be a covered entity under Title III, they must be considered a public accommodation as defined by the statute. Title III defines a public accommodation as a facility, operated by a private entity (regardless of size), whose operations affect commerce and fall within at least one of the 12 specified categories identified in the statute. The commercial operations of publishers do have an effect on commerce because when one considers the myriad of ways a publishing company can conduct its business, through the telephone, mail, and the Internet, it seems more than obvious that its operations affect commerce. In addition to a publisher's commercial activities, the entity must fall within the statutory list of 12 categories of private entities considered to be public accommodation. Further, no cases have been reported indicating that publishers are places of public accommodation. Presently, whether a publisher is a public accommodation and therefore required to provide reasonable accommodations pursuant to the mandates of Title III is an open question. Whether a publisher is considered a place of public accommodation is largely dependent on how it is characterized. Publishers are public accommodations. First, a publisher needs to be defined as falling within the twelve listed categories and thus is a place of public accommodation within the meaning of Title III [ADA, 42 U.S.C. § 12181(7)].[9] Second, the definition of a place of public accommodation must be defined more broadly than merely as the physical location where the disabled individual is seeking access. To limit the category of entities to mere "facilities" will render the meaning of the general rule of Title III superfluous. The general rule prohibiting discrimination makes no explicit reference to physical access to physical structures. The section states: "No individual shall be discriminated against ... in the full and equal enjoyment of the goods, services, facilities, privileges, advantages, or accommodations of any place of public accommodation by any person ... who operates a place of public accommodation" [ADA, 42 U.S.C. § 12182(a)]. If the intent of Congress was to limit Title III to mere physical access, it makes more sense to strike out the terms *goods, services, privileges,* and *advantages* from 42 U.S.C. § 12182(a). The general rule would thus be drafted as follows: "No individual shall be discriminated against ... in the full and equal enjoyment of the facilities." To adopt that view would render certain words and purposes of the statute meaningless. Finally, a private entity considered to be a public accommodation should be defined by the nature of the transactions it provides to the general public.

---

[9]To be considered a public accommodation, a publisher must fit into one of the 12 categories listed. However, this task is not as simple as it may appear. One argument is that if the entity does not appear in the list, Congress did not intend to cover it under Title III (in other words, Congress could have included it, but chose not to) (see *Stoutenborough v. National Football League Inc.*, 59 F.3d 580, 583). A contrary argument is that if an analogous covered entity could be found, this is enough to satisfy the broad mandates of the statute (see *Carparts Distribution Center, Inc. v. Automotive Wholesalers Association of New England, Inc.*, 37 F.3d 12, 20). A second layer of arguments surrounds the fact that even if an entity was found in the list, the statute is only concerned with the removal of physical barriers to these facilities, and does not address whether the goods and services are provided in a nondiscriminatory manner [see *Parker v. Metropolitan Life Ins. Co.*, 121 F.3d. 1006, 1011 (Sixth Circuit *en banc,* 1997)].

## Publishers Are Within the 12 Categories of Public Accommodations

Publishers will argue that Title III never even uses the word "publisher" in either the 12 categories or the examples provided within each category. This does not necessarily preclude placing publishers within the coverage of Title III. An important distinction must be made between the list of 12 categories, which is considered exhaustive, and the examples of each category that represent the type of entities within the 12 categories and are meant to be illustrative and therefore should be interpreted broadly. The illustrative nature of the examples is evidenced by the use of the terms "other similar entities" after each list of examples given for each category described in the statute [ADA, 42 U.S.C. § 12181(7)(A)–(L)]. From the legislative history of Title III, it can be ascertained that the congressional reviewing committee intended the "other similar" terminology to be construed liberally. This is consistent with the intent of the statute to provide the broadest opportunity possible of full and equal access by individuals with disabilities to the goods and services that their non-disabled peers receive.[10] The question is, can an entity that is not specifically mentioned among the 12 categories be considered a public accommodation? Recent legal challenges against private web sites have sought to find an answer to the question.

In the past few years, several cases have considered the question whether private web sites and other institutions using electronic technology in their business plans fall under the coverage of Title III of the ADA. The first and leading case was a lawsuit filed by the National Federation of the Blind (NFB) on behalf of its members against America Online (AOL). The charge was that AOL failed to provide reasonable access for its blind users by using its graphically driven software on its web site. As part of the settlement, AOL promised to create a new version of its software that would be more compatible with the screen readers used by its blind customers. Other guidelines for better technical support and consistent operating standards would be adopted to facilitate greater access.[11]

---

[10]S. Rep. No. 101-116, at 59 (1989); see also H. R. Rep. No.101-485, pt. II, at 100 (1990), reprinted in 1990 U.S.C.C.A.N. 303, 382-83. Case law adopting a broad interpretation includes *Florida Paraplegic Association, Inc. & The Association of Disabled Americans, Inc. v. Miccosukee Tribe of Indians of Florida*, 166 F.3d 1126, 1128 (11th cir., 1999). The 11th Circuit Court of Appeals noted, "In fact, it is precisely the sort of facility within "the array of establishments ... available to others who do not currently have disabilities" that Congress intended to make "equal[ly] access[ible]" to disabled individuals through enactment of Title III of the ADA."

[11]The text of the AOL settlement with the NFB can be obtained from the NFB web site at http://204.245.133.32.agreement.htm. The NFB AOL press release is available at http://204.245.133.32/nfbaolr.htm. See also Weiss (2000). "AOL Promises Access for Blind," Computerworld, July 31, 2000, at 8. Available at 2000 WL 2176778, or http://www.pcworld.com

In April 2000, the Attorney General of Connecticut and the National Federation of the Blind settled an action against Gilman & Ciocia, H&R Block, H. D. Vest, and Intuit, alleging that the companies failed to make their online tax services accessible to the blind and visually impaired in violation of Title III. The companies agreed to change the coding of their sites for the 2000 tax filing season. More recently, the California Council of the Blind reached a settlement with the Bank of America whereby the bank agreed to install 2,500 talking ATMs in Florida and California, and to make its web site and online banking services compatible with screen reading technology. Although all of these three cases were settled, they are nonetheless significant in the resulting positive social changes from the litigation.

Private web sites, which are similar to publishers, are not listed among the exhaustive list of 12 categories nor can they be found in the examples within each category. Nevertheless, legal commentators have noted that the e-commerce transactions that occur at these web sites fall squarely within the coverage of Title III of the ADA (Blanck & Sandler, 2000). Many people, including the disabled, are buying, selling, and trading goods and services online. According to these commentators, there is no reason why these web sites should not be categorized as sales and rental establishments and subject to the accessibility guidelines under Title III [ADA, 42 U.S.C. § 12181(7)(E)]. An analogous argument can be applied to publishers. There is no reason why a publisher cannot also be considered a covered entity under the category of sales and rental establishments. Publishers often have dedicated sales departments within the organization that are solely responsible for selling and distributing textbooks to educational institutions. Publishers are turning to electronic textbooks, the Internet, and other digital media to attract parents and teachers to education built around a business plan focused on increased technology (White, 2001). Goods and services are exchanged within interstate commerce. These are exactly the types of transactions the ADA was drafted to cover. Thus, the mere absence of publishers from the categories or examples does not indicate an intention to exclude them from the coverage of Title III.

Arguments by publishers that they are not mentioned in the statute may ironically work in favor of the plaintiffs. If it were the intention of Congress to exclude publishers from Title III, it would have been listed as an exempt organization in the statute. Title III shall not apply to "private clubs, or establishments exempted from coverage under Title II of the Civil Rights Act of 1964 or religious organizations or entities controlled by religious organizations, including places of worship" (ADA, 42 U.S.C. § 12187). For example, despite their service to the public, religious institutions are exempt and not considered a public accommodation. This indicates that when Congress wanted to exempt a particular category or certain type of entity, it knew how to do so (as in the case of religious institutions). Therefore, a reasonable interpretation is that publishers are not exempted from coverage under Title III.

To the extent that the question of whether publishers are exempt is ambiguous, deference is accorded to the legislative history and intent of the statute. From the language of the legislation itself and from the legislative history, it is evident that the ADA is a general statute that Congress intended to have broad applicability.[12] The purpose of the ADA is "to invoke the sweep of congressional authority, including the power to enforce the fourteenth amendment and to regulate commerce, in order to address the major areas of discrimination faced day-to-day by people with disabilities" [ADA, 42 U.S.C. § 12101(b)(4)]. To adopt a narrow interpretation of Title III by excluding publishers as a place of public accommodation only serves to undermine the congressional intent and purpose of the Act. A narrow interpretation of Title III renders substantive terms in the statute superfluous, incorrectly assumes that the statute is only concerned with physical access, and further undermines the remedial purposes of the ADA.

## Is a Public Accommodation Limited to Access or Does It Mean More?

The second major contention in clarifying the meaning of a public accommodation is whether the definition is limited to the access to physical structures. This "access approach" was adopted by the Sixth Circuit Court of Appeals sitting *en banc* in *Parker v. Metropolitan Life Insurance Co.* (1997). The plaintiff in *Parker*, who suffered from mental anxieties, sued her employer's disability insurance company for disparities in their coverage under Title III. Under the policy, physical disorders were covered until the age of 65, while coverage for mental disorders was limited to 2 years.[13] The *en banc* majority held that a Title III claim is limited only to the access of a *facility*. The term "facility" constitutes "all or any portion of buildings, structures, sites, complexes, equipment, rolling stock or other conveyances, roads, walks, passageways, parking lots, or other real or personal property, including the site where the building, property,

---

[12] A broader application of the statute should be adopted in order to be consistent with the overall purpose of Title III as a remedial statute to eliminate disability based discrimination. See Department of Justice (1992) *Technical Assistance Manual*, III-3.11000, reprinted in *Americans with Disabilities Manual* (BNA) 90:0917. See also *Charrow v. Bailey*, 910 F.Supp. 187. The obvious intent of Title III is to preclude the denial of services available to the public generally by reason of an individual's disability. This remedial purpose of the ADA should be emphasized.

[13] One of the factors that seems to affect the disparities in coverage for mental disabilities compared to physical disabilities lies in the certainty of diagnosis of such conditions. For additional information, see Geeter (2000). See Firak (1998).

structure, or equipment is located" as defined by a "place" (physical structure) where the business is located (insurance offices), but it is not applicable to the goods and services sold on those premises (insurance policies) (28 C.F.R. § 36, Appx. B, p. 602). Because the plaintiff was not denied physical access to the insurance offices, her Title III claim was subsequently dismissed. In many cases, a motion to dismiss is filed on the grounds that an insurance company is not a public accommodation. Plaintiffs must survive this threshold attack before pursuing their claim of insurance discrimination on the policy itself (Firak, 1998). Thus, if a plaintiff intends to pursue a Title III action against publishers in a jurisdiction that follows the *Parker* precedent, a requirement of entry into a physical structure (place) is necessary despite discrimination in the provision of goods and services. Hypothetically, the publisher can make the same argument as the insurer in *Parker* (2000) that no discrimination existed because the plaintiff was never denied physical access to its offices or facilities.

The First Circuit in *Carparts Distribution Center, Inc. v. Automotive Wholesaler's Association of New England* (1994) ruled that a public accommodation does not have to be a physical structure that a person has to physically enter in order to gain the protections of Title III. Unlike *Parker*, the *Carparts* court found that the terms in a disputed health insurance policy were covered under Title III. In arriving at this conclusion, the court looked at other entities within the service category under the statute, such as a travel service, and found that it is unnecessary to physically enter into a physical structure to acquire such services. The *Carparts* court further noted:

> Neither Title III nor its implementing regulations make any mention of physical boundaries or physical entry. Many goods and services are sold over the telephone or by mail with customers never physically entering the premises of a commercial entity to purchase the goods or services. To exclude this broad category of businesses from the reach of Title III and limit the application of Title III to physical structures which persons must enter to obtain goods and services would run afoul of the purposes of the ADA. (*Carparts*, 1994, p. 19)

The First Circuit reasoned that the significant aspect of a travel service is not physical access to the office, but instead is the planning and arranging of the vacation through various means other than physical entry of the facility.[14]

---

[14] Although the First Circuit did not explicitly mention that Title III applies to the goods and services provided by a private entity considered to be a public accommodation, its broad treatment of a travel agency clearly indicates that the scope of the statute can cover such areas of a business. On remand, the district court held that an insurance company and its policy could be subjected to the scrutiny of Title III. See *Carparts*, 987 F.Supp 77, 81.

The reasoning proposed by the *Carparts* court can plausibly be applied to publishers. Many publishing companies conduct business without requiring customers to enter their facilities. Many customers place book orders and revise their business plans by telephone or other means to their publishers without ever entering an actual publishing office. Consequently, as noted by the First Circuit, "[It] would be irrational to conclude that persons who enter an office to purchase services are protected by the ADA, but persons who purchase the same services over the telephone or by mail are not. Congress could not have intended such an absurd result" (*Carparts*, 1994, p. 19).

## Publishers Are Not Exempt Wholesalers

A final contention in deciphering the meaning of a public accommodation is being able to distinguish the transactions conducted by publishers from other wholesale industries who are exempt from Title III.[15] Under the controlling regulations proffered by the Department of Justice (DOJ), "The Department intends for wholesale establishments to be covered ... as places of public accommodation except in cases where they sell exclusively to other businesses and not to individuals" (DOJ, 1996). By likening publishers to wholesale establishments that sell certain goods and services (textbooks in this case) only to university bookstores, a logical conclusion is that such publishers are exempt wholesalers and beyond the reach of Title III. However, this interpretation goes beyond the scope of the controlling regulations.

The selling of textbooks at bookstores is distinguishable from general wholesalers who only sell to other businesses. The purpose behind the wholesale exception is to recognize the limited scope of Title III in its ability to interfere with the contracting activities between businesses. The example provided by the DOJ regulations was that of a food-producing wholesaler considered to be exempt in its transactions with a food processing company. However, a distinction can be made between the supplied example and the problem of inaccessible textbooks. The DOJ example of the food producer and food processor is addressing a pure wholesale dealer with another wholesale dealer. These transactions are exempt under Title III. This exemption becomes inapplicable if a business becomes a wholesale retailer selling its goods and services to individual customers. Thus, a bookstore or publisher may be categorized as either an ex-

---

[15] As defined by *Black's Legal Dictionary* (Black, Nolan, & Nolan-Haley, 1990), a wholesale dealer is "one whose business is the selling of goods in gross to retail dealers, and not by the small quantity or parcel to consumers thereof." In addition, a wholesaler is "one who buys in comparatively large quantities, and then resells usually in smaller quantities, but never to the ultimate consumer." Publishers will argue that they fit. If they do, Title III does not apply to them.

empt wholesaler or not, depending on who it is selling its products to. Considering that many blind students are making individual requests through these entities, the transaction is with a wholesale retailer, and is not exempt from Title III scrutiny. The relationship between a bookstore and a publisher is distinguishable from the example provided by the DOJ regulations. As indicated by the regulations, a sale establishment that markets its goods "wholesale to the public" and sells to individuals is not exempt from ADA coverage despite its use of the word "wholesale" as a marketing technique (DOJ, 1996). Among the list of businesses identified by the DOJ regulations, sale establishments such as jewelry stores, pet stores, and bookstores are considered places of public accommodations and not treated as exempt wholesalers because of the nature of those businesses.

The key distinction between a food-producing wholesaler who only sells to a food processing plant and a jewelry store, pet store, or a bookstore is that the former typically sells only to retailers whereas the latter entities typically sell to individuals. Therefore, the wholesale food producer who sells to food processing companies would not consider an individual a potential customer for its crops. However, in the context of publishers, bookstores request book orders based on the number of individuals enrolled in a particular class and then sell them to those individuals. Although the bookstore negotiates directly with the respective publishers, the demand and supply of textbooks are driven by student requests. The potential customer who will eventually bear the costs and reap the benefits is not the bookstore, but the individual student.

In addition, the mere fact that it is the bookstore that directly places the book orders from publishers does not excuse such entities from complying with Title III. Nothing stops a student from requesting the same textbooks found in the bookstore directly from the publisher. In that situation, a publisher may not directly discriminate, just as it cannot do so indirectly through a bookstore. Unlike the food-producing wholesaler, a publisher is not exempt as a wholesaler because it must not only consider its business interactions with the educational institution, but must also consider the individual student as a potential customer (whether directly or indirectly) essential to its success.

## Reasonable Accommodation

Even if a plaintiff can show that a publisher is a covered entity (place of public accommodation) under Title III, he or she must then address whether his or her requests for electronic textbooks are deemed reasonable accommodations. Title III includes in its definition of discrimination the failure of a place of public accommodation "to make reasonable modifications [accommodations] in policies, practices and procedures, when such modifications are necessary to afford such goods, services, facilities, privileges, advantages or accommodations to individuals with disabilities" [ADA, 42 U.S.C. § 12182(b)(2)(A)(ii)]. Title III does not use the term *reasonable accommodations*, but instead uses the term *reasonable modifications* (same as Title II). Despite the difference in terminology, the concepts are the same. A place of public accommodation may escape from such responsibilities if the entity can demonstrate that making such a modification would fundamentally alter the nature of the provided programs or services. The fundamental alteration and undue hardship language are affirmative defenses that covered entities can assert to avoid complying with the requirements of Title III.

The leading Title III case addressing whether an accommodation is deemed reasonable is the U.S. Supreme Court decision rendered *PGA Tour, Inc. v. Casey Martin* (2001). Casey Martin is a professional golfer who suffers from Klippel–Trenaunay–Weber syndrome, a degenerative circulatory disorder that obstructs the flow of blood from his right leg back to his heart. This progressive disease prevents him from walking for long periods of time without extreme pain, fatigue, and anxiety. Martin's substantial limitation is his inability to walk the entire golf course. Nonetheless, "he does walk while on the course—even with a cart, he must move from cart to shot and back to the cart. In essence, he still must walk approximately 25% of the course. On a course roughly five miles in length, Martin will walk 1 1/4 miles" (*Martin*, 1998, p. 1251). To force Martin to walk and play golf would run the significant risk of causing a hemorrhage in his leg, developing blood clots, and possibly leading to a severe fracture in his tibia that could require amputation. The trial court noted, "[Martin] is in significant pain when he walks, and even when he is getting in and out of the cart. With each step, he is at risk of fracturing his tibia and hemorrhaging. The other golfers have to endure the psychological stress of competition as part of their fatigue; Martin has the same stress plus the added stress of pain and risk of serious injury" (*Martin*, 1998, pp. 1251–1252). Because of these reasons, Casey Martin requested the use of a golf cart for the qualification rounds of the PGA Tour.[16]

Martin was denied the accommodations due to the "walking rule," which was the PGA's rule to inject a level of fatigue in the shot-making aspect of the game for the last round of the qualifications. The PGA stated that allowing Martin to use a golf cart for the final round would fundamentally change the character of the tournament and provide Martin with an unfair advantage over his peers. Thus, the issue became whether allowing a disabled golfer to use a golf

---

[16]The PGA conducted three rounds for golfers competing in its Q-school tournaments in order to qualify to play in the subsequent tours. Golf carts were allowed for the first two rounds, but were not permitted for the third and last round.

cart and waiving the walking rule was a reasonable accommodation under Title III.

At trial, the federal court for the District of Oregon found that the use of a golf cart by a disabled golfer did not fundamentally alter the nature of the game and required the PGA to permit Martin to use a golf cart in competition (*Martin*, 1998). The PGA appealed and the Ninth Circuit Court of Appeals affirmed the lower district court's opinion (*Martin*, 2000).

At the same time, the Seventh Circuit Court of Appeals was addressing a similar set of facts involving another disabled golfer and held in favor of the PGA (*Olinger*, 2000). In the Seventh Circuit case, that court found that the PGA was not considered a public accommodation and that golf carts would fundamentally alter the nature of the competition.[17] *Certiorari* was granted and the U.S. Supreme Court finally settled the dispute, ruling in favor of Casey Martin.[18]

On review, for the U.S. Supreme Court, Justice Stevens noted that Martin paid $3,000 as a member of the public to have the opportunity to obtain a slot to compete. Despite his status as a participant-player in the tournament, he does not lose that designation as a member of the public seeking access. Thus the PGA's tournament is considered a public accommodation. The court found that allowing Mr. Martin to use a golf cart did not alter the essential aspects of the game and that the association's walking rule was not an indispensable feature of tournament play. As Justice Stevens noted, "the waiver of a peripheral tournament rule that does not impair its purpose cannot be said to fundamentally alter the nature of the athletic event" (*PGA Tour*, 2001, p. 1888). The court understood that although the walking rule injected an element of fatigue into the skill of shot making, it recognized that Martin endured greater fatigue even with the cart than his able-bodied competitors did by walking.

Extending the logic of the *PGA Tour* decision to publishers, the issue is whether a request for electronic textbooks will fundamentally alter the nature of the goods and services offered by publishers. A fundamental alteration may occur if a request is inconsistent with the goods and services traditionally offered by the covered entity. However, as noted by Justice Stevens in the *PGA*

---

[17]The U.S. Golf Association (USGA) argued that its tournament, the U.S. Open, was not a public accommodation under Title III. The USGA did not dispute that a golf course was among the list of private entities considered a public accommodation in 42 U.S.C.A. § 12181(7)(L). However, according to the USGA, the statute is referring only to the designated public areas behind the rope for spectators and not to the players of the tournament where Mr. Olinger was seeking public access (*Olinger*, 2000, p. 1005).

[18]The Casey Martin decision from the Ninth Circuit Court of Appeals reached a contrary decision from *Olinger* in the Seventh Circuit Court of Appeals. The Ninth Circuit struck down the PGA's argument that it was considered an exempt private club and that Martin was not a proper customer falling within the coverage of Title III because he was a player and not a public spectator. See *Martin v. PGA Tour, Inc.*, 204 F.3d. 994, 997.

*Tour* decision, "the use of carts is not itself inconsistent with the fundamental character of the game of golf. Golf carts started appearing with increasing regularity on American golf courses in the 1950s. Today they are everywhere. And they are encouraged" (PGA *Tour*, 2001, p. 1884). Similarly, the request for electronic textbooks seems reasonable in light of the enormous reliance of publishers to produce and store their textbooks on an electronic medium. The request is not for any special or unique good or service that a publisher would not typically have access to in its normal business operations.[19] The fundamental character of a textbook is to convey information. An electronic textbook is only a change in the format and not in the substantive content of the textbook. To protect the publisher's property interest, students obtaining electronic textbooks are subject to the same transaction costs and copyright restrictions as if they were buying a hard copy version. Because publishers are concerned with royalty rights of the author(s) of the textbook, they need some assurance that the student intends to buy and use this for school and not for some other commercial gain. Taking all of this into consideration, requests for electronic texts will not fundamentally alter the mix of goods and services provided by the publishers.

A situation may arise where producing an electronic version of a textbook may cause an undue hardship for publishers due to time constraints, costs, or other unforeseeable restrictions.[20] The scope and extent of what constitutes an undue hardship will vary from case to case and is, therefore, beyond the scope of this chapter. Rather than speculating where that threshold of costs and benefits may be, it is clear that despite this, a covered entity must engage in a conscientious effort to provide the requested accommodation or a reasonable alternative unless it would constitute an undue hardship (Wong, 1999). This often

---

[19]From the various interviews with publishing representatives, there is no consistent standard for storing textbooks that have already been published. The publishing company does keep a copy of the published textbook, but not necessarily in some electronic archive. Many companies are starting to develop electronic libraries, because it saves space and allows for easier revisions in subsequent editions. Further, these companies are operating on multiple information technology platforms, and having textbooks in a digital format gives them flexibility to integrate these goods for future multimedia packages. One publishing representative noted that the problem is not that the textbook is not available in some electronic format; the challenge lies in finding it in a finished product that can be released to the student through computer disks. If a finished product is not available, the publisher will simply not provide the student with that information.

[20]Because the electronic textbooks are not readily available, it will take some time for publishers to react to a student's request. No rule of thumb exists on how much time is unreasonable or how high the costs should be before an undue hardship exists. One plausible approach is that it should not take the whole semester because by the end of the semester, the book is useless to that particular student. Moreover, the costs of producing the electronic files should not be more than the number of students presently enrolled for that class who will buy the book. Thus, if there are 100 students enrolled and the textbook costs $50, then the costs should not exceed $5000 to produce an accommodated version (the cost of lost sales if the professor chose a different textbook publishing company, preferring to do business with a company that does not discriminate).

13. Access to E-Texts for Disabled Students  255

requires the covered entity to engage in an interactive-communications process with the student to identify the appropriate accommodations, possible alternatives, relevant time frames and deadlines, and the available resources to accomplish these goals (Beck, 1996). Thus, for a publisher to simply assert that an accommodation cannot be achieved will not satisfy the undue hardship test. Given the vast resources of some publishers and the revenues generated by selling textbooks, it is in the best interests of publishers to cooperate rather than destroying the goodwill between the company and its customers.

Whether plaintiffs choose to pursue a Title II or a Title III claim, they will encounter legal hurdles. Under Title III, it will be difficult to place publishers into the category of a public accommodation. However under Title II, the challenging task is to determine the reasonableness of such accommodations. Because of these reasons, pursuing a discrimination claim under state law may be a more viable alternative.

## STATE ACCESSIBILITY LAWS

### Recent State Developments

Recent developments to increase the availability of electronic textbooks for the disabled from publishers can be seen in state laws requiring that such accommodations be provided. Generally, the state laws addressing the issue of providing electronic textbooks to the disabled are supplements to a state's education code; they are not statutes addressing general discrimination concerns, such as the Americans with Disabilities Act. However, the number of states enacting laws providing access to electronic texts remains small.[21] Despite the small number of states providing such rights, the mere presence of these statutes provide additional evidence that electronic textbooks are perceived to be an increasingly valuable tool in a disabled person's education.

### Benefits of State Accessibility Laws

State laws addressing accessibility to electronic textbooks provide several benefits. First, the explicit mention of a requirement that publishers provide electronic textbooks to all qualified disabled students seeking such accommodations makes it clear that these materials are essential for the individuals requesting them. By

---

[21]The following states and their respective statutes addressing the issue of electronic textbooks are: Arizona (A.R.S. § 15-1425–115-1425 and A.R.S. § 15-1626–115-1626); California (West's Ann. Cal. Educ. Code § 67302); Washington (WA ST § 28B.10.912); and West Virginia (WV ST § 18-10J-5). Of the 50 states, only 4 states have legislation addressing accessibility to electronic textbooks at the postsecondary level. These states are West Virginia, Arizona, California, and Washington.

passing such progressive legislation, these states are making an affirmative statement recognizing that the technology is available for disabled students. With the presence of such laws, disabled individuals can finally take advantage of such advancing technology.

Second, unlike the ADA, the state laws that do exist remove the ambiguities surrounding the determination of a covered entity or whether electronic textbooks are even considered reasonable accommodations. These laws are designed for a specific group and purpose. Publishers are specifically mentioned for the sole purpose of providing electronic texts as accommodations. Publishers are well aware that if they wish to conduct business in these particular states, they must comply with the accessibility mandates of these laws. When considering a large state such as California and all of the universities in that jurisdiction, a strong economic incentive exists for publishers to cooperate, as a failure to do so may result in lost revenue. Finally, these laws may save the state the money it would have spent on other forms of accommodations in order to provide the necessary services for these disabled students. Many states provide cash subsidies and services such as vocational rehabilitation pay for readers, textbooks, and other necessary expenses for a disabled student to attend school.[22] State vocational rehabilitation programs (in the Department of Economic Securities) generally provide educational support services by assisting students with the payment of tuition, textbooks, and the purchase of requisite adaptive equipment for school, such as a computer system. From interviews with many vocational rehabilitation students, having the ability to read textbooks on computers greatly enhanced their independence from readers. If anything, it is a wonderful complement to meeting the needs of their education. Although no present study exists to support the amount of savings, it seems likely that as more disabled students acquire and use electronic textbooks the need for other equivalent services (such as readers) will diminish.

In addition, the states incur no direct costs for the implementation of the accessibility laws. The state laws deal with compliance and nondiscrimination and are not concerned with appropriations. The marginal cost of enacting state legislation to require publishers to produce electronic textbooks is minimal. Unlike the guidelines for vocational rehabilitation or other provisions in a state's education code, no appropriations are required to administer these ser-

---

[22]Some states will allow children of blind parents to attend school for free. In Alabama, where the head of the household is blind and certain economic needs can be shown, a child can attend a state university for little or no cost. See AL ST § 16-33-4. Several states will pay for readers for blind students attending postsecondary education. Examples include New York (see NY EDUC § 4210), Kansas (K.S.A. § 76-157), Missouri (MO ST § 178.160), and Ohio (OH ST § 3325.05). This list is by no means unlimited, but rather shows how some states are attempting to assist disabled students in the pursuit of their education.

vices. Whether a publisher complies with the law or not, the state is not paying for it. The greatest obstacle to any law expanding the rights of the disabled to electronic textbooks will be the political and lobbying efforts of publishers to minimize their responsibilities under such laws. One possible indirect cost might be lost revenue from publishers who are not in compliance; however, it is unlikely that these losses would be significant or continuous.[23] States adopting accessibility laws have nothing to lose and their disabled students have everything to gain by the increased access afforded by such laws.

## Shortcomings of State Accessibility Laws

Despite the existence of these laws, accessibility to electronic textbooks varies from state to state. There are several possible explanations for this. First, disabled students, educators, and publishers are generally unaware of the existence and scope of these laws. If they are aware of the law, it is often not clear how the law can be used to acquire access to electronic textbooks. Presently, access to electronic textbooks is at its infancy. Publishers are still wary of delivering electronic textbooks because of copyright concerns. States are unwilling to give up traditional support structures for the blind, such as the provision of readers or the use of tape recorders, for more progressive approaches such as the use of computer screen reading programs and computer systems. Further, the efficacy and costs of these new learning methods still need to be tested. Even if a student is aware of the law and manages to fax a copy to the publisher, a lack of compliance and enforcement may still occur. Because these laws are relatively new, many publishers, students, and educators are unaware of the laws. The direction and impact of these laws are unclear. For instance, in a recent survey of how many disabled individuals use the Internet, the results indicated that "only 10 percent of people with disabilities use the Internet, as compared to 38 percent of people without disabilities" (Blanck & Sandler, 2000). Due to the fact that only one state, California, has a law with an enforcement remedy in the statute to encourage publishers to cooperate, lack of compliance becomes a problem.[24] There are no real consequences for publishers who choose not to

---

[23]The business of publishing and supplying educational textbooks to universities and colleges is a multi-billion-dollar industry. Although the demand for education has declined slightly from the high-demand years of the mid 1960s–1970s when the baby boomers were going back to school, competition for the education market remains stiff.

[24]West's Ann. Cal. Educ. Code Section 67302(j) added in 1999 through assembly bill (AB) 422. The particular section of the California statute states, "Failure to comply with the requirements of this section shall be a violation of Section 54.1 of the Civil Code." When the California Civil Code Section 54.1 is cross-referenced, the remedies are those consistent with Title II and Title III of the ADA. See CA Civil Code Section 54.1.

comply with the accessibility requirements of the other three states' statutes. Thus, in order to encourage more consistent compliance, greater awareness of the law needs to be established and more comprehensive enforcement measures need to be enacted. Each state needs to weigh the costs and benefits of these accessibility laws and to determine the criteria for its enforcement that will be fair and reasonable for consumers and publishers involved.

## POLICY ARGUMENTS AND PRACTICAL SOLUTIONS

### Universal Design

Any attempt to change the law implies an attempt to change public policy. Although numerous policies may be invoked by this research, the specific policy encouraged by increased availability and use of electronic textbooks is one of universal design.[25] Constructing technology from a universal design is a basic recognition by computer software and hardware designers that technology should be developed in a format that is accessible for all individuals, disabled or not (Dispenza, 2002). Publishers creating textbooks through these universal platforms should be able to provide alternative electronic formats to anyone using computer technology. Educators and scholars, who are the primary source of many textbooks used in college settings, should encourage the development and use of technology embracing the universal design concept. This not only promotes greater options for learning, it also provides greater social utility. No one should be shut out from participating in the present information age, especially the disabled. Electronic textbooks represent a potential solution capable of bridging the gap of rapidly developing technology with the practical realities of using it for a positive social purpose. Electronic textbooks represent information that the disabled can use to empower themselves to learn, grow, and become more independent in our society. Social utility is best served when everyone can benefit from the changes in technology, not just the non-disabled.

*Greater Accessibility Leads to Greater Opportunities.* Consistent with the idea of a universal design is the continuity that electronic textbooks can provide for users of such technology. Professors often remind students that this is what it is like in the real world, that what you practice in college will eventu-

---

[25] The core element in electronic textbooks is data. In our everyday lives, the data may be an e-mail from someone's parents wishing them a happy birthday, a colleague checking in, or simply just a grocery list for the weekend cookout. Data in the education context for a blind student is the ability to access information without the assistance of someone else. It is true freedom and independence. Greater accessibility enhances the educational experience for these individuals and provides them with opportunities that were not available without such technology.

13. Access to E-Texts for Disabled Students  259

ally help you out in the real employment world. As that world continues to rely on computers and other information technologies, it becomes essential for disabled students to learn how to use that technology in order to be marketable to future employers.

## Practical Application

A policy is only useful if it can be put into practice. It is one thing to say that the ADA may require a publisher to provide electronic texts as a reasonable accommodation, but it is something else to say that the publisher actually provides those texts in an efficient manner. There are critical steps that must be followed to acquire electronic textbooks from the respective covered entities. First, the disabled student must initiate the interactive process of requesting a reasonable accommodation. This should be initiated as soon as possible after acquiring the list of required textbooks from professors. Students can identify the relevant publishers from the textbooks listed in class syllabi. Telephone numbers and e-mail addresses for publishers can be obtained from the managers of university bookstores responsible for ordering these textbooks. Information can also be acquired through administrators of academic departments responsible for coordinating the ordering of textbooks. Once the correct information has been obtained, students should then call the respective publishers. If possible, writing an e-mail message to the appropriate point of contact can clarify the issues surrounding the requested accommodations. Written communications are preferable because then both the student and the publisher have a record of what has transpired. Further, publishing companies, especially the larger ones, may require several attempts in order to reach the appropriate person who can assist with accommodations.

What is involved in the interactive process? It is important for students to identify their specific needs for the accommodation to be effective. Compatibility with screen readers and other systems requirements of individual computers must also be addressed.[26] Just because a textbook has been computerized does not guarantee that screen-reading programs can automatically access these text files. Text files in Microsoft Word, WordPerfect, and ASCII standard text are the most compatible with current screen readers. Electronic texts must also be provided in a timely manner. Providing electronic versions of textbooks serves

---

[26]If a blind student wanted to upgrade from the older Windows 98 operating system to the latest Microsoft XP operating system, he or she would also have to buy the updated screen reader (JAWS) corresponding with the new operating system. Compatibility problems such as these occur often among software and hardware requirements for a computer. Thus, a student must be clear what operating system he or she is using, and what supporting software is on such a system (i.e., Word or WordPerfect).

no purpose if they are provided at the end of the semester. Exercising common sense and assertiveness may help success in acquiring the textbooks.

Publishers will require the student to meet certain conditions before any electronic texts are provided. Evidence that the student has purchased the books will be required. Written contracts signed by the student agreeing to respect all copyright and patent rights of publishers will also be required. Many of these contracts are reasonable and do not pose any threats or legal concern. No additional costs should be imposed to acquire the electronic formatted textbooks. The final product can be sent through conventional mail, via e-mail as attachments, or the students can download many of these products online.

Requesting the accommodations of an electronic text is an educational process. The more it is practiced, and the more familiar it becomes for publishers, the more efficiently such requests will be met. Students taking a proactive role in this educational process will guarantee their future success and open doors for other individuals seeking similar accommodations.

## CONCLUSION

Presently, whether or not a blind university student can acquire electronic textbooks depends on the circumstances. In some situations, publishers are more than willing to cooperate and provide electronic textbooks. In others, however, publishers wait until the end of the semester to finally inform the student that the requested electronic textbooks cannot be provided. Disability resource centers on campus offer to help, but their resources are limited because they must meet the demands of all students requesting accommodations. Because of these inconsistent results in acquiring electronic textbooks, students are left with no guidance on how to pursue requested accommodations in a more efficient manner.

The guidance many students are seeking is a better understanding of their rights in pursuing accommodations. Under the Americans With Disabilities Act (ADA), students need to consider the challenges of demonstrating that electronic texts are reasonable accommodations under Title II, and whether publishers are even considered a public accommodation as defined by Title III. Failure of students to satisfy these threshold questions under the ADA will result in the dismissal of their complaints, regardless of the merits of their requests. The most promising avenue of change is to exercise the right to acquire these electronic textbooks through state law. However, students must realize that not all states have such laws, and those states that do have this progressive legislation are limited in their enforcement. Access is often associated with equality. However, access is not necessarily equivalent to full participation. The term *access* can be interpreted broadly or narrowly depending on a person's point of view. No one is disputing that disabled students do not have access to textbooks. Blind university students can have their textbooks read to them, recorded on cassette tapes, or translated into Braille. The existence of these alternatives to accommodate blind students could raise questions as to why blind students even need electronic textbooks at all. Answering the previous question forces us to reflect on just how much our society has changed because of the tremendous availability and reliance on computer technology and the information it generates. A decade from now, personal computers will cost less than $300 and will pack 64 times the muscle of today's models. In fact, Moore's law (named after former Intel Corp. Chairman Gordon Moore) holds that computer power doubles every 18 months for the same price. The power of computers coupled with the proliferation of new forms of adaptive technology to meet such demands has facilitated a new learning environment in which electronic texts and files are the basic foundations of the infrastructure. Denying the disabled access to that medium will effectively shut them out from full participation in the present information society. Adopting a narrow interpretation of accessibility to electronic texts only serves to retard the tremendous progress technology has provided for disabled students. Change must occur. A major impetus in this change is recognizing that mere access is not sufficient. Access must allow for full and meaningful participation by individuals with disabilities.

The future of accessibility to electronic texts holds much promise. However, "it takes about 30 years to absorb an idea into a culture and we're just ten years into a revolution" (Benfield, 1992). Both the ADA and technology are still in their infancy. The main event is still to come. Computer technology is sweeping across our campuses, with more than 20% of students owning computers, and that figure is far higher at top colleges—for example, 42% of students at the University of Michigan in Ann Arbor have PCs and 70% at Case Western Reserve University in Cleveland (Cox, 1993). More significantly, a research survey in California found that more than 95% of colleges and universities have computer labs for their students. Computers are the tools that will define our future. This future will allow the disabled to read via scanners, to access computers through screen readers, and to use voice recognition software programs for those individuals who cannot access a keyboard through traditional means. Technology will continue to amaze us by tearing down barriers of accessibility for the disabled, opening up a rich world of information. As technology continues to grow and as we become more educated about these alternative means of accessing information, electronic texts can move into mainstream society as a major force in educating our disabled students.

## ACKNOWLEDGMENT

This research could not have been accomplished without the mentorship provided by Professor Jane Korn, Professor of Law at the University of Arizona James E. Rogers School of Law.

## REFERENCES

Americans with Disabilities Act (ADA), 42 U.S.C. et seq. (1990); Title I, 42 U.S.C. Sections 12111–12117; Title II, 42 U.S.C. Sections 12131–12150; Title III, 42 U.S.C. Sections 12181–12189.
Arizona Revised Statute, A.R.S. Section 15-1626(14) (2004).
Beck v. University of Wisconsin Board of Regents, 75 F. 3d 1130 (7th Cir. 1996).
Benfield. (1992, September 29). The brave new world of books on discs [quoting M. Saffo of the Institute for the Future]. *Wall Street Journal,* p. A14.
Black, H. C., Nolan, J. R., & Nolan-Haley, J. M. (1990). *Black's Law Dictionary* (6th ed., pp. 526–527). St. Paul, MN. West.
Blanck, P., & Sandler, L. A. (2000). ADA Title III And the Internet: Technology and civil rights. *Mental & Physical Disability Law Reports, 24,* 855.
Bulkeley, W. M. (1998, November 16). Technology (A special report): Crystal ball. *Wall Street Journal,* p. R4.
California Civil Code, Educ. Code Section 67302. (1999).
*Carparts Distribution Center, Inc. v. Automotive Wholesaler's Association of New England, Inc.,* 37 F.3d 12 (1st Cir. 1994).
Charrow v. Bailey, 910 F.Supp. 187 (M.D. Pa. 1995).
Cox. (1993, June 1). Electronic campus: Technology threatens to shatter the world of college textbooks. *Wall Street Journal,* p. A1.
Department of Justice. (1996). 28 C.F.R. pt. 36, App. B at 604.
Department of Justice. (1992). *Technical assistance manual* (II-3.6100 [January 24]; II-7.1100 [January 24]; III-3.11000 [January 24]). Retrieved from www.usdoj.gov/crt/ada
Dispenza, M. (2002). Overcoming a new digital divide: Technology accommodations and the undue hardship defense under the Americans With Disabilities Act. *SYR. Law Review, 52,* 159–181.
*Dyer v. Jefferson County School District R-1,* 905 F. Supp. 864 (D. Colo. 1995).
Firak, N. (1998). Threshold barriers to Title I and Title III of the Americans with Disabilities Act: Discrimination against mental illness in long term disability benefits. *Journal of Law & Health, 12,* 205.
*Florida Paraplegic Association, Inc. & The Association of Disabled Americans, Inc. v. Miccosukee Tribe of Indians of Florida,* 166 F.3d 1126 (11th Cir., 1999).
Geeter, J. (2000). The condition dilemma: A new approach to insurance coverage of disabilities. *Harvard Journal of Legislation, 37,* 521.
Hall v. Claussen, 6 Fed. Appx. 655 (10th Cir. 2001).
Hurley-Bardige v. Brown, 900 F.Supp. 567 (D. Mass. 1995).
Johnsen v. Mel-Ken Motors, Inc., 894 P.2d 540 (Or.App. 1995).
Jones v. First Commercial Bank, 18 F.Supp.2d 974 (E.D. Ark. 1998).
Kan. Stat. Ann. § 76-157 (2000).

Martin v. PGA Tour, Inc., 994 F.Supp. 1242 (D.Or. 1998).
Martin v. PGA Tour, Inc., 204 F.3d 994 (9th Cir. 2000).
Mo. Ann. Stat. § 178.160 (2001).
*National Disability Law Reporter.* (1994). 5, 423 [Case #09-93-2214-I]. April 21.
*National Disability Law Reporter.* (1999). 15, 251. [Case#10992002]. January 22.
N.Y. Educ. § 4210 (2001).
Ohio Rev. Code Ann. § 3325.05 (Banks-Baldwin 2001).
*Olinger v. United States Golf Assn.*, 205 F.3d 1001 (7th Cir. 2000).
*Parker v. Metropolitan Life Ins. Co.*, 121 F3d. 1006 (6th Cir. 1997).
PGA Tour, Inc. v. Casey Martin, 121 S.Ct. 1879 (2001).
Rehabilitation Act of 1973, 29 U.S.C. Section 794 (1973).
*Singer v. Office of Senate Sergeant at Arms*, 173 F. 3d 837 (Fed. Cir. 1999).
*Stoutenborough v. National Football League, Inc.*, 59 F.3d 580 (6th Cir. 1995).
Waddell, C. D. (1999, May 25). *The growing digital divide in access for people with disabilities: Overcoming barriers to participation.* Remarks at Understanding the Digital Economy Conference, Washington, DC. Retrieved from http://www.digitaleconomy.gov
Wash. Rev. Code Ann. § 28B.10.912 (2001).
W. Va. Code § 18-10J-5 (1996).
Weiss, T. R. (2000, July 31). AOL promises access for blind. *Computerworld*, p. 8. Available at http://www.pcworld.com
White, E. (2001, January 11). McGraw-Hill to launch learning net site. *Wall Street Journal*, p. C12.
*Wong v. Regents of the University of California*, 192 F.3d 807 (9th Cir. 1999).
*Wooten v. Acme Steel Co.*, 986 F.Supp. 524 (N.D. Ill. 1997).
*Zukle v. Regents of the University of California*, 166 F.3d 1041 (9th Cir. 1999).

# 14

# Making the Case for Meaningful Reasonable Accommodations for Employees With Physical Disabilities: A Legal Analysis of Part-Time and Flexible Work Schedules Under the Americans With Disabilities Act (ADA)

Nonnie L. Shivers

True individual freedom cannot exist without economic security and independence.
(President Franklin D. Roosevelt, State of the Union Address, 1944)

Qualex Incorporated hired David Lamb as a full-time account specialist on December 2, 1996. Lamb was in poor mental and physical health and missed one-half of his work time during his 10-month tenure at Qualex. When Lamb became unable to fulfill his responsibilities as a full-time account specialist, Qualex granted him granted medical leave to cope with the physical and emotional toll of his disability. When he sought to return to his job, Lamb requested a part-time work schedule as an accommodation. Qualex management quickly asserted it had never and would never have a part-time account specialist position and summarily terminated Lamb from his position with no further discussion of other plausible accommodations.

Lamb subsequently brought suit against his employer, alleging he was discharged in violation of the Americans with Disabilities Act (ADA; 2004) as his employer discriminated against him by refusing to accommodate his request for a part-time or flexible work schedule; *Lamb v. Qualex Inc.* (2002). The court determined Lamb was not a qualified individual with a disability because he was unable to perform an essential function of his job—working on a full-time basis with regular attendance. Specifically, the court held the ADA does not require an employer to "rehire" a full-time employee as a part-time employee as a reasonable accommodation or to allow the employee to work a sporadic, flexible schedule.

Although a primary goal of the ADA is to ensure individuals with disabilities are "afforded a full panoply of employment opportunities" (O'Neil & Reiss, 2001, p. 347) through equality of opportunity, full participation, independent living, and economic self-sufficiency, Lamb found no such protection or relief in the ADA's lofty goals (Americans With Disabilities Act, 2004). Moreover, although reasonable accommodation is a core feature of the ADA, Qualex was not even required to consider or attempt to reasonably accommodate David Lamb.

Most of the litigation surrounding the ADA in the employment context has revolved around the definition of disability (Lewis & Murray, 1999). Most recently, the U.S. Supreme Court determined a person exhibiting physical or mental manifestations of HIV is protected by the ADA as a disabled person (*Bragdon v. Abbott*, 1998). Prior to the passage of the ADA, however, critics predicted that the terms *reasonable accommodation, undue hardship*, and *essential job functions* would be the greatest source of litigation under the new legislation. (Wilkinson, 1997). Courts are only just beginning to interpret the meaning and extent of the reasonable accommodation requirement (Befort, 2002). In fact, the Supreme Court decided its first reasonable accommodation case in 2001, over 10 years after the ADA was passed (*PGA Tour, Inc. v. Martin*, 2001). Now that the definition of disability has been "resolved" and the judiciary tackles this secondary "battle," employers covered by the ADA must grapple with fragmented and inconsistent court opinions, Equal Employment Opportunity Commission (EEOC) enforcement guidelines that are given varying weight, and vague statutory language and regulations offering few precise definitions or requirements. Likewise, employees with disabilities face little consistency on what rights they do have in the workplace and achieve few victories in the courtroom on such ADA claims.

This chapter examines the extent to which legal decisions have warped the ADA's underlying structure and goals of protecting employees with disabilities in the workplace. Specifically, courts have interpreted the term *reasonable ac-*

*commodation* to exclude part-time or flexible work schedules for individuals with disabilities, despite the weight of EEOC regulations, legislative history, and simple statutory interpretation that demand the inclusion of such reasonable accommodations. The next section of this chapter details the ongoing employment crisis facing disabled Americans, even 14 years after the ADA was implemented. The third section explains the relevant provisions of Title I of the Americans With Disabilities Act of 1990. The terms and processes associated with reasonable accommodations, undue hardship, and essential function are addressed individually and as an interactive process. An in-depth analysis of part-time, flexible and sporadic work schedules as reasonable accommodations follows in the fourth section. This section shows how courts believe "employers bend over backwards to accommodate disabled workers" and often rule as a matter of law that regular and predictable attendance or full-time work schedules are essential functions of any job (*Amadio v. Ford Motor Co.*, 2001, p. 929). This section further illustrates how per se rules foisted on individuals with disabilities to protect employers have vitiated some of the key protections the ADA claims to offer. Finally, the fifth section calls for legislative action to further study the ADA's implementation and to amend the ADA's amorphous definitions to enhance the effectiveness of the act. Practical recommendations for maximizing the accommodation process at the employer–employee level are also offered to assist applicants and employees seeking part-time and flexible work schedules while also offering a critical and practical interpretation of the ADA for employers, in spite of the judicial interpretations plaguing the construction of the ADA in the courtroom.

## THE EMPLOYMENT CRISIS FOR INDIVIDUALS WITH DISABILITIES

David Lamb is one of millions of Americans with disabilities who have faced or will face adverse employment decisions with no recourse under the ADA. Even more staggering, however, is the number of individuals with disabilities who are simply unable to secure employment. In fact, "not working is perhaps the truest definition of what it means to be disabled" (Lipman, 2003, p. 398). When the ADA was enacted in 1990, an estimated 43 million Americans had one or more physical disabilities. They often faced constant discrimination in every aspect of their lives, including employment (Andrikopoulos & Gould, 2003). This discrimination has been characterized as an evil on par with racial and sexual discrimination (Moberly, 1996).

Disability discrimination law, however, is one of the newest areas of civil rights protection in the United States (Colker, 1997). Indeed, the "history of discrimination against individuals with disabilities, while less than racial or sex discrimination, is no less a story of a group that has traditionally suffered ... the badge of inferiority emplaced by a society that often shuns their presence" (*Trautz v. Weisman*, 1993, pp. 294–295). Prior to the enactment of the ADA, discrimination and prejudice denied disabled individuals the opportunities available to able-bodied individuals, thereby preventing their ability to live independently and productively (Americans With Disabilities Act, 2004). Unlike other minorities, individuals with disabilities "have often had no legal recourse to redress such discrimination" (Americans With Disabilities Act, 2004). As a result, this discrimination and denial of equal opportunity have "cost the United States billions of dollars in unnecessary expenses resulting from dependency and nonproductivity" (Americans With Disabilities Act, 2004). Only 26% of America's 43 million individuals with disabilities were employed full-time when the ADA was enacted in 1990 (Pack, 2001). Further, only 13% of the nation's disabled women were engaged in full-time employment when it was enacted (Berkery, 1990). Individuals with disabilities were forced to live with two limitations on their lives until the ADA was passed: the physical or mental impairment itself, and societies' differential treatment caused by reactions to or beliefs about the impairment (Morin, 1990).

Since the passage of the ADA, the number of individuals with disabilities has increased, yet the number of individuals with disabilities employed has not significantly improved and the proportion of individuals with disabilities living in poverty has remained high. In 2003, the number of individuals with disabilities in the United States grew to an estimated 50 million (Andrikopoulos & Gould, 2003). Individuals with disabilities now comprise the nation's largest minority (Morin, 1990). Despite the dramatic increase in individuals with disabilities, employment rates are dismal for this marginalized population; unemployment rates for people with disabilities are more than double those for the general population (Erb, Rich, & Rich, 2002). The unemployment rate for people with severe disabilities is about 70%, while non-disabled adults have an unemployment rate just over 5% (Erb et al., 2002). People with nonsevere disabilities have an unemployment rate of 18% (Erb et al., 2002). Probably the most telling statistic is that of the Americans with disabilities who are not working, 66% of these individuals want a job and prefer to work (S. Rep. No. 101-1116, 1989). The statistics reflect that individuals with disabilities are less likely to work, and when they do work, it is more likely to be part-time, with lower wages and benefits.

The drafters of the ADA were deeply troubled by the widespread unemployment of disabled Americans resulting in the poverty of these individuals; however, it does not appear the ADA has decreased the employment disadvantages individuals with disabilities suffered before passage of the act (Malloy, 2001). No reason is evident for why people with disabilities are not being employed at higher rates since the passage of the ADA (Buchholz, 2002). Former President Clinton summed up this unemployment divide when he stated: "Not everyone has shared in the American economic renaissance. We all know there are people who have been left behind, including millions of Americans with significant disabilities who want to go to work" (Tomko, 2002, p. 1033).

Although individuals with disabilities are eagerly seeking employment, most have no realistic expectation of finding it and will likely be relegated to living in poverty. In 2003, 29% of individuals with disabilities lived in poverty, with a household income of $15,000 or less (DeFord, 2003). In comparison, only 8% of non-disabled individuals live in poverty (Erb et al., 2002). Sadly, such statistics are not startling but merely reflect this population's continuing poverty, which existed prior to passage of the ADA. The poverty rate for families in which either one or both partners has a disability has been shown to increase drastically (Elwan, 1999). Indeed, "the combination of poverty and disability is a fearsome one. Either one may cause the other and their presence in combination has a tremendous capacity to destroy the lives of people with impairments and to impose on their families burdens that are too crushing to bear" (Elwan, 1999, p. 1). Although the ADA was passed to address these and other concerns, its effectiveness was doubted even before it was signed into law in 1990 (Colker, 1997).

## THE AMERICANS WITH DISABILITIES ACT (ADA) OF 1990

### Relevant Provisions of Title I of the ADA

The ADA specifically requires employers to provide reasonable accommodations to otherwise qualified employees with disabilities. A reasonable accommodation is a modification or adjustment to the work environment or to the manner or circumstances under which the position held or desired is customarily performed that may enable a qualified individual with a disability to perform the essential functions of that position (Regulations to Implement the Equal Employment Provisions of the Americans With Disabilities Act, 2003). A *disability* is defined as a physical or mental impairment that substantially limits one or more major life activities of the individual; having a record of such impairment; or being regarded as having such an impairment (Regulations to Implement the Equal Employment Provisions of the Americans With Disabilities Act, 2003). The accommodation must enable the employee to perform all essential functions of the job without causing the employer any undue hardship (Americans With Disabilities Act, 2004). Both of these determinations are critical in determining whether the individual is "qualified" for the job (Regulations to Implement the Equal Employment Provisions of the Americans With Disabilities Act, 2003). The employee must demonstrate that the reasonable accommodation is possible (*US Airways v. Barnett*, 2002). If this showing is made, the burden then shifts to the employer to prove that the accommodation would impose an undue hardship and is therefore not required under the ADA (*US Airways v. Barnett*, 2002).

Neither the statute nor the regulations offer a specific definition of reasonable accommodation, instead opting to list examples of what may possibly constitute a reasonable accommodation (Regulations to Implement the Equal Employment Provisions of the Americans With Disabilities Act, 2003). Reasonable accommodations may include "job restructuring, part-time or modified work schedules, reassignment to a vacant position, acquisition or modification of equipment or devices, appropriate adjustment or modifications of examinations, training materials or policies, the provision of qualified readers or interpreters, and other similar accommodations" (Americans With Disabilities Act, 2004). Additionally, the regulations interpreting the ADA list sample factors that may help an employer, employee, or court determine whether a function of a job is an essential function or whether an accommodation would impose an undue hardship (Regulations to Implement the Equal Employment Provisions of the Americans With Disabilities Act, 2003). While the regulations provide useful factors, the lists are not exhaustive and leave immense discretion to employers and courts. For instance, the undue hardship standard is set ambiguously somewhere between "a ceiling of bankruptcy and a floor of *de minimus*" (Lee, 1997, p. 179).

Failure to reasonably accommodate an employee with a disability is considered employment discrimination under the ADA and may give rise to a private right of action for damages (Americans With Disabilities Act, 2004). If the employer violates Title I of the ADA, the employee may bring a private cause of action to enforce his or her rights, acting as a "private attorney general to enforce the paramount public interest in eradicating invidious discrimination" (*Mardell v. Harleysville Life Ins. Co.*, 1994, p. 1235). A successful employee-plaintiff may recover compensatory and punitive damages, as well as attorneys' fees (*EEOC v. Wal-Mart Stores, Inc.*, 1997).

Generally, the ADA presumes individuals with disabilities can work and seeks to ensure equal access to equal employment opportunities based on merit. (Regulations to Implement the Equal Employment Provisions of the Americans With Disabilities Act, 2003). To achieve this ideal, the ADA prohibits employers from discriminating against a qualified individual with a disability because of the disability (Americans With Disabilities Act, 2004). The fundamental concept behind the ADA's accommodation provision is that the workplace is mutable (Karlan & Rutherglen, 1996). It is an antidiscrimination statute that was "designed to remove barriers which prevent qualified individuals with disabilities from enjoying the same employment opportunities that are available to persons without disabilities" (Regulations to Implement the Equal Employment Provisions of the Americans With Disabilities Act, 2003). The employment provisions in Title I of the ADA adopt a flexible, case-by-case approach, recognizing the inherent differences of each employer, employee and job (Robinson, 2003). The ADA does not "simply mandate that a group be treated differently; it requires that each person within a group be treated differently" (Malloy, 2001, p. 609). This flexible "case-by-case approach is essential if qualified individuals of varying abilities are to receive equal opportunities to compete for an infinitely diverse range of jobs" (Smith, 1995, p. 172). A flexible approach is also consistent with the concepts of reasonable accommodation and undue hardship as espoused throughout the legislative history and the statutory language itself (Robinson, 2003).

As the primary vehicle for integrating employees with disabilities into work environments and society, the EEOC recommends that: (a) The employer should analyze the particular job involved and determine its purpose and essential functions; (b) the employer should consult with the individual with a disability to ascertain the precise job-related limitations imposed by the individual's disability and how those limitations could be overcome with reasonable accommodation; (c) the employer should consult with the individual to be accommodated, identify potential accommodations, and assess the effectiveness each would have in enabling the individual to perform the job's essential functions; and (d) the employer should consider the preference of the individual to be accommodated and select and implement the accommodation that is most appropriate for both the employee and the employer (Regulations to Implement the Equal Employment Provisions of the Americans With Disabilities Act, 2003).

## EMPLOYEE WORK SCHEDULES AND ATTENDANCE

### Full-Time Work Schedules as Essential Functions of All Jobs

Both employers implementing the ADA in the workplace and courts interpreting the ADA see full-time work as an essential function of most jobs. In the ADA, however, Congress stressed that part-time schedules may be a reasonable accommodation for employees with disabilities [H.R. Rep. No. 101-485(II), 1990]. The EEOC guidelines reinforce the congressional position by stating that an employer must provide a modified or part-time work schedule when it is a reasonable accommodation and does not cause an undue burden on the employer (EEOC Enforcement Guidance, n.d.). Despite Congressional intent apparent in the ADA and through EEOC interpretation, employers and courts have almost universally demanded full-time work from employees regardless of reasonable accommodations.

### Part-Time Work: Reasonable Accommodation or Undue Hardship?

To determine what is reasonable, it is important to remember what is not required of an employer. Regulations, statutory language, and case law all help define what may constitute a reasonable accommodation and what lengths an employer may be required to go to. First, the ADA does not relieve a disabled employee from performing the essential functions of his or her job (Regulations to Implement the Equal Employment Provisions of the Americans with Disabilities Act, 2003). For example, if working full-time for 6 months without an absence is required for all employees to pass a probationary period, it is possible this requirement will be found to be an essential function and any absence will lead to the employee's termination, no matter how valid the reason for the absence may be (*Jackson v. Veterans Administration*, 1994). Second, the ADA may not require the employer to allow the employee with a disability who works full-time to change to a part-time work schedule if such a schedule is simply incompatible with the job functions or requirements which the employee was hired to fulfill (*Terrell v. U.S. Air*, 1998). In *Terrell v. U.S. Air* (1998, p. 626), the Eleventh Circuit held that "although part-time work, as the statute and regulations recognize, may be a reasonable accommodation in some circumstances (particularly where the employer has part-time jobs readily available), [the employer] was not required to create a part-time position for Plaintiff." Finally, the employer is not mandated to pick the best accommodation for the employee, only an accommodation that allows the employee to do his or her job effectively. The Eleventh Circuit recently stated that the "ADA's use of the word reasonable as an adjective for the word accommodate connotes that an employer is not required to accommodate an employee in any manner in which that employee desires" (*Terrell v. U.S. Air*, 1998, p. 626). The court went on to state "the word reasonable would be rendered superfluous in the ADA if employers were required in every instance to provide employees the maximum accommodation or every conceivable accommodation possible" (*Terrell v. U.S. Air*, 1998, p. 626).

Employers cannot and should not assume an employee with a disability is unable or uninterested in working full-time; rather, the employer must identify the potential accommodation that would allow the employee to work. Many Americans with disabilities have been precluded from the personal and financial satisfaction that full-time work can provide because of bald assumptions about individual abilities (Pack, 2001). Instead of passively assuming the employee is unable to work full-time, the employer should determine if a part-time schedule is a reasonable accommodation by thoroughly investigating the impact such an accommodation would have upon the organization. Of course, such an accommodation may not even be necessary. If a part-time schedule is a potential accommodation, the employer should then investigate the impact part-time schedules would have in the workplace. For instance, other employees may be asked or required to take on the nonessential functions the disabled employee will no longer perform when working part-time. Permitting a part-time schedule may "detrimentally affect management's overall flexibility and productivity" (Befort, 2002, p. 448). Hiring an employee for full-time work and then permitting part-time work on a long-term or short-term basis may mean that employers will not receive the work effort of employees who are trained and experienced in their current positions (Befort, 2002).

Most courts have found that working full-time is probably an essential function of a full-time job and largely defer to the employer's definition of what constitutes an "essential function" (*Kuehl v. Wal-Mart Stores, Inc.*, 1995; Malloy, 2001). In *Devito v. Chicago Park District* (2001), the Seventh Circuit Court of Appeals affirmed that a full-time job requires the individual with the disability to be capable of working full-time, because working full-time is an essential function of a job. The Seventh Circuit stated that it is "oddly assumed" rather than stated in Seventh Circuit and Eight Circuit precedent that full-time jobs require ability to work full-time at the work-site (*Devito v. Chicago Park District*, 2001, p. 534). Apparently by asserting this statement as truth, rather than merely assuming, the court in *Devito* has made its conclusion a matter of law, because no support for the statement was necessary.

Courts have also generally deferred to employer judgment on whether full-time work is an essential function of a particular job instead of merely utilizing the employer's definition of the job's essential functions as persuasive. Unless the employee produces "specific and compelling proof that the job is different than the employer states," courts have generally been unwilling to second-guess an employer's assessment of what constitutes an essential function (Lee, 1997, p. 170). Generally, an employee's bald assertions or generalized disagreement over full-time work being an essential function is insufficient. (Lee, 1997). Interestingly, the ADA merely requires that courts give consideration to the employer's judgment regarding the essential functions of the job; however, courts have interpreted this provision to mean that under the ADA, "the employer's definition is *persuasive* in determining the essential functions of the job"

(*Kuehl v. Wal-Mart Stores, Inc.*, 1995, p. 802). Instead of taking the position that the "employer is always right," however, courts should instead carefully examine the party's evidence of essential functions and reasonable accommodations and allow juries to make determinations of fact rather than enter findings as a matter of law. For example, in *Kinlaw v. Alpha Baking Co., Inc.* (2003), the court permitted the jury to weigh the evidence of the employer's full-time work preference, the job description, and hiring practices to determine if full-time work was required in the job. In *Kinlaw*, the employee became permanently physically disabled from a work injury and was unable to work for more than 6 hours per day. Instead of determining Kinlaw was unable to work full-time and therefore could not be accommodated because full-time attendance was a requisite of his job, the jury was allowed to determine if a reasonable accommodation was possible without resulting in an undue hardship on the employer.

### Must the Employer Follow Its Own Rules and Policies When Accommodating?

Employers may have policies or rules in place that prohibit part-time or flexible work schedules. Frequently, however, the reasonable accommodation is an individual exception to just such a workplace practice, policy or rule. As the U.S. Supreme Court noted in *US Airways v. Barnett* (2002, p. 398), an accommodation may allow a worker with a disability "to violate a rule that others must obey." The very definition of accommodation means that "the employer must be willing to consider making changes in its ordinary work rules, facilities, terms, and conditions in order to enable a disabled individual to work" (Smith, 1995, p. 180). Indeed, reasonable accommodations "may require employers to alter existing policies or procedures that they would not change for non-handicapped employees" because "that is the essence of reasonable accommodation" (*Ransom v. Arizona Board of Regents*, 1997, p. 902). An employer should therefore approach all requests for reasonable accommodation with a requisite degree of caution and reserve. An employer should not automatically reject an employee's request for a reasonable accommodation under the mantra "it's never been done, and it never will be."

The EEOC specifically considered whether an employer must allow an employee with a disability to work a modified or part-time schedule even if the employer has a policy prohibiting or no policy permitting such schedule modifications (EEOC Enforcement Guidance, n.d.). The EEOC acknowledged that a modified schedule might include "adjusting arrival or departure times, providing periodic breaks, altering when certain functions are performed, allowing an employee to use accrued or paid leave, or providing additional unpaid leave" (EEOC Enforcement Guidance, n.d.). The EEOC noted that the "employer must provide a modified or part-time schedule when required as a reasonable accommodation, absent undue hardship, even if it does not provide such schedules for other employees" (EEOC Enforcement Guidance, n.d.). Failure to change a work policy absent proof of undue hardship may result in liability for discrimination or disparate treatment under the ADA (EEOC Enforcement Guidance, n.d.).

The employer's enactment and enforcement of attendance and part-time work schedule policies may also be determinative of if attendance requirements or full-time schedules are in fact essential functions. In cases where the employer either allowed the employee to work a flexible or part-time schedule in the past or allowed other employees to work the modified schedule the disabled individual requests, courts have found the attendance requirements may not be essential functions. The inquiry focuses on whether the employer actually required the specific employee or employees generally to perform the functions the employer asserts are essential (Regulations to Implement the Equal Employment Provisions of the Americans With Disabilities Act, 2003).

For instance, a federal district court in Minnesota recently held that an employee who could work only half of her scheduled 12-hour shift because of a disability could not be forced to work full-time after the employer allowed her to work part-time for nearly 11 years (*Larson v. Seagate Technology, Inc.*, 2001): Long-time employee Patricia Larson suffered a series of work-related injuries that led to her physical disability. After 17 years on the job full-time, she was medically restricted to a 6-hour workday due to her disability. Both Larson and Seagate attempted to increase her hours for the first 2 years; however, her doctor refused to approve the request. After nearly 11 years of working part-time shifts, Seagate simply tired of "enduring" Larson's accommodation and told Larson it could not accommodate her reduced work hours. Seagate then terminated her when she was unable to work the 12-hour shifts it demanded. The court noted, however, that "in light of the fact that [Seagate] had previously offered [Larson] a part-time schedule without undue hardship," the determination of whether the ability to work a 12-hour shift was an essential function was a question of fact, not a question of law, and would be decided by a jury (*Larson v. Seagate Technology, Inc.*, 2001, p. 2).

### Flexible Work Schedules: Inherently Reasonable Accommodations

Congress could easily have been envisioning Kevin Terry when it drafted the ADA to include flexible work schedules as a reasonable accommodation. Terry suffered from nocturnal seizures due to epilepsy while working as a customer service representative at Time Warner (*Runkle v. Potter*, 2003). Due to his nighttime seizures, Terry found it difficult to arrive at work consistently in the morning. His supervisor accommodated his disability by allowing Terry to arrive at work after the regular starting time in the morning and to stay later in the evening to make up missed time. When a new manager arrived, employees began to complain about Terry's "special treatment," and the manager responded that Terry "should not be treated different than any other employee" (p. 1193). Terry and his supervisor were accused of falsifying time sheets when an agent of the new manager conducted surveillance on Terry while he worked after hours. His supervisor was terminated for "colluding with Terry in falsifying his timesheets," and Terry was told the managers would no longer be forced to accommodate him; he was fired soon thereafter (pp. 1193–1194). Although the court was critical of the employer's surveillance and discriminatory comments, Terry lost his suit against his former employer (*Runkle v. Potter*, 2003).

Although many permutations of a flexible work schedule exist, flexible work schedules generally permit the employee to arrange a predetermined schedule that varies from that of other employees but still allows the employee to fulfill his or her job duties and hour requirements. A flexible work schedule may entail allowing the employee to perform the essential functions of the job at alternate times or allowing the employee to take different shifts to accommodate her physical needs, such as treatment or side-effects of treatments (EEOC Enforcement Guidance, n.d.). The employee will likely be required to work a predetermined number of hours per week; however, the hours may fall outside of the typical Monday through Friday, 9:00 a.m. to 5:00 p.m. schedule. The employee may be allowed to work 10:00 a.m. to 6:00 p.m. or to work additional hours for 9 days on the job, allowing an additional day to be taken off on the 10th day.

The ADA specifically recognizes modified or flexible work schedules as a typical reasonable accommodation that may assist employees with disabilities to be successful in finding a job, acclimating to the work environment and demands as it interplays with the disability, and retaining the job through good performance. Flexible or modified work schedules are only one of a number of examples of reasonable accommodations specified in the text of the ADA. According to the EEOC, an employee who needs a flexible schedule because of his or her disability is entitled to such a schedule if there is no other effective accommodation and it will not cause undue hardship for the employer (EEOC Enforcement Guidance, n.d.). The ADA is not the first congressional acknowledgment that flexible work schedules are a reasonable accommodation for employees. Indeed, Congress has already determined that uninterrupted attendance in the face of a family emergency is not a necessary job requirement and does not unduly burden employers (Family Medical Leave Act, 2004).

Flexible work schedules are important reasonable accommodations for employees with disabilities. Mobility-impaired employees who face commuting problems may find a flexible schedule a necessity if accessible transportation is only available at specific times. Employees with disabilities who need a modified or flexible work schedule could plausibly include people who require special medical treatment for their disability, such as cancer patients or those with AIDS; people who need rest periods, including those with multiple sclerosis, cancer, or respiratory conditions; people whose disabilities are affected by eating or sleeping schedules, such as individuals with diabetes; and people with mobility or other impairments who find it difficult to use public transportation during peak hours or who must depend on special paratransit schedules.

Some employers view flexible schedules not as a burden, but as simple accommodations more akin to bending the dress codes to allow for special footwear; however, other employers have determined that flexible schedules are not reasonable accommodations (Buchholz, 2002). When employers determine flexible schedules are not reasonable accommodations, the court hearing the ADA discrimination complaint filed by the employee should not impose a per se rule of law that flexible schedules are not reasonable, but should instead address the facts presented on a case-by-case basis looking at reasonable accommodations, essential functions, and undue hardship. For example, in *Varone v. City of New York* (2003), Varone worked as a computer programmer for the City of New York Human Resources Administration (HRA) for over 22 years. A disability prevented Varone "from maintaining a fixed schedule for any length of time" and for fifteen years, Varone worked from home "at any time of the day" (p. 5). Varone primarily worked from 10:00 p.m. to 8:00 a.m., coming into the office when needed for client or staff meetings. After 15 years, the employer determined Varone's flexible schedule was no longer acceptable and required Varone to work on a fixed schedule in the office. The court found that determining whether Varone was entitled to a fully flexible schedule as a reasonable accommodation, or whether such a schedule would prevent Varone from performing the essential functions of his job, was an inappropriate finding for judgment as a matter of law (*Varone v. City of New York*, 2003).

## (Un)Reasonably Accommodating Sporadic Attendance?

Offering an employee with a disability a flexible work schedule may constitute a reasonable accommodation without imposing any undue hardship on the employer. Unlike a flexible yet defined schedule, an employee will likely not be accommodated by being allowed to come to work when he or she is able or willing to do so. Sporadic attendance is not an accommodation recognized by the ADA and is not embraced by employers due to the effect unannounced, repetitive absences have on workers and productivity. Likewise, courts are unwilling to impose such burdens on employers.

Employers undoubtedly have a clear interest in employee attendance and productivity. Nearly all employers have attendance policies that provide for and regulate the use of vacation, medical leave, and sick leave to facilitate appropriate employee attendance leading to success for the employee on the job and the company overall (Rosenberger, 2001). Employers regularly tolerate some level of absenteeism by their employees and typically apply the same standards to all similarly situated employees to maintain employee equality (Rosenberger, 2001). When employees exceed the allotted leave time by a "great deal," however, the absences or flexibility might be rightfully deemed excessive and prevent an employee from performing the job or an essential function of the job (*Jackson v. Veterans Admin.*, 1994, p. 282). Employers "should be permitted to take reasonable steps to secure a steady, reliable, and adequate work force" since an employee's absence from work "impairs the efficiency of an office or agency" (*Malone v. Aramark Services, Inc.*, 2000, p. 678). Many employers accommodate employee absenteeism by overstaffing or reassigning duties for short durations (Smith, 1995).

For employees with disabilities, intermittent leave may be a crucial form of accommodation because many disabilities may entail "flare-ups" or "episodes." In fact, "sporadic, unpredictable, and sometimes lengthy absences are the natural result of many chronic illnesses" (Smith, 1995, p. 184). Such leave may be "especially burdensome for employers because of the difficulty of predicting when an individual who requires such an accommodation will be present at work" (Befort, 2002, p. 465). Temporary, nonchronic impairments of short duration which have little or no long-term impact, may not even be considered disabilities under the ADA and therefore may not require any reasonable accommodation (Colker, 1997). When attendance is found to be an essential function (as it most often is), an employer may discharge an employee for excessive absences if a reasonable accommodation will not enable the employee to maintain regular attendance (*Hypes v. First Commerce Corporation*, 1998).

Despite the ADA provisions calling for part-time or flexible work schedules as reasonable accommodations, businesses are not compelled under the ADA to tolerate erratic, unreliable, or even less-than-perfect attendance (Malloy, 2001). When an employee cannot meet or simply fails to meet uniformly applied reasonable attendance requirements due to sporadic attendance, the ADA does not function as a "job insurance policy" (*Tenbrink v. Federal Home Loan Bank*, 1996, p. 1160). This line of reasoning first emerged in *Wimbley v. Bolger* (1986), a case under the Rehabilitation Act in which the plaintiff was discharged for violations of the U.S. Postal Service's attendance policy requiring advance notice of absences. The court stated that "it is elemental that one who does not come to work cannot perform any of his job functions, essential or otherwise" (*Wimbley v. Bolger*, 1986, p. 481). The court did not require the Postal Service to show why accommodating Mr. Wimbley's absences would impose an undue hardship, instead stating that the employer "must have employees who can be counted on to come to work on a regular basis" (*Wimbley v. Bolger*, 1986, p. 481). The court found it was "obvious why the Postal Service could not simply allow plaintiff to come and go as he pleased" but left its reasoning woefully incomplete (*Wimbley v. Bolger*, 1986).

Since *Wimbley*, courts have followed suit and imposed a per se rule that presence or attendance is an essential function of nearly all jobs, despite statutory and regulatory guidance to the contrary (Smith, 1995). Courts cite a litany of on-point cases to support this per se rule and ignore the statutory requirements and regulatory guidance on reasonable accommodation and undue hardship analysis. The courts state emphatically, time and time again, that an employee "who does not come to work cannot perform any of his job functions, essential or otherwise" and that "when an employee is unable to perform the essential function of attending his employment, few, if any reasonable accommodations exist" (*Amadio v. Ford Motor Company*, 2001, p. 928; *Tyndall v. National Education Centers*, 1994, p. 213). This per se rule has been applied to myriad types of jobs. For example, the Seventh Circuit Court of Appeals held that attendance without excessive or sporadic absences is an essential function of clerical workers, teachers, forklift drivers, account representatives, production employees, and plant equipment repairman, among others (*Amadio v. Ford Motor Co.*, 2001). Employers argue, and most courts agree, that sporadic attendance is disruptive to the work environment, that regular attendance is an essential function of nearly all jobs, and that allowing sporadic attendance is an "unreasonable" accommodation not mandated by the ADA (Malloy, 2001; Robinson, 2003).

Courts following *Wimbley* and imposing such a per se rule have ignored the statute and EEOC Guidance statements that are in direct opposition to the *Wimbley* rule. The regulations interpreting the ADA clearly state: "Attendance is not an essential function as defined by the ADA because it is not one of the fundamental job duties of the employment position" (EEOC Enforcement Guidance, n.d.). However, the EEOC regulations are not persuasive authority in many courts. For instance, in *Lamb* the court chastised the plaintiff for overstating the consideration that must be afforded to EEOC directives. Instead, the court stated that the EEOC interpretive guides are not controlling upon the courts because they do not have the force and effect of law in the adjudicatory process (*Lamb v. Qualex*, 2002). Absent the EEOC guidelines, which many courts find unpersuasive, commentators still believe the ADA language mandates no presumption should exist that attendance is an essential job requirement (*Cehrs v. N.E. Ohio Alzheimer's Research Ctr.*, 1998).

Courts have determined that attendance or presence as an essential function is a matter of law, rather than a question of fact to be determined on a case-by-case basis (Rosenberger, 2001). This outcome is very likely in two types of cases: first, cases involving specific types of jobs that might require an actual physical presence, and second, cases where the employer has a neutral policy regarding attendance or tardiness (Befort, 2002). Specific types of jobs requiring attendance might include jobs that must be done by one or more persons for safety reasons (e.g., digging a ditch must be done by more than one person for safety reasons) or because of a cooperative process required to complete the task (e.g., an assembly-line worker who is the only person qualified to complete a certain crucial task). On the other hand, courts have been more receptive to absences on the job where the jobs are of a nature that allows complete flexibility. Jobs that may be accomplished without a set schedule might include a computer programmer or a sales representative who can makes sales calls at any time during a week.

Courts universally chastise employees with disabilities who seek fully flexible work schedules that cater to their needs and desires and deride disabled employees who are excessively absent, even with accommodations (*Svarnas v. AT&T Communications*, 1999). Employee requests to work only when able or willing have been perfunctorily rejected by employers and courts alike (Lee, 1997). This is not to be confused with mere flexibility in a job, where an employee uses "flex time" or makes alternate arrangements temporarily, sporadically, or on a regular basis for treatment or illness. Unlike a flexible schedule, sporadic absences are unpredictable and may vary wildly from week to week. Even where a flexible schedule may be a reasonable accommodation, an open-ended schedule permitting the employee to work when he or she sees fit is not a reasonable accommodation where the employee's work affects the schedule, efficiency, and duties of others in the employee's work group or department (*Deo v. Candid Color Sys.*, 1998). As one court wrote in response to a service representative's contention that she be allowed to work on a schedule revolving around her migraine headaches:

> This is unreasonable and not an accommodation [the employer] should be required to make. The court recognizes that "job restructuring" or "part time or modified work schedules" are included in the ADA's definition of "reasonable accommodation".... But plaintiff asks too much of [the employer]. (*Barfield v. Bell S. Telecommunications, Inc.*, 1995, p. 1327)

This judicial creation of a "sweeping, unnecessary, and misleading rule of law in contravention of the case-by-case approach mandated by the ADA" is ill-conceived and effectively eliminates the ADA's most important protections (Smith, 1995, p. 163). The per se rule widely adopted by the courts discourages "many from seeking work or fighting discriminatory practice where they occur" (Smith, 1995, p. 184). Courts have been unwilling to let go of the idea that perfect attendance is an essential function of most jobs, resulting in cursory treatment of the reasonable accommodation and undue hardship requirements under the ADA. Amid these decisions invoking the per se rule, a few select courts have cautioned that there should be no presumption that attendance is an essential function of a job (*Cehrs v. N.E. Alzeheimer's Research Ctr.*, 1998). The definition of essential function refers to the performance of duties related to crucial tasks or obligations, not an "ethereal concept of presence" (Smith, 1995, p. 169). Scholars argue the "presence is an essential function" myth is erroneous because it assumes that most jobs can only be performed at the employer's work site and because all employers are able to and do in fact accommodate some degree of employee absenteeism (Smith, 1995). In fact, "perfect attendance is not a necessary element of all jobs ... the necessary level of attendance and regularity is a question of degree depending on the circumstances of each position" (*Walders v. Garrett*, 1991, pp. 309–310). To ascertain the degree of necessary attendance "requires close scrutiny ... this is necessarily a fact intensive determination" (*EEOC v. AIC Sec. Investigation, Ltd.*, 1993, p. 1064).

Instead of imposing a per se rule, courts have an obligation under the ADA to consider whether a leave of absence or the absences themselves (if no leave is desired, needed or possible) would place an undue hardship on the employer (*Cehrs v. N.E. Ohio Alzeheimer's Research Ctr.*, 1998). If the employee with the disability cannot adhere to a regular work schedule, the employer and court should both first ask: What reasonable accommodation would allow the employee with the disability to accomplish the actual job duties (Smith, 1995)? Many courts that have decided attendance is an essential function have skipped this crucial step in analyzing reasonable accommodations. Other courts have convoluted this step with an employer's right to discipline employees who do not meet standards of attendance without seeking a reasonable accommodation. In order to remain true to the spirit of the ADA, however, courts must be "more stringent in requiring employers to delineate factors that constitute undue hardship" (Smith, 1995, p. 179). This inquiry is a crucial mandate of the ADA because it forces employers to recognize and address subtle ways in which the workplace is biased against disabled individuals (Malloy, 2001). Employers are typically unaware of their biases with respect to disability, and the reasonable accommodation inquiry helps employers focus on unintentional discrimination and whether a disabled employee can perform the essential functions of the job with an accommodation (Smith, 1995). The reasonable accommodation inquiry also forces employers to "recognize that workplaces are not structured neutrally—they are shaped by and for a non-disabled majority" (Smith, 1995, p. 179). Courts can no longer "allow employers to circumvent the undue hardship analysis by simply making a conclusive statement that they cannot reasonably accommodate absenteeism" (Smith, 1995, p. 183). Even if flexible schedules are potentially problematic in jobs where essential functions are performed during a specific or inalterable time frame, this inquiry must still be conducted on a case-by-case basis.

The ADA itself may be responsible for this lack of judicial analysis because it does not require a quantitative basis for undue hardship; the ADA only requires that the accommodation be an action requiring significant difficulty or expense to impose an undue hardship. The ADA

> threatens employers with liability for discrimination unless they accurately distinguish between accommodations which would cause them undue hardship and those which would not. Consequently, employers must be provided with a method which enables them to make this distinction. To simply say that "the courts, over time, will provide such a method" is an insufficient response. It is unfair to impose liability on an employer for failure to comply with an obligation Congress has consciously decided not to define clearly. Congress' failure in this regard was northing short of an abdication of its responsibility. (Epstein, 1995, pp. 440–441)

Despite Congress's failure, however, the judiciary must force employers to demonstrate what is required in the statute to assert attendance or full-time schedules are an essential function. An "employer cannot simply assert that a needed accommodation will cause it undue hardship ... and thereupon be relieved of the duty to provide an accommodation. Rather an employer will have to present evidence and demonstrate that the accommodation will, in fact, cause it undue hardship" (EEOC Enforcement Guidance, n.d.).

Although no standard clearly delineates what constitutes an undue hardship, the First Circuit took the position that an employer must produce "at least some modicum of evidence showing that an open-ended schedule would be a hardship, financial, or otherwise" to show that the flexible schedule would not be a reasonable accommodation under the ADA (*Ward v. Mass. Health Research Inst.*, 2000, p. 29). The employer should document factors such as financial loss, disruption of the workplace, loss of business or productivity with specificity, and morale problems that might result from accommodating the employee's absences or schedule. A determination of undue hardship must be made on a case-by-case basis after presentation of specific evidence that the accommodations would impose financial difficulty, that the accommodations are unduly extensive, substantial, or disruptive, or that the accommodations would fundamentally alter the nature or operation of the business (EEOC Enforcement Guidance, n.d.). Courts ignoring such factors and instead applying a per se rule that attendance or full-time schedules are always required are blatantly misapplying the ADA and subverting the accommodation process by blindly following such a per se rule.

## MAXIMIZING REASONABLE ACCOMMODATIONS

### Legislative Recommendations

*Encourage Voluntary, Quasi-Binding Mediation of Reasonable Accommodation Complaints.* Congress specifically authorized the use of alternative means of dispute resolution under the ADA, and this explicit integration of alternative dispute resolution processes indicates congressional awareness of the intrinsic efficiency of mediation and other alternative dispute resolution approaches (Cohen, 2001). By preserving the employee's private right of action against an employer for discrimination, the ADA did not intend mediation or some other form of alternative dispute resolution to be the employee's sole remedy for alleged acts of discrimination (Ferrier, 1996). The EEOC completed a pilot project mediating ADA claims in the mid-1990s with great success (Hodges, 1996). Out of 300 mediated cases, 267 of the claims were fully resolved in the mediation process (Hodges, 1996). Although the pilot project did not include reasonable accommodation cases under the ADA, "reasonable accommodation cases are precisely the types of cases that should be mediated. In reasonable accommodation cases, the parties can work out an accommodation that enables the employee to retain employment, thus preserving the [employer-employee] relationship" (Hodges, 1996, p. 1024).

Congress or individual state legislatures should consider funding pilot or permanent programs creating nonbinding mediation, allowing the employer and employee to settle the ADA dispute. The program should not deny employees the right to file the ADA claim in court should the accommodation not materialize or if the discrimination does not cease within the workplace as a result of the terms of the settlement. The pilot or permanent program should have the following elements: informed and voluntary participation; use of neutral facilitators; confidential deliberations; and nonbinding agreements (Hodges, 1996). Employer efforts to develop voluntary internal mediation programs for ADA claims could also be funded and tested. A mediation program on the federal, state, or local level should be carefully designed to minimize the disadvantages of mediation and maximize the advantages and active participation discussed below.

Although both pros and cons face an employer engaging in mediation, the tangible and intangible benefits the employer will gain may persuade the employer to voluntarily choose to mediate reasonable accommodation disputes. First, mediators, unlike juries, are unlikely to render large punitive damage awards against the employer (Ferrier, 1996). Rather, the mediator will likely be working toward an amicable resolution of the charge, keeping media attention to a minimum and damage awards minimal or even limiting remedies to workplace accommodations. Mediators will seek to ease tension between the employer and employee through mutual settlement and to allow the work relationship to resume unharmed. Second, if the mediation is successful, both the employee and employer will be spared the time and expense associated with litigation (Ferrier, 1996). The employer may save even more money if it does not have to hire and train a new employee to replace the employee who chose to file suit or quit his or her job (Ferrier, 1996). The employer may also be spared larger damage awards because, due to the timeliness in which mediation occurs, the employee will not accrue further damages in the form of back pay while a winning case sits on a court docket awaiting trial (Ferrier, 1996). Of course, the potential downfalls for an employer must be weighed against the benefits. Other employees may begin to come forward with claims of discrimination under the ADA due to the small cost of bringing the complaint to mediation (Ferrier, 1996). Because protracted litigation often forces the employee into a settlement that is favorable to the employer, mediating claims may position employers in a less advantageous bargaining position than enjoyed in litigation.

Employees with disabilities must also carefully weigh the benefits and risks of mediating their reasonable accommodation complaint. Ostensibly, mediation is less adversarial than a traditional lawsuit. The "win–win" mediation process may allow the employee to maintain a positive relationship with the employer and return to work quickly with the necessary accommodation in place (Ferrier, 1996). By focusing on the underlying interest of the employee in mediation, namely, seeking a reasonable accommodation allowing them to continue working, this goal is more easily achieved in mediation than through litigation (Hodges, 1996). Mediation also provides the employee with quicker resolution, because the EEOC has an enormous backlog of cases that must be investigated before an employee can proceed with a lawsuit, a case that may then take years to meander through the judicial dockets and pretrial litigation before coming to the courtroom for trial (Hodges, 1996). Quicker resolution through mediation may result in a more timely damage award without a protracted delay resulting from the EEOC's investigation or subsequent litigation (Ferrier, 1996). The cons facing an employee submitting his or her ADA discrimination claim to mediation are not inconsequential. Mediation may be inherently biased in favor of employers, especially in light of the "lack of diversity with respect to gender, race and social status" among mediators (Ferrier, 1996, p. 1303). Furthermore, employees may be giving away their right to have the ADA claim heard in court if the settlement is binding (Ferrier, 1996).

In addition to the pros and cons that face employees and employers, critical public policy and social justice arguments abound rallying for and against mediation of ADA claims. Despite the statutory support for mediation, one might question whether mediation has an appropriate role in ADA disputes, given the nature of the public rights involved (Hodges, 1996). Resolution of ADA disputes through mediation may result in "diminished ability to identify and resolve systemic discrimination problems," which is an underlying purpose of the ADA (Hodges, 1996, p. 1057). In order to achieve the ADA's lofty goal of eradicating discrimination against individuals with disabilities in the workplace and in society at large, employers must be aware that the ADA will be judicially enforced. (Ferrier, 1996). One commentator argues that by allowing mediation of ADA claims, employers will not be deterred from future discrimination. (Ferrier, 1996). If mediation becomes a mainstay of ADA claims, "few legal opinions will be elicited, resulting in little judicial precedent. Employees will become wary of filing an ADA suit because of the uncertainty surrounding judicial resolution" (Ferrier, 1996, p. 1301). Another commentator noted that "courts also play a role in establishing norms—a process of giving meaning to our public values," and this function of the courts will be limited if mediation becomes widespread (Hodges, 1996, p. 1054).

Without mediation, however, some commentators argue that public support for the ADA will be undermined (Ferrier, 1996). Without the relatively inexpensive option of mediation, the average employee with a disability will be faced with the immense cost and expense of litigation, which will in turn render the ADA meaningless (Ferrier, 1996). The employee must be wary of the potential power imbalances inherent in mediation between an individual with a disability and a business or government agency with more power, resources, and experience with the mediation process (Hodges, 1996). Employees may be at a disadvantage during mediation "because of the historical discrimination they have endured and their lack of resources" (Hodges, 1996, p. 1054). To achieve a balance of power in mediation, employees should be encouraged to bring a representative or advocate to the mediation, adequately trained mediators should be used, and mediations should be monitored to ensure acceptable performance by all parties during and after process (Hodges, 1996). In creating a mediation program on the employer, state, or federal level, the pros and cons facing the employer, employee, and the public at large must be carefully weighed.

**Require Empirical Studies of Reasonable Accommodations and Costs.** The ADA has no provision to track the type, number, or costs of reasonable accommodations offered to employees with disabilities under the auspices of the legislation. Almost no empirical studies exist regarding what reasonable ADA accommodations are employed within the workplace, the number of employees with disabilities employers accommodate or the cost of those accommodations (Stein, 2003). Employers currently have no benchmarks to compare their own reasonable accommodations or any chance of reviewing a list of reasonable accommodations for a particular disability (Blanck, 1997). The lack of information about the actual implementation of the ADA in workplaces throughout the nation is a significant problem, which could be remedied with a legislative provision and requisite funding to track and study the implementation, effects, and outcomes of the ADA on employees and employers.

As some of the ADA's most outspoken critics, private employers believe reasonable accommodations are expensive and detract from their bottom line, despite limited research studies concluding most reasonable accommodations are virtually cost-free. Critics contend that reasonable accommodations unfairly place high financial burdens and administrative costs on the operation of businesses; however, such critiques are made without reliance on data, because no such data even exist (Blanck, 1997; Stein, 2003). Without tracking and studies, the employers holding this outdated belief will likely discriminate against individuals with disabilities due to fears of rising costs and lower earnings.

The limited studies which have been conducted dispel many if not all of the typical employer's fears about hiring and accommodating an individual with a disability. The leading empirical study of accommodation costs examined 500 accommodations made by Sears, Roebuck and Co. from 1978 to 1992 (Stein, 2003). From 1978 to 1992, the average cost for an accommodation was about $120 (Stein, 2003). The average cost dropped to $45 from 1993 to 1996. (Stein, 2003). Overall, 72% of accommodations required no cost, 17% cost less than $100, 10% cost between $101 and $500, and only 1% cost between $500 and $1,000 (Stein, 2003). Nearly all legal scholarship refers only to the small Sears study as definitive proof that reasonable accommodations are not cost prohibitive; indeed, it is one of only a handful of such studies that even exist in legal or social sciences scholarship. In the absence of reliable, applicable information, "it is no surprise that the attitudes and behavior of many employers reflect the view that the costs of accommodations outweigh the benefits" (Blanck, 1997, p. 899).

Studying reasonable accommodations must extend beyond the Sears study to validate the ADA's success and encourage employers to hire employees with disabilities. If, as economists believe, ADA-required accommodations act as a disincentive to the voluntary hiring of people with disabilities, more accurate, updated, and universal data may dispel the myths in which employers shroud ADA provisions (Stein, 2003). The studies that currently exist are incomplete and ineffective to dispel these myths. Corporate cultures, internal policies, and economies differ. Furthermore, the Sears study merely represents a large company's policy toward employees with disabilities. The Sears study also does not report the costs of accommodations that were sought but not provided, presumably due to expense. Ultimately:

> The accuracy of the few studies assessing the costs of providing accommodations to workers with disabilities have to verified, refuted or debated further through subsequent empirical testing. These studies may show accommodation costs to be more or less expensive than they are currently perceived, but additional and rigorous analysis is necessary in order to better understand the impact of accommodations costs. (Stein, 2003, p. 109)

Defining the parameters, methods, and goals of further studying the ADA's reasonable accommodations provisions is a complex task on which every scholar seems to demand something unique in order for the study to pass muster. Minimally, future examination into the type, effectiveness, and cost of accommodation at all businesses subject to and implementing the ADA (including large, medium, and small businesses) must be implemented using a standardized means for gathering, reporting, and analyzing information. Additional analysis is also needed of the patterns and magnitude of the costs and benefits associated with Title I implementation, compliance and litigation (Blanck, 1997). Extrapolating data on reasonable accommodations merely from court cases provides an inadequate view of the ADA's implementation because most accommodations likely occur well before litigation. Of course, without studying the ADA's implementation, even this simple statement is mere conjecture, further highlighting the need for additional studies.

Outside of these basic parameters, the data could address any number of other variables. Some call for closer examination of the "direct and indirect costs and benefits of Title I implementation and who bears the costs and receives the benefits associated with workplace accommodations" (Blanck, 1997, p. 906). An analysis of job retention and advancement is also viewed as crucial to help qualified individuals keep their jobs and achieve their potential after they have been reasonably accommodated (Blanck, 1997). The data collection could also examine the fears and stigmas associated with disclosure of actual and hidden disabilities, because many employees with disabilities may chose not to request a reasonable accommodation due to fear of disclosure (Blanck, 1997). The study might also include an examination of the external benefits some employers have reported from offering accommodations. Employers have reported that accommodations are often profitable for employers. For example, one federal agency found that every dollar spent on accommodations saved almost $50 in net benefits (Stein, 2003). Quantitative evidence found that "disabled workers receiving accommodation had lower job turnover rates and equivalent or lower absenteeism rates, thus saving their employers replacement expenses" (Stein, 2003, pp. 104–105). Although the challenge of designing, funding and implementing such an instrument does pose immense challenges, collecting more information and administering studies is crucial to understanding the qualitative and quantitative impact the ADA has had and further improving the statute.

**Clarify the Statutory Ambiguity Inherent in the ADA Definitions, Including the Definition of Reasonable Accommodation.** The ADA's insistence that employers and courts utilize a case-by-case determination of what constitutes reasonable accommodation is simultaneously the strongest and weakest part of the ADA. The statute leaves as a "great unsettled question" the matter of what can or should be considered a reasonable accommodation and has led to "inconsistent and unpredictable court decisions" (Hoffman, 2003, p. 231). In permitting the facts surrounding each accommodation request and complaint to be adjudicated, drafters hoped to best meet the needs of each unique employee and employer. The process envisioned in the ADA eschews rote decisions and "one-size-fits-all" blanket rules, which would have preempted individual consideration of all circumstances and information attendant to a particular request for accommodation.

The result of the ADA's amorphous definition of reasonable accommodation, in tandem with the case-by-case determination requirement, has been the creation of burdens not only on courts, but also on employees and employers. One commentator noted that the interaction of the ADA's open-ended definitions and individualized process creates "a particularly onerous burden for employers attempting to avoid ADA lawsuits" (Willis, 1994, p. 725). Indeed, the ADA's ambiguity and insistence on case-by-case adjudication leave "employers and persons with disabilities uncertain of their rights and duties, hinders settlement of disputes and causes risk averse parties to accept too little. The result may be hostility, distrust and an erosion of society's commitment to persons with disabilities" (Malin & Moss, 1998, p. 198). Commentators have speculated that the "reason why the Supreme Court and other federal courts have been so strict in their interpretation of the ADA's definition of disability is because they have sought to create a high threshold for qualifying as disabled in order to avoid having to deal with the amorphous reasonable accommodation requirement" (Long, 2003, p. 897). Even Supreme Court Justice Sandra Day O'Connor explicitly criticized the ADA for failing to specify the intent of Congress (Hoffman, 2003).

Although the inherently fact-specific approach to what constitutes a reasonable accommodation should remain part of the ADA, creation of clear guidelines for both employers and courts to follow in interpreting the ADA may resolve the judicial misinterpretation. Creating bright-line rules to cover all potential ADA situations is virtually impossible, given the uniqueness of each job and employee (Long, 2003). The solution to this problem may be to attack the ADA's elusive definitions and rewrite into the ADA simple, categorical guidelines to be used with the case-by-case determinations when the ADA is enforced. Addressing all possible accommodation situations is unrealistic; however, adding additional guidance to the regulations or specificity to the statute based on the implementation of the ADA from the past 15 years may illuminate the process for all involved. Although a solution must necessarily balance the competing interests of employers and employees, there is clearly room for improvement.

***Offer Tax Incentives, Grants, or Subsidies to Encourage the Hiring and Accommodation of Employees with Disabilities.*** Congress adopted the goals of the ADA as a social goal; however, the cost of achieving the equality envisioned in the ADA has fallen almost solely on the business community. Federal or state funds could be used to defray the expense of reasonable accommodations, thereby allowing employers to make personnel decisions based on merit rather than the costs of an accommodation. Shifting the costs of accommodation to the federal or state government would help "achieve the equality the ADA seeks but has not delivered" (Malin & Moss, 1998, p. 199). The ADA is regarded as a costly, unfunded mandate that needs to be funded (Hoffman, 2003). Critics argue that if "society chooses to assist the disabled, the government should pay for accommodation out of tax revenue so that the burden is spread over the entire population" (Malin & Moss, 1998, p. 224). Due to the lack of studies on accommodations and the associated costs, it is unclear how much accommodations cost businesses, however, it is estimated that public funding of accommodations would require a federal outlay of roughly $1.3 to $2.5 billion (Malin & Moss, 1998).

Many different forms of public funding may be viable solutions to fund the ADA and reasonable accommodations in the workplace. Currently, some limited tax credits and deductions permit employers to receive credits for expenses associated with tangible personal property acquired to provide employees with disabilities accommodations pursuant to Title I of the ADA (Hoffman, 2003). For example, the disabled access credit provides qualifying small businesses with an election to receive a 50% tax credit for "eligible access expenditures," such as acquiring or modifying equipment, devices, materials or services for individuals with disabilities under Title I of the ADA (Lipman, 2003). Notably, only qualified small businesses are eligible for the credit, and the credit is limited to $5,000 or 50% of up to $10,000 of eligible access expenditures per tax year (Lipman, 2003).

There are pros and cons to each public funding program, but any successful program must be familiar to the business community and the program parameters and processes must be easily communicated and not too complex (Lipman, 2003). Business, government, and disability advocates all agree that the primary barriers to increasing use of available public funds are "unfamiliarity with these incentives and misconceptions regarding the difficulty involved in qualifying for them" (Lipman, 2003, p. 419). The prospective positive outcomes from publicly funding the ADA's reasonable accommodation provision are threefold. First, by subsidizing reasonable accommodations, litigation of ADA discrimination cases will decrease dramatically. Reduced litigation should "facilitate the building, rather than the destruction, of enabling relationships between employers and employees" (Lipman, 2003, p. 426). Second, employers will no longer offer inadequate accommodations or attempt to pass the cost of accommodation on to employees with disabilities. Finally, businesses will no longer have a financial incentive not to hire individuals with disabilities. The ADA will only continue to be better understood and enforced by expanding current programs or creating new incentives or subsidies.

## Maximizing Profits and Effectiveness While Offering Reasonable Accommodations

*Instill in Employees and Employers Understanding That Accommodations Are Not Social Welfare, Affirmative Action, or Mere Preferences.* The way the ADA and accommodations made under the ADA provisions are viewed in the workplace will play a key role in how effective the accommodation will be for the employee and employer. The ADA has been less effective than some hoped because it is viewed as a social welfare statute rather than as an antidiscrimination law (Travis, 2003). The U.S. Supreme Court recently fueled this debate when it repeatedly referred to reasonable accommodations as "preferences" (US Airways v. Barnett, 2002, p. 1521). It is critical that the employer not label a reasonable accommodation as a preference or as affirmative action for the employee with a disability. When a reasonable accommodation is labeled a preference or affirmative action, those who are not accommodated may harbor resentment, which, in turn, "risks further devaluing and stigmatizing the qualities associated with the beneficiaries' right to accommodation in the first place" (Travis, 2003, p. 329). Other employees may be hostile or less supportive of accommodations when such measures are seen as unfair advantages to the employee with the disability. An employer may and should certainly respond to a question from an employee about why a coworker is receiving "different" or "special" treatment by emphasizing its policy of assisting any employee who encounters difficulties in the workplace (EEOC Enforcement Guidance, n.d.). The bottom line for many employers and employees may have been summarized by Sears & Roebuck executives during congressional testimony on the ADA prior to passage: "It is hard to believe that [Sears could make its entire national headquarters accessible] for that cheap a price. But if a person wants disabled people, the accommodations really don't become a burden. If they don't, they always do" (H.R. Rep. No. 101-485(II), 1990).

***Utilize Federal and State Expert Resources to Create a Joint and Interactive Accommodation Process.*** An employer can avoid the cost of litigation and loss of productivity by clarifying how the ADA in general and the reasonable accommodation provision specifically will be interpreted for the company and for specific positions. Reasonable accommodations may be viewed as unclear or indecipherable by human resources professionals, especially where reasonable accommodations intersect other federal laws such as FMLA or state regimes like worker's compensation (Postol, 2002). Instead of permitting the ADA to become a legislative Rorschach test, an inkblot whose meaning and significance is determined through years of litigation and judicial lawmaking, employers should attempt to implement the intentionally open-ended provisions with the flexibility the ADA permitted to maximize the employer's productivity and output while accommodating and empowering the disabled. Merely having forms and procedures for handling reasonable accommodation requests will help keep clarifications out of the courtroom. Indeed, Congress may have intended the contours of the ADA to be defined by the courts or for employers to take initiative to implement the act because a fixed standard of reasonable accommodation or undue hardship could not possibly be applied fairly in all situations due to "the infinite permutations of disabilities, need for accommodation, and the levels of employer resources" (Epstein, 1995, p. 427).

An employer can take proactive steps to implement policies and procedures that will assist disabled employees and non-disabled employees. The first step the employer should take is to prepare and regularly update descriptive and thorough job descriptions for all positions in the organization. This will serve as a protective measure for the employer and the employee in the interactive accommodation process and in the event a lawsuit emerges. For example, if a function is not included in a job description, an employer might find it challenging to argue later that the function was in fact essential. An employee with a disability may seek to have such a "nonessential" function of his or her job transferred to another employee if the function is not clearly listed as essential. Also, a job applicant with a disability who applies for a job but is not hired because he or she is not "otherwise qualified" to perform the essential function that is not listed may bring, and be successful in, a nondiscrimination suit.

A second simple step employers should take is to establish effective written procedures for processing reasonable accommodation requests from employees. The ADA does not require employers to have any specific procedures in place to handle reasonable accommodation requests; however, the EEOC Guidelines (n.d.) do suggest each employer have a policy in place to guide the accommodation process. On July 26, 2000, President Clinton signed an executive order requiring each federal agency to establish effective written procedures for processing requests for reasonable accommodations under the Rehabilitation Act of 1973 (Exec. Order No. 13164, 2000). Although the order does not apply to the ADA, the history, language, purpose, and jurisprudence surrounding the Rehabilitation Act and the ADA are virtually identical, and the recommendation can be seen as a forward-looking glance at what may be to come for the ADA. There is little doubt that such a policy would be beneficial, although optional, for those employers falling under the ADA and not the Rehabilitation Act.

Effective written procedures for processing reasonable accommodation requests will "enable agencies to handle requests in a prompt, fair and efficient manner; they will assure that individuals with disabilities understand how to approach the system and know what to expect; and they will be a resource for both individuals with disabilities and for agency employees, so that all parties can understand the legal requirements" of the act (EEOC Enforcement Guidance, n.d.). Recommendations to make procedures effective include: informing individuals about their rights and responsibilities under the ADA and other relevant laws that might intersect the ADA, such as the FMLA or worker's compensation; explaining relevant terms such as *essential functions*, *undue hardship*, and, of course, *reasonable accommodation*; making the company's reasonable accommodation procedures readily available to all employees; and identifying the decision maker and putting all decisions in writing concerning reasonable accommodations offered and accepted or rejected (EEOC Enforcement Guidance, n.d.).

Finally, employers should consider developing a comprehensive process to guide all employees and managers through the reasonable accommodation process by tapping into available resources. Numerous federal and state resources provide methods for the mutual, cooperative, and ongoing process Congress envisioned when it passed the ADA. Employers have ample guidance assisting them in successfully using the interactive accommodation process central to the ADA. First, the Job Accommodation Network (JAN) provides key information and procedures regarding work-site accommodation options (JAN, n.d.). JAN was established in 1983 and is a service of the Office of Disability Employer Policy of the U.S. Department of Labor. JAN recommends using its five-step "Job Accommodation Process" to research and implement accommodations arising at any stage of employment, including application, retention, or return to work. JAN's first step is to define the situation. Employers and employees should ask: What specific symptoms and functional limitations are creating barriers to accessing the workplace, performing job tasks, or benefiting from an equal employment opportunity; whether the individual's condition is progressive, stable or unpredictable; whether documentation is needed to support the accommodation; and what specific job tasks, work environments, equipment or policies are creating barriers to successful job performance. JAN's second step is to perform a needs assessment. Employers and employees should ask whether it is necessary to modify the job; whether it is necessary to modify a policy, and whether it is necessary to modify the facility, product or equipment. JAN's third step explores alternative placement options. Employers and employees should explore whether reassignment is a possibility; whether the employee is qualified for reassignment; and whether there are any vacant, equivalent positions. The fourth step involves redefining the situation if a reasonable accommodation cannot be found or agreed upon during the interactive process. Step four may include seeking additional resources, assembling an accommodation team to address the issue, or returning to the possible accommodations to determine if something was overlooked. JAN's fifth and final step is to monitor the reasonable accommodation once implemented. A reasonable accommodation today may become unreasonable a year from now for the employer or employee, depending on the circumstances. Establishing who will be responsible for monitoring the accommodations, who the employee should communicate with in case problems arise with the accommodation or a change in their disability or limitations, and ensuring that the accommodation enables the employee to perform the essential functions of his or her position are all critical to ongoing implementation and success of the accommodation.

## Methods Employees With Disabilities Can Employ to Maximize Accommodations

The enactment of the ADA did not simply erase the deeply embedded societal disdain for the disabled. Although touted as the "Emancipation Proclamation" for individuals with disabilities, the act truly achieves little without the front-line collaboration between employers and employees seeking to find practical solutions through its terms and suggestions. Employees have several paths by which they may be able to maximize the ADA on their own behalf.

***Pursue Mutually Beneficial Accommodations Such as Telecommuting.*** New technology abounds that may allow employees and employers to develop mutually beneficial alternatives to a physical, full-time presence in the workplace (Travis, 2003). With the accessibility and relative inexpense of cell phones, high-speed Internet, fax machines, and other real-time communication devices, it is no longer the case that an employee must always be physically present in the workplace in order to perform his or her job. Telecommuting is being touted as a new means for achieving workplace equality for women and may hold similar promise for the employees with disabilities (Travis, 2003). Working at home may be a required accommodation, depending on the essential job functions of the employee's position and the supervision of that position (EEOC Enforcement Guidance, n.d.). Certain types of jobs may easily be performed by a telecommuting employee, including such jobs as a proofreader, medical transcriptionist, or telemarketer (EEOC Enforcement Guidance, n.d.). Other types of jobs cannot easily be performed outside the workplace, such as food server or cashier (EEOC Enforcement Guidance, n.d.).

To determine if a job can be performed effectively at home, the employer and employee should consider all possible implications, drawbacks, and benefits, including the employer's ability to adequately supervise the employee; the employee's need to work with certain tools or equipment that cannot be replicated at home; whether the essential functions of the job may be performed at home and what additional technology, time, and expenses this would incur; whether the accommodation would be effective; and finally, whether allowing the employee to work at home would cause undue hardship for the employer (EEOC Enforcement Guidance, n.d.). Courts that have rejected working at home as a reasonable accommodation focused on evidence that personal contact, interaction, and coordination were needed for the employee's specific position (*Misek-Falkoff v. IBM Corp.*, 1995; *Whillock v. Delta Airlines*, 1995).

The potential of such technological advances "is not inherent in the technology itself" (Travis, 2003, pp. 285–286). Collaboration between the employee and employer will still be necessary to effectively utilize the technology available. The company and supervisor must create collaborative solutions so the employee is not simply working unsupervised in the home (*Vande Zande v. Wisconsin Department of Administration*, 1995). Although critics argue that telecommuting magnifies existing segregation and hierarchies within the workplace—and the weight of current case law supports the view that working at home is an extraordinary accommodation warranted only in exceptional cases—this form of modified work schedule is a viable option between an employee and employer and should be pursued when possible (Travis, 2003).

*Research and Present the Accommodation's Cost-Effectiveness to the Employer.* Most reasonable accommodations are likely relatively inexpensive; however, many employers do not have this information or may believe otherwise. Studies conducted prior to the passage of the ADA anticipated that the total cost to businesses for reasonable accommodations would range between $50 and $100 dollars for each employee who needed an accommodation (*Questions and Answers*, 1989). One governmental study determined that among reasonable accommodations provided by federal contractors, the lowest costing accommodations included "changing work hours, work procedures, task assignments; transferring the workers to a new job; and orienting coworkers" (*Americans With Disabilities Act Hearing*, 1990). The studies also predicted that 51% of the employees needing accommodation would require no expense at all (*Americans With Disabilities Act Hearing*, 1990). Because the ADA does not track the cost of accommodations for employees with disabilities, the employee may find it useful to conduct his or her own "study" of the potential cost of an accommodation based on the employee's information and research.

Even if proof of the cost-effectiveness of an accommodation does not persuade an employer that the accommodation is reasonable, the information gathered and presented by the employee may prove important if the complaint the employee lodges is mediated, settled, or litigated. Specifically, information presented regarding cost-effectiveness will be important if the court engages in undue hardship analysis. The employee should focus on how accommodation of his or her disability would not place too onerous a burden on the operations of the employer in order to prove the employer is legally obligated to provide such an accommodation (Smith, 1995). While cost-benefit analysis may be a useful tool for an employee to use in negotiating the most beneficial reasonable accommodation, employers cannot simply rely on the accommodation's cost to determine if the accommodation is reasonable (EEOC Enforcement Guidance).

*Become Familiar With the Employer's Reasonable Accommodation Policies, Leave Policies, and Work Schedules.* Despite vague standards in the text of the ADA, forward-looking employers may have policies or procedures in place to accommodate individuals with disabilities. Employees seeking accommodations should become intimately familiar with all such policies. The policies may detail the process of how to make a request, how a decision will be made, which accommodation best suits the employer and employee, or even policies giving guidance on whether such an accommodation is allowed or if exceptions can be made to an employer's general policy. Employees who are unaware of employer policies or practices are put in the "awkward position of not knowing what accommodations they can rightfully demand from their potential or current employers" (Epstein, 1995, p. 442). The more informed an employee is, the more likely it is that a request for a reasonable accommodation will not result in tense or hostile relations between employers and employees with disabilities, both of whom are merely trying to facilitate accommodations.

If an employee with a physical disability is absent for reasons associated with his or her disability, the employee should provide the employer sufficient information to show the disability and absence are related. This information will help the employer and employee engage in an ongoing discussion of whether the accommodation being provided, such as an allowance of time off for care and treatment, is reasonable and sufficient. Under the ADA, an employer has the right to request this documentation, and providing the information up front will create open, ongoing communication and trust. It also allows the employer to dispel any myths in the work environment that the disabled employee is being given preferential treatment by taking leave or incurring absences that are unrelated to the disability. Employees must show that they are both willing and able to demonstrate that they have the skills to do the job by coming to work. Poor attendance may give employers and the courts the necessary proof to show the reasonable accommodations are infeasible.

## CONCLUSION

When an employer consciously or subconsciously structures a workplace around majority norms with a narrow vision that all employees will be able-bodied, nondiscrimination requires more than a mere passive avoidance of bias. Nondiscrimination requires employers, often at the urging of the judiciary, to actively modify the work environment, policies, and procedures to allow employees with disabilities an equal opportunity to participate and compete. By definition, a reasonable accommodation requires the employer to treat the employee with a disability differently than able-bodied employees or even other employees with disabilities. The laudable goals of the ADA rely on this highly individualized and contextual vision of equality. The goals of the ADA have not been realized, however, because employers (empowered by proemployer courts) have undermined the ADA's affirmative treatment principle despite clear statutory language and regulatory guidance to the contrary. The ADA requires employers to consider whether reasonable accommodations could remove the barriers created by a disability, and in this respect, the affirmative requirements are quite unique compared to other federal legislation. Although no specific form of accommodation is guaranteed under the ADA, the reasonable accommodations, in particular part-time and flexible work schedules, that Congress contemplated would ensure equal opportunity and access for individuals with disabilities are not being protected in court. The "continuing existence of unfair and unnecessary discrimination and prejudice" perpetrated by the courts "denies people with disabilities the opportunity to compete on an equal basis and to pursue those opportunities for which our free society is justifiably famous" (Americans With Disabilities Act, 1990).

Neither the ADA nor the EEOC guidance can mandate or even predict the "correct" answer in advance of each employment decision concerning an individual with a disability. Congress did not intend, however, to allow employers to maintain "rigid work schedules that permit no flexibility as to when work is performed" (EEOC Enforcement Guidance, n.d.). The courts have largely ignored Congress's mandate that reasonable accommodations be considered on a case-by-case basis and instead have developed hard and fast rules to define what will or will never constitute a reasonable accommodation. This court-imposed burden shifting to the employee is improper and ineffective. The demoralizing effects of these decisions that deny individuals with disabilities the ability to be self-supporting is still being felt by individuals with disabilities due to such per se rules despite the enactment of the ADA.

To fully reach its potential, the ADA must be amended and augmented to clarify gaps that exist in the amorphous statutory definitions of reasonable accommodation, essential function and undue hardship. Congress or state legislatures could also fund and implement ancillary programs such as mediation pilot programs or tax incentives to further expand the ADA's implementation. As implementation of the ADA's provisions are tracked and studied, judges may feel freer to expand construction of the ADA and to facilitate the kind of workplace flexibility, experimentation and collaboration envisioned by the ADA's creators. Until then, the responsibility for successful implementation of the ADA will rest on informed and mutual employer–employee collaboration to find and attempt creative solutions that benefit everyone.

# REFERENCES

Amadio v. Ford Motor Co., 238 F.3d 919, 929 (7th Cir. 2001).
Americans With Disabilities Act of 1990, 42 U.S.C. § 12101 et seq. (2004).
Americans with Disabilities Act: Hearing before the House Committee on Small Business, 101st Cong., 19 (1990).
Andrikopoulos, S., & Gould, T. E. M. (2003). Living in harmony? Reasonable accommodations, employee expectations and US Airways v. Barnett. Hofstra Labor Law Journal, 20, 345.
Barfield v. Bell S. Telecommunications, Inc., 886 F. Supp. 1321, 1327 (S.D. MS. 1995).
Befort, S. (2002). The most difficult ADA reasonable accommodation issues: Reassignment and leave of absence. Wake Forest Law Review, 37, 441.
Berkery, P. M. (1990). The Americans with Disabilities Act: Its impact on small business. National Public Accountant, 35, 42.
Blanck, P. D. (1997). Individual rights and reasonable accommodations under the Americans with Disabilities Act: The economics of the employment provisions of the Americans with Disabilities Act. DePaul Law Review, 46, 877.
Bragdon v. Abbott, 118 S.Ct. 2196 (1998).
Buchholz, B. B. (2002, October 27). Disabled job seekers struggle to find work. Chicago Tribune. Retrieved October 23, 2003, from Westlaw Allnews database.
Cehrs v. N.E. Ohio Alzeheimer's Research Ctr., 155 F.3d 775 (6th Cir. 1998).
Cohen, J. (2001). The ADA mediation guidelines: A community collaboration moves the field forward. Cardozo Journal of Conflict Resolution, 2, 1.
Colker, R. (1997). Hypercapitalism: Affirmative protections for people with disabilities, illness and parenting responsibilities under United States law. Yale Journal of Law and Feminism, 9, 220.
DeFord, S. (2003, January 28). Independent living's real costs. Washington Post. Retrieved October 23, 2003, from Westlaw Allnews database.
Deo v. Candid Color Sys., 156 F.3d 726 (10th Cir. 1998).
Devito v. Chicago Park District, 270 F. 3d 532, 534 (7th Cir. 2001).
EEOC v. AIC Sec. Investigation, Ltd., 820 F. Supp. 1060, 1064 (N.D. IL, 1993).
EEOC v. Wal-Mart Stores, Inc., 198 F.3d 257 (10th Cir. 1997).
EEOC Enforcement Guidance. (n.d.). Reasonable accommodation and undue hardship under the Americans with Disabilities Act. Retrieved October 1, 2003, from EEOC: http://www.eeoc.gov/docs/accommodation
Elwan, A. (1999, December). Poverty and disability: A survey of the literature. The World Bank, Social Protection Unit, Human Development Network. Retrieved August 1, 2003, from http://www.worldbank.org/sp
Epstein, S. B. (1995). In search of a bright line: Determining when an employer's financial hardship becomes "undue" under the Americans with Disabilities Act. Vanderbilt Law Review, 48, 391.
Erb, C. T., Rich, R. F., & Rich, R. A. (2002). Critical legal and policy issues for people with disabilities. DePaul Journal of Health Care Law, 6, 7–8.
Executive Order No. 13164 (2000).
Family Medical Leave Act, 29 U.S.C. § 2601 et seq. (2004).
Ferrier, J. (1996). ADA and ADR: Approaching an adequate adjudicatory allocation. Catholic University Law Review, 45, 1281.

Hodges, A. C. (1996). Dispute resolution under the Americans with Disabilities Act: A report to the administrative conference of the United States. *American University Administrative Law Journal, 9*, 1007.

Hoffman, S. (2003). Corrective justice and Title I of the ADA. *American University Law Review, 52*, 1213.

H.R. Rep. No. 101-485(II) at 34, 62 (1990).

*Hypes v. First Commerce Corp.*, 134 F.3d 721, 726 (5th Cir. 1998).

*Jackson v. Veterans Administration*, 22 F.3d 277 (11th Cir. 1994).

Job Accommodation Network. (n.d.). Retrieved October 21, 2003, from http://www.jan.wvu.edu/media/JobAccommodationProcess.html

Karlan, P. S., & Rutherglen, G. (1996). Disabilities, discrimination, and reasonable accommodation. *Duke Law Journal, 46*, 38–39.

*Kinlaw v. Alpha Baking Co., Inc.*, No. 02 C 1014, 2003 U.S. Dist. LEXIS 8319 (N.D. IL. May 14, 2003).

*Kuehl v. Wal-Mart Stores, Inc.*, 909 F.Supp. 794, 801-802 (D.C. CO. 1995).

*Lamb v. Qualex*, No. 99-1188, 2002 WL 500492, at *1 (4th Cir. April 3, 2002).

*Larson v. Seagate Technology, Inc.*, No. 00-2507, 2001 U.S. Dist. LEXIS 20489 (MN. 2001).

Lee, M. (1997). Searching for patterns and anomalies in the ADA employment constellation: Who is a qualified individual with a disability and what accommodations are courts really demanding? *Labor Lawyer, 13*, 179.

Lewis, T. M., & Murray, P. J. (1999). The Americans with Disabilities Act and reasonable accommodation: Are employers required to reassign disabled individuals who can no longer perform their jobs? *Labor Lawyer, 15*, 1.

Lipman, F. J. (2003). Enabling work for people with disabilities: A post-integrationist revision of underutilized tax incentives. *American University Law Review, 53*, 398.

Long, A. B. (2003). The ADA's reasonable accommodation requirement and "innocent third parties." *Missouri Law Review, 68*, 863.

Malin, D. A., & Moss, S. (1998). Public funding for disability accommodations: A rational solution to rational discrimination and the disabilities of the ADA. *Harvard Civil Rights–Civil Liberties Law Review, 33*, 197.

*Malone v. Aramark Services, Inc.*, 334 N.J. Super. 669, 678 (2000).

Malloy, E. W. (2001). Something borrowed, something blue: Why disability laws are different. *Connecticut Law Review, 33*, 605–606.

*Mardell v. Harleysville Life Ins. Co.*, 31 F.3d 1221, 1235 (3rd Cir. 1994).

*Misek-Falkoff v. IBM Corp.*, 854 F. Supp. 215, 227-28 (2nd Cir. 1995).

Moberly, M. D. (1996). Perception or reality? Some reflections on the interpretation of disability discrimination statutes. *Hofstra Labor Law Journal, 13*, 346.

Morin, E. C. (1990). Americans with Disabilities Act of 1990: Social integration through employment. *Catholic University Law Review, 40*, 189.

O'Neil, T. F., & Reiss, K. M. (2001). Reassigning disabled employees under the ADA: Preferences under the guise of equality. *Labor Lawyer, 17*, 347.

Pack, A. L. (2001). The Americans with Disabilities Act after *Sutton v. United Airlines*— Can it live up to its promise of freedom for disabled Americans? *Kentucky Law Journal, 89*, 541.

*PGA Tour, Inc. v. Martin*, 532 U.S. 970 (2001).

Postol, L. P. (2002). Sailing the employment law Bermuda triangle. *Labor Lawyer, 18*, 165.

*Questions and Answers on the Substitute Amendment to the Americans with Disabilities Act of 1989 before the Senate Committee on Labor and Human Resources*, 101st Cong. (1989).

*Ransom v. Ariz. Bd. of Regents*, 983 F. Supp. 895, 902 (D. AZ. 1997).

Regulations to Implement the Equal Employment Provisions of the Americans With Disabilities Act, 29 C.F.R. 1630 et seq. (September 12, 2003).

Robinson, M. B. (2003). Reasonable accommodation v. seniority in the application of the Americans with Disabilities Act. *St. Louis Law Journal, 47,* 186.

Rosenberger, M. G. (2001). Absenteeism and the ADA: The limits and loopholes. *Catholic University Law Review, 50,* 957.

*Runkle v. Potter*, 271 F. Supp.2d 951 (E.D. MI. 2003).

S. Rep. No 101-1116 at 9 (1989).

Smith, A. E. (1995). The "presence is an essential function" myth: The ADA's trapdoor for the chronically ill. *Seattle University Law Review, 19,* 172.

Stein, M. A. (2003). The law and economics of disability accommodations. *Duke Law Journal, 53,* 79.

*Sutton v. United Airlines*, 527 U.S. 471, 479 (1999).

*Svarnas v. AT&T Communications*, 326 N.J. Super. 59 (App. 1999).

*Tenbrink v. Fed. Home Loan Bank*, 920 F. Supp. 1156, 1160 (D. KS. 1996).

*Terrell v. U.S. Air*, 132 F.3d 621, 626 (11th Cir. 1998).

Tomko, C. M. (2002). The economically disadvantaged and the ADA: Why economic need should factor into mitigating measures disability analysis. *Case Western Reserve Law Review, 52,* 1033.

*Trautz v. Weisman*, 819 F.Supp. 282, 294-295 (S.D.N.Y. 1993).

Travis, M. A. (2003). Equality in the virtual workplace. *Berkeley Journal of Employment and Labor Law, 24,* 283.

*Tyndall v. Nat'l Educ. Ctrs.*, 31 F.3d 209, 213 (4th Cir. 1994).

*US Airways v. Barnett*, 122 S.Ct. 1516, 1523 (2002).

*Vande Zande v. Wis. Dep't of Admin.*, 44 F.3d 538 (7th Cir. 1995).

*Varone v. City of New York*, No. 02-1089, 2003 U.S. Dist. LEXIS 13604 (S.D.N.Y. August 1, 2003).

*Walders v. Garrett*, 765 F. Supp. 303, 309-310 (E.D. VA. 1991).

*Ward v. Mass. Health Research Inst.*, 209 F.3d 29 (1st Cir. 2000).

*Whillock v. Delta Airlines*, 926 F.Supp. 1555, 1564 (N.D. GA. 1995).

Wilkinson, W. (1997). Judicially crafted barriers to bringing suit under the Americans with Disabilities Act. *South Texas Law Review, 38,* 907–908.

Willis, C. J. (1994). Title I of the Americans with Disabilities Act: Disabling the disabled. *Cumberland Law Review, 25,* 715.

*Wimbley v. Bolger*, 642 F. Supp. 481 (W.D. TN. 1986).

# 15

# The Adequacy and Enforcement of Emergency Evacuation Laws in the Workplace for People With Disabilities

Marina Hadjioannou

> The challenge of social justice is to evoke a sense of community that we need to make our nation a better place, just as we make it a safer place.
> (Marian Wright Edelman, 2001)

On September 11, 2001, a stunned world witnessed thousands of people stream out of the World Trade Center in New York City in a live evacuation from a terrorist attack on the Twin Towers. Shortly thereafter, thousands more perished, stranded with no way to escape before the buildings collapsed.[1] The loss of lives on that day is all the more tragic because the emergency evacuation plan in the Twin Towers of the World Trade Center was known to be one of the most exemplary plans in existence.

After the first terrorist attack on the World Trade Center in 1993, the Port Authority in New York City revised its evacuation plan so that the buildings exceeded minimum standards required by federal and New York law (International Labor Organization [ILO], 2001). Reflective lighting was installed, stairwells were widened, and every person in a wheelchair was provided an evacuation chair (ILO, 2001; National Commission on Terrorist Attacks Upon the United States [9/11 Commission], 2004). Subsequently, every 6 months, emergency drills that included the use of the evacuation chairs were conducted (ILO, 2001).

---

[1]For a detailed accounting of the events leading to and following September 11, 2001, see the National Commission on Terrorist Attacks Upon the United States (2004), *9/11 Commission Report*.

This preparation on the part of the New York Port Authority likely saved many lives on September 11, including lives of people with disabilities. Tina Hansen, a woman with rheumatoid arthritis who worked on the 68th floor in one of the Towers, escaped from death when two of her colleagues carried her in an evacuation chair to safety, a perilous descent that took over an hour (see Baker, 2002; Barkley, 2001). Others, such as Abe Zelmanowitz, were not so lucky. Abe, a paraplegic, was one of the World Trade Center employees in wheelchairs who never made it out of the building (Barkley, 2001). Many lives were lost on that day, and improved evacuation planning may not have saved the life of Abe Zelmanowitz, but his story serves as a reminder that people with disabilities could benefit from disaster prevention planning that is specific to the needs of individual employees at the workplace.

In response to these horrific events, the federal government launched a number of initiatives across the nation to increase security measures. Many of these programs, including the development of the Department of Homeland Security, focus on terrorism prevention. Government plans have been created and funding set aside to evaluate and implement disaster prevention plans, but criticism has been widespread on the distribution, or lack thereof, of funding for disaster response planning (see National Council on Disability [NCD], 2003). Despite a call to action by disability advocates, government attentiveness to people with disabilities post September 11 has been weak (NCD, 2003).

The 9/11 Commission Report (9/11 Commission, 2004) is an example of the federal government's lack of attention to the needs of people with disabilities in the midst of a national disaster. Although the commission offers a comprehensive account of the events leading up to and following the terrorist attack on September 11, nowhere in the report does the commission specifically address the issue of disability, nor does it provide any recommendations for future initiatives that would provide protection for people with disabilities (9/11 Commission, 2004).

When an emergency strikes, people with disabilities are one of the highest risk groups for injury and death. For this reason, it is very timely for disability advocates to create and expand protection programs in the public and private sectors. As the events of September 11 demonstrated, a workplace can be a vulnerable place to be when a disaster strikes. When an emergency occurs, employers should provide accommodations necessary to evacuate employees with disabilities. Tragically, this duty is neither articulated nor practiced by many businesses. Furthermore, although antidiscrimination statutes attempt to protect people with disabilities, federal, state, and local building guidelines and fire codes do not effectively protect the interests of people with disabilities. As a result, many employers fail to create or maintain evacuation plans that accommodate their employees with disabilities.

The adequacy of emergency evacuation procedures is a topic only recently included in public debate (U.S. Department of Homeland Security, 2004) and academic publication (Hollis, 2003). Prior to September 11, little had been written about emergency evacuation laws in the workplace for people with disabilities. The issue had only been addressed in other contexts, such as prisons (e.g., Carnahan, 1999; Gardner, 1994) and airline flights (e.g., Cameron, 1999). For example, *Armstrong v. Wilson* (1997), a class action suit heard in the U.S. Court of Appeals for the Ninth Circuit, challenged the lack of accommodations for inmates with disabilities. The court concluded that a California state prison did not have adequate emergency evacuation plans for disabled inmates and was in violation of the Americans with Disabilities Act of 1990 (ADA). Academics responded with policy papers regarding inmates with disabilities (e.g., Carnahan, 1999; Gardner, 1994).

Another wave of writings has addressed the importance of including people with disabilities in the evacuation planning process (Batiste & Loy, n.d.; Blanck, 1995). Although these papers do stress important issues for individuals with disabilities, such as consultation in the planning process, accessible egress, accessible communications, and ongoing training, these publications do not adequately address state and local requirements and enforcement mechanisms that provide incentives for employers to create nondiscriminatory evacuation plans.

Although funding is being set aside to improve disaster planning and homeland security safety procedures, legislators must be made aware of the prevalent problems that exist with emergency evacuation planning for people with disabilities. State and local authorities must commit to implementing clear guidelines and effective enforcement mechanisms that support federal mandates of equality in the workplace. Furthermore, employers should be provided specific guidance as to how to go about creating a nondiscriminatory emergency evacuation plan for their employees with disabilities.

## THE PROBLEM: INEQUALITY IN EMERGENCY PLANNING

### The Community Defined

People with disabilities have been described as being the "hidden minority" in the United States as a result of persistent denial of equal opportunity to fully access mainstream society (Percy, 1995). In order to understand the consequences that inadequate evacuation procedures have on employees with disabilities, it is first necessary to realize the prevalence of disability in general and the scope of the problem of emergency evacuation in the workforce.

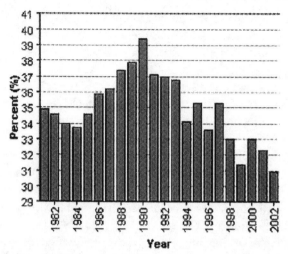

FIG. 15.1. Employment Rate: The percentage of men and women with a disability employed in the United States from 1981 to 2002.[2]

According to the U.S. Census (2000), 49.7 million people in the United States, nearly 1 in 5 people, are living with a disability.[3] In the age group of 21 to 64 years old, 30.6 million are reported to have a disability. Of those 30.6 million people, only 56.9% were employed. Likewise, in the state of Arizona, the rate of disability is 19.4% or 536,733 people in the employable age group of 21 to 64 years old. As demonstrated in Fig. 15.1, the employment rate for people with disabilities across the nation has been steadily decreasing and in 2002 was at its lowest rate the past 20 years.

It is worth considering that very capable individuals may be refusing to seek employment because they are not willing to compromise their capabilities or sacrifice their safety in exchange for employment. A recent poll reported that 58% of people with disabilities claimed that they do not know whom to contact in their community about emergency plans in the event of a crisis (Harris Poll, 2001). Among the people surveyed that were employed, 50% reported that no

---

[2]From Houtenville, Andrew J. 2004. *Disability statistics in the United States*. Ithaca, NY: Cornell University Rehabilitation Research and Training Center, www.disabilitystatistics.org. Posted May 15, 2003. Accessed September 27, 2004. These statistics were calculated by the Cornell University Rehabilitation Research and Training Center (Cornell RRTC) using data from the Current Population Survey (CPS), which is conducted by the Census Bureau and the Bureau of Labor Statistics. Persons with a disability are those who have a "health problem or disability which prevents them from working or which limits the kind or amount of work they can do."

[3]Census 2000 statistics are based on the Census taken on April 1, 2000, and include information on over 281.4 million people in 115.9 million housing units across the United States. Census 2000 used a functional limitation definition of disability. Six questions on the 2000 Census Long Form collected information on disability, including employment, and can be used to identify the total population with disabilities.

plans have been made for them to safely evacuate their workplace (Harris Poll, 2001). These statistics highlight the fact that there is—at the very least—a perception of inequality in terms of safety at the workplace, and a larger problem with emergency response planning.

## Inadequate Protections

Although both federal and Arizona state laws mandate equal opportunity and reasonable accommodation for people with disabilities in the workplace, emergency evacuation plans included, these mandates are inadequate based on two factors. First, these laws and regulations are often not accompanied by adequate—or any—enforcement mechanisms. As a result, employers are neither monitored nor provided incentives to follow these regulations. Federal and state government agencies have articulated guidelines for emergency evacuation for the general public, but most do not protect individuals with disabilities nor do they have an enforcement arm. (Access Board, 2002). Nongovernmental advocacy groups make recommendations for disaster planning, but do not have compelling influence on employers to enforce compliance with the recommendations. Second, the existing laws and regulations concerning emergency evacuation are not specific enough to meet the needs of disabled employees in the workforce. In other words, some laws and regulations may touch on emergency evacuation, such as the Emergency Planning and Community Right to Know Act in Arizona (A.R.S. 3326-341, et seq.), but do not make specific accommodation or mention of individuals with disabilities. Furthermore, a law may mention or even make accommodation for individuals with disabilities, but may not do so in a specific manner that adequately protects the wide range of disabilities represented by the community at large.

The state of Arizona serves as an example of a state government attempting to create protections for people with disabilities, but falling grossly short of offering adequate protection. The Arizona Administrative Code (A.A.C.) provides that emergency evacuation procedures and evacuation drills are required for people living in group homes who are developmentally disabled (A.A.C., R9-33-201, 2004). However, no Arizona state law exists that pertains specifically to the needs of other people with physical impairments or employees with disabilities.

Legislators must be informed that the needs of people with disabilities are complex and, moreover, will vary from person to person because individuals with disabilities demonstrate a large range of capabilities, type of disability and degree of disability (Percy, 1995). Likewise, even when an employer makes an effort to meet minimum requirements under a standard evacuation plan, minimum requirements are not satisfactory in many ways. The result is not likely to provide full protection for the array of disabilities, such as mobility impairments, visual and auditory impairments, and a broad range of comprehensive disabilities. Federal law creates an obligation on the part of employers to make comprehensive accommodations to their employees with disabilities (see the Americans with Disabilities Act of 1990 [ADA]), but states, such as the state of Arizona, have a large gap to bridge between existing policy and the comprehensive accommodation required by federal law.

## THE FEDERAL MANDATE OF NONDISCRIMINATION AND STATE OBLIGATIONS

### The Americans With Disabilities Act of 1990

In 1990, Congress enacted the Americans with Disabilities Act of 1990 (ADA) in order to provide government protection against discrimination of people with disabilities in the following contexts: (a) private employment; (b) public accommodation; (c) telecommunications; and (d) institutional organizations. The primary goal of the ADA is to support full social participation for all Americans with disabilities (Scotch, 2000). By 1992, most of the primary sections of the ADA came into effect through the issuing of compliance guidelines and an outreach campaign to put the public on notice of the new legislation (Sullivan, 1995). However, almost 15 years later the ADA has yet to have an effect on many public spaces.

The failure of full implementation of the ADA can be explained by a persistent social prejudice against people with disabilities. Richard K. Scotch (2000) stated:

> I would contend that, at least in its first ten years, the ADA appears to have fallen short of its more optimistic goal of fundamentally changing the lives of most Americans with disabilities .... While survey data suggest that most Americans are supportive of the ADA's goal of inclusion and nondiscrimination, stigma that constrains individuals with disabilities persists in individual attitudes and institutional processes. (p. 275)

For example, companies regularly maintain discriminatory policies and practices, including companies that have failed to make accommodations in emergency evacuation plans for employees with disabilities (Scotch, 2001). These failed accommodations not only violate federal mandates, but literally put employees' lives at risk.

Protection for people with disabilities in emergency evacuations can be found within Title I of the ADA. Title I prohibits private employers, state and local governments, employment agencies, and labor unions from discriminating against qualified individuals in employment situations. A qualified individual is an individual with a disability who, with or without reasonable accommodation, can perform the essential functions of the job that the employee is hired to perform. Reasonable accommodation is to occur on a case-by-case basis and includes any modification or adjustment to a job or the work environment that enables a qualified applicant or employee to participate in the application process or to perform essential job functions. Title I also guarantees equal rights and privileges to employees with and without disabilities, meaning that all employees should be treated equally by their employer. Some of the accommodations that an employer might be required to make under Title I include renovation of existing facilities, modification of work schedules, and modification or acquisition of equipment that allows people with disabilities to carry out job responsibilities. Furthermore, Title I provides employees with disabilities the right to enjoy the same benefits as employees without disabilities in the workforce.

The Federal Emergency Management Agency (FEMA) and the U.S. Fire Administration (USFA) (2000) noted that the ADA's reasonable accommodation provision requires employers to provide the same level of safety to people with disabilities as it does to other employees.

Another area of protection that will not be addressed in this discussion is protection under Title II of the ADA. Title II of the ADA prohibits all public entities from discriminating in employment against qualified individuals with disabilities. Title II protects people with disabilities from being excluded from activities, services, and programs because a building is not accessible. Following the lead of disability advocates, and in an attempt to focus this particular discussion on expanded protections in the workforce, the focal point here is on Title I of the ADA.

Although it appears that emergency evacuation procedures fall clearly within the scope of ADA requirements, neither the ADA nor its enforcement agency have regulations that directly address the question of emergency evacuation procedures in the workplace (see 29 C.F.R. 1630, 2002). For this reason, courts have not interpreted the ADA consistently with respect to evacuation plans. In *EEOC v. Wal-Mart Stores, Inc.* (2000), deaf and hard-of-hearing plaintiffs alleged that Wal-Mart refused to hire them based on their disability status and illegally refused to make the necessary accommodations for their employment. As part of the remedy granted in that case, the court ordered Wal-Mart to revise its emergency evacuation policies and to install flashing emergency lights to notify plaintiffs in the case of an emergency. Similarly, in *Spoon River College* (1992), where emergency evacuation procedures pertained only to persons without disabilities, the court found that the college had not taken adequate steps to plan for the emergency evacuation of persons with disabilities in violation of Title II of the ADA. Finally, in *Fayetteville State University* (1991), the university was held to be in violation of Title II when buildings lacked a posted evacuation plan or adequate emergency warning system for disabled students. These cases demonstrate some attention by the courts to compel changes to emergency evacuation procedures in public accommodations, such as in schools, but a scarcity of case law regarding private employers.

### The Equal Employment Opportunity Commission

Although the ADA mandates nondiscrimination, and the courts have held this mandates applies to emergency evacuations, the enforcement agency that polices Title I gives neither notice nor incentive to employers on the issue of nondiscrimination in emergency evacuation. The Equal Employment Opportunity Commission (EEOC), the federal agency charged with enforcing Title I of the ADA, publishes regulations and interpretive guidelines that provide notice to employers by specifically enumerating obligations to employees with disabilities. For example, an employer is *not* required to assist an employee in transferring from a car to a wheelchair upon arrival to work. On the other hand, the employer *is* required to provide reasonable accommodations that eliminate physical barriers within the work environment. Although the guidelines promulgated by the EEOC include a nonexhaustive list of reasonable accommodations that might need to be made in any particular workplace, these guidelines are strikingly silent on the question of emergency evacuation, emergency egress, and disaster planning. Hence, the ADA provides a clear mandate of nondiscrimination in the workforce, but the EEOC has failed to enumerate accommodations that must be made during an emergency evacuation, and has furthermore failed to provide notice or sanctions if this obligation is not met.

The EEOC complaint mechanism available for victims of discrimination exemplifies one of the federal government's methods to enforce the ADA. If a victim of discrimination files a complaint at the EEOC, the EEOC's policy is to seek full and effective relief for each and every victim of discrimination. The remedies may include posting a notice to all employees advising them of their rights, including their right to be free from retaliation; corrective or preventive actions taken to cure or correct the source of the identified discrimination; job placement in the position the victim would have occupied if the discrimination had not occurred; compensatory damages; back pay and lost benefits; and ending the specific discriminatory practice. Hence, if the ADA and the EEOC guidelines provided specific policies on nondiscriminatory evacuation, this agency would seemingly be the place where an employee could go to compel enforcement of these standards.

The EEOC is not the only federal agency charged with the responsibility for promulgating guidelines for emergency evacuation plans. Guidelines are published by the Access Board, the federal agency that promulgates standards for buildings under the ADA, in the ADA Accessibility Guidelines (ADAAG), and by the Federal Emergency Management Agency (FEMA), the agency that provides emergency procedures for public settings and private offices.

The primary difference between the EEOC and these other organizations is that the EEOC functions as an enforcement agency, whereas the Access Board and FEMA set policy without having an enforcement arm. The Access Board specifically addresses standards including specifications for accessible means of egress, emergency alarms, and signage, and FEMA provides guidelines for employers who have disabled individuals in the office.

Ironically, the EEOC, the federal agency charged with enforcing the ADA, has no clear regulations or guidelines for enforcing evacuation standards, whereas the Access Board and FEMA have detailed guidelines but no mechanism to enforce them. This apparent gap in federal policy demonstrates the inadequacy of relying on federal law alone to seek protection for employees with disabilities.

This lack of enforcement is not an oversight by the federal government, but the result of a restriction in the U.S. Constitution. The ADA was enacted by congress under its powers found in section 5 of the 14th Amendment in the Bill of Rights. Congress can make laws under this power, but cannot apply any sanctions to states because of the 11th Amendment. Therefore, in order to provide incentive for employers to follow guidelines, states must create enforcement mechanisms and impose sanctions against noncompliant employers (Willborn, 2000).

## THE STATE RESPONSE: ARIZONA CODES AND REGULATIONS

Although the federal government passed legislation mandating equal protection for people with disabilities in the workplace, because of the enforcement gap already explained, the onus falls on the states to create comprehensive enforcement mechanisms to compel employers to follow local and federal laws.

In Arizona, the Arizonans with Disabilities Act of 1992 (AzDA) mirrors the Americans with Disabilities Act of 1990. The purpose of the state act is to provide an enforceable mandate for the elimination of discrimination based on disability within the state of Arizona. The AzDA enables a victim of discrimination to file a civil legal action against an offender. In addition to a civil action, a victim can file a complaint at the Civil Rights Division of the Arizona Office of the Attorney General. In turn, the Attorney General's office has a responsibility to investigate all claims that it believes are related to employment discrimination (see A.R.S. §41-1481, 2004). The Attorney General's office, in a manner similar to the EEOC, follows administrative guidelines that are set forth in the Arizona Administrative Code.

The Arizona Administrative Code addresses emergency and evacuation drills for individuals that are developmentally disabled and living in group homes (A.A.C. R9-33-201, 2004). However, nothing in the code addresses the standards for emergency evacuation in public places or in places of employment. Although the State of Arizona Division of Emergency Management has a response and recovery plan with guidelines on evacuation, there are no specific recommendations for people with disabilities, nor is there an enforcement arm of this division (State of Arizona, 1998).

Building codes provide another opportunity for state or local governments to promulgate regulations for emergency evacuation. In Arizona, local recommendations and regulations for accommodations to inform the building process do exist—such as the minimum number of accessible parking lot spaces, the number of accessible telephones that must be provided, and exact specifications for water-fountain dimensions—like federal policies, little guidance is provided for emergency evacuation plans (Access Board, 2002). Mention of emergency evacuation is contained in instructions for emergency communications in elevators and detectible warning systems. These instructions are designed to protect the general public, as well as protecting some—but certainly not all—employees with disabilities.

## COMPREHENSIVE PLANNING

The success of the evacuation of the World Trade Center is not an accurate measure of the condition of evacuation plans in the United States. Quite the opposite is true—the World Trade Center had the most advanced evacuation plan of all high-profile towers (ILO, 2001). Most high-rise buildings adopt only the minimum standards of emergency evacuation necessary to pass fire code inspections that are often conducted by local agencies during the construction stage. Routine inspections may be made by elevator companies (to maintain license requirements) and alarm systems (as a courtesy of the company), but these inspections are technical in nature and do not provide extensive monitoring of employee behavior during evacuation drills.

Federal agencies offer inspections for evacuation safety, but these inspections do not specifically protect individuals with disabilities. The Occupational Safety and Health Administration (OSHA) offers detailed instructions on the creation of an evacuation plan as well as the requirements for training and maintenance of the plan. OSHA states that employers' emergency action plans must include emergency escape procedures with specified escape route assignments (29 C.F.R. 1910.38, 2002). The plan must be in writing and must be made available to employees on request. A business with 10 or fewer employees is permitted to communicate its plan orally. Missing from these regulations is any mention of special needs, special accommodations, or employees with disabilities. Alternatively, FEMA has issued a guide for instituting emergency procedures in offices for disabled employees, but it does not provide any requirements for inspections of the worksite (FEMA and USFA, 2000).

Some municipalities have taken it upon themselves to create standards for emergency evacuation and enforce those standards. As of October 2002, all high-rise businesses in Pittsburgh must comply with a city ordinance that requires each building to file for an emergency preparedness certificate with the Office of Emergency Preparedness (Pittsburgh City Ordinance, Bill No. 2002-088, 2002). This procedure ensures that the requirements of the ordinance are being fulfilled, that at least two evacuation drills are being practiced per year, and that an "All Hazard Plan" has been developed for the building. Under this plan, people who have requested special assistance will be specifically mentioned in the written plan, along with those people's usual location and specific needs during evacuation.

Likewise, Chicago's municipal code was amended shortly after September 11 (Chapter 13-78, 2001) to require that all high-rise buildings prove compliance with local emergency evacuation guidelines in order to acquire a "Certificate of Fitness." Similar to Pittsburgh, the Chicago ordinance requires a listing of names and normal floor location for all occupants with an ambulatory restriction or any other condition or disability that could delay a swift exit from the high-rise building in the event of an emergency. Each plan is required to designate and describe the location of one or more places of refuge or rescue each occupant if an emergency were to occur.

The most progressive state legislation to date can be found in Illinois, where the Emergency Evacuation Plan for People with Disabilities Act (430 I.L.C.S. 130/10 et seq., 2002) mandates that every high-rise building owner must establish and maintain an emergency evacuation plan for disabled occupants of the building who have notified the owner of their need for assistance. The evacuation plan calls for evacuation drills at least once per year with written records of the procedure. Failure to comply with this act is a petty offense, however, punishable only by a fine of $500, an amount not likely to result in full compliance. Arizona and other states should use this law as a template to build their own Emergency Evacuation for People with Disabilities Act that provides both specific instructions to employers as well as compliance incentives to ensure enforcement of the act.

## SOCIAL BARRIERS TO COMPLIANCE: IGNORANCE AND EMPLOYER RESISTANCE

### Social Disparities and the Problem of Awareness

In addition to problematic evacuation models and inadequate regulations, a number of dangerous assumptions work against the equal protection of people with disabilities in the workplace (Baynton, 2001). Both the community at large and legislators might mistakenly assume that regulations and enforcement measures that serve to protect employees with disabilities are already in existence, even though the same people likely cannot explain what those regulations are or which body is responsible for enforcing them.

Even among those aware that regulations do not exist, there may be some who assume that when an emergency situation occurs, employees will take care of one another. Although this may be true in individual cases, when faced with an emergency, impaired judgment, and trauma, people may seek self-preservation above all else.

Furthermore, it might be assumed that even in the absence of an evacuation plan, and even if employees do not help each other out, the disabled individual will have a plan of his or her own. Along the same lines of thinking, faith may be placed in a rescue crew that will have the expertise to evacuate those who require assistance. As demonstrated by September 11, even a highly experienced rescue crew might not be able to execute an effective plan (9/11 Commission, 2004).

Further complicating the problem is the fact that when an emergency evacuation plan to address people with disabilities exists, those most affected are often unaware of them. The plan may appear in written form in an employee manual or a book of policies and procedures, but until and unless the plan is practiced, and practiced regularly, employees never take the time to learn it. Although no data exist to prove these plans are not being practiced, ask a random sampling of 10 people you know when was the last time an evacuation drill was conducted in their office and this problem will become painfully apparent.

Reluctance on the part of the courts to compel revision of emergency disaster plans demonstrates the social resistance to acknowledging disparities in protection between people with disabilities and the public at large. For example, in *Massachusetts Coalition of Citizens with Disabilities, et al. v. Civil Defense Agency and Office of Emergency Preparedness of the Commonwealth of Massachusetts, et al.* (1981) an evacuation plan for a nuclear power plant emergency did not adequately protect people with disabilities, non-English speakers, and individuals without an automobile. An injunction sought to require modification of the plan to accommodate those groups. The claim invoked section 504 of the Rehabilitation Act of 1973 (29 U.S.C. 701-18), which reads, "No otherwise qualified handicapped individual shall be excluded from participation in, be denied the benefits of, or be subjected to discrimination under any program or activity receiving federal financial assistance" (p. 73). Without proof of "immediate irreparable injury" nor evidence that the deficiencies in the plan constituted discrimination "sufficient to compel a court to curtail the operation of the power facility," the injunction was denied. (p. 73). In justifying its decision, the First Circuit Court of Appeals explained:

> If at the time of a nuclear accident some persons, handicapped and non-handicapped, automobiled and non-automobiled, become subject to some inequality of the plan's effects, such inequality is not the fault of the plan, the provisions of which bear a reasonable relationship to the evacuation objectives sought to be fulfilled by adoptions of the plan. (p. 77)

Attitudes such as this demonstrate society's blatant disregard for and misunderstanding of the specific needs of people with disabilities.

## Employers' Defenses to Compliance

One of the largest barriers to the implementation of accessible evacuation plans for people with disabilities is resistance on the part of employers who may use legal defenses and public policy arguments to avoid implementing comprehensive emergency plans. First and foremost, the employer's duty to accommodate an employee or applicant with disability comes with limitations in the form of legal defenses. These defenses can be used by an employer in rebuttal to a discrimination charge under the ADA. The direct threat defense is relevant to the duty to provide accommodation for emergency evacuation as it is a defense that refers to the health and safety of other individuals in the workplace.

If a person with a disability poses a "direct threat" to the health or safety of others, or to themselves (see *Chevron USA, Inc. v. Echazabal*, 2002) the employer may exclude that person from the workforce. This defense has most commonly been seen in case law dealing with employees who have infectious diseases such as HIV/AIDS (e.g., *Estate of William C. Mauro v. Borgess Medical*

Center, 1998) and diabetes mellitus (e.g., *Miller v. Sioux Gateway Fire Department and Hathaway*,1993).

The events of the evacuation of the World Trade Center that occurred on September 11 exemplify the added risk to other employees who take it on themselves to evacuate a disabled coworker. One example, already mentioned briefly in the beginning of this chapter, is the story of Michael Benfante and John Cerqueria, who encountered a woman in a wheelchair on the 68th floor of the South Tower (Baker, 2002). These two men placed her in an evacuation chair and the two of them took turns carrying her down the remaining 67 flights of stairs (Baker, 2002). Over an hour later and only moments before the tower collapsed, all three exited the building (Baker, 2002) These men clearly put their lives at increased risk by deciding to help a third person.

Is it reasonable to request an employer to institute a "buddy system" that would compel third-party participation in an evacuation plan for workers with disabilities? Due to potential liability, the employer may elect to avoid additional risk to non-disabled or other workers and reject the most accommodating evacuation plan if it would place a direct threat to others in the workplace (see Hollis, 2002). Furthermore, the company might argue, after a recent U.S. Supreme Court decision, that an employee with a disability constitutes a direct threat to his or her own health and safety during emergency evacuation, and therefore should not even be in the workplace at all (see *Chevron USA, Inc. v. Echazabal*, 2002). These types of arguments certainly do not expand accessibility for people with disabilities, but rather have the potential to create additional barriers for employees with disabilities in the workforce.

Another defense available to the employer under the ADA is undue hardship. If the employer can demonstrate that it would cause undue hardship to accommodate the person with the disability as an employee, reasonable accommodation need not be made. To determine whether the creation of a comprehensive evacuation plan would create undue hardship for an employer, several variables, including cost, the functions of the workforce, and the abilities of other employees, would be assessed. This is likely the largest issue for employers who are ultimately concerned with the bottom line of costs, resources, and additional liability that could accrue once they begin to establish comprehensive and inclusive emergency evacuation procedures (Rothman & Herman, 2001; Waterman, 2003).

## RECOMMENDATIONS

A parting goal in this discussion is to provide guiding principles for use in the development of an emergency evacuation plan for employees with disabilities. Although employers may be intimidated by increased liability and costs of implementation, the fact remains that these companies are under an obligation, imposed by the ADA and state civil rights legislation, to provide accommodation to all employees in the event of an emergency evacuation.

To compel employers to implement these recommendations, it should be noted that the ultimate expense of implementing policies before an emergency occurs would certainly be less costly than the liability that could be assigned to a company if taken to court by employees in a negligence action.

A few simple principles can provide guidance to employers who take it upon themselves, even without the pressure of local or state certification requirements, to create a comprehensive and accessible plan (Blanck, 1995). These principles are consultation with the disability community, individual evacuation planning, creating alliances with local enforcement agencies, and community education and social marketing efforts.

## Consultation

The most important element to incorporate into any new emergency plan is a consultation process with people who have disabilities. Consultation has been endorsed by disability organizations that represent the needs and interests of individuals with disabilities (Cameron, n.d.; National Organization on Disability, 2001). The purpose of consultation is to directly address concerns that come from individuals with disabilities and to incorporate their personal experiences and ideas into an effective emergency plan. Ideally, the members consulted will be people with a variety of disabilities, including the physically impaired, hearing impaired, sight impaired, and people with mental and developmental disabilities. This group should be consulted prior to the drafting of the emergency procedure, invited to help in the drafting process, and consulted for review after the procedure has been developed. If direct consultation with individuals with disabilities is not feasible, consultation should be sought with a local and national disability rights organizations.

## Individualizing Plans

After a general plan is instituted in the workplace, individual assessments should be required for every individual with a disability. The purpose of individualizing an emergency plan is to ensure that it accommodates the employee's specific needs during evacuation. This concept is modeled after the reasonable accommodation determination required under the ADA for all employers that have employees with disabilities. Section 12111(9) of Title I provides that reasonable accommodation may include: (a) making existing facilities used by employees readily accessible to and usable by individuals with disabilities; and (b) job restructuring, part-time or modified work schedule, reassignment to a vacant position, acquisition or modification of equipment or devices, appropriate adjustment or modifications of examinations, remaining materials or policies, the provision of qualified readers or interpreters, and other similar accommodations for individuals with disabilities. The EEOC (29 C.F.R.1630.9, 2002) provides interpretative guidance on this process:

> The employer must make a reasonable effort to determine the appropriate accommodation. The appropriate reasonable accommodation is best determined through a flexible, interactive process that involves both the employer and the [employee] with a disability.

Much like a reasonable accommodation assessment made for employment of individuals with disabilities, the burden of requesting this assessment must be on the part of the employee, given that not all disabilities will be obvious to an employer (EEOC, 2002). However, once an assessment has been deemed necessary, it should be up to the employer to make all necessary accommodations to meet the individual needs of employees.

## Affiliations With Local Monitoring and Enforcement Agencies

After a plan has been developed in consultation with a number of people with disabilities and tailored to meet the needs of individuals at the workplace, the next recommendation is to distribute the plan to emergency response agencies and local enforcement agencies. The purpose here is twofold: first, to educate all potential participants in an emergency response situation, and second, to establish accountability through community education and awareness. Emergency response teams can use evacuation plans to coordinate rescue efforts, while meeting the specific needs of individual employees. In 2001, a nationwide assessment of fire departments revealed that approximately 84 million United States residents (roughly 29% of the population) are under the jurisdiction of fire departments that do not provide review of emergency plans (U.S. Fire Administration, 2002). By following the Chicago model, an employer would file a plan with the city and then periodically update the plan as required. Proactive submission of evacuation plans would enable a city to guide other employers in emergency plan development and would demonstrate general preparedness for emergency response.

## Workplace Education and Social Marketing

To most effectively advocate for employees with disabilities, employers should incorporate an education and social marketing scheme into the workplace. First and foremost, employee education is necessary. Beyond basic evacuation drills, every employee should receive a copy of the plan during the first employee orientation day or the first day of work. With each modification, the updated evacuation plan should be posted in the break room or bathroom of the workplace. Periodically, meetings should be scheduled to address concerns about a disaster and questions about the evacuation plan. This internal education provides accountability among employees and benefits everyone, employer and employee alike, in terms of developing a sense of community.

Beyond internal education, if the place of employment is open to the public, a social marketing plan should be formatted to inform the public that a nondiscriminatory evacuation plan is practiced on site. Currently, these sorts of notices are common for "hate-free zones," "weapon-free zones," and in work sites that wish to openly denounce race and gender discrimination. The University of Arizona has used this type of marketing in a campaign against sexual harassment. Posted in various locations, such as the recreation center and the university hospital, signs read "Mutual Respect. Sexual Harassment" and "Don't Do It. Sexual Harassment."

A clear notification in the form of a posting on a bulletin board at the employer's site puts anyone on notice that certain protections are in place. It also serves to dispel myths that people with disabilities are automatically protected without proactive measures. Ideally, this will compel people to inquire whether other work sites have nondiscriminatory disaster plans in place. A universal icon could be developed to denote that a "disabled-emergency" plan is enforced at the employer's site. Job postings could include reference to the emergency plans as part of the nondiscrimination statements that accompany human resource information. The importance of raising awareness and gaining commitment on the part of the workforce and the community at large should not be overlooked, as it is an essential component of implementing an effective evacuation plan.

These four suggestions (consultation, individual assessment, affiliation, and social marketing) are a starting point for the development of a nondiscriminatory emergency evacuation plan for the workplace. This discussion does not address the details of the different devices and techniques that can be used in the event of an emergency evacuation for people with disabilities, but rather only suggests methods to go about drafting the plan and distributing the plan. Various resources are available to provide guidance for employers attempting to design and implement an emergency evacuation plan, or for people with disabilities looking for information to provide to employers (see U.S. Department of Labor, n.d.).

## CONCLUSION: A CALL TO ACTION

It is tragic to consider that until a disaster occurs and an individual sues under the ADA or files a complaint with a state enforcement agency, employers are not provided any incentive to follow guidelines for emergency evacuation of people with disabilities. The greatest problem with existing remedies is that disaster planning is only effective if it occurs preventatively. This research seeks response through preventative planning. Following the lead of other states and municipalities, states, such as Arizona, have an opportunity to create much-needed protection for millions of people with disabilities of working age. Additionally, employers can take it upon themselves, in the absence of state and local protections, to create an access plan in collaboration with disabled employees by following the guidelines set forth in this discussion. In an era of increasing security and emergency planning, it is an appropriate time for employees with disabilities to gain equal protections in the workplace.

## ACKNOWLEDGMENTS

The research necessary for writing this article was supported by the David and Minnie Meyerson Foundation's project on Research, Advocacy and Policy Studies on Disability at the University of Arizona. I would like to thank Jane Korn, John D. Lyons Professor of Law, at the University of Arizona Rogers College of Law for her support and guidance during this project. I also owe my deepest gratitude to friends and fellow writers, Joan Zerrien and Karen Pepper, for their insights and editorial assistance.

## REFERENCES

Access Board. (2002). *Americans With Disabilities Act accessibility guidelines for buildings and facilities (ADAAG)*. Published in 69 Fed. Reg. 44083 (July 23, 2004) (to be codified at 36 CFRpt. 1190-1191).
Americans With Disabilities Act of 1990, 42 U.S.C. §12101 *et seq.* (2004).
Arizonans With Disabilities Act of 1992, A.R.S. §§41-1492 *et seq.* (2004).
*Armstrong v. Wilson*, 124 F. 3d 1019, 1024-25 (9th Cir. 1997).
Baker, S. (2002). Meet Tina Hansen: A World Trade Center survivor. *Arthritis Today*. Retrieved September 30, 2004, from http://www.arthritis.org

Barkley, M. (2001). *World Trade Center locked stairwells: Accumulating comments on evacuation problems.* Retrieved September 30, 2004, from http://www.mjbarkl.com/locked.htm

Batiste, L. C., & Loy, B. (n.d.). *Emergency evacuation procedures for employees with disabilities.* Job Accommodation Network. Retrieved September 30, 2004, from http://www.jan.wvu.edu/media/emergency.html

Baynton, D. C. (2001). Bodies and environments: The cultural construction of disability. In P. D. Blanck (Ed.), *Employment, disability, and the ADA* (pp. 387–411) Evanston, IL: Northwestern University Press.

Blanck, P. D. (1995). *Disaster mitigation for persons with disabilities: Fostering a new dialogue.* Washington, DC: The Annenberg Washington Program in Communications Policy Studies of Northwestern University.

Cameron, C. T. (n.d.). *Emergency Planning for People with Disabilities and Other Special Needs.* Urban Energy & Transportation Corporation. Retrieved September 30, 2004, from http://www.disabilitypreparedness.com/Planning%20for%20People%20With%20Disabilities%20article.doc

Cameron, K. (1999). Are United States airlines prepared to handle in-flight medical emergencies? *Indiana International & Comparative. Law Review, 9,* 573.

Carnahan, S. J. (1999). The Americans With Disabilities Act in state correctional institutions. *Capitol University Law Review, 27,* 291.

*Chevron USA, Inc v. Echazabal,* 536 US 73 (2002).

Edelman, M. W. (2001, October 12). *A prayer for the children in the 21st century.* Paper presented at the 2001 Symposium, The Call to Serve: Renewing the University's Social Justice Mission. Abstract retrieved September 1, 2004, from http:// www.georgetown.edu/publications/bluegray/2001/1022/features/A061022B.htmEEOC

Emergency Action Plan, 29 CFR 1910.38 (2002).

Equal Employment Opportunity Commission. (2002). *Enforcement guidance: Reasonable accommodation and undue hardship under the Americans With Disabilities Act* (No. 915.002). McLean, VA: Equal Employment Opportunity Commission Clearninghouse.

EEOC v. Wal-Mart Stores, Inc., 2000 U.S. Dist. LEXIS 61 (Arizona, 2000).

Emergency Evacuation Plan for People with Disabilities Act, 430 ILCS 130/10 et seq. (2002).

Emergency Planning and Community Right to Know Act, A.R.S. §§26-341, et seq. (2004).

Enforcement Procedures for Discrimination in Employment, A.R.S. § 41-1481 (2004).

*Estate of William C. Mauro v. Borgess Medical Center,* 137 F.3d 398 (6th Cir. 1998)

*Fayetteville State University* (NC) 2 NDLR 301 (October 11, 1991).

Federal Emergency Management Agency & U.S. Fire Administration. (2000). *Emergency procedures for employees with disabilities in office occupancies* (No. FA-154). Emmitsburg, MD: U.S. Fire Administration.

Gardner, E. (1994). The legal rights of inmates with physical disabilities. *Saint Louis University Public Law Review, 14,* 178.

Group Home Requirements for Individuals Who Are Developmentally Disabled, Emergency Procedures and Evacuation Drills, A.A.C. R9-33-201 (2004).

Group Home Requirements for Individuals Who Are Developmentally Disabled, Fire Safety Requirements, A.A.C. R9-33-202 (2004).

Harris Poll. (2001, December 5). *The Harris Poll #60: Many people unprepared for terrorist attacks or other disasters.* Rochester, NY: Harris Interactive.

High Rise Buildings, Emergency Procedure, Municipal Code of Chicago, Chapter 13-78 (2001).

Hollis, W. C. (2002). The rights of people with disabilities to emergency evacuation under the Americans With Disabilities Act of 1990. *Journal of Health Care Law & Policy, 5,* 524.

Houtenville, A. J. (2000). *Disability statistics in the United States.* Retrieved September 27, 2004 from Cornell University Rehabilitation Research and Training Center website.

International Labor Organization. (2001). How an evacuation plan saved lives. *World of Work,* No. 41.

*Massachusetts Coalition of Citizens with Disabilities, et al. v. Civil Defense Agency and Office of Emergency Preparedness of the Commonwealth of Massachusetts, et al.,* 649 F.2d 71 (1st Cir. May 26, 1981).

*Miller v. Sioux Gateway Fire Department and Hathaway,* 497 N.W. 2d 838 (Iowa 1993).

National Council on Disability. (2003). *National Disability Policy: A Progress Report, December 2001-December 2002.* Washington, DC: National Council on Disability.

National Commission on Terrorist Attacks upon the United States. (2004). *The 9/11 Commission Report: Final report of the National Commission on Terrorist Attacks Upon the United States* (pp. 279–281, 316). Washington, DC: U.S. Government Printing Office.

National Organization on Disability. (2001, November 7). *Disability disaster mobilization initiative: Response to September 11th.* Retrieved September 30, 2004, from www.nod.org

Percy, S. L. (1995). *Disability, civil rights and public policy in power. Privilege and law: A civil rights reader, 424.* (Leslie Bender & Daan Draveman, Eds.). St. Paul, MN: West Group.

Pittsburgh City Ordinance Number 29 (October 10, 2002), Bill No. 2002-088.

Regulations to Implement the Equal Employment Provisions of the Americans with Disabilities Act, 29 C.F.R. 1630 *et seq.* (2002).

The Rehabilitation Act of 1973, 29 U.S.C. 701-18.

Rothman, R. A., & Herman, M. I. (2001, Winter). Potential employer liability arising out of an incidence of terrorism. *Employer Update, 1.*

Scotch, R. K. (2000). Making change: The ADA as an instrument of social reform. In L. P. Francis & A. Silvers (Eds.), *Americans with disabilities: Exploring implications of the law for individuals and institutions* (p. 275). New York: Routledge.

Scotch, R. K. (2001). *From good will to civil rights: Transforming federal disability policy* (2nd ed.). Philadelphia: Temple University Press.

*Spoon River College* (IL), 3 NDLR 183 (September 1, 1992).

State of Arizona. (1998). *Division of Emergency Management Emergency Response and Recovery Plan.* Phoenix, AZ: Arizona Division of Emergency Management.

Sullivan, P. V. (1995). The Americans with Disabilities Act of 1990: An analysis of Title III and applicable case law. *Suffolk University Law Review, 29,* 1117.

U.S. Census Bureau. (2000). *2000 Census of Population and Housing Demographic Profile.*

U.S. Department of Homeland Security. (2004). *Every business should have a plan.* Retrieved March 5, 2005, from http://www.ready.gov

U.S. Department of Labor, Occupational Safety and Health Department. (n.d.) *Evacuation plans and procedures e-tool.* Retrieved September 30, 2004, from http://www.osha.gov/SLTC/etools/evacuation/index.html

U.S. Fire Administration. (2002). *Needs assessment of the U.S. Fire Service* (No. FA-240). Emmitsburg, MD: U.S. Fire Administration.

Waterman, S. (2003, April 9). D.C. businesses worry for terror liability. *The Washington Times*.

# Author Index

## A

Abbot, N. C., 85, *100*
Abbott, R. D., 146, 147, *159*
Achenbach, T. M., 223, *234*
Adams, P. F., 40, *64*
Adamson, L. A., 89, 91, 92, *101*
Agostinelli, S., 86, *101*
Aguirre, A., 134, 137, *139*
Akande, A., 179, *185*
Akerblom, M., 127, *139*
Alafaci, M., 72, *82*
Allen, E. H., 137, *138*
Allen, R., 168, 177, *183*
Allen, T. E., 58, 62, *64*
Allred, E. N., 132, *139*
Al-Shibabi, T., 78, *82*
Amaya, C., 4, *13*, 75, *82*
American Psychiatric Association, 10, 11, *13*
Ames, R. G., 125, 128, 129, 130, 131, 137, *138, 140*
Anderson, C. W., 144, 145, 148, *159, 160*
Anderson, G. B., 42, *64*
Anderson, J., 76, *82*
Anderson, R., 87, *100*
Andrikopoulos, S., 267, 268, *298*
Anglin, G. J., 112, 118, *121*
Appel, S., 85, 86, *101*
Aprea, C., 129, *138*
Aquilar, M. G., 129, 133, 137, *138*
Arakane, S., 75, *82*
Archambault, D., 72, *82*
Armstrong, T., 221, *233*
Arnau, L. M., 231, *233*

Aro, H. M., 28, *36*
Arora, C. M. J., 188, 189, *197*
Ashford, J. B., 30, 34, *35*
Astin, J. A., 85, 86, *100, 101*
Atkins, D. L., 150, *159*
Atkins, M. S., 223, 226, *233*
Attree, E. A., 78, *82*
Avorn, J., 95, *102*

## B

Bade, 209, *219*
Baerger, D. R., 149, 150, *158*
Bahan, B., 43, *65*
Baker, S., 104, *121*, 302, 314, *318*
Balderson, K., 28, *35*
Baldwin, C. M., 86, 98, *100, 101*
Balinky, J. L., 226, *233*
Bandura, A., 191, *197*
Barenbaum, E., 169, 177, 178, *184*
Barkley, M., 302, *319*
Barkley, R. A., 226, 227, 228, 229, 230, 231, 232, *233*
Barnes, J., 85, *100*
Barnhart, S., 129, 137, *140*
Barnicle, K., 45, 46, 47, 61, *65*
Barrett, R. P., 167, 175, 178, *184*
Barrios, B. A., 164, *183*
Bartini, M., 187, 192, *200*
Bassano, J. C., 70, *82*
Bates, J. E., 192, *201*
Batiste, L. C., 303, *319*
Batsche, G. M., 187, *197*
Battersby, S. J., 80, *82*
Bauer, D., 73, *82*

# AUTHOR INDEX

Baxter, J., 4, *14*
Baynton, D. C., 312, *319*
Beach, J., 137, *140*
Beck, A. J., 18, 19, 20, 21, 32, *35*, 36
Beck, C., 74, *83*
Befort, S., 266, 273, 278, 280, *298*
Behan, A. M., 27, *37*
Beidel, D. C., 164, *183*
Beitchman, J. H., 28, *35*
Bell, I. R., 86, 98, *100, 101*
Bellinger, D., 132, *139*
Bellini, J. L., 62, *65*
Bemark, F., 187, *197*
Bender, B. G., 117, *122*
Benfield, K., 261, *262*
Benson, H., 95, *100*
Bentley, K. M., 188, *197*
Benz, M. R., 194, 195, *198*
Berger, S., 27, *35*
Berkery, P. M., 268, *298*
Berkowitz, G. S., 136, *139*
Berry, H., 137, *140*
Berry, J., 104, *120*
Berry, L. L., 47, 66, *67*
Berry, M. R., 136, *138*
Berts, M., 190, *199*
Bethel, M., 88, 89, *100*
Bexten, E. M., 70, *83*
Bhojak, M. M., 27, *35*
Biesecker, G. E., 132, *139*
Björkqvist, K., 190, 191, *199, 201*
Björnsson, J. K., 190, *199*
Black, H. C., 250, *262*
Blackwell, D. L., 41, *65*
Blades, F., 45, 46, 47, 50, 61, *65*
Blanck, P. D., 257, *262*, 286, 287, 288, *298*, 303, *319*
Bledsoe, C., 71, *83*
Blenkhorn, P., 72, *82*
Block, A. K., 143, *157*
Blum, R. W., 172, *183*
Boersam, E. R., 133, *139*
Boone, S. E., 42, *64*
Bor, R., 29, *35*
Borg, M. G., 189, *197*
Borg, W. R., 61, *65*
Borthwick-Duffy, S., 209, 210, *219*
Bos, C. S., 232, *233*
Boulton, M. J., 187, 188, *197*
Bourquin, E. A., 43, *65*
Bozzi, N., 129, *138*

Bradley, N., 70, *83*
Bradman, A., 127, 133, 135, 136, *138*
Brain, P., 188, *201*
Braunwarth, M., 70, *82*
Brenner, B. L., 136, *139*
Bricout, J. C., 76, *82*
Bridges, M. W., 27, *37*
Brier, N., 146, 147, *157*
Broder, P. K., 147, *158*
Brooks, A. J., 86, *101*
Brooks, B. M., 76, 80, *83*
Brooks, F., 187, 192, *200*
Brown, C., 149, *160*
Brown, D. J., 80, *82, 83*
Brown, R. T., 227, *234*
Brownlie, E. B., 28, *35*
Bruden, T., 105, *123*
Bruner, J. S., 106, *120*
Brunschwig, L., 165, 170, 180, *185*
Bruyere, S. M., 3, *13*
Bryson, S. E., 163, 166, 174, *184*
Buaud, A., 72, *82*
Buchholz, B. B., 269, 277, *298*
Buck, E. S., 86, 89, 91, 93, *100*
Bulkeley, W. M., 243, *262*
Bullis, M., 144, 145, *159*, 194, 195, *198*
Bullock, L. M., 147, *157*
Buntinx, W. H. E., 209, 210, *219*
Burcar, P. J., 130, 131, 137, *140*
Burger, D., 72, *82*
Burke, B., 89, 91, *100*
Burke, J. M., 136, 137, *138*
Burnette, J., 230, *233*
Burrell, S., 143, *157*
Butcher, P., 28, *35*

## C

Caesar, R., 150, *159*
Calhoun, G. B., 150, *157*
Calkins, D. R., 85, 86, *101*
Calvert, I. A., 137, *140*
Cameron, C. T., 315, *319*
Cameron, K., 303, *319*
Campbell, D. T., 33, *35*
Campbell, S. B., 228, *233*
Campbell, T., 28, *35*
Capella, M. E., 42, *65*
Carey, S. P., 227, *235*
Carnahan, S. J., 303, *319*
Carney, R. N., 111, 112, 118, *120, 121*

Cary, P. T., 187, 201
Casey, K., 147, 157
Cassidy, C. M., 97, 98, 99, 100
Castorina, R., 127, 133, 135, 136, 138
Catalano, R. F., 188, 198
Ceci, S. J., 209, 219
Chang, E., 76, 83
Chen, C. H., 76, 83
Chen, M. C., 79, 83
Chen, R., 76, 83
Cheok, A. D., 70, 83
Chesney-Lind, M., 150, 151, 159
Chien, D. H., 192, 201
Chrislip, D., 125, 128, 129, 130, 131, 137, 138, 140
Chu, N. C., 79, 83
Civit, A., 4, 13, 75, 82
Claudio, L., 136, 139
Claypoole, K., 130, 131, 137, 140
Cohen, J., 283, 298
Cohen, R., 109, 120
Coie, J. D., 187, 188, 191, 192, 198, 199, 201
Cole, K., 40, 66
Coles, C. D., 227, 234
Coles, R., 41, 65
Colker, R., 267, 269, 278, 298
Collier, S., 226, 231, 234
Collins, J. G., 41, 45, 46, 47, 50, 61, 65
Colvin, G., 187, 202
Conoley, J. C., 187, 191, 198
Conti-Ramsden, G., 195, 198
Cook, A., 76, 83
Cook, D., 45, 67
Costabile, A., 188, 189, 198
Coulter, D. L., 209, 210, 219
Covell, A. B., 63, 65
Cowie, H., 189, 201
Cox, P., 261, 262
Craig, E. M., 209, 210, 219
Craig, W. M., 190, 191, 192, 196, 197, 199, 202
Creswell, J., 150, 160
Crick, N. R., 190, 191, 197, 198
Crockett, D., 189, 197
Crombie, D., 72, 82
Cromer, W., 110, 120, 123
Croog, V. J., 132, 140
Cropley, A., 104, 123
Cross, M., 28, 35
Cullen, F. T., 141, 159

Cummins, R. A., 167, 183
Cunha, B., 80, 83
Curran, M., 75, 83
Curtin, S., 91, 92, 100
Curtin, T., 104, 122
Curtis, S. E., 136, 138

**D**

Dacher, E. S., 98, 101
Dahle, K. B., 144, 145, 157
Dale, B., 28, 35
Danek, M., 42, 43, 44, 65
Daniell, W. E., 129, 130, 131, 137, 140
Davies, M. L., 28, 36
Davis, R. B., 85, 86, 101
Dawkins, J. L., 194, 195, 197
Dayton, J., 231, 233
DeFord, S., 269, 298
Delbanco, T. L., 85, 86, 101
DeLuca, J., 78, 82
DeMarinis, R. K., 3, 13
Demers, P., 129, 137, 140
Derevensky, J. L., 167, 183
Derwent, G., 78, 82
DeVoe, J. F., 187, 197
Diessner, R., 105, 122
Dilley, M., 109, 120
DiMatta, P. H., 75, 83
Dishion, T. J., 187, 200
Dispenza, M., 258, 262
Dixon, D. N., 86, 91, 93, 101, 109, 123
Dodge, K. A., 187, 188, 191, 192, 197, 198, 201
Doll, B., 190, 191, 196, 201
Donelson, E. G., 27, 36
Dong, Q., 163, 164, 179, 183, 185
Donnenwerth-Nolan, S., 109, 123
Doolittle, G., 45, 67
Doreleijers, T. A. H., 152, 158
Doren, B., 194, 195, 198
Douglas, G., 105, 122
Dowds, B. N., 89, 90, 91, 101
Drakeford, W., 148, 158
Duff, R., 167, 174, 178, 183
Dunivant, N., 148, 158
Dunn, D. S., 27, 36
DuPaul, G. J., 226, 227, 228, 230, 231, 232, 233
du Plessis, P., 29, 35
Dutot, A., 72, 82

Dutton, G., 78, 83

## E

Eagle, J. W., 187, 201
Ecobichon, D. J., 127, 138
Edelman, M. W., 301, 319
Efran, J. S., 88, 89, 91, 92, 101
Egan, S. K., 191, 192, 200
Eggleston, C. R., 149, 157
Eisenberg, D. M., 85, 86, 101, 102
Elder, N. C., 86, 101
Elias, A., 28, 35
Ellis, J. W., 209, 210, 218
Elwan, A., 269, 298
Engelbert, K., 150, 160
Engelkamp, J., 109, 121
Enticknap, A., 78, 82
Entzeroth, L., 217, 218
Epstein, S. B., 282, 291, 296, 298
Erb, C. T., 268, 269, 298
Erlich, J., 149, 150, 158
Ernst, E., 85, 100
Eskenazi, B., 127, 133, 135, 136, 138
Espelage, D. L., 189, 198
Ettner, S. L., 85, 86, 101
Evans, G., 72, 82

## F

Fagan, J., 217, 218
Fairbairn, L., 193, 199
Falek, A., 227, 234
Farrington, D. P., 188, 189, 191, 198
Fejes-Mendoza, K. E., 152, 157, 158
Feld, B., 142, 158
Fels, D., 74, 83
Fenske, R. A., 137, 138
Ferguson, A. C., 133, 140
Ferrier, J., 283, 284, 285, 298
Finke, M., 73, 82
Fiorello, C. A., 136, 138
Firak, N., 248, 262
Fisher, B. L., 168, 177, 183
Fishman, C. S., 216, 219
Fiske, D. W., 33, 35
Floyd, S., 4, 14, 76, 78, 83
Foley, R. M., 148, 149, 158
Fondacaro, M. R., 142, 161
Fontana, A. F., 89, 90, 91, 101

Fonzi, A., 188, 189, 198
Forness, S. R., 192, 198
Forsyth, E. M., 47, 65
Foster, C., 85, 86, 101
Frantz, J., 157, 159
Freeman, N. C., 133, 134, 136, 137, 138, 139, 140
Freidman, R., 95, 100
Fujioshi, M., 72, 83
Furlong, M. J., 187, 194, 199
Furniss, F., 80, 83

## G

Gable, R. A., 187, 198
Gall, M. D., 61, 65
Gallagher, B., 72, 82
Gallini, J. K., 112, 122
Gammel, D. L., 225, 233
Gammlin, B., 43, 66
Garcia, I. E., 129, 133, 137, 138
Gardner, E., 303, 319
Garrett, J. F., 27, 35
Gates, M., 75, 83
Gatsonis, C. A., 132, 139
Gaucher, P., 74, 83
Geeter, J., 248, 262
Genta, M. L., 188, 189, 198
Germer, C. K., 88, 89, 91, 92, 101
Gersten, R., 104, 121
Ghatala, E. S., 117, 121
Gibson, J. J., 114, 121
Gilden, D., 70, 84
Gillcrist, A., 86, 101
Gilman, A., 45, 46, 47, 61, 65
Gingerich, K. J., 222, 229, 233
Gips, J., 75, 83
Glenberg, A. M., 114, 115, 117, 118, 119, 120, 121, 122
Gluckman, I. B., 224, 235
Glueckauf, R. L., 4, 14
Godbold, J. H., 136, 139
Godfrey, C., 86, 101
Goffman, E., 29, 36
Goldstein, A. P., 187, 191, 198
Goldstein, S., 103, 122
Goodman, R., 194, 202
Goodwin, D., 117, 121
Gore, A. C., 136, 139
Gould, T. E. M., 267, 268, 298
Graziano, A. M., 170, 183

Graziano, J., 132, *140*
Greenhouse, J. B., 132, *139*
Griffin, E., 149, 150, *158*
Griller-Clark, H. M., 144, 145, 148, *159, 160*
Groden, G., 167, 175, 178, *184*
Groden, J., 167, 175, 178, *184*
Grotpeter, J. K., 190, 191, *197, 198*
Gu, J., 76, *83*
Guarnaccia, V. J., 167, *183*
Guillet, V., 72, *84*
Guillette, E. A., 129, 133, 137, *138*
Gullone, E., 165, 166, 167, 169, 170, 171, 172, 173, 174, 175, 178, 182, *183, 184*
Gutierrez, T., 117, 118, 119, *121*
Guttmann, J., 112, 113, *121*

## H

Hakola, S. R., 225, 229, *233*
Hall, T. S., 217, *219*
Halman, M., 28, *35*
Hamlin, K., 164, *183*
Hammer, S., 79, *84*
Hara, S., 72, *83*
Harachi, T. W., 188, *198*
Hardy, R. E., 166, 171, *184*
Harkness, E. F., 85, *100*
Harlow, C. W., 21, *36*
Harnad, S., 114, *121*
Harootunian, B., 187, *198*
Harper, D. C., 193, *198*
Harper, P., 45, *66*
Harrington, J. M., 137, *140*
Harris, M., 89, 90, 91, *101*
Harrison, A., 78, *82*
Hartman, C. A., 152, *158*
Hartman, D. P., 164, *183*
Haverkamp, F., 79, *84*
Hawkins, J. D., 146, 147, *159*, 188, *198*
Hayes, L. M., 30, *36*
Hazelwood, D., 46, 61, 63, *66*
Hazler, R. J., 188, 189, *198*
Heaton, R. K., 130, 131, 137, *140*
Hechtman, L., 229, *235*
Heinze, A., 165, 171, 172, 179, *184*
Helsel, W. J., 163, 164, 166, 171, 172, 175, *184, 185*
Hendershot, G. E., 40, *64*

Hendrickson, J. M., 187, *198*
Herman, M. I., 314, *320*
Hetherington, R. W., 98, *101*
Hewa, S., 98, *101*
Hodges, A. C., 283, 284, 285, *299*
Hodges, E. V. E., 191, 192, *198, 200*
Hoffman, S., 288, 289, 290, *299*
Hoffmeister, R., 43, *65*
Hollis, W. C., 303, 314, *320*
Holmes, L., 4, *14*
Holt, J., 40, *66*
Homzie, M., 109, *121*
Hoover, J. H., 168, 176, 177, *185*, 188, 189, *198*
Hotto, S., 40, *66*
Houtenville, A. J., 304, *320*
Howery, K., 76, *83*
Hubal, E. A. C., 136, 137, *138*
Hudson, D., 28, *36*
Hufford, B., 4, *14*
Hugo, K. E., 152, *158*
Hung, B. K. M., 163, 166, 173, *184*
Huttunen, A., 190, 191, *200*
Huurre, T. M., 28, *36*

## I

Ibrahim, F. A., 87, *101*
Ikeda, M. J., 226, *234*
Ikeuchi, H., 75, *82*
Imado, K., 75, *82*
Inglis, A., 28, *35*
Ingram, J. L., 132, *140*
Ioannidis, G. T., 72, *82*
Ishihara, Y., 74, *84*
Itoh, K., 72, *84*
Ivanoff, A., 30, *36*

## J

Jacobson, J. L., 133, *138*
Jacobson, S. W., 133, *138*
Japuntich, S., 117, 118, 119, *121*
Jenkins, B., 125, 128, 129, 130, 131, 137, *138, 140*
Jimenez, G., 4, *13*, 75, *82*
Jimenez, M., 133, *140*
Johnson, J. A., 89, 91, 92, *101*
Jones, K., 28, *35*
Jonson-Reid, M., 150, *158*

Jordan, I. K., 64, 66
Josephs, A., 167, 169, 178, *184*
Jung, M., 70, *83*

## K

Kagee, S. A., 86, 91, 93, *101*
Kahan, B. S., 86, *102*
Kahn, H., 87, *101*
Kain, J., 4, *14*
Kampfe, C. M., 43, 66
Kamphaus, R., 104, *121*
Kamrin, M. A., 125, 127, *139*
Kanaya, T., 209, *219*
Kapp, M. B., 95, *101*
Kapperman, G., 165, 171, 172, 179, *184*
Kaptchuk, T. J., 85, *102*
Karlan, P. S., 271, *299*
Karlsson, J. S., 28, *36*
Karon, M., 166, 173, *185*
Karshmer, A. I., 71, *83*
Kaschak, M., 117, 118, 119, *121*
Kato, N., 74, *84*
Katsiyannis, A., 104, *123*
Kauffman, J. M., 221, *234*
Kaufman, P., 187, *197*
Kaukiainen, A., 191, 194, 195, 196, *198, 201*
Kavale, K. A., 192, *198*
Kawamitsu, R., 72, *83*
Kaynak, M. N., 70, *83*
Keefe, T. J., 130, 131, 137, *140*
Keifer, M., 130, 131, 137, *140*
Keilitz, I., 146, 147, 148, *157, 158*
Kelly, N., 80, *82*
Kelso, D., 45, 46, 47, 61, *65*
Keogh, B., 104, *121*
Kessler, R. C., 85, 86, *101*
Kewman, D. G., 27, *37*
Keys, S., 187, *197*
Kim, J. A., 163, 166, 174, *184*
King, E., 190, *199*
King, J. J., 165, 166, 172, 173, *184*
King, N., 72, *82*
King, N. J., 163, 164, 165, 167, 169, 170, 171, 172, 173, 178, 179, *183, 184, 185*
Kingsley, C., 45, *67*
Kirk, J., 86, *101*
Kirkham, C., 189, 190, *200*
Kirkland, J., 87, *100*

Kissel, J. C., 137, *138*
Klaus, J., 4, *14*
Klein, O., 127, *139*
Knapp, L. G., 167, 175, 178, *184*
Knoblich, G., 109, *122*
Knoff, H. M., 187, *197*
Knox, E., 195, *198*
Ko, C. C., 70, *83*
Kochenderfer, B. J., 187, *199*
Kochenderfer-Ladd, B., 187, *199*
Kormi-Nouri, R., 109, *121*
Kose, G., 168, 177, *183*
Kosovich, G. N., 42, 66
Krager, J. M., 221, *234*
Kratochwill, T. R., 163, 164, 165, 167, 171, 172, *184, 185*, 231, *234, 235*
Krauss, H. H., 86, *101*
Krieger, R. I., 128, 137, *139*
Kroesen, K., 86, *101*
Kupersmidt, J. B., 187, *199*
Kusel, S. J., 187, 188, *200*
Kusunoki, K., 72, *83*

## L

Ladd, G. W., 187, *198, 199*
Lagerspetz, K., 190, 191, 194, 195, 196, *198, 200, 201*
Lagerspetz, K. M., 190, *199*
La Greca, A. M., 175, *184*
Lancee, W., 28, *35*
Lancioni, G., 80, *83*
Landrigan, P. L., 132, 133, 136, *139, 140*
Lane, B. A., 146, 147, *158*
Lane, E. C., 151, *158*
Lane, H., 43, *65*
Lannen, T. L., 80, *82*
Lanting, C. I., 133, *139*
La Rocca, J., 167, 174, 178, *183*
Larson, K. A., 146, 147, *158*
Lazarro, J.J., 70, *84*
Leckie, J. O., 133, *140*
Lee, M., 270, 273, 280, *299*
Lee, P. W. H., 163, 166, 173, *184*
Lees, D., 75, *83*
Leiss, J. K., 127, 135, *139*
Leloup, J., 74, *83*
Lengenfelder, J., 78, *82*
Lenssen, S. A. M., 152, *158*
Lentz, R., 112, *121*

Lenz, W. A., 132, *139*
Leone, P. E., 148, 149, 150, *158, 159*
Lesgold, A. M., 112, 113, 117, *121, 122*
Levie, W. H., 112, *121*
Levin, J. R., 107, 108, 109, 110, 111, 112, 113, 117, 118, 119, *120, 121, 122, 123*
Leviton, A., 132, *139*
Levy, L. S., 137, *140*
Lewis, J. A., 80, *83*, 130, 131, 137, *140*
Lewis, T. M., 266, *299*
Li, A. K. F., 188, *197*
Li, H., 169, 178, 180, *184*
Li, T. Y., 74, 79, *83*, 84
Liefooghe, A. P. D., 189, *201*
Lieh-Mak, F., 163, 166, 173, *184*
Lilienthal, C., 207, *219*
Limber, S. P., 187, 188, *199*
Lioy, P. J., 133, *140*
Lipman, F. J., 267, 290, *299*
Litfin, J. K., 222, 229, *233*
Littlejohns, D., 28, *35*
Lizzet, A., 167, 174, 178, *183*
Loewenherz, C., 137, *138*
Long, A. B., 289, *299*
Long O, 41, 66
Love, S. R., 166, 174, *184*
Lovelace, E., 109, *121*
Low, R., 109, *122*
Loy, B., 303, *319*
Lu, C., 137, *138*
Luckasson, R., 209, 210, *219*
Luk, S. L., 163, 166, 173, *184*
Lunghini, L., 129, *138*
Lustig, S., 210, *219*
Lyddon, W. J., 89, 91, 92, *101*
Lyon, G. R., 103, *122*
Lyons, J. S., 149, 150, *158*

# M

Maag, J. W., 226, *234*
MacDonald, J. M., 150, 151, *159*
MacMillan, D., 104, *121*
Madden, C., 167, 169, 178, *184*
Mager, A., 72, *82*
Maggi, L., 207, *219*
Magnotti, R., 127, *139*
Maher, P., 60, 66
Maizlish, N., 129, 137, *139*

Mäki, H., 194, 195, 196, *198*
Malespin, O., 127, *139*
Malin, D. A., 289, *299*
Mallory, W., 143, 146, *159*
Malloy, E. W., 269, 271, 278, 279, 281, *299*
Malmgren, K., 146, 147, *159*
Mandl, H., 112, *122*
Manikam, R., 165, 171, 172, 179, *184*
Marano, M. A., 40, *64*
Marcotte, P., 141, 142, *159*
Margalit, M., 168, 176, 178, *184*
Marini, Z., 193, *199*
Markowitz, S. B., 136, *139*
Marley, S. C., 118, 119, *122*
Martin, P., 167, 174, 178, *183*
Maruschak, L. M., 18, 19, 20, 21, 32, *35*, 36
Matheis, R. J., 86, *101*
Mather, N., 103, *122*
Mathias, D., 106, *122*
Matson, J. L., 163, 164, 165, 166, 171, 172, 174, 175, 179, *184, 185*
Matte, T. D., 136, *139*
Mayer, R. E., 109, 112, *122*
McArthur, P., 147, *157*
McConachie, H., 194, *202*
McConaughy, S. H., 223, *234*
McConnell, R., 127, 130, 131, 137, *139, 140*
McCullough, C., 105, *122*
McCurdy, T. R., 136, *138*
McGarvey, E. L., 143, 145, *159*
McKenna, S. J., 75, *84*
McKinley, W., 4, *14*, 76, 78, *83*
McShane, D., 105, *122*
Meers, G., 151, *159*
Meisel, S. M., 148, *158*
Mekaouche, A., 70, *82*
Menesini, E., 188, 189, *198*
Meng, L., 74, *84*
Meng, M., 76, *83*
Meyers, K., 157, *159*
Meza, M. M., 129, 133, 137, *138*
Mickelson, W. T., 187, *201*
Micozzi, M. S., 98, *101*
Miesenberger, K., 4, *14*
Miller, A. K., 187, *197*
Miller, M. T., 132, *139*
Miller, S. L., 146, 147, *158*
Millus, D., 150, *159*

Mina, S., 74, 83
Minagawa, H., 74, 84
Minz, R., 86, *101*
Mishna, F., 193, *199*
Miyagawa, H., 75, 82
Moate, T. F., 137, *138*
Moberly, M. D., 267, *299*
Modukuri, R., 72, 84
Mohammed, Y., 79, 84
Montgomery, L., 150, *159*
Moon, M. M., 141, *159*
Morato, P., 80, 83
More, A. J., 104, *122*
Morgan, D. P., 127, 128, 129, *139*, 143, 145, 146, *159*
Morgan, R., 105, *123*
Morin, E. C., 268, *299*
Morita, Y., 187, *201*
Morris, N., 29, 30, *36*
Morris, R. J., 72, 84, 163, 164, 172, *184*, 189, 196, *201*, 209, *219*, 221, 226, 231, *234*
Morris, T. L., 164, *183*
Morris, Y. P., 209, *219*, 221, 226, *234*
Morrison, G. M., 187, 194, *199*
Morrison, K., 75, 84
Morrison, R. L., 187, *199*
Morton, J. B., 150, 151, *159*
Moss, S., 289, *299*
Mossman, D., 213, *219*
Mounce, L. M., 130, 131, 137, *140*
Mourant, R. R., 78, 82
Mousavi, S. Y., 109, *122*
Mueller, A. D., 27, *36*
Mulder, P. G., 133, *139*
Mulhall, J., 165, 170, 171, 172, 173, *184*
Mumola, C. J., 21, *36*
Murakami, H., 74, 84
Murphy, D. M., 145, 148, *159*
Murray, D., 127, *139*
Murray, P. J., 266, *299*

**N**

Nabuzoka, D., 194, 195, *199*
Naglieri, J., 105, *122*
Nahmias, M. L., 232, *233*
Naito, I., 74, 84
Nakamura, K., 43, 66
Nansel, T. R., 188, *199*
Nathawat, S. S., 27, *35*

Nayak, S., 86, *101*
Nearing, J., 228, *235*
Needham, L. L., 137, *139*
Needleman, H. L., 132, *139*
Nelson, C. M., 143, 145, 148, 149, *158*, 160
Newcomer, P. L., 169, 177, 178, *184*
Nicholas, J. J., 27, *37*
Nidiry, J., 128, *140*
Niehaus, M., 79, 84
Nilsson, L. G., 109, *121*
Nishioka, T., 73, 84
Noice, H., 116, *122*
Noice, T., 116, *122*
Noker, M., 79, 84
Nolan, J. R., 250, *262*
Nolan-Haley, J. M., 250, *262*
Noon, J. M., 94, 95, 96, *101*
Norlock, F. E., 85, 86, *101*
Novelli, M. T., 129, *138*
Noyes, E., 109, *121*
Nozawa, M., 75, 84
Nyberg, L., 109, *121*
Nybro, C., 150, *159*

**O**

O'Brien, M., 127, 135, 136, *139*
O'Connell, P., 191, *199*
Oda, K., 72, 84
Ohnishi, K., 75, 82
Olafsen, R. N., 189, *199*
Ólafsson, R. F., 189, 190, *199*, *201*
Ólafsson, R. P., 190, *199*
Oliver, R., 188, 189, *198*
Olivier, D., 72, 82
Ollendick, T. H., 163, 164, 166, 167, 169, 170, 171, 172, 173, 175, 178, 179, *183*, *184*, *185*
Olsen, J. M., 95, *102*
Olweus, D., 187, 188, 189, 190, 191, 192, 196, *200*, *201*
O'Malley, M., 125, 126, 127, 128, 130, 137, *139*, *140*
O'Moore, A. M., 189, 190, *200*
O'Neil, T. F., 266, *299*
O'Neill, A., 72, 82
Opfer, T., 150, *160*
Orenstein, M., 176, *185*
O'Rourke, M. K., 134, 137, *139*
Osada, H., 72, 84

Österman, K., 191, *201*
Overpeck, M., 188, *199*
Overton, W. F., 88, 89, 91, 92, *101*

**P**

Pacheco, F., 127, *139*
Pack, A. L., 268, 273, *299*
Paget, K. D., 168, 176, *185*
Paivio, A., 109, *120, 122, 123*
Panek, P., 74, *83*
Panksepp, J., 221, *234*
Paramore, L. C., 86, *101*
Parasuraman, A., 47, *66, 67*
Patandin, S., 133, *139*
Pattern, M. D., 168, 176, *185*
Patterson, G. R., 187, *200*
Patterson, J. B., 4, *14*
Pavel, D., 104, *122*
Pearce, L., 167, 174, 178, *183*
Peck, C., 167, 174, 178, *183*
Peeck, J., 112, 118, *122*
Pelham, W. E., 223, 226, *233*
Pellegrini, A. D., 187, 192, *200*
Pelletier, K. R., 85, *101*
Pepler, D. J., 190, 191, 192, 196, *197, 199, 202*
Pepper, S. C., 87, 89, 97, *102*
Percy, S. L., 303, 305, *320*
Perry, D. G., 187, 188, 191, 192, *198, 200*
Perry, L. C., 187, 188, 192, *200*
Peter, K., 187, *197*
Petrie, H., 72, *82*
Pettit, G. S., 188, 191, 192, *198, 201*
Piaget, J., 106, *122*
Pieper, M., 79, *84*
Pierce, C. A., 27, *37*
Pilla, R. S., 188, *199*
Pinon, J., 72, *84*
Pintner, R., 165, 170, 180, *185*
Planty, M., 187, *197*
Plas, J., 105, *122*
Platzman, K. A., 227, *234*
Plinge, A., 73, *82*
Podboy, J., 143, 146, *159*
Pollard, C. J., 151, *159*
Pollard, R. R., 151, *159*
Popovac, D., 132, *140*
Poppen, W., 70, *83*
Porter, A., 61, *66*

Postol, L. P., 291, *299*
Powell, D. M., 3, *14*
Powell, E., 150, *159*
Powell, H. M., 80, 82, *83*
Power, T. J., 226, *234*
Prazak, B., 79, *84*
Pressley, M., 112, 117, *121, 122*
Price, J. M., 188, 191, *198*
Proctor, L. J., 192, *201*
Prosser, F., 43, *66*
Pumariega, A. J., 150, *159*

**Q**

Quigley, P., 149, 150, *158*
Quinn, M. M., 148, 149, *159*

**R**

Ramirez, S. Z., 167, *185*
Ramsey, E., 187, *202*
Rand, M. R., 187, *197*
Randall, A., 157, *159*
Ranjan, 98, *102*
Rapport, M. K., 146, *159*
Rassmus-Gröhn, K., 71, *84*
Raven, R., 28, *35*
Raviv, A., 168, 176, 178, *184*
Redmond, S. M., 28, *37*
Reed, J. K., 4, *14*, 76, 78, *83*, 133, *140*
Reeve, A., 209, 210, *219*
Reid, J. B., 187, *200*
Reid, R., 226, 230, *234*
Reid, W., 30, 34, *35*
Reif, S. F., 231, *234*
Reinberg, J., 45, 46, 47, 61, *65*
Reiss, J. A., 132, *139*
Reiss, K. M., 266, *299*
Repp, B. H., 109, *122*
Reynolds, C. R., 168, 176, *185*
Rice, M. L., 28, *37*
Rich, R. A., 268, 269, *298*
Rich, R. F., 268, 269, *298*
Richard, M. A., 47, *67*
Richards, J. S., 27, *37*
Riding, R. J., 105, 106, *122*
Ries, P. W., 41, *67*
Rigas, M. L., 136, *138*
Rigby, K., 188, *200*
Rigler, D., 166, 173, *185*

Rio, F. D., 4, *13*, 75, *82*
Roberts, C. M., 192, *200*
Robertson, D. A., 114, 115, *121*
Robinson, M. B., 271, 279, *300*
Robinson, T. R., 146, *159*
Rocha, N., 80, *83*
Rodier, P. M., 132, *140*
Rodriguez, C. M., 168, 177, 178, *185*
Rodriguez, M. A., 4, *13*, 75, *82*
Rogan, S. P., 134, 137, *139*
Rogers, K., 150, *159*
Rohner, R., 104, *123*
Romero, H., 136, *139*
Rose, F. D., 76, 78, 80, *82, 83*
Rosen, L. A., 222, 229, *233*
Rosenberger, M. G., 278, 280, *300*
Rosenstock, L., 129, 130, 131, 137, *140*
Ross, D. M., 188, 189, *200*
Ross, M., 95, *102*
Rothlind, J., 226, *234*
Rothman, D. J., 29, 30, 36, 141, *159*
Rothman, T. A., 314, *320*
Routh, D. K., 168, 177, 178, *185*
Ruan, W. J., 188, *199*
Rubman, C. N., 112, 115, *123*
Rudy, S. A., 187, *197*
Rumpler, B., 72, *84*
Rumrill, P., Jr., 62, *65*
Russek, L. G., 96, 98, *100, 102*
Russo, J., 125, 128, 129, 130, 131, 137, *138, 140*
Rutherford, R. B., 143, 144, 145, 148, 149, 152, *158, 159, 160*
Rutherglen, G., 271, *299*
Rybarczyk, B., 27, *37*

**S**

Sabers, D., 105, *123*
Sabornie, E. J., 194, *200*
Safer, D. J., 221, *234*
Saint, C. G., 134, 137, *139*
Saito, Y., 75, *82*
Sales, B. D., 3, *14*, 18, 21, 23, 30, 34, *35, 37*
Salkind, N. J., 62, *67*
Salmivalli, C., 190, 191, 194, 195, 196, *198, 200, 201*
Saltz, E., 109, *123*
Salvia, J., 227, *234*
Samuels, S., 129, 137, *139*

Sánchez Lizardi, P., 127, 134, 135, 137, *139, 140*
Sandler, L. A., 257, *262*
Sanger, D., 146, 150, *160*
Sankai, Y., 75, *84*
Sasso, G. M., 187, *198*
Sato, H., 72, *83*
Sauer, P. J., 133, *139*
Savage, E. P., 130, 131, 137, *140*
Savitz, D. A., 127, 135, *139*
Schaffart, B., 150, *160*
Schauer, J., 45, 46, 47, 61, *65*
Schaughency, E. A., 226, *234*
Scheidt, P., 188, *199*
Schell, A., 132, *139*
Schenker, M., 129, 137, *139*
Schettler, T., 132, 133, *140*
Schlieder, C., 72, *82*
Schneider, M., 81, *84*
Schneider, N. R., 18, 21, 23, *37*
Schneider, P., 4, *14*
Schultheis, M. T., 78, *82*
Schulz, S. C., 149, *160*
Schwartz, D., 129, 137, *140*, 192, *201*
Schwartz, G. E., 96, 98, *100, 102*
Schwartz, R. K., 95, *102*
Scotch, R. K., 306, *320*
Scullin, M. H., 209, *219*
Seawright, K. W., 47, *67*
Seedhouse, P., 80, *83*
Seiber, J., 129, 137, *139*
Seiden, J., 217, *219*
Seisenbacher, G., 74, *83*
Semple, W. E., 149, *160*
Sengupta, K., 70, *83*
Severson, R. A., 108, *123*
Sevillano, J. L., 4, *13*, 75, *82*
Sexton, K., 137, *139*
Shapiro, A. K., 94, *102*
Shapiro, E. S., 230, *235*
Shauffer, C. B., 144, *161*
Sheldon, L. S., 136, 137, *138*
Shepherd, R. E., Jr., 141, *160*
Shiflett, S. C., 86, *101*
Shimron, J., 112, 113, *121*
Shopland, N., 80, *83*
Shrout, P., 132, *140*
Shu, S., 190, *201*
Shubert, J., 104, *123*
Shulz, R., 27, *37*
Shum, L., 150, *160*

# AUTHOR INDEX  333

Sickmund, M., 142, 146, 147, *160*
Silverman, C., 74, *83*
Simcox, N. J., 137, *138*
Simons-Morton, B., 188, *199*
Siple, L. A., 44, *67*
Sitter, P., 4, *14*, 76, 78, *83*
Sjöström, C., 71, *84*
Slee, P. T., 188, *200*
Slobogin, C., 142, *161*
Small, M. A., 187, 188, *199*
Smith, A. E., 271, 274, 278, 281, 282, 295, *300*
Smith, G., 194, *199*
Smith, I. E., 227, *234*
Smith, M., 189, 190, *200*
Smith, P. K., 187, 188, 189, 190, 191, 192, 193, 194, 195, 196, *198*, *199*, *200*, *201*, *202*
Snyder, H. N., 146, 147, *160*
Snyder, T. D., 187, *197*
Solberg, M. E., 189, *201*
Song, S. Y., 187, *201*
Soto, A. D., 129, 133, 137, *138*
Soumerai, S. B., 95, *102*
Spinetta, J. J., 166, 173, *185*
Spreen, O., 146, 147, *160*
Spurgeon, A., 137, *140*
Stafford, C., 165, *184*
Staghezza-Jaramillo, B., 132, *140*
Standen, P. J., 80, *82*
Steenland, K., 125, 128, 129, 130, 131, 137, *138*, *140*
Stein, J., 132, 133, *140*
Stein, M. A., 286, 287, 288, *300*
Stein, P. A., 168, 176, 177, *185*
Stephens, R., 137, *140*
Stevens, G., 229, *235*
Stone, W. L., 175, *184*
Stoner, G., 227, *235*
Stoy, M. R., 227, *234*
Strambi, M., 129, *138*
Straus, J. L., 95, *102*
Streiner, D. L., 163, 166, 174, *184*
Strock, M., 150, *159*
Strömland, K., 132, *139*
Strong, J. W., 216, *220*
Sudoh, Y., 72, *84*
Sullivan, P. V., 306, *320*
Sundt, J. L., 141, *159*
Sutton, J., 191, *201*
Sveinsson, A. V., 189, 196, *201*

Svensonn, H., 72, *82*
Swami, D. R., 27, *35*
Swearer, S. M., 187, 189, 190, 191, 196, *198*, *201*
Sweeting, H., 193, 195, 196, *201*
Sweller, J., 109, *122*
Swirczynski, D., 45, *67*
Swisher, K., 106, *123*
Szatmari, P., 163, 166, 174, *184*
Szymanski, L., 27, *37*

**T**

Tamminen, M., 194, 195, 196, *198*
Tanner-Talverson, P., 105, *123*
Taylor, E., 222, *235*
Tebarth, H., 79, *84*
Tewksbury, M. A., 4, *14*, 76, 78, *83*
Thomas, A. D., 86, 102, 176, *185*
Thomas, K. W., 137, *138*
Thompson, D., 193, 194, 195, 196, *202*
Thompson, V., 109, *123*
Timmons-Mitchell, J., 149, *160*
Tisdale, B., 132, *140*
Tobin, M. J., 132, *139*
Toch, H., 29, *37*
Tomás de Almeida, A. M., 189, *202*
Tomko, C. M., 269, *300*
Touchstone, J., 137, *138*
Travis, M. A., 290, 291, 294, 295, *300*
Turner, K. D., 146, 147, *158*
Turner, S. M., 164, *183*
Turnock, P., 222, 229, *233*
Tynan, W. D., 228, *235*

**U**

Underwood, K., 187, 188, *197*
Underwood, L. A., 149, *160*

**V**

Valenti, M., 132, 133, *140*
Vandenberg, B., 167, 175, *185*
Vandenheiden, G., 45, 46, 47, 61, *65*
Van Dijk, M. E., 152, *158*
Van Duizend, R., 3, *14*
van Dulmen-Krantz, J. J., 208, 217, *220*
Van Meter, P., 113, *123*
Van Rompay, M., 85, 86, *101*

Varley, W. H., 108, *123*
Vauras, M., 194, 195, 196, *198*
Viemerö, V., 189, *199*
Vogelgesang, S., 4, *14*
von Ammon Cavanaugh, S., 95, *102*

## W

Waddel, N., 80, *83*
Waddell, C. D., 242, *263*
Wahlberg, K., 127, *139*
Wainapel, S. F., 86, *102*
Waite, D., 143, 145, *159*
Wake, H., 72, *84*
Waldie, K., 146, 147, *160*
Walker, B., Jr., 128, *140*
Walker, H. M., 187, *202*
Walker, J., 105, *122*
Wallinga, D., 132, 133, *140*
Walter, J. E., 60, *66*
Walters, H., 28, *35*
Wang, H., 74, *84*
Warboys, L. M., 143, 144, *157, 161*
Ward, A., 80, *83*
Wasserman, G. A., 132, *140*
Waterman, S., 314, *321*
Waters, H. S., 112, 115, *123*
Watson, D., 42, *64*
Watts, M. S., 28, *37*
Webb, A., 157, *159*
Webster, D., 150, *158*
Webster, S. E., 149, *160*
Weil, A., 98, *102*
Weisglas-Kuperus, N., 133, *139*
Weiss, B., 127, 132, 133, 135, *140*
Weiss, G., 229, *235*
Weiss, R. L., 167, *183*
Weiss, T. R., 246, *263*
Weisskopf, C., 129, 137, *139*
Weitzel, A., 28, *37*
Welmur, J. C., 136, *139*
Wenar, C., 163, 164, *185*
West, M. D., 76, *82*
West, P., 193, 195, 196, *201*
Wetzel, M. S., 85, *102*
White, E., 247, *263*
Whitney, I., 189, 193, 194, 195, 196, *202*
Whitten, P., 45, *67*
Whitton, J., 4, *14*
Whorton, J., 105, *123*
Whyatt, R., 129, *140*
Wiemer, S. A., 163, 165, 171, 172, *185*
Wiener, M., 110, *123*
Wigle, D. T., 125, 135, 136, *140*
Wilhelm, J. G., 165, *185*
Wilkey, S., 85, 86, *101*
Wilkinson, W., 266, *300*
Williams, J. H., 150, *158*
Williams, M., 167, 174, 178, *183*
Williams, N., 47, 61, *67*
Williamson, G. M., 27, *37*
Williard, J. C., 192, *200*
Willis, C. J., 288, *300*
Wilson, B., 28, *35*
Wilson, F. J., 163, 166, 174, *184*
Wilton, M. M. M., 192, *202*
Wolff, M. S., 136, *139*
Wolff, P., 107, 108, 110, *123*
Wolford, B. I., 143, 145, 149, *160*
Woolard, J. L., 142, *161*
Wright, J. P., 141, *159*
Wu, F. G., 76, *83*
Wu, T., 74, *84*
Wu, W., 74, *84*

## Y

Yang, B., 163, 164, 179, *183, 185*
Yeatman, J., 28, *35*
Young, D. J., 46, *67*
Young, S. T., 47, *67*
Ysselduke, J. E., 227, *234*
Yude, C., 194, *202*

## Z

Zagler, W. L., 4, *14*, 74, *83*
Zaremba, B. A., 147, *158*
Zartarian, V. G., 133, 136, *138, 140*
Zeithaml, V. A., 47, 66, *67*
Zhang, D., 104, *123*
Zimmer, H. D., 109, *121*
Zirkel, P. A., 224, 225, 230, 231, *235*
Zuber, R., 193, *199*
Zufall, M. J., 137, *138*

# Subject Index

## A

Abuse, in prison
　need for research on, 33
　potential for, 23–26
Accessibility issues
　with e-text textbooks, 237–263
　in prison, 21–23
　state laws on, 255–258
Accommodations. *see also* Reasonable accommodations
　cost-effectiveness of, employee research on, 295
　employee understanding of, 290–291
　for physically disabled offenders, 31–32
　for students with disabilities, e-text textbooks, 237–263
　Title II on, 238–243
　Title III on, 244–255
Acetylcholinesterase inhibition, pesticide exposure and, 128, 131
Activity, and learning from text, 111–113
Activity-based cognitive processes, 106–111
Activity-based learning model, 103, 113–119
　Native American children and, 104–106
ADA. *see* Americans with Disabilities Act
Adaptive behavior limitation requirement, modifications of, 213–214
Adaptive web browser (AWB), for learning-disabled individuals, 79–80
ADHD. *see* Attention deficit–hyperactivity disorder

Age of onset requirement, modifications of, 214
Alternative medicine. *see* Complementary and alternative medicine
Ambulatory disabilities, offenders with, abuse of, 24–25
Americans with Disabilities Act (ADA)
　ambiguities in definitions in, need for clarification of, 288–289
　and evacuation planning, 306–308
　on interpreters for the deaf, 44
　Title I, 269–271
　Title II, 17
　　scope of, 238–243
　Title III, scope of, 244–255
America Online (AOL), 246
Amputation, coping with, 27
Anxiety, in children with disabilities, 163–185
　cross-disability comparison of, 169t, 177–179
　need for research on, 179–183
Applying, 111
Arizona
　demographics of, 40
　emergency evacuation codes and regulations, 309–310
Arizona Rehabilitation Services Administration (ARSA), 39–67
Asperger syndrome (AS), children with, fears and anxieties in, research on, 166t, 174
Assistive technology, 81t
*Atkins v. Virginia*, 206–208
　retroactivity of, 217

ATMs, 69, 72
Attendance, sporadic, accommodations for, 277–283
Attention deficit–hyperactivity disorder (ADHD)
  assessment of, legal issues in, 226–227
  definition of, 222
  diagnosis of, developmental issues in, 228–229
  law on, 221–235
Augmented reality, 73
Autism, children with, fears and anxieties in, research on, 166t, 174
Automated teller machines (ATMs), 69, 72
AWB. see Adaptive web browser

**B**

Behavior, pesticide exposure and, 125–140
Blindness, computer technology and, 70–73
Braille
  for mathematical expressions, 70–71
  printing systems, 72
Briseno, Jose, 211
Bullying
  of children with disabilities, 187–202
    need for research on, 195–197
  literature on, 188–195
  theoretical frameworks regarding, 190–191
Burden of proof, on mental retardation, 215–216

**C**

CAA. see Computer access assessment
CAM. see Complementary and alternative medicine
Camera mouse, 75–76
Career preferences, worldview and, 89–90
*Carparts Distribution Center, Inc. v. Automotive Wholesaler's Association of New England*, 245, 249–250
Children
  with disabilities
    bullying and victimization of, 187–202
    fears and related anxieties in, 163–185, 163t–169t
  Native American, with learning disabilities, instructional modalities for, 103–123

Chronic medical conditions
  computer technology and, 74–78
  and sporadic attendance, 278
Classroom functioning, pesticide exposure and, 135–136
Classroom issues, with ADHD, 230–231
Cognitive processes, pesticide exposure and, 125–140
Cognitive representation, modes of, 106–107
Communication modes
  expressive, 53t
  receptive, 53t
Complementary and alternative medicine (CAM), 85–102
  worldview and, 93–94
Comprehension, activity-based model of, 113–119
Computer access assessment (CAA), 74
Computer technology, 69–84
  and developmental disabilities, 80
  e-text textbooks for students with disabilities, 237–263
  and hearing impairment/deafness, 73–74
  and learning disabilities, 79–80
  and physical disability, 74–78
  and visual impairment/blindness, 70–73
Conduct disorder, children with, fears and anxieties in, research on, 169t, 177–178
Constructivism, 106
Consultation, in emergency evacuation planning, 315
Contextualism, 87
Conventional medicine
  philosophy of, 98–99
  worldview and, 93–94
Costs, of reasonable accommodations, empirical studies of, need for, 286–288
Counseling preferences, worldview and, 92

**D**

Deaf individuals
  rehabilitation counselors for, 42–43
  video remote interpreting services for, 39–67

## SUBJECT INDEX    337

vocational rehabilitation services for, 41–42
Deafness
  computer technology and, 73–74
  definition of, 40
  videoconferencing technology and, 45–47
Death penalty, mental retardation and, 205–220
Deficit-poor readers, 110–111110
Delay, 46
Developmental disabilities, computer technology and, 80
*Devito v. Chicago Park District*, 273
Diabetes, inmates with, abuse of, 25
Difference-poor readers, 110–111
Differential treatment hypothesis, 146–147
Digital speech signal processing, 73
Disability(/ies)
  children with
    bullying and victimization of, 187–202
    fears and related anxieties in, 163–185, 163t–169t
  definition of, 143–144, 269
  employees with
    maximization of accommodations, 294–296
    prevalence of, 303–305, 304f
    reasonable accommodations for, 265–300
    understanding of accommodations, 290–291
  individuals with
    and complementary and alternative medicine, 85–102
    computer technology for, 69–84
    definition of, 18
    emergency evaluation laws for, 301–321
    employment crisis for, 267–269
  juvenile delinquents with, 141–161
    educational services for, 148–149
    mental health services for, 149–150
    need for research on, 156–157
    prevalence and incidence of, 145–148
    relationship between, research on, 152–156, 154t–155t
  students with, e-text textbooks for, 237–263
Disability research, 3–14
Dual coding theory, 109

### E

Educational services
  issues with ADHD, 221–235
  for juvenile delinquents with disabilities, 148–149
EEOC. *see* Equal Employment Opportunity Commission
*EEOC v. Wal-Mart Stores, Inc.*, 307
Electro-oculographic potential, 75
Emergency evacuation laws
  adequacy and enforcement of, 301–321
  compliance with, barriers to, 312–314
  comprehensive planning for, 310–312
  recommendations for, 314–318
Emotional disorder, among juvenile delinquents, 146–148
Employers
  and compliance with evacuation planning, 313–314
  and own rules and policies, 274–275
  and reasonable accommodations with work schedules, 265–300
Employment. *see* Work
Enactive representation, 106–108
Equal Employment Opportunity Commission (EEOC), 274–275
  and evacuation planning, 308–309
  on reasonable accommodations, 271
Equal protection claims, retroactivity of, 217
E-text textbooks, for students with disabilities, 237–263
Evacuation planning
  comprehensive, 310–312
  inequality in, 303–306
  laws on
    adequacy and enforcement of, 301–321
    compliance with, barriers to, 312–314
    recommendations for, 314–318
Exempt wholesalers, limitations of, 250–251
Expert resources, for accommodation process, 291–293
Expressive communication modes, 53t

### F

Fear, in children with disabilities, 163–185
  cross-disability comparison of, 169t, 177–179
  need for research on, 179–183
Federal Emergency Management Agency (FEMA), on evacuation planning, 307, 311

Federal law
  and educational services with ADHD, 222–226
  and evacuation planning, 306–309
Females, with disabilities
  fears and anxieties in, research on, 179
  in juvenile justice system, 150–152
Fingerspelling, difficulties with, on video remote interpreting, 57, 57t, 61
Flexible work schedules, as reasonable accommodation, 265–300
Formism, 87
Friendships, worldview and, 90
Full-time work schedules, as essential function, 271–275
*Furman v. Georgia*, 205–206

## G

Gait training systems, 75
Gesture recognition systems, 75
Global positioning system (GPS), 72
Good behavior, rewards for, physically disabled offenders and, 26
Grants, for hiring and accommodation of employees with disabilities, 289–290
Graphic user interphase (GUI), and visually impaired individuals, 71

## H

*Habitat Mobile pour Personnes Handicapées*, 74
HAL. *see* Hybrid assistive leg
Hansen, Tina, 302
Hard of hearing, definition of, 40
Health care
  philosophical congruence in, 85–102
  philosophies of, worldviews and, 96–97
Health impairment, children with, fears and anxieties in, research on, 166t, 172–174
Health promoting behavior, worldview and, 93
Hearing aids, with digital speech signal processing, 73
Hearing impairment
  children with, fears and anxieties in, research on, 165t, 170–171
  computer technology and, 73–74
Hidden Markov models (HMM), 75
HIV/AIDS
  and ADA protections, 266
  offenders with, abuse of, 24
  outside of prison, 28–29
Honors points, physically disabled offenders and, 26
Hybrid assistive leg (HAL), 75
Hyperactivity, definition of, 222

## I

Iconic representation, 106–107
IDEA. *see* Individuals with Disabilities Education Act
IEP. *see* Individualized education program
Illinois, emergency evacuation codes and regulations, 311–312
Imagery-based cognitive processes, 106–111
Imaginal representation, motor activity and, 107–110
Imposed strategies, 110
Imprisoned intelligence, 176
Impulsivity, definition of, 222
Inattention, definition of, 222
Indexing propositions, research on, 115–119
Individualized education program (IEP), 225
Individualized plans, for emergency evacuation, 315–316
Individuals with Disabilities Education Act (IDEA), and ADHD, 223–225
Induced strategies, 110
Interpreters, 43–44
Interpreter training programs, 44

## J

Jitter, 46
Job Accommodation Network (JAN), 293
Juvenile delinquency, disability and, 141–161
  educational services for, 148–149
  mental health services for, 149–150
  need for research on, 156–157

# SUBJECT INDEX 339

prevalence and incidence data on, 145–148
relationship between, research on, 152–156, 154t–155t
Juvenile justice system
females within, 150–152
history of, 141–143

## K

*Kinlaw v. Alpha Baking Co., Inc.*, 274

## L

Lamb, David, 265–266
*Larson v. Seagate Technology, Inc.*, 275
Law
on ADHD, 221–235
on death penalty and mental retardation, 205–220
state, on accessibility, 255–258
Lead exposure, effects of, 132
Learning, activity-based model of, 113–119
Learning disabilities (LD)
among juvenile delinquents, 146–148
children with
bullying of, research on, 192–193
fears and anxieties in, research on, 168t, 175–177
computer technology and, 79–80
Native American children with
characteristics of, 103–106
instructional modalities for, 103–123
Learning strategies, types of, 110–111
Learning styles, types of, 110–111
Leave policies, employees and, 296
Lip-reading, 73

## M

Maps, electronic, 72
Martin, Casey, 252–254
*Massachusetts Coalition of Citizens with Disabilities, et al. v. Civil Defense Agency and Office of Emergency Preparedness of the Commonwealth of Massachusetts, et al.*, 313
Mechanism, 87
Mediation, for reasonable accommodation complaints, 283–286

Medical model worldview orientation, 97
Medical treatment, in prison, 20
Memory
activity- and imagery-based strategies and, 106–111
activity-based model of, 113–119
Mental disorder, definition of, 144–145
Mental health services, for juvenile delinquents with disabilities, 149–150
Mental retardation
among juvenile delinquents, 146–148
children with, fears and anxieties in, research on, 167t, 174–175
and death penalty, 205–220
definitions of, 208–210
statutory, 210–214
determination of, criminal procedures on, 215
Metacognitive hypothesis, 146–147
Meyerson Disability Research Project (MDRP), ix–x
Microsoft programs, for visually impaired individuals, 70
Minority students, with ADHD, issues regarding, 229–230
Mobility impairment, computer technology and, 74–78
Motor activity, and imaginal representation, 107–110

## N

National Federation of the Blind (NFB), 246–247
Native American children
with learning disabilities
characteristics of, 103–106
instructional modalities for, 103–123
learning style of, 104–106
Neurodevelopment, pesticide exposure and, 133–135

## O

Occupational Safety and Health Administration (OSHA), on evacuation planning, 311
Organicism, 87–88
Organicism-Mechanistic Paradigm Inventory (OMPI), 88–89

# SUBJECT INDEX

Organophosphate (OP) pesticides
    and cognitive and behavioral functioning, 129–135
    exposure to
        and classroom functioning, 135–136
        effects of, 125–140
        signs and symptoms of, 127
    metabolites of, 128
OSHA. *see* Occupational Safety and Health Administration
Other health impaired, definition of, 223

## P

*Parker v. Metropolitan Life Insurance Co.*, 248
Part-time work schedules
    legal status of, 272–274
    as reasonable accommodation, 265–300
Patient satisfaction, worldview and, 92–93
PCBs. *see* Polychlorinated biphenyls
PD. *see* Physically disabled
*Penry v. Lynaugh*, 206
Pepperian worldviews, 87–91
Personal computers (PCs), 4, 69
Personality traits, and health care preferences, 91–92
Pesticides
    and cognitive and behavioral functioning, 129–135
    exposure to
        and classroom functioning, 135–136
        effects of, 125–140
        signs and symptoms of, 127
*PGA Tour, Inc. v. Casey Martin*, 252–254
PHANTOM, 71, 71f
Philosophical congruence, 91–94
    in health care, 85–102
Physical disability
    computer technology and, 74–78
    employees with, reasonable accommodations for, 265–300
    epidemiological research on, need for, 32
Physically disabled (PD) individuals, outside of prison, 27–29
Physically disabled (PD) offenders
    accommodations and services for, 31–32
    epidemiology of, 17–20
    need for research on, 32–34
    in prison, 17–37
    psychological breakdown of, need for research on, 33–34
    unique problems of, 21–26
Physician compatibility, worldview and, 92–93
Pictures, and learning from text, 111–113
Pixilization, 46
Placebo effect, 94–96
Polychlorinated biphenyls (PCBs), 132–133
Population validity, 61–62
Presence, as essential function, 281
Prison
    abuse in, potential for, 23–26
    accessibility issues in, 21–23
    injury occurring in, prevalence of, 19
    non-physically disabled individuals in, 29–30
    physically disabled offenders in, 17–37
Profits, maximizing, while offering reasonable accommodations, 290–293
Psychopathology, in individuals with disability, 163
Public accommodations
    publishers as, 246–248
    scope of, 248–250
    Title III on, 244–245
Publishers
    not exempt wholesalers, 250–251
    as public accommodations, 246–248

## Q

Qualex Incorporated, 265–266
Quarter Video Graphics Array (QVGA), 73

## R

Rat, definition of, 23
RCDs. *see* Rehabilitation counselors for the deaf
Reasonable accommodations
    definition of, need for clarification of, 288–289
    empirical studies of, need for, 286–288
    for employees with physical disabilities, 265–300
    e-textbooks as, 239–243

# SUBJECT INDEX  341

legislative recommendations for, 283–290
maximizing, 283–296
and profits, 290–293
for sporadic attendance, 277–283
Title I on, 269
Title III on, 251–255
Receptive communication modes, 53t
Registry of Interpreters for the Deaf, 43
Rehabilitation
  computer-aided, 75
  vocational, deaf clients of, video remote interpreting services for, 39–67
Rehabilitation Act, 224, 292
Rehabilitation counselors for the deaf (RCDs), 42–43
Related services, definition of, 223
Remembering, 111
Representation, types of, 106–107
Research needs
  on bullying of children with disabilities, 195–197
  on fear and anxiety in children with disabilities, 179–183
  on juvenile delinquency and disability, 156–157
  on physically disabled offenders, 32–34
  on video remote interpreting, 58–61
Robotics, 69, 76
*Runkle v. Potter*, 275–276

## S

School bullying
  of children with disabilities, 187–202
    need for research on, 195–197
    literature on, 188–195
    theoretical frameworks regarding, 190–191
School failure hypothesis, 146–147
Schools, responsibilities regarding ADHD, 221–235
SCIs. *see* Spinal-cord injuries
Sears & Roebuck, 291
See-through head mount display (ST-HMD), 73
Self-performed task (SPT) effect, 109
September 11, 2001, and emergency evacuation, 301–302

Services, for physically disabled offenders, 31–32
  need for research on, 34
SES. *see* Socioeconomic status
Sign language
  computer technology and, 73–74
  video remote interpreting for, 39–67
SignWorks Project, 45–46
Sketch boards, digitizer, 75
Social marketing, for evacuation planning, 317–318
Socioeconomic status (SES)
  and fear contents, 170
  of students with ADHD, issues regarding, 229
Special education, definition of, 223
Speech recognition, 70
Spinal-cord injuries (SCIs)
  assistive technology and, 76, 77t–78t
  coping with, 27
SPT. *see* Self-performed task effect
State law
  on accessibility, 255–258
    benefits of, 255–257
    shortcomings of, 257–258
  and evacuation planning, 309–310
ST-HMD. *see* See-through head mount display
Students
  with disabilities, e-text textbooks for, 237–263
  rights regarding ADHD, 221–235
Subsidies, for hiring and accommodation of employees with disabilities, 289–290
Susceptibility hypothesis, 146–147
Symbolic representation, 106–107

## T

Tax incentives, for hiring and accommodation of employees with disabilities, 289–290
Technical assistance (TA) system, 74–75
TeDUB system, 72
Telecommuting, 76–78
  as accommodation, 294–295
Telemedicine, and video remote interpreting, 44–45
Televisits, 78
Terry, Kevin, 275–276

Thalidomide, 132
Tim Language (TL), 72
Training with Animated Pedagogical
    Agents (TAPA), 79
Treatment modalities, worldview and,
    90–91

## U

Understanding, 111
Unified modeling language (UML), 72
United States Department of Defense, and
    telemedicine, 45
United States Fire Administration (USFA),
    on evacuation planning, 307
Universal design, policy arguments for,
    258–259
US Airways v. Barnett, 274
USERfit framework, 76

## V

Veterans Affairs (VA), and telemedicine,
    45
Victimization, of children with disabilities,
    187–202
    literature on, 191–195
    need for research on, 195–197
Videoconferencing technology, and deaf-
    ness, 45–47
Videophones, 78
Video remote interpreting (VRI)
    for deaf vocational rehabilitation clients,
    39–67
        best practices in, 63
        need for research on, 58–61
    definition of, 39
    satisfaction with, 47, 54–57, 55t–57t
Violence, in schools, against children with
    disabilities, 187–202

Virtual reality, and disabled individuals, 78
Visual impairment, children with, fears
    and anxieties in, research on,
    165t–166t, 171–172
Visually impaired individuals
    adjustment of, 28
    computer technology for, 70–73
Visually impaired offenders, abuse of, 24
Vocational rehabilitation, deaf clients of
    services for, 41–42
    video remote interpreting services for,
        39–67
VRI. see Video remote interpreting

## W

WHS. see World Hypothesis Scale
Wimbley v. Bolger, 279
Work
    crisis in, for individuals with disabili-
        ties, 267–269
    developmentally disabled individuals
        and, computer technology
        for, 80
    in prison, 21–22
    schedules, 271–283
        ADA and, 265–300
        employees and, 296
    telecommuting, 76–78
Workplace education, on evacuation plan-
    ning, 317–318
World Hypothesis Scale (WHS), 88–89
Worldviews, 87
    Pepperian, 87–91

## Z

Zelmanowitz, Abe, 302